"I Cease Not to Yowl"

"I Cease Not to Yowl"

Ezra Pound's Letters to

Olivia Rossetti Agresti

Edited by
Demetres P. Tryphonopoulos
and Leon Surette

University of Illinois Press
Urbana and Chicago

© 1998 by the Board of Trustees
of the University of Illinois
Previously unpublished letters of
Ezra Pound © 1998 by Mary de
Rachewiltz and Omar S. Pound
Manufactured in the
United States of America
C 5 4 3 2 1
This book is printed on
acid-free paper.

Library of Congress
Cataloging-in-Publication Data
Pound, Ezra, 1885–1972.
I cease not to yowl : Ezra Pound's
letters to Olivia Rossetti Agresti /
edited by Demetres P. Tryphonopoulos
and Leon Surette.
p.   cm.
Includes bibliographical references
(p.) and index.
ISBN 0-252-02410-9 (acid-free paper)
1. Pound, Ezra, 1885–1972—Correspon-
dence. 2. Agresti, Olivia Rossetti—
Correspondence. 3. Poets, American—
20th century—Correspondence.
I. Agresti, Olivia Rossetti.
II. Tryphonopoulos, Demetres P., 1956–
III. Surette, Leon. IV. Title.
PS3531.082 Z4815   1998
811'.52—ddc21
[b] 98-8909
CIP

For Litsa, Panayiota, and Panyiote

D.P.T

Contents

Acknowledgments

In particular we wish to thank Mary de Rachewiltz for her generous cooperation—not only in extending permission to publish these letters without elisions but also in providing photos of Ezra Pound and of Olivia Rossetti Agresti. In addition we want to thank Helen Guglielmini for her generous cooperation and the provision of the photograph of Agresti, her great-aunt, addressing the Italian parliament. We are also grateful for the assistance of many colleagues, research assistants, students, and friends who have made this book possible.

Timothy Materer read an earlier version of the manuscript, made numerous invaluable suggestions, and saved us from many mistakes—indeed, he has been remarkably helpful. We would also like to thank Marjorie Perloff and Timothy Redman, who also read this work in manuscript and made many helpful comments.

The late John Walsh, who originally wanted to publish this correspondence through Black Swan Books, is remembered here for his encouragement and his efforts on our behalf in locating various items at the Beinecke Rare Book and Manuscript Library at Yale University. Richard Taylor, who alerted us to the presence of many Pound letters in the New York Public Library, is also gratefully acknowledged.

We are also most indebted to the following colleagues, research assistants, and friends for help, advice, and encouragement: the late James Laughlin, Andrzej Sosnowski, Joseph Webster, Roger Ploude, Jacqualine Cox, Michael Mills, Diane A. Read, John Wooden, Tony Fabianjic, Shawn Malley, Lance Callahan, Stephen Sloan, John Heinstein, and Julie Dennison.

Our copyeditor at the University of Illinois Press, Becky Standard, has been extraordinarily helpful—her expert advice on matters both editorial and literary has made our work immeasurably better than it was when she first received it in manuscript. Though it may have exasperated us, her steady stream of questions and suggestions no doubt improved this work immensely. Our thanks as well to Richard Wentworth, director of the University of Illinois Press, for having the courage to take on this project and to several other members of the staff for assistance.

The book could hardly have been written without the support we received from the faculty and staff of the English departments at the University of New Brunswick and the University of Western Ontario. Wilfrid Laurier University, where Demetres taught while first working on this project, provided financial support through a research grant, making it possible for him to visit for the first time the Beinecke Rare Book and Manuscript Library.

We are deeply grateful to all the research librarians who have helped us. Special thanks go to Patricia Willis, curator of the Collection of American Literature at the Beinecke Rare Book and Manuscript Library at Yale University; Francis O. Mattson, curator of the Berg Collection at the New York Public Library; and Saundra Taylor, curator of manuscripts at the Lilly Library at Indiana University. As well, we are grateful to Peggy Fox, director of New Directions Publishing, for all her efforts on our behalf.

While working on this book, both editors held Social Sciences and Humanities Research Council grants and would like to acknowledge the council's important contribution to this project.

Grateful acknowledgment is made to the following individuals and estates for permission to use the previously unpublished archival material: the Ezra Pound Literary Property Trust for Ezra Pound's correspondence with Olivia Rossetti Agresti, and Mary de Rachewiltz and Omar Pound; and Helen Dennis Guglielmini for Olivia Rossetti Agresti's letters to Ezra Pound.

Introduction

LEON SURETTE

The first task of an introduction to an edition of a long-neglected correspondence must be to account for the neglect—after all if the neglect is justified, then the edition is not. Part of the explanation in the case of the Ezra Pound and Olivia Rossetti Agresti correspondence is doubtless that Agresti is not a figure well known to literary scholarship. Although a member of the illustrious Rossetti family of London, she is a distinctly minor literary personality. Another factor is that—though English born—she was an Italian patriot and numbered many Fascists among her friends. As a result the correspondence touches frequently upon sensitive political, religious, and racial topics and reveals attitudes that many may find offensive.

We suspect that this latter feature accounts in greatest part for the neglect, because the strongly pro-Fascist, pro-Axis sentiments of both correspondents cannot be disguised. The corollary of these sentiments is a hostility toward the Allies, especially Great Britain and the United States. Somewhat surprisingly, there was little softening of this hostility toward and suspicion of the Allies even as late as the cold war. Despite its sentiments, this correspondence cannot be ignored because it contains the most frank expression we have of Pound's political, religious, and racial views during the years 1937 to 1959—and, perhaps, for any period.

Many will find these letters painful reading. Pound's epistolary style is not only cryptic and disconnected but also often rude and offensive—even toward the gentle Agresti. Even more difficult for most readers are the targets of his rhetorical abuse. No one is surprised any longer to learn that Pound routinely expressed anti-Semitic sentiments, but this hatred is by no means the only one. We find him demonstrating equal scorn for the Catholic church and the papacy, for Roosevelt and Churchill, for John Maynard Keynes and A. C. Pigou, for Clare Boothe Luce and Bernard Baruch.

Pound's hatreds are directed at liberals, capitalists, Catholics, Americans, Britons, orthodox economists, and Marxists as well as at Jews. Agresti, though she is a gentle soul, shares many of his hostilities, but not those directed at Catholics or Jews. One value of this correspondence is that it demonstrates that hatreds need not come as a package. It further suggests that anti-Semitism, undeniable though it might be, was not the fount or source of Pound's "paideuma," as he came to call his worldview.

On the other hand, no one can come away from a reading of this correspondence without recognizing that Pound believed that the balance of virtue and wisdom in the great conflicts of this century was with the political Right and not with the Left or with the liberal center. Pound's analysis led to alienation from his homeland and his attachment to Italy. Such an alienation is not uncommon among American artists, many of whom threw in their lot with Europe—amongst them Pound's most illustrious literary friend, T. S. Eliot. Indeed, Pound and Eliot shared the right-hand portion of the political spectrum, which put them out of sympathy with liberals and Marxists alike. But we should not repeat Pound's errors by condemning him and all his works on the grounds that his political posture is offensive to us. Pound's great weakness was to demonize those with whom he disagreed. We ought not to follow him in this error.

Nor should we exaggerate the novelty or unexampled nature of the political and racial views expressed in this correspondence. In point of fact, they have all been expressed by Pound in more public forums, occasionally with equal vehemence. This correspondence permits us to follow Pound's iteration of these views to a single correspondent over more than two decades—and what decades they were for the world and for Pound personally. In 1937, when the correspondence began, war clouds were gathering ominously. Pound's career was well launched, if in a bit of a lull. He had just published *The Fifth Decad of Cantos* and thought himself poised to save the world from a second catastrophe. Four years earlier he had finally got *Jefferson and/or Mussolini* into print, a work which expressed his conviction that he had found in Mussolini an Augustus for whom he could be a Virgil. Of course, events turned out very differently and Pound became infamous beyond any fame he had previously earned.

There is a gap in the correspondence after the collapse of Mussolini's regime in 1943 and the disruptions that followed. The correspondence rebegins in 1947 and the vast bulk of it belongs to the period of Pound's incarceration at St. Elizabeths Hospital in Washington, D.C., to which he was committed when he was found mentally unfit to stand trial for treason on 14 December 1945. He was indicted on the grounds that his broadcasts over Rome Radio during the war had contained treasonous statements. He never stood trial but was eventually released from confinement on 18 April 1958 on the condition that he leave the United States. Despite his incarceration, these are the years of Pound's greatest fame and influence. *The Pisan Cantos* won the Bollingen Prize in 1949. He also completed his Confucian translations and wrote *Rock Drill* (1955) and *Thrones* (1959). As a result the correspondence contains much of interest to scholiasts of the late cantos. Pound continuously discusses the books he is reading with Agresti, and his reading is either motivated by composition of *The Cantos* or simply finds its way into that compendious and memorious work. Agresti herself earns a mention at the beginning of canto 76 (452) and another at the end of canto 78 (483).

Olivia Rossetti Agresti's letters from Ezra Pound were the first original letters acquired for the Ezra Pound Papers at the Beinecke Rare Book and Manuscript Library at Yale University. Donald Gallup reports that "upon his return to Italy in 1958, Pound discovered that she [Agresti] needed money. He proposed to Professor [Giovanni] Giovannini at the Catholic University of America in Washington that he edit the Agresti-Pound correspondence" (Gallup, *Pigeons on the Granite* 193). This initiative of Pound's amounted to a gift to Agresti since his letters to her were technically his property. However, the letters proved too expensive for Giovannini's university; they were subsequently purchased by Yale. Agresti received six hundred dollars in payment. For whatever reason, Giovannini never carried out the proposed edition, and the letters languished unedited and uncited for thirty years.

I first came across this correspondence at the Lilly Library at Indiana University in 1985. Busy with other projects, I was not lucky enough to find someone willing to share the labor of collating and editing the Pound-Agresti correspondence until 1989. The Pound estate immediately and graciously granted permission to undertake the work, but Demetres Tryphonopoulos had other projects underway and the labor of annotation proved far greater than we had imagined. Thirteen years later we have finally brought the work to completion. I trust that the following assessment of its intrinsic interest is not entirely an artifact of long and arduous labor.

One totally unexpected bonus was the discovery that Olivia Rossetti Agresti was of historical interest in her own right as well as an intelligent and informed correspondent. She is the daughter of William Michael Rossetti and hence the niece of Dante Gabriel Rossetti and Christina Rossetti. She was born in London on 30 September 1875 and grew up in an intensely cultural and political environment. In 1892, when Agresti was eighteen and Helen, her sister, fourteen, the girls (who did not attend school) took over the premises and printing press of *The Commonweal*, whose editor and publisher, David Nichol, had been sentenced to eighteen months in jail for an article judged to be an incitement to murder. The best account we have of this incident is written by Agresti herself in a never-finished and unpublished memoir provisionally entitled "The Anecdotage of an Interpreter." *The Commonweal* had been founded in 1885 by William Morris and the Socialist League, but by 1890 David Nichol and some other more radical Socialists had taken it over from Morris (though he continued to pay the bills). In 1892 a group of working men were found in possession of explosives and sentenced to ten years of penal servitude. According to Agresti, "This savage sentence aroused the indignation of all the libertarians and Nichol published in *The Commonweal* an ill judged article which laid him open to the charge of inciting to murder Chief Police Inspector Melville. He was arrested, tried, and given 18 months hard labour and *The Commonweal* came to an end. The printing-press, type, etc. belonging to the paper were left derelict in the loft over a mews off the Clerkenwell Road, where they were lodged" ("Anecdotage," chap. 6: "The Red Romantics" 10).

Agresti and her sister took possession of the printing paraphernalia and began to publish their own Anarchist journal, *The Torch*, in the basement of their home. Agresti gives an account of this enterprise in a letter:

> I wrote it [*A Girl among the Anarchists*] jointly with my sister Helen: we had lived the experience together. Our Anarchist days began when I was 14 and she was 10 and ended as far as active participation went, when I was 20 and she was 16. Of the 12 chapters of the book Helen wrote 5 and I 7; we were not together at the time; she was in London, and I was married (to an anarchist) in Rome, but though they were written quite separately and neither revised the work of the other, it seems to me quite homogeneous. I remember I wrote the 1st and the last chapters, but have not a very distinct recollection of the authorship of the others. As you see, we both entered political life when other girls are in high school. . . . We were anarchist communists, but we heartily disliked the Marxist variety of the animal, and used to go to Social-Democratic meetings to disturb them, which was doubtless very ill-mannered but what are you to expect of young anarchists cock-a-hoop with the exuberance of teenagers? How did we come to be anarchists? I grew up on Plutarch and Corneille, followed by the French Revolution and then came Sunday mornings in Regent's Park listening to one of Wm. Morris anarchist proselytes of the old *Commonweal*, a certain Nichols, and Kropotkin's "Appeal to the Young" which made a tremendous impression on us, and Whitechapel commemorations of the Chicago

"martyrs." It was in the air, not anarchy but a tardy awakening of the English well-to-do to the iniquities of the social system in days when the mass of the working-people were housed in filthy verminous lodgings, a family to a room, with no kitchens, or decencies of any kind. We felt ashamed of our comforts. All those years my poor mother was in very bad health (she died of consumption in the spring of 1893 in San Remo), my Father, an ardent lover of Shelley and freedom, was rather amused and rather proud of us, and believed in leaving us alone; and so we set up our printing press, and wrote our paper (great trash I have no doubt) and got round us a whole job-lot of people, from fine intellectuals of the type of Kropotkin and Stepniak and Tcherkhesof, to Bohemians like Alexandre Cohen, who came from Paris to London when anarchist outrages made the place too hot for him, to old Chartists like Harrigan who took part in the London riots of 1886, looted a shop, and on the proceeds enjoyed some months of comfortable seclusion with Shakespeare and Dictionaries, his favourite reading, until he had finished his funds and took again to the road as a tramp. He used to like to give himself out as our Grandfather, and would give me advice about the way to deal with the capitalist world of our days. "We must get round them with our insidious means, and then go in for wholesale assassination" was his remedy for social ills; but he was the nicest old man, and used to call himself an "eleuthero-maniac," one of the words he had put together from his study of the dictionary. (27 Oct. 1950)

According to their cousin, Ford Madox Ford, the girls were expelled from the basement in 1893:

My uncle William [William Michael Rossetti] was a man of the strongest—if slightly eccentric—ethical rectitude and, as soon as my aunt was dead and the house became his property, he descended into its basement and ordered the press and all its belongings to be removed from his house. He said that although his views of the duties of parenthood did not allow of his coercing his children, his sense of the fitness of things would not permit him to sanction the printing of subversive literature in the basement of a prominent servant of the Crown. *The Torch* then had to go.

It removed itself to Goodge Street, Tottenham Court Road—a locality as grim as its name. There it became a sort of club where the hangers-on of the extreme Left idled away an immense amount of time whilst their infant hosts and hostesses were extremely active over their forms. I did not myself like it much and only went there I think twice—to see about the printing of my first poem. (*Return to Yesterday* 113)

Ford tells us that they also published George Bernard Shaw's *Why I Am an Anarchist.*

A Girl among the Anarchists is a slightly fictionalized account of their experiences as Anarchist publishers. The two girls become Isabel Meredith, the pseudonymous author of the work published by Duckworth in 1903. In this account *The Torch* (called *The Tocsin*) is finally closed down in a police crackdown following upon an Anarchist's attempt to assassinate the Spanish prime minister in Madrid in 1898 (we have been unable to match this incident to a historical one).

Agresti has not given any other account of the demise of *The Torch*, but Ford provides a colorful one. According to him, the girls attempted to hawk copies of *Why I Am an Anarchist* during Shaw's address to a group of Socialists in Hyde Park:

> Every time he opened his mouth that anthem: "Why I am an Anarchist by the lecturer. One penny," began again. Every now and then they added: "And worth it!" I suppose it would be worth ten thousand pence today. And then some!
>
> Those people shortly afterwards arrived at the conclusion that they were being victimised, and *The Torch* was discontinued. (*Return to Yesterday* 114)

Ford also tells us that he first heard about the Greenwich Observatory incident at the offices of *The Torch*. Martial Bourdin was found horribly mutilated on 15 February 1894 near the Royal Observatory at Greenwich. He later died from the accidental explosion of the bomb he was carrying. Bourdin's brother-in-law, H. B. Samuels, editor of an Anarchist newspaper, was also an undercover police agent. Samuels was suspected of persuading his rather simple brother-in-law to plant a bomb in hopes of fomenting public outrage against the Anarchists. Ford's recounting of the incident and of the Anarchist ambience of *The Torch* to Joseph Conrad provided the inspiration for *The Secret Agent* (114).

A more certain and enduring consequence of Agresti's Anarchist period was her marriage to the Florentine Antonio Agresti (1866–1926) in 1897. Agresti describes him as the son of the "head of a big chemical works in Tuscany." His father died when he was sixteen. Antonio was "one of some 80 'internationalists' prosecuted for 'associazione a delinquere' ("associating with delinquents") and escaped to Paris where he lived an adventurous life." Agresti was "a convinced anarchist, and an equally convinced anti-marxist. We married and he returned to Florence, and took up journalism, came to Rome and was taken on the staff of the Tribuna" (10 Dec. 1950). He wrote several books, among them an account of the pre-Raphaelites, and translated several of George Bernard Shaw's plays into Italian. He died in 1926.

Another element of Agresti's biography important to the correspondence is her involvement with David Lubin. Lubin was born near Krakow, Poland (then part of Russia), on 1 June 1849 to a Jewish family that fled the pogroms and emigrated to New York in 1855. He left school at twelve, went to California at sixteen to seek his fortune, and became prosperous in more than one career. In 1900 he published a utopian plan for the future called *Let There Be Light* and toured Europe in an attempt to promulgate his ideas. When in Rome on this tour in 1904 he hired Agresti as a translator. Quite unexpectedly, Lubin was granted an audience with Victor Emmanuel, the king of Italy, and with his blessing was able to found the International Institute of Agriculture (IIA) in Rome in 1906. The IIA was the first modern international organization and a significant forerunner of the League of Nations. Indeed, Lubin engaged in a correspondence with H. G. Wells between October 1916 and May 1918. Though the correspondence was mostly concerned with Lubin's utopian ideas as expressed in *Let There Be Light*, we may plausibly credit him with showing the way for the League of Nations, since H. G. Wells was a principal progenitor of that organization, and the IIA preceded Wells's proposals for such a league by several years (Mackenzie and Mackenzie 314–15). The IIA ceased to exist only when it was absorbed by the agricultural body of the League of Nations, the Food Agriculture Organization.

Agresti remained with Lubin as secretary and translator until his death on 31 December 1918 during the great flu epidemic of that year. In 1919 she moved to Geneva as a translator for the Italian delegation to the League of Nations. She returned to Rome in 1921 to edit the newsletter of the Italian Association of Joint Stock Companies. While in that position she published a biography of Lubin, *David Lubin: A Study in Practical Idealism*.

Agresti's close association with Lubin is important to the correspondence for two reasons. Firstly, it had rendered Agresti literate in economics. Although Agresti never warmed to Pound's Social Credit analysis of economic phenomena, she and Pound were in broad agreement on the role of interest rates, on the Fascist policy of autarchy—or economic self-sufficiency—and on the necessity of private property. Secondly, because Lubin was Jewish, their discussion of his ideas brings us face to face with Pound's anti-Semitism, which Agresti vigorously opposes. She berates him on several occasions, including the following reproach: "On the subject of Jews all I will say is that I am profoundly convinced that it is wrong to foster generalisations that make a whole people or race responsible for the actions of some. In the matter of monetary crimes, Samuel Lloyd and Hamilton seem to me good Bt. [British] names. Montagu Norman and Benjamin Strong were not Jews" (28 Aug. 1954).

For his part, Pound's struggle to detach any merit he finds in Lubin's ideas from his racial identity reveals the precise nature of his anti-Semitism at this period and leaves no doubt that he believed that the genetic endowment of Jews somehow renders them greedy, unprincipled, and destructive of civilized values. In 1953 Pound read *Hitler's Table Talk*. His response to the Nazi leader is astonishing, for he is so blinded that he characterizes Hitler's Caesarism as a "dirty jew mania": "The Hitler Conversations very lucid re/ money/ unfortunately he was bit by dirty jew mania for World DOminion, as yu used to point out/ this WORST of German diseases was got from yr/ idiolized and filthy biblical bastards. Adolf clear on the baccillus of kikism/ that is on nearly all the other poisons. but failed to get a vaccine against that" (letter 70).

Agresti will have none of this admiration for Hitler (18 Nov. 1953):

> I have not read Hitler's Table Talk and do not know whether an Italian translation is being published. But do not trouble to send it to me. [. . .] I look upon as Hitler as a madman, and a dangerous one; it is all very well to speak in a more or less flippant way of "better deads", but when from such talk one sets down to really killing off all those belonging to such categories as one can lay hands on, it is a case of criminal lunacy. Besides, as articles in the Ecrits de Paris, reviewing books by some of the German Generals, show, he was a megalomaniac and ruined his own plans by his idiotic behaviour.

Pound is unrepentant and replies with an incredible defense of Hitler: "Yes, my Dear O.R.A. BUTTT we shd/ ask WHAT kind of a bloody lunatic, and what druv him/ and NOT allow *ourselves* to be intoxicated by the very filth of propaganda which you so rightly deplore" (letter 71).

It is painful to confront the magnitude of Pound's misreading of history. That is an intellectual failure, but his failure to recognize the unspeakable crimes of the Nazis is surely a moral failure of the greatest magnitude—and one for which no palatable excuse is imaginable. On the other hand, his inhumanity toward groups is in strong contrast to his humane generosity to Agresti—shown both by his interest in her family's affairs and by acts of financial generosity—extended in spite of the straitened financial circumstances of his own family.

In "Political Immaturity," a brief article written for *Front* but never published, Agresti articulates her admiration for Mussolini's corporate state, but—in contrast to Pound—disapproves of his adoption of Nazi racist policies (25 Feb. 1948). She accepted Mussolini's characterization of fascism as a continuation of socialism and considered her old Anarchist/Socialist friends to be "Red Romantics": "They represented in politics very much what the French romantics of the 1830(s) represented in literature. Individualists to the backbone, sworn enemies to Marx and his totalitarian State. Though they were professed atheists, their mental attitude was not materialistic. Rebels against the social injustices and suffering they saw around them, they were altruistic and disinterested, free from all wish to use their political activities to make for themselves a position or to gain any personal advantages" (24 Sept. 1956). Such "National Socialists," as they were called, abandoned Marx in favor of Proudhon and Sorel, largely because of Marxism's materialism. Atheism was not part of their program and many, like Agresti, who converted to Catholicism in her middle age, were drawn to Christianity. In response to Pound's remark, "Wd/ be almost BUT NOT QUITE worth a muscovite invasion to get rid of the Vatican, and the Pacelli gang/ as it is you hv/ had a barbarian invasion and NOT got rid of the vatican" (letter 22), Agresti replied:

> Of course I do not agree with your views of the Vatican; indeed, as I see it, the world is lining up for one great struggle, that between Marxian materialism which leads to slavery, with the (its) total contempt for human personality—whole generations ruthless, ploughed under, like green-manure, with the pretence that this will fertilise the (hypothetic) milennium to come, and when—if ever—it did (does) come, it would be that most unstable of utopias, Huxley's *Brave New World* than which I can conceive of nothing more detestable—and Christian conception of the supreme value of human personality and the sacred duty of respecting it. That idea will rally those like your good self, who profess detestation of Xianity, and those like myself who believe that it is the one idea that gives a *raison d'être* for life with all its sufferings and distresses, the one idea that transmutes values and can make the words "Blessed are they who suffer" to have a real meaning. (25 Sept. 1949)

However, she was no democrat. In a letter of 5 September 1954 she registers her distrust of "the present forms of parliamentary democracy": "I came to the conclusion that they were outlived when I was 18, and read with great interest 'Les Assemblées Parlantes' by Leverdays (1883) which was given me by Peter Kropotkin and which is a destructive criticism of the myth of popular representation."

Of course as an Anarchist she ought to have been suspicious of all forms of government. Some survivals of Anarchist sentiment can be detected in the following letter of 31 January 1959, which sounds very much like contemporary right-wing doctrine as found in Europe and North America: "I was an Anarchist in my young days, and I find myself becoming more distrustful than ever of all governments. I am *not* a communist, for the idea of placing the whole economy of a country in the hands of bureaucrats is to me detestable. I am a firm believer in private enterprise as the thing that makes progress in all fields possible. And the best government is the one that governs least. [Mussolini's idea of] vocational representation should replace geographica{l} representation. But you do not need me to tell you what you know much better than [I do]."

At the age of seventy-nine, reminiscing about her Anarchist youth, she reveals a reformist zeal, which is perhaps what she and Pound most shared: "we were anarchists and wrapped up in poetry (not as makers but as lovers) and dreams of an approaching millennium and belief in the perfectibility of man and in that myth of progress" (25 Sept. 1954).

By the time Pound met Agresti she was a widow and had abandoned her early agnosticism for the Catholicism of her Italian ancestors, a circumstance that elicits exchanges between them on Christianity, which Pound regarded as a Jewish corruption of paganism: "the jewish impertinence of the god damned Xtians in sticking their label on [illegible deletion] a decent style of conduct practiced and formulated 2000 years before the publicity agent from Tarsus messed up the decent teachings of a possibly mythical, but traditionally immature protagonist in the dirtiest and most-trouble making district of a distracted planet" (letter 15). That egregiously offensive remark elicited the following response:

> Where I must definitely part company with you is about the Pope and the Vatican and St. Paul. I cannot understand how you can speak of the man who wrote XIII Corinthians as you do. The fact that the Pope for all the materialistic breed of communists and exploiters is Public Enemy N° 1 shows where he stands. [. . .] Catholicism is neither racial nor national, but universal, as a respectable religion should be. I came to it late in life after a full experience of the various agnostic, anti-religious and materialistic outlooks on life, and I find it the one rational, consoling, and satisfying attitude to life. But never fall into the fatal error of trying "to justify the ways of God to man". We are surrounded by mysteries far beyond our very limited forces of comprehension, we are far less to God than an ant is to us, and when we attempt to "justify" what we cannot understand we become simply ridiculous. (3 Aug. 1949)

Pound was unrepentant, and responded:

> The Church of Rome decayed, got steadily stupider pari passu as the jew books were put into circulation, and stupidities engrafted on the clean greek and roman ideas of the early Church.
> The New Test is ANTI the old, or anti all but a very few pages of it./ a few good ideas, and much and increasing corruption. (letter 18)

The points on which Pound and Agresti disagree serve to underline how extreme Pound's political partisanship was in these years. For example, Pound is willing to endorse Senator Joseph McCarthy's anticommunism despite his trampling over individual rights. His position on this is elicited by Agresti's casual remark that some American visitors gave her "the impression that in witch-hunting activities are cowing people into joining the Baa Baa flock of 1984 which seems to be advancing threateningly" (28 Aug. 1953). Pound replied:

> have I got to start on YOU, to keep even YOU from swallowing the god damned lies of the same god damned liars who lied re/ Mus and Adolph. There is no witch hunt.
> They lie about McCarthy, the press in the hands of dirty jews and worse goyim. (letter 66)

She did not reply to this blast.

Despite these serious disagreements, and an inability to find much in Pound's poetry to which she could relate, Agresti retained a great admiration for Pound, expressed effusively in a letter to Giovannini in which she enclosed eighty-six letters from Pound:

> Ezra Pound for whom I have a great admiration, not only as a most distinguished innovator in the field of poetry, as a man of high and extraordinary wide culture and critical faculty, but as an all too rare example of fearless courage and great dignity during all these 11 years of most unjust treatment. Never was an American truer to the great principles for which his country stands than Ezra Pound, and it is this unswerving fidelity which in these years (times) of widespread degeneracy has brought on him the vindictive hatred of those whose acts and policies he denounced. (14 May 1958)

The correspondence includes a kaleidoscope of references to people and events that make Pound's already difficult prose virtually impenetrable without a road map. We have tried to identify all those people and events that were unfamiliar to us as well as many we judged likely unfamiliar to a significant proportion of our probable readership. No doubt we have erred on the side of officious pedantry for some and on the side of elitist exclusivity for others. We can only beg our readers' indulgence and hope that we have hit it right for most.

The historical and personal events that lie behind the correspondence cannot be adequately presented here and are available in standard sources. Where specific details are required for comprehension, we have supplied them in notes or the glossary. We must assume a general knowledge of the history of Italy and the United States for this period in our readers, since to do otherwise would render an already large volume quite unwieldy. Still, a few remarks might be in order.

When Pound first wrote to Agresti in June 1937, Italy's invasion of Ethiopia begun on 3 October 1935 had been triumphantly concluded; Mussolini had begun speaking of a Berlin-Rome axis; and Germans and

Italians were fighting in Spain side by side with Franco's Royalists against the Anarchist and Communist Republicans. Pound had been much distressed that Italy had become an international pariah after the Ethiopian invasion, for he thought of Italy as the vanguard nation in a worldwide political movement that would bring peace and prosperity to all. That movement was Social Credit, not fascism, but he dreamed that he could capture fascism for Social Credit. Instead, fascism captured Pound, and Social Credit drifted off to the former British colonies of Canada and New Zealand.

Mussolini did not enter the war when it broke out on 3 September 1939 but waited until 28 May 1940, when the defeat of France was apparent and many expected Britain to sue for peace. The United States, of course, did not enter the war until 8 December 1941, the day after the Japanese attack on Pearl Harbor. Pound's vigorous journalistic support of Mussolini's regime did not, therefore, put him in a position of potential disloyalty to his country until that date.

So far as Italy was concerned, its war was very short. Mussolini took responsibility for the Balkans and North Africa, where his army did not do well. A quarter of a million Italian soldiers surrendered to the British early in 1941. Another quarter million ill-equipped Italian soldiers assisted in the invasion of the Soviet Union. Largely because of these military disasters, Mussolini was overthrown by Marshall Badoglio in July 1943. Badoglio arrested Mussolini and negotiated a peace with the Allies. Unfortunately for Italy, the Germans rescued Mussolini in a daring paratroop raid in September and set him up in northern Italy in a new Fascist regime known as the Salò Republic. Fighting continued in Italy, essentially now a civil war fought by proxy between the Germans and the Allies. Through all of this Pound remained loyal to Mussolini.

Pound's residence in Italy was in the Ligurian resort town of Rapallo, distant from Rome, a city he could seldom afford to visit unless his way was paid. From his remote retreat he engaged in a tireless letter-writing campaign to further the cause of modern literature and Social Credit economic reform. The latter occupied more of his time and energy than the former during the entire period of the correspondence. He wrote many letters every day—to private correspondents like Agresti, fellow Social Crediters, editors, dignitaries, celebrities, politicians, economists, old friends and acquaintances, and anyone he thought he might recruit for his reform of the world.

His letters to Agresti clearly reflect his preoccupation with economic reform, as well as his conviction that his opponents were legion, depraved, and implacable, and that his supporters were slackers, thick-headed, or insufficiently committed to the cause.

Agresti was not really a supporter of Pound's economic project so much as a sympathetic ear. She was almost exactly ten years Pound's senior and in her sixty-second year in 1937. She and her husband had no children, but Agresti adopted an Italian family and its two girls, Rosamaria and Malù. Rosamaria was a small child when she first appears in the correspondence, but Malù, who was diagnosed with tuberculosis in 1948, must have been an adolescent, for she married in 1954. Her illness caused Agresti a great deal of anxiety and obliged her to give language lessons to raise money for the doctor's bills. Her sister Helen spent the war in London nursing their invalid sister, Mary. Their house was destroyed in the Blitz, and Helen moved to Rome in 1949.

Agresti became part of the extended Pound family. Pound's daughter, Mary de Rachewiltz, first wrote to her in March or April of 1946, and Agresti met Mary's husband, Boris Barrati, Count de Rachewiltz, late in 1947. She visited them at their home, Schloss Brunnenburg, Dorf Tirol, in July 1949 with Rosamaria, whom she left behind for an extended visit since she was about the same age as Siegfredo, the de Rachewiltzes' son, whose pet name was "Cricri." Dorothy Pound had sent twenty dollars from Washington to cover the cost of the trip from Rome. Agresti reported on the visit to Pound: "I enjoyed the three days complete rest at Schlossbrunnenburg very much, and the company of your very nice Mary and of the beautiful little Cricri, all April showers, with his pure spun-gold hair and blue eyes" (3 Aug. 1949). From that point on there was fairly regular contact between Agresti's and Mary's families.

The surviving correspondence between Ezra Pound and Olivia Rossetti Agresti numbers 328 letters and cards written between 1937 and 1959, just one year before Agresti's death in 1960. Our transcriptions of the letters printed here are drawn from both originals and carbons housed in folders 17–25 (1937–59), box 1, series 1, general correspondence, of the Ezra Pound Papers and folder 6, box 1, series 1, correspondence, of the Ezra Pound Papers Addition, both in the Yale Collection of American Literature at the Beinecke Rare Book and Manuscript Library at Yale University, and housed in the Ezra Pound–Boris de Rachewiltz Correspondence in the Henry W. and Albert A. Berg Collection of English and American Literature at the New York Public Library. Some duplicates of letters at the Beinecke Library have found their way to the Lilly Library at Indiana University, but the collection at the Lilly Library includes no letters that are not already part of the collection at the Beinecke Library.

All of these letters have remained unpublished until now. Though we wanted to present the complete record, that would have required a book of some eight hundred pages. Although we have included only approximately 75 percent of Pound's extant letters, we present each of these in full. Primarily, we have dropped repetitive letters and those of intensive commentary (for example, lists of and comments on Alexander Del Mar's works and a series of letters in which Pound is responding to his reading of Daniele Varè's *The Two Imposters*). We have not dropped any letters because they contain information that may place Pound in an unfavorable light, and we have tried to retain most of the letters that include vivid anecdotes and character revelation. We include samples of Agresti's writing to give a taste of her personality and role in the correspondence. Our objective throughout is to give as accurate an impression as we can of an important friendship.

Transcriptions

Each letter is preceded by a tag giving its number in the present edition, its form, and the number of pages in its original version. The great majority of both Pound's and Agresti's letters are in typescript. The following codes have been used to distinguish between the various forms of correspondence: TLS (Typed Letter Signed), TLU (Typed Letter Unsigned), and ALS (Autograph Letter Signed).

Unless otherwise indicated, the letters are from the collection at the Beinecke Library. Those letters from the Henry W. and Albert A. Berg Collection are indicated by the abbreviation NYPL.

We have appended to each letter a date in a standard location and format, even though many of Pound's letters are undated. In most cases probable dates could be derived from either Agresti's habit of recording on the envelopes (and more rarely in the margins) of Pound's letters the date of her answer (indicated by "ans." in the heading), from postmarks of original mailing envelopes for most of the letters Pound wrote from St. Elizabeths, or (when necessary and possible) from internal evidence. When a date is especially speculative, it is enclosed in square brackets and usually discussed in accompanying notes. We have deleted all of Agresti's own dates since they are generally presented in standard form and because we have for the most part included only excerpts from her letters. Pound's dates appear as he wrote or typed them except that we have standardized their location.

We have deleted the place of origin for all of Agresti's letters since each was written from Rome. The origin is included for one of Pound's letters only if it did not originate at St. Elizabeths, the site of most of the correspondence, and its location has been standardized. Our indications of origins appear in square brackets.

The position of salutations, complimentary closes, and signatures, where they appear, has been standardized as much as possible, but occasionally Pound's habit of continuing a letter long past his signature or closing has made this impossible.

With the exception of a few deleted places of origin, each letter written by Pound appears in its entirety. Our deletions of portions of Agresti's letters are indicated by bracketed ellipses.

Every attempt has been made to produce a readable text. Pound's idiosyncratic typing, composition, and writing habits, however, do not conform to typographical conventions and, thus, his letters often test the transcriber's and editor's mettle. Agresti's letters present no such challenge, since her prose, syntax, and typography are generally conventional. To preserve both Pound's and Agresti's letter-writing styles we have decided to reproduce each letter as exactly as possible. Inadvertent misspellings, accidentally transposed letters, typographical errors, repeated words, miswordings, missing or incorrect punctuation, and grammatical errors have been retained. No errors have been silently corrected, no material has been silently deleted, and no material has been silently introduced in the body of the letters, even when it is clear that words or marks of punctuation have been omitted. On a few occasions when comprehension seemed especially difficult, we have supplied missing words or punctuation in square brackets. When a name, word, or phrase is spelled idiosyncratically or is abbreviated, the full name, word, or phrase is supplied in the notes when confusion might result. Underlined words or phrases are presented in italic type, and double underlined words or phrases are presented in underlined italic type. The single instance of triple underlining and the sole use of quadruple underlining have each been presented in underlined italic type.

We have attempted to preserve Pound's and Agresti's habits of revision and correction as much as possible. Interlinear corrections, some of which are also noted in the margins, have been silently incorporated into the line where they belong. Marginal additions, however, have been identified as such. Since Dorothy Pound and Agresti occasionally annotated Pound's letters, their additions have been identified. Handwritten text, whether a single letter or several words, is included in braces. When a deletion is legible, it has been included and marked with strikethroughs. When Pound or Agresti has typed or written over text to make it illegible, "[illegible deletion]" has been inserted. On rare occasions we have inserted a question mark within square brackets to signify that we are uncertain about the accuracy of the transcription or cannot make out what was intended.

Agresti's letters thus appear virtually in facsimile. For Pound's letters, however, we have had to make some further adjustments. Pound's habits of spelling, punctuation, abbreviation, and capitalization have been retained with a few exceptions. We have included all of Pound's unusual punctuation, but because of his propensity for varying space, all marks of punctuation—even his ubiquitous slash marks—have been closed up to the nearest letter. His habit of varying spacing between words, sentences, lines, and paragraphs has been ignored and standard spacing has been used. To signal a new paragraph Pound uses indentions of various lengths—or sometimes has none at all—that do not comply with typographical conventions; we have chosen to standardize such indentions.

Annotations

Because we have prepared this edition for both scholars and general readers, we have had to tread a fine line between excessive explanation and insufficient assistance. The glossary entries and the annotations following the letters are thus designed primarily to clarify cryptic and little-known references and to provide sufficient information for informed readers to make sense of the letters. Although we have assumed that readers will recognize references by name to people such as Montaigne and Langston Hughes, we have occasionally provided birth and death dates of well-known people when Pound's allusion was especially obscure, he had misspelled the name, or confusion might result. We have also sometimes provided glossary entries when a significant connection exists between Pound and a well-known person. For such a lengthy and dense correspondence, however, it is impossible to locate, annotate, and explain every name, idea, or opinion. We have tried to avoid explicating well-known references and hope that other scholars will fill the gaps.

Although we have assumed that readers will recognize common foreign words, some notes contain translations for the many foreign terms used in this multilingual correspondence. When Pound has misspelled a foreign word or phrase, the correct spelling has been supplied in a note along with a translation.

Items with glossary entries are signaled by bold type in the notes. When we were uncertain about the identity of a person mentioned in the letters, we have occasionally provided brief biographies of possibilities in the notes. Only short citations appear in the notes unless the publication information is significant or a comment about it was necessary. Complete references, where possible, appear in the bibliography.

In addition to containing works referred to in the correspondence and in the glossary, the bibliography lists the many books we have relied on for information. Furthermore, we must acknowledge that, like anyone else working on Pound's correspondence, we are indebted most to all those editors of previously published letter collections (especially D. D. Paige, Donald Pearce, Herbert Schneidau, Timothy Materer, Hugh Witemeyer, David M. Gordon, and Barry Ahearn) and Pound biographers (especially Charles Norman, Noel Stock, John Tytell, Humphrey Carpenter, and J. J. Wilhelm), and to Carroll F. Terrell, whose *A Companion to the Cantos of Ezra Pound* stores so much useful information. Donald Gallup's bibliography has also proved indispensable.

For the sake of brevity (and at the risk of appearing too familiar) we have decided to refer in the notes and glossary to our principal subjects by their initials—hence Ezra Pound is EP and Olivia Rossetti Agresti is ORA.

EP's passport photo, circa 1930–40.
(Courtesy of Mary de Rachewiltz)

EP with Luigi Villari, circa 1930–40.
(Courtesy of Mary de Rachewiltz)

ORA addressing the Italian
parliament following the war.
(Courtesy of Helen Guglielmini)

ORA drinking tea at
Schloss Brunnenburg,
circa 1955. (Courtesy of
Mary de Rachewiltz)

ORA with her sister
Helen Rossetti Angeli
at Schloss Brunnenburg,
circa 1955. (Courtesy of
Mary de Rachewiltz)

O.R.A.   CONtinuing /

7 Az

        You wd/ in any case not write anything idiotic / and (B)
it wd/ be extremely useful to have several facts in print
set down by someohe who had been in position to know.
        Gt/ struggle with people absolutely without circle of
reference/ i.e. totally IGnorant/   still calling russians
" red fascists " /
The young too young to remember Romain Rolland up in Svizzera
during other war , bleating about being above the conflict.
        I said (radio) that I was NOT above but down under
with it going on over me / material interests in England/
no one in Ital/ forces as near me as young Angold .
        I was in fact working on translation into italian of a
prose book of his when the partigiani came to door with
tommy-gun / not at precice moment / at that partic/ moment
I was working on Mencius.
        The false picture of Italy/ SMEAR so heavy that
takes rock drill to get it into anyone that a FASCIST govt/
had given me freedom of microphone/   as per statement
in Mercure de France. (You have a copy ? if not will
send at once).
        Dick degli Uberti wrote a good note in Merlo Giallo
years ago / but one note in Merlo dont hold up against
avalanche of yid lies/ note Thos. Mann STILL lying
in a pocket vol/ Seven Arts/ and Rose Benet with THREE
straight lies in a book of reference/ which Paige has
spotted. (Chapter and verse if you can use 'em).
        If you have freedom to print and B/ nerve to
print it / wd/ cert/ be useful to state exactly what I
was doing/   having virtually kidnapped a microphone/
yesterday a young man with good intentions, getting garbled
" monitorings" of discorsi , starts after Pearl Harbour/
    inexact plus lapse of time and no knowledge of
what preceded , makes 'em a bit incomprehensible/ also
I seem to have been more severe BEFORE the war started
but in papers of small circulation or stray interviews.
        The Fr.Hesse bk/ wd/ give chance to mention men
who tried to PREvent the war . Hesse, v. Hoesch. Edward viii
DID stave it off for three years. Include Ian Monro
(M.Post corresp / in Rome) and I think R.Packhard
        at least a few tried to get real news into the
U.S.
        As to being RIGHT , there is now a faint perception
that Roose was NOT a blessing to the U.S./ Churchill)
god damn him, has admitted the war was unnecessary , and
wanted at the end to attack thru the Balkans.
The IF they had listeded to E.P. is at least proper
subject for speculation / and the NON-use of E.P.'s
knowledge AFTER the 600 days is mentionable.
        If you think feasable and WANT any particular
details, they can be sent you. Monotti and Pellizzi
and Vicari can fill in a few more /   I dont know
whether v.Hoesch is remembered by ANYone. Even a man
in Hesse's position did not know about gas ovens till Sept. 1944
and they were not particularly german, I mean not
spirito del popolo / and there were none in ITALY
tho I have only seen ONE statement of that fact , forget
if in Degnac or Spampanato/ also my geo-politik
to use a large word was NOT germanic/
        Martine HY having got out of Morocco says her
red opinion of same is " sobered" "tussel from crossing Libya
c. H/ and Cirenaica & countries where a dream was, in process of
crystalizationed , then someone   actually being
tore up the mould and we were left a half imaginary
civilization. It'll take more than a race of fonctionaires
in pijamas and chemises de nuit to fulfill birthright
of N.Africa.

2/ there is a young new eye/ coming out of french sphere.
what.else./La vera storia will get writ
sometime. The Hesse manifestly a straight statement. very
much NOT in Papen class. H/.saw it over Ribbentrops
shoulder. von P/ considered very light (but that is not in
the Spiel um D/ld). We ought to have known more
about Feder (again a different compartment, haven't found
him mentioned in the Hesse as far as I hv/ read.
Sigura in Barcelona shd/ send his ¼ stuff to ABC.
/ he has translated some of it into english, but I suppose
the spanish wd/ be more useful in Roma ? or not ?
The struggle to prevent the 2nd/ war from making
a third/ ... well Korea is a police action ... etc.
anyhow , apparently Edward and v. Hoesch saved Europe three
years of hell / and v.H. died of the strain. Hesse
takes pains to say he saw the body and that Hoesch hadn't
been poisoned. They say , or rather bedside physician

said Boris of Bulgaria WAS.
Any of yr/ friends know a man named Robin Saunderson ?
(I dont, but have heard him well spoken of)/ also does
yr/ or any's memory touch Richatson-Hat (VERY suspicious sound)
connected with the still more louche name of Reuter.??
Returning to opening sentence. I shd/ think you could
be about as good a witness to my INtentions from 1939 onward
as anyone. Whether it shd/ go back to first meeting I dont
know . or rather I dont know that it wd/ be helpful to use
that chapter at this moment. Though it might. all depends on
treatment. No use creating such panic and dither as
THOUGHT did at that time in little Suvitch (if that was
his name) . dd d dreamamite , s-si sI , dinamite.
the overall picture , possibly less timely now
that the

banzAI

robin red-breast line.

6 Jan/ 55 annon Dom. AUG.

I dont understand how Helen had the Cantos ., they were ordered
sent to you. Unless this is some other provenienzaaaa.

I still marvel(changing the subject) at the pussilanimity
of some fauna/ the infantilism. etc. You wd/ think that
any adult , instead of saying what USE ? etc. of something
printed in rural paper / wd/ have sense enough to know that
a QUOTATION from same , in far country where NO damn wop
paper has ever been heard of (except the vile Corriere)
wd/ be as useful as a quote from an official organ in a
despised etcH

And in the same breath bemoaning the lack of
spirit in his concitoyens.... (YES, I have a case in mind).

My friends are THE most chaRRRRming idiots on earth ,
among whom about 8 or 10 have traces of intelligence.
Among whom , you (I gather , when Helen) Mary and Boris.

New adult arruv/ from Calif / from la PoLOGne
via Australia. Now translating R. de St Victor. I want
connections to get him into print as soon as possible/
he can get some of his cash out of Australia AFTER May 1st/
(has to be OUT of there a year before the brit/sods/ will
permit transfer.

Baynes and Moss "BYZANTIUM" / Andreades chapter on Byzantine
Byzantine econ/ DID anyone in the Ventennio make ANY
use of corporatism in Byzantium ? LOTS of propaganda
value. Prefect's edict re / trade unions functioned from
time of Leo the Wise, right down to Mustapha Kemal/
the dirty Manchersterians , crabbed ALL Byzantine history,
part of black out/ AND Pearson reports that the churrch of
Rome , damned giudianity and perversion, is trying to
prevent publication of facts in archives of the greek church.

I seem to remember Villard being damned dull/ may be
that was some other book of his.

Anyhow, ALL out of date. as atomic energy for
industry busts ALL previous calculation /. No use
thinking as from the Tin-Lizzy days. Mania of even
better radio mutts , for, OMITTING Italy in all american
yawp re/ Europe / they have heard of france, the
decaying heap/ and EVEN of Spain as a factor. Inferiority
complex of all the lousy journalists re/ Mus/ who HAD
been a journalist/

Naturally D.G.R. Hand and Soul and Vita Nuova
basic in E.P's paideuma / also that " I have been here
before" poem./ AND yr/ quote from Dant/ the general
theme , or Cantos , beginging with Pisans/ . The first
½ being attempt to set up circle of reference.

Am now trying to learn a little greek / never had
patience to use largest size dic/ before. Whether anyone
can read the Odyssey until they have translated the ODES,
I don't know. Chang , as per clip that wil send to Mary ,
is tootin fer Kung in Frisco.

IF there are any ITALIAN italians left, they ought to make
USE of J.Brown's " Panorama de la literature contemporaine aux
Etats Unis. " to castigate Brown AND illustrate the
rise of Italy as an intellectual power (however weak and
dithering in the 3rd /decennio AFTER)

TOTAL lack of any controversial writing in the J.S.
NO one has noted the improvement by translation in Eva's
version :

Redefreiheit ohne Radiofreiheit
gleich null ist.

OR that knowing what one did, one had a duty , to warn the
dupes.

Some Spanish friend of Jimenez (Juan Ramon) notes
the   scant   solidarity of intellectuales americanos.

NOT'noting the contradiction of noun and adjective. Cocteau

made a remark when he said: I thought I was among men of letters
and was suddenly aware that they were a group of garage
mechanics.

FIRST FOLD

AIR LETTER
AÉROGRAMME

Ch/ma Sig/a O.R. AGRESTI

36 via Ciro Menotti

ROMA

ITALY

VIA AIR MAIL
PAR AVION

MESSAGE MUST APPEAR ON INNER SIDE ONLY
NO TAPE OR STICKER MAY BE ATTACHED
IF ANYTHING IS ENCLOSED, THIS LETTER
WILL BE SENT BY ORDINARY MAIL

WASHINGTON
JAN 7
6 PM
1955
D.C.

BY AIR MAIL
U.S. 10¢

ROMA 4-5
10-1
1955

SECOND FOLD

Aug. 31. I '55

"I Cease Not to Yowl"

1937

[Rapallo]

7 June {37}

Dear Madame Agresti

I am sending you a note, in my damn bad Italian, re paper money, Chicago Credit etc/[1]

I trust you to correct the grammar. In fact for vetting service you ought to have a % IF we get it past the editor.

I also want yr/ opinion of its fitness for Rev/ Polit Econ//[2]

Do you think they want MORE detail.?? or that I have put in too much theory and ethics??

I have tried to stick to narrative. And can't get it much shorter.

The chinese is for yr/ personal diversion/ tho' the Matin[3] might act as shoe horn with edtr??

I have omitted break of London gold market, from prudence.

Wd/ it be better to try to convince the edtr/ of my watchfulness by risking the remark that Russian dumping,[4] and increase of gold production may have contributed to the break BUT that there is possibly another factor. Even the god damn rot/schilds[5] may suspect that the public wont be ass enough to go back into the cage.

I can either cut the article or I can EXPLAIN or lengthen parts you think more suited to rev. pol/ ec/

If the WHOLE is just wrong for the purpose, please say so

Not a matter where my "feelings" are entangled.

1. Probably EP's "A che serve il danaro?" which ORA translated. This is also mentioned in the next letter.

2. Since EP's article was written in Italian, the journal he meant was probably *Revista Politica Economica*. We have been unable to locate either the journal or EP's article.

3. *Le Matin*, the Paris daily.

4. A reference to the gold scare of 1937 precipitated by an increase in Russia's gold production. See "Financial Notes."

5. The Rothschild family of bankers, a favorite target for EP's fulminations against "usurocracy."

2. TLU-1   [7–26 June] 1937
[Rapallo]
{1937}

Dear Signora Agresti
 I have tried to keep this foot note in bounds. It wd. take another whole
article to go into the reasons for Alberta[1] etc.
 I dont think I can get the note shorter. I hope it is clear/ or will be when
the office has vetted it and put it into Italian.
 If I say any more it will merely overbalance the article on paper money.
 IF they accept this, I can of course go on.. But we agreed, I think, that
this article was no place for theories and arguments.
 anyhow/ R.S.V.P.

 1. The province of Alberta, Canada, elected a Social Credit government in 1935
led by **William Aberhart**. Social Credit was the economic theory of **Major Clifford Hugh Douglas** to which EP had been converted as early as 1917.

1938–40

There are no extant letters from EP that can be dated to 1938–40.

1941

3. TLU-1   29 July 1941
[Rapallo]
29 Lug/ {[1941]}

Dear Signora Agresti
 A talk by Princess Troubetzkoi[1] on Bolchevik in English During/ traslit-
teo [illegible deletion] yesterday evening, THE most important I have
heard from Rome Radio/ should be printed and diffused in ten languages/
 To save time, can you get in touch with her and make an Italian trans-
lation/ which I shall try to have published in Meridiano.[2]

cordially yrs/

 1. **Princess Amélie Troubetzkoi.** ORA responded on 5 August 1941 that she had
acquired a transcript of the talk, which was broadcast on the American Hour of
Rome Radio.
 2. *Meridiano di Roma,* the journal edited by the outspoken **Cornelio di Marzio.**

4. TLU-1   25 October [1941]
[Rapallo]

Car Signore Agresti

Quanto fretta avete? per i nomi?[1] Tinkham[2] wd/ understand it/ IF he saw it, if it cd/ be drawn to his attention.

Fish[3] probably wd/ neither understand nor read it. Si batte a ferri corti adesso, non con idea.[4] Non so che posizione Voorhis[5] ha preso. Se io potrei vedere il fascicolo potrei giudicare meglio.[6]

The American Exporter/[7] weekly (or monthly). I may be able to find the address. solo giornale ch io conosco/ che ha un interesse speciale nel sojetto.[8]

Chicago Tribune;[9] utile/[10]

Mandatelo a Packhard ed altri giornaliti Americani rimasti a Roma.

se sanno leggere Italiano, leggerano molto piu presto una cosa in lingua loro.

Pensero ad altri nomi/

Molto immerso nella traduzione Confucio/ mente non molto disponibile per altro.

cordiali saluti.[11]

1. It.: "In how much of a hurry are you for the names?" Presumably of members of the American First Party.

2. **George Holden Tinkham.**

3. **Hamilton Fish Jr.**

4. It.: "One beats with a short iron now, not with ideas."

5. **H. J. Voorhis.**

6. It.: "I don't know what position Voorhis has now. If I could see the dossier, I could judge better."

7. Monthly journal of foreign trade, based in New York City.

8. It.: "[it is] the only journal I know that has a special interest in the subject."

9. EP contributed numerous articles, notes, and letters to the Paris edition of the *Chicago Tribune* between 1921 and 1934. His friend William Bird was a correspondent at the *Tribune* throughout this period.

10. It.: "useful."

11. It.: "Send it to Packhard and other American journalists remaining in Rome. If they can read Italian, they would [nonetheless] read much more quickly in their own language. I will think of other names. I am much immersed in the translation of Confucius. [I have] not much intelligence left for other things. Cordial regards." EP means **Reynolds Packard.**

1942

There are no extant letters from EP that can be dated to 1942.

1943

5. TLU-1   29 November [1943]
[Rapallo]
29 Nov.

Dear O/R/A

Thanks for bulletin. Somewhere between here and Tokyo is an article beginning: I belong to a learned society, that is to say I subscribe to a comic paper, eh, that is to say I BElong to a learned society.

Poor Donaldson[1] has to hold down a job in a pseudoversity. However he did admit at end of article/ what I have said more clearly.

Aint MY pt/ of view also American, namely that the unutterable hog or jew pimp Morgenthau;[2] working with Roosenstein[3] has taken ten billion out of the American pocket/ whereof FOUR billion excess profits to hell filth and co/ now being used to speculate in munitions etc/

Believe I have sent a meditation (another) to Meridiano on Um' Accademia per far ridere pelli.[4]

Had I been able to get to Washington[5] I shd/ have tried to mention the matter in conversation to the thief in chief.

Mac N/Wison[6] thinks (or thought) it was messianic urge. J.C.[7] about due again in the White House.

Am soothing myself with Flaubert's correspondence.

                                                              yours

1. **John Donaldson.**
2. **Henry Morgenthau Jr.**
3. Franklin Delano Roosevelt. EP invents many derisive names for Roosevelt, including Oozefelt, Oozesmelt, Oozenstein, Oozenstink, the Ooze, Roosenstein, Sowbelly, Roosenbelly, the great he-sow, SowJowl, Jewzfeld, Roose, and Goosenstein.
4. It.: "the American Academy, which would make one laugh oneself silly."
5. EP tried to leave for the United States in mid-1941, hoping to speak to Roosevelt and imagining he could avert U.S. involvement in the war.
6. **Robert McNair Wilson.**
7. Jesus Christ. A sardonic reference to Roosevelt, who was reelected in 1943.

1944–47

There is a long break in the correspondence from 1944 to 1946 as a consequence of the turmoil in Italy and EP's arrest, detention at Pisa, and incarceration at St. Elizabeths Hospital in Washington, D.C., as mentally unfit to stand trial for treason.

6. ALS-2   [ans. 22 June 1947]

Dear ORA

Tanti saluti a Rosamaria.[1] Credo che sia la stessa (e sola) persona che mi ha mai chiamato "gigante".[2]

No I did NOT know Villari[3] had Procida'd.[4] I have heard NOTHING about le vicende[5] of Anyone. & Monotti[6] is a pig for not having sent me items. Villari can now send a whole census & show that age is (properly) superior to the 1/2 baked. Prefer chinese order.

Fanaticisms are from abstract statements. & a religion hatched in slums & cut off from agriculture is a *curse* whether of 1000 or 3000 years.

I wish Varé[7] wd/ overcome etc. & go see (as if I were present) George Santayana,[8] at the convent. S. Stefano Rotond (6. via S.S. Rotond.). I think hardly anyone does & Varé is the suitable person.

of course if the *young* had started reading me 20 years ago the world *wd* be brighter

Try Frobenius[9] instead of the trype you list in yrs.[10]

ever

EP

& do see Vicari[11] even if his modesty makes him wait for an invitation

1. **Rosamaria** is one of ORA's adopted granddaughters.

2. It.: "Many greetings to Rosamaria. I believe she is the same (and only) person who has ever called me 'giant.'"

3. **Luigi Villari.**

4. It.: "been jailed."

5. It.: "the goings on."

6. **Francesco Monotti.**

7. **Daniele Varè.** EP usually has *Varé* in the letters; ORA, however, uses the correct accent.

8. EP had met **George Santayana** in 1939 in Italy. By this time Santayana lived in a nursing home run by the Blue Nuns. On 16 December 1947 ORA reported that Villari did visit Santayana.

9. **Leo Frobenius.**

10. Presumably Koestler's *Darkness at Noon* and Papini's *Lettere agli uomini di Papa Celestino VI*, books ORA mentions in a 25 May 1947 letter.

11. **Giambattista Vicari.**

7. ALS-1   13 August 1947

13 Ag.

Dear ORA

The patrimoniole[1] is of course completely iniquitous And idiotic. a penalization of merit. I told you the answer some years ago. I didn't invent it. Wot about Coppola??[2] can he see it yet. The objection to thought rather strong.

The Brit Emp now rotted probably rose because Herbert of Cherbury[3] had more sense than Mac/yevelly[4]—(I spose a slimy scot??)[5] Anyhow Herb. saw need of ethos.—So did Gucciardini.[6] or @ least a use for it. I spose Di Marzio[7] was shot for digging up that line in Gcdi.[8]

&. so on.

I still hunger for news of people in particular.

{EP}

There is only
one tax that
is not blasphemy
&. bestialitas.

1. Presumably *patrimoniale*, It.: "property tax."
2. Probably Francesco Coppola (1878–1957), a Nationalist party intellectual and Fascist political writer who supported the Nationalist fusion with the Fascist party in 1923, or **Coppola d'Anna.**
3. **Edward Herbert, Baron of Cherbury.**
4. Niccolò Machiavelli.
5. The Herbert family was not Scottish but Welsh.
6. **Francesco Gucciardini.**
7. **Cornelio di Marzio.**
8. Possibly "A chi stima . . . l'onore assai" (92/618), It.: "to him who esteems . . . honor enough"—a quotation EP also uses as a postscript in his *Confucius:* "Nothing is impossible to him who holds honor in sufficient esteem." See Terrell 1:556. In a letter to **Boris de Rachewiltz** EP wrote: "Gucciardini. It was Di Marzio the real Di M/ who dug up Guic/ in fact ABC might well put up THAT motto" (30 May 1954; NYPL).

8. TLS-3 6 October 1947

We include the following letter of ORA's partly for its intrinsic interest in revealing the circumstances in Italy and her assessment of the postwar period and partly because the correspondents had it published in the little magazine Four Pages *in January 1948.*

Dear Ezra Pound:

We sit here watching Europe dying; the physicians all want to bleed the patient though they disagree as to the best way of doing so; but bleeding hardly seems the right cure for haemorrage. England, under an ultra fascist government[1] is now trying autarchy,[2] which was a capital offence when tried by Italy; but to become autarkic under the best circumstances takes time, and to try it now in England is rather like saying (to a starving horse) "aspetta cavallin' che l'erba cresce!"[3] Here we had this year a disastrou(s)ly bad harvest, and so did the rest of Europe, and so grain must be imported from North and South America, and that means dollars, and the problem is to find them. Meantime Einaudi,[4] a hidebound orthodox economist of the gold-standard school(,) is trying credit deflation in the hopes that by bankrupting the big business firms he will force them to put their goods on the market at liquidation prices (and lower the price level), but the immediate result of this is further unemployment, and the need for further currency inflation to distribute unemployment doles, and so the snow-ball keeps growing. The Communist remedy here for high cost of living is strikes(;) to stop the little production there is in order to meet famine conditions sounds an Alice in Wonderland remedy.

The Government has a grand plan for increasing production by irrigation and land-reclamation, but it is a long-term plan. FAO[5] is urging arachidi and soja,[6] and something is being done, but only in a half-hearted way. This year there is a good olive-crop, though recent heavy hail storms in Apulia have done much damage. [. . .]

1. The Labour party quit the wartime coalition government under Winston Churchill on 26 May 1945. **Clement Attlee**'s Labour party won the subsequent election (5 July 1945). It seems highly idiosyncratic to characterize Attlee's government as "ultra fascist." ORA must have been thinking of Churchill, for whom such an epithet would still be a canard, but not such a ludicrous one.

2. A self-sufficient economy functioning without need for exports or imports.

3. It.: "wait horse, until the grass grows!"

4. **Luigi Einaudi.**

5. The Food Agriculture Organization of the United Nations, with headquarters in Washington and a European Bureau in the former International Institute of Agriculture in Rome. The institute was founded by **David Lubin.**

6. It.: "peanuts and soybeans." The recurring peanuts and soybeans relate to ORA's and EP's interest in nutrition, especially of the poor. Peanuts and soybeans are inexpensive sources of protein and niacin, a deficiency of which causes pellagra. EP had reviewed Paul de Kruif's *Hunger Fighters* (1928), an account of the discovery of the cure for the disease, in *New English Weekly* (see "Hunger Fighters").

1948

9. TLS-2   25 February 1948

"Political Immaturity" was sent by ORA to **Dallam Simpson,** *editor of* Four Pages, *who had already published part of letter 8. So far as we know, this article did not appear in* Four Pages. *We include it because it presents a definitive statement of ORA's political attitudes at the time.*

"Political Immaturity"!!

To talk as "liberators" often do, of the "political immaturity" of the Italian only proves the "historical incipiency" of the "liberators".

Call the Italians bad or mad or whatever you like, but don't talk of the "political immaturity" of a people who down 3000 years of history have done more to mould European civilisation than any other single influence.

Of the Roman Empire we will only say that it offers perhaps the only case in which the late descendants of the conquered recognise by general consent that the influence of their conquerors was beneficial. (Can the Irish, the Hindus, the Red Indians say as much?)

Let us leave Rome for Italy. In the Vth century Italians fleeing from Attila and his Huns found refuge in the desolate lagoon(s) of Venetia and founded there a State which evolved a form of Government that lasted until the treaty of Campoformio (1798).[1] During the intervening thirteen centuries the Venetian Republic was the most prosperous and stable government in Europe. It grew rich in commerce, held its own with the most powerful States of Europe, was instrumental in saving Europe from the Turks, and left behind an unrivalled heritage of beauty, of such universal appeal that not even two world wars with their air bombardments dared destroy it.

Another example: the internal government of the Roman Catholic Church. Italian genius was the main force in building up that system, at once democratic and autocratic, flexible in detail, unbending in principle, infinitely adjustable yet unalterable, that stepped with its hierarchy into the place left vacant by the Roman Empire, gradually civilised the Barbarians, gave sp{i}ritual unity to Europe until the XVIth century, then spread to the furthest confines of the globe and has dealt in unbroken continuity down nineteen centuries, yesterday with Roman Emperors, today with American Presidents.

Compare such achievements with the pitiful record of the League of Nations[2] and the still less promising UNO[3] and say on which side "political immaturity" is found!

The Italian is a realist wedded to an idealist. Passionately parochial yet irresistibly attracted to universal ideas. He is not, never has been, a nationalist. When Mazzini[4] wanted to create United Italy he had to convince himself and his followers that they were working not only for Young Italy but also for Young Europe, for the Poles, the Hungarians, the Germans, the South Slavs, that all might enjoy as peoples that individual personality the Italian holds sacred in man.

When Fascism fired the Italian imagination it was above all by seeking a solution for a world-felt need, that of harmonising the interests of capital, management, and labour in the Guild[5] or Corporative State.[6] Time may yet show that the "politically immature" Italian has blazed a path along which others are travelling in many climes. The {"}Guild State{"} may yet save the world from the "Servile State".[7]

It was when Mussolini ceased to be guided by his Italian instinct, when he attempted to link up Italy to an aggressive military power, to teach the Italian to feel contempt for the African and hatred for the Jew, that he failed. The Italian neither despises the African nor hates the Jew, in whom he sees facets of the great unitarian whole, humanity, of which each individual deserves respect and the whole forms the mystical body travelling towards its ultimate destiny.

When Fascism rejected parochialism (the individual) and internationalism (mankind) for nationalism it ceased to be Italian, and it died before the "Liberators" arrived. But a day will come when the contribution fa{s}cist Italy made to the solution of both local and universal problems will be studied and perhaps understood.

1. The 1797 treaty between France and Austria.

2. Created in the aftermath of World War I by the incorporation of the Covenant in the Treaty of Versailles and other Treaties of Peace in 1919.

3. United Nations Organization.

4. **Giuseppe Mazzini.**

5. The Fascist state.

6. See letters 54 and 55.

7. A reference to *The Servile State*, in which **Hilaire Belloc** argued for the abandonment of capitalism and the avoidance of socialism in favor of a "collectivist state," in principle not unlike Mussolini's Fascist state. Its epigraph concluded: "if we do not restore the Institution of Property, we cannot escape restoring the Institution of Slavery; there is no third course." George Bernard Shaw, representing the Socialist, or Fabian, side, debated the question of slavery versus service with Belloc at a Fabian meeting. See Cole.

10. TLU-2 [1948]

O.R.A.

O DAMN

If people wd. listen to grampaw WHEN he speaks and not 30 years after. American wypers plugging for Scandinavian union, and dont know
it was Quisling's[1] idea in 1937 or before.

And mebbe you better contact some nice young anarchists[2] who print
(I mean they work the press) in Bearsville N.Y. BUT I hv/ to tell 'em. The
state is not THE supreme evil, it is supremely dangerous, and has to be
watched EVERY minute/ a world without honour is a dungheap, fit only
for people like R, and C.[3]

of course (damn all, I must get you a copy of all the Cantos.)

coin royal prerogative, i.e. THE essence of sovereignty. of course the
republic (after the death of Cato ETC,) {kaput}

glad Villari has got to that.[4] now make him READ the U,S, constitution, wot I been talking about ever since ever.

AND get the Confucius into print and circulation. I think a VERY far
country will probably beat the wops to it. But hate to mention promises
till they turn into facts.

Walter[5] is only ¼ wop/ one wafty grammaw is a Hrooshun, related I
believe to respectable teutonic line, so mebbe not so DAMN-russ.

Glad his education has been properly started amid the family reliques,
after passin' my first youth among 'em at S.Lodge[6] etc.

How is Malú.?[7]

An error of FACT in Mercure de France,[8] Jan. 1. shd/ be corrected. review otherwise friendly and sane.

A bloke signing C.Ruggieri[9] in Momento-Sera, 23/24 Feb. makes mis-
statement, possibly from vagueness, and fact that wop NEVER hears ~~fHH~~
the difference between one word and another. I dont remember the MAN,
but do remember saying PART of what he records. I never said Lao Tze[10]
had a mentalità massonica.[11] I said he was subversive, damnably subversive.

It is a case where a wrong word can stir ~~malie~~ malice and make trouble. There were TWO Adams presidents.[12] etc. and the scandal, bad press
etc. of second part of Faust due (on examination) to something more interesting than betrayal of mystic secrets. Mebbe wd/ be more stimulat-
ing to MAKE 'em hunt for it.

I'll tell YOU in a later letter, if you don't know, and care to.

You shall also have my early poEMS if the new edtn. ever comes off
the press. I have seen proofs.

Somebody might compliment Einaudi on having exchanged me for
Lucky Luciano[13] and the rotogravure section of l'Europeo. and doing
NOTHING to get the swap put into reverse.

The lack of magnanimity is undecorative, vide treatment of Petain.[14]
Glad to see reporter hadn't the faccia tosta[15] to visit Knut Hanson.[16]

The BASTARDS don't KNOW that the right to coin IS the sovereignty. case of OPEN power or secret power. the open is preferable.

Pellizzi's "Rivoluzione Mancata"[17] shd. be useful, couldn't J.Drummond[18] translate it?

shd. be SEVERELY criticized IN Italy by friends, for UNCONSCIOUSNESS of meaning of american constitution/ callit TAINT of his years in Univ. of Sodom on Thames,[19] where he did NOT assassinate Laski.[20]

Pel's own fault if certain ideas were boycotted by his Instituto

1. **Vidkun Quisling.**
2. **Dachine Rainer** and **Holley Cantine.**
3. Roosevelt and Churchill.
4. Perhaps to the notes EP sent him via ORA.
5. **Siegfredo Walter Igor Raimondo de Rachewiltz.**
6. South Lodge, that is, 80 Campden Hill, London, the home of **Isabel Violet Hunt,** daughter of the Pre-Raphaelite painter Alfred William Hunt and mistress of **Ford Madox Ford.**
7. **Malù.**
8. See Vallette's "Quelques poètes américains récents (1)," in which he reviews the January–March issue of *Sewanee Review,* especially the article in it by F. O. Matthiessen. Presumably both the "sanity" and the "error of fact" EP mentions are in the following: "La division entre poètes américains et poètes anglais devient de plus en plus artificielle à mesure que l'art devient plus international. Eliot et Pound sont Américaine d'origine. Mais le premier est incorporé à la littérature anglaise contemporaine, et tous deux ont exercé en Angleterre, sinon par delà les frontières de ce pays, une influence capitale" (148). (The division between American and English poets is becoming more and more artificial as art becomes more international. Eliot and Pound are American in origin, but the first is incorporated into English literature and both have exercised a great influence—in England, if not elsewhere.) The unidentified "error" is perhaps the denial of EP's and T. S. Eliot's influence outside England.
9. Ruggeri, "Invece del capestro il premio 'Bollingen.'"
10. Lao-tzu (sixth century B.C.).
11. It.: "masonic mentality."
12. EP is referring to John Adams (1736–1826) and John Quincy Adams (1767–1848). Presumably a synecdoche for "public enemy."
13. Presumably a synecdoche for "public enemy."
14. **General Philippe Pétain.**
15. It.: "cheek," that is, audacity.
16. Possibly Harald Franklin Knudsen, author of *Jeg var Quislings sekretar.*
17. **Camillo Pellizzi's** *Una rivoluzione mancata.*
18. **John Drummond.**
19. No doubt the University of London, where Pellizzi taught Italian literature for a time.
20. **Harold Joseph Laski.**

11. TLU-2   [1948]

O.R.A.

Villari's interesting,[1] will be dealt with at first opportine.

The weariness, reading Cione,[2] in fact ALL of 'em.[3] Does V/[4] meet or correspond with any of 'em. There were honest men like Soldato[5] who went with the republic[6] DESPITE the socialization, sacrificing their good sense to desire for unity. Now PRIMO: I never in the 20 years met an anti-fascista who wasn't a god damned fool. But to socialize from under the wheels INSTEAD of from the Credit/ is plain stupidity. There is all C.H. Douglas'[7] THOUGHT to consider. There is Bryan's confession to Kitson[8] etc.

B. Abbot[9] and others see danger of centralization of power. and there is DANGER. The evil is not private issue of private money but private[,] private AND irresponsible, and they haven't even read the American constitution. (and monopolistic issue of PUBLIC purchasing power.)

pur/ pow[10] INCLUDES credit and money. Money being properly PRESENT tense, the product of WORK and NATURE, or certificate of deposit of same, existence of same, DELIVERABLE existence of same, not Lawes'[11] error. Cannot issue money against LAND, or anything undeliverable. Credit is the future of money.

Must reexamine Aristotle's terminology. ~~XPEA~~ XREIA,[12] if I remember rightly, obscured in Loeb edtn/ translation.

needed (or wanted) deliverable goods. [illegible deletion] Work as MEASURE now assumed, even in Mercure de France 1947. Measure of value not the same thing as certificate of existence of product. arguments re/ Russia now mostly based on how many hours work the goddam moscovite has to do to get a given object (overcoat or whatever).. As for consumer credit......Douglas 30 years ago; ERP.???

I shall prob/ die of stroke from rage at idiocy of people who nevr read the authors I recommend, at least not without 30 or more years time lag.

Villari has got to Mommsen.[13] he NEEDS Douglas and Gesell.[14]

He needn't write about 'em. It's Cione who needs the light. Socialists nearly as bad as Hen. Georgites.[15] Pellegrini[16] rather "dumb". Then of course a lot of 'em dont read english. Bodrero,[17] hopeless?

Pini[18] left out a question mark?? when talking about sanita morale[19] of the eyetalyans? I grant Pini's sanita morale, but wish it were more contagious

Who's the DiMarzio[20] mentioned without prenom? now doing something or other.

and of course goddamit ALL over the occident, this bestial stopping of the mind at the Tigris and Euphrates, ham ignorance of Chinese history and thought.

Notes from E.P. received recently.

Have Villari or someone get in direct touch with Ronald Duncan[21]
Meade Farm
Welcombe, nr/Bude, [illegible deletion]
Cornwall, England
for Duke of Bedford[22] and agronomy.
Report from Italian conversation—7 campi, rendered QUATTRO milioni from PEANUTS, in the Veneto. But [illegible deletion] used for oil.
Got to get BUTTER idea into their blocks re/ arachidi. And into ALL of 'em: Alberi e Cisterni.[23] Arachidi, Acero[24] Soja.
If AMERICAN U.S. Embassy in London can get Japanese Kadzu[25] seed for [illegible deletion] Duncan; the same gang in Rome can be made to do the decent re American seed for Italy. If somebody TELLS, goddamit, t'ell with 'em.
When is plenty you money-reform.
When abundance has been bitched you AGRONOMY.
None of the Italian papers has yet mentioned, arachidi, soja, acero
(Not clear {w}hether Brooks Adams HAS been translated—published—in Italian?[26] Or what other of books recommended by E.P.
as Jean Cruet's *La vie du droit*—pubd 1914[27]
Wm. E. Woodward's New American History[28]
(pubd by Farrar and Rinehart—said to
be a stunning thing)

1. Villari's *Italian Foreign Policy under Mussolini*. ORA sent the original Italian edition of this work to EP in mid-June 1948.

2. Presumably Edmondo Cione, mentioned by Villari while giving an account of the Milanese general strike of March 1944: "In the meantime, attempts were being made within the territory of the Italian Social Republic, with approval of the Duce himself, to bring about an understanding between Fascists and anti-Fascists on a patriotic basis, among others by Professor Edmondo Cione, a Neapolitan scholar and author, who then professed himself an anti-Fascist but was attracted by the personality of Mussolini" (336).

3. Presumably former Fascists.

4. **Luigi Villari.**

5. **Giuseppe Soldato.**

6. Presumably the Salò Republic (9 September 1943–28 April 1945). It was Mussolini's counter government, established for him by the Germans, who rescued him from Italian authorities on 12 September 1943. Victor Emmanuel had arrested Mussolini on 25 July 1943.

7. **Major Clifford Hugh Douglas.**

8. William Jennings Bryan's (1850–1925) so-called Free Silver campaign for president in 1896 advocated the fight against the interests of the banking class. Though an advocate for the demonetization of silver, **Arthur Kitson** supported Bryan. According to Eva Hesse, EP wrote to **Noel Stock** on the subject: "William J. Bryan admitted to Arthur Kitson many years ago that the 'Free Silver' campaign was window dressing" (183). This "confession" is mentioned in canto 97.

9. **Beatrice Abbott.**

10. Purchasing power.

11. EP has in mind John Law (1671–1729), a Scottish financier active in France who founded the Banque Général in 1716 that first issued paper currency. Later he formulated the Mississippi Scheme, an ultimately disastrous speculation plan for the development of the French territories in the Mississippi Valley and Louisiana. He would thus have been involved in issuing "money against LAND."

12. Gk.: "use." See letter 67.

13. **Theodor Mommsen.** In *Italian Foreign Policy under Mussolini* Villari noted Mommsen's influence on Mussolini: "Quoting from the German historian . . . who said years ago . . . that one does not remain in Rome without a universal idea, he [Mussolini] declared: 'I believe and affirm that the only universal idea existing in Rome today is that which radiates from the Vatican'" (10).

14. **Silvio Gesell.**

15. Followers of **Henry George.**

16. **Domenico Pellegrini-Giampetro.**

17. **Emilio Bodrero.**

18. **Georgio Pini.**

19. It.: "healthy morality" or "moral sanity."

20. It is not clear if EP is thinking here of **Cornelio di Marzio.**

21. **Ronald Duncan.**

22. **Twelfth Duke of Bedford.**

23. It.: "trees and cisterns."

24. It.: "maple trees."

25. Kudzu.

26. EP probably means **Brooks Adams's** *The Law of Civilization and Decay.*

27. For EP's view on Cruet's book, see "Rosanov e Cruet."

28. **William E. Woodward's** *A New American History.* EP found much in the book to admire. He and Woodward exchanged several letters between January 1933 and May 1936. For a selection of these letters, see "Letters to Woodward."

12. TLU-1   [ans. 18 June 1948]

O.R.A.

anonimo/[1] and anybody can incorporate it an article over their own signature or quote as from an observer of the interregnum. all or part.

"Lo Stato è lo spirito del popolo."[2] Mussolini. And Mussolini's state fell when it ceased to be the italian spirit, which is one of order and moderation, as anyone who observed the quiet and good order ~~that~~ with which north italy functioned during the 600 days *preceding* the "liberation" can testify from experience. The basic spirit of italy is abstentionist so far as politics are concerned. It is regional rather than factional. Hence the slowness in union.

[in ORA's hand:] {18.VI.'48}

1. It.: "anonymous."
2. It.: "The State is the spirit of the people."

13. TLU-1   23 October 1948

Dear O.R.A.

Another Meridiano come, a bit dull. Will NONE of these well inten-
tioned socialoid nuts EVER understand that to "control the econ/ forces
and equate 'em to needs of nation" is O.K. but that to try to do it by socialization of EVERYTHING or anything save money issue is like trying
to run a locomotive from the cowcatcher or from under the wheels.

Socialists are idiots, and liberals a mere shop front for usury and inter-
nat/ money lenders (some of whom despite your fanatical defence of 'em
are yidds, and the dirtiest sort of yidds.)

No literate nation will go on having its pockets picked by redshield/
BUT socializing dishclothes and diapers won't stop 'em.

Really Varé or Villari ought by now to attained sufficient mental maturity to begin to see that. Not that I suspect Varé of being socialoid or
anything but royalist and snob.

Personally have no objection to an honest king or even an honest pope
(if that be conceivable). "Make him of wood with steel springs", perpet/
not heredit/

Note from Alden[1] showing that he had done what he personally cd/...as
he wd/ have to account to auditors etc.

He tries to tell me there is honesty in second hand book trade (like you
stickin' up for money lenders), I spose someone will discover an honest
antiquary or art-dealer (specimen for the Smithsonian).

benedictions

1. **John Alden,** who, at EP's request, arranged for ORA's copy of **Gabriele Rossetti's** *Il mistero dell' amor platonico del medio aevo* to be bought by the University of Pennsylvania Library.

14. TLU-1   [ans. 2 July 1948]

AGRESTI

If childs[1] lung trouble is TB/ might be useful to know that late Dr
Tweddell[2] cured TB (pulmonary) with finely powdered borax, blown into
air of bed room with ordinary flit squirt, of DDT atomizer.[3]

no publicity obtainable because it hits the TB industry. two dollars
worth of borax, treatment at home, no use for swank hospitals.

Check up with Ronald Duncan who I think used this method at least
in part, and his wife nearly cured.

Borax must be in very fine dust to get down into alveoli of lungs.

Was to have seen Tweddell in U.S. in '39[4] but he died. However, I once had his notes from medical journals.

he was convinced. and cert/ disinterested. Heard later of swank specialist in Paris working it with nickel plated tubles tibes de luxe and soc. ladies nude on (may have been onyn divans.)

dollars two $ worth of borax lasted six months. Might get some publicity now in stricken europe.

WHAT has become of Umberto Notari?[5] His {"}Due Monete{"} writ several years before Worgl experiment,[6] brilliant. a couple of blurrs, which I cd/ clear up: p. 129 imobiliare, and 145 immobiliare redditizia,[7] where he dont see implications. but one of few clear minds, not afraid to think. IMBECILITY of those damnd literary circles, that never know when an author exists. Fierar Letteraria,[8] froust[9] etc. Wd anything persuade Notari to look at my Orientamenti?[10]

I tried to find a pub r/ for trans/ of Notari's Terrorista, years ago, but nobody had sense enough to mention his Saggi to me. TOO dumb. the blinkin lot of 'em. Marinetti[11] should have.

1. **Malù.**

2. **Francis I. Tweddell.**

3. ORA seems to have ignored EP's suggestions. Instead, the family had **Malù** treated by **Eugenio Morelli.** She wrote of him: "(by the way an impenitent Fascist, for he found under it the means to carry out ideas for saving lives which would have required years and years to get through under a purely parliamentary regime) as he still compresses the lung with the pneumo-thorax method, injecting air every five or six days" (15 May 1943).

4. EP visited the United States in 1939.

5. **Umberto Notari.**

6. An experiment with stamp scrip money (a monetary reform recommended by **Silvio Gesell**) in the small Tyrolean town of Wörgl in the early 1930s. See EP's "A Visiting Card," in *Selected Prose, 1909–1965*, 314–16, and cantos 41/205 and 74/441.

7. It.: "real estate property."

8. *La Fiera Letteraria* (The literary beast), a Roman literary journal that published EP's works in translation between 1928 and 1961.

9. "To rest lazily, lounge." EP is condemning literary groups in general.

10. Many times in the correspondence EP betrays his eagerness to have his *Orientamenti*, or at least part of it, translated and republished.

11. **Emilio Filippo Tommaso Marinetti.**

15. TLU-2   [ans. 12 Dec. 1948]

Dear O.R.A.

the jewish impertinence of the god damned Xtians in sticking their
label on [illegible deletion] a decent style of conduct practiced and formulated 2000 years before the publicity agent from Tarsus[1] messed up
the decent teachings of a possibly mythical, but traditionally immature
protagonist in the dirtiest and most-trouble making district of a disthra-
cted planet surpasses even Fordie's[2] capacities as an exaggerator to define.
That there are respectable arab physicians, and medicos of other semitic
tribes I wd/ be the last to deny. In fact I am about to elucubrate a declaration that I am not anti-semite, but want to find a candid mode of defining a position in regard to certain diseases of thought which do seem to
afflict even Spinoza (whom they kicked out) and Montaigne[3] whom I
believe they did not. Find me {a} nice adjective that will damn Lao-tze
along with the other pollutors or perverters of the human mind, and I will
try to get you an american radio prize. I think you wd/ make more by
candid memoirs than by translating work inferior to yr/ own, but yr/ title is too long for the ang/am market. cut it down to three pejoratives and
"some exceptions". No market for saints. Vide the quote from Yeats in
4 P/ "has appeared in the Punjab[4] etc." well to save you looking up lost
files. "A saint has appeared in the Punjab, but the public need feel no
anxiety, the police are already on his trail."

That for the British Raj/ as per also Travaso 26 Sept. where Weinstein
Kirkeberg[5] has got J.Bull[6] to.

I have been using Geryone in Cantos[7] for a long time, no use taking
NEW photos, when perfect ones already exist. L'Europa sarà...../// waaaal
a young Englishman is now getting enthusiastic over a vol/ by the sotto
scritto J. and/or M.///[8] too little and too late.

Harpies, humbugs, sycophants and a few exceptions "might land a
pubr/

As I gather the joke re/ the F. fambly[9] was that they didn't and dear
Violet's[10] old family retainer supplied V/ with conversational matter in
proposito...in fact for two of the most lovable people gawd ever turned
loose on the planet...etc...and I remember at Rap/[11] having pointed out
his egregious inaccuracy re/ the undersigned, in fantasia and Fordie trying to find out by search of mental scenario what initial fact had given
rise to which bit of decorative phantasmagoria. Opium smokers also [il-
legible deletion] start from a point. Dont feel obliged to answer my
exuberances..in fact, dont write till there is something to answer, but as
in the recipe for french stage/ never prevent anyone else from doing so. I
want all the Rome news I can get. And I take it the noble Romans can

now correspond with republicans without being sent to Regina Coeli[12] or assassinated in open piazza. Evvia il Merlo.[13] and I hope you follow Tobia's gattiloscritti[14] in Travaso.

You consume yr/ own smoke to such an UNfordian extent that I never knew you had a sister till saw Angeli[15] signature in brit/paper and asked who and if/.

Sorry I never met yr/ father. I was consulted by pubr/ and approved printing his trans/ of I think the Convito. Mathews[16] prob/ knew no one else who wd. have known what it (Il Convito) was/ but even he wd/ have felt the inadvisability of injecting me (a.d. 1908 or 09 into the so serious ambience.) Wdn̶t it hv/ been a bit like de Gourmont's[17] marquise who had "never before met an american". Or had Emerson called?

Where the deuce is yr/ sister? I dont recommend manicomii[18] for war nerves...charming as some of the criminal patients are. She prob/ cdn't qualify for a criminal ward.... I dont mean that ALL murderers are genial souls, but still, take 'em by and large... I have had some good friends among 'em. Greatly regret dear old S/[19] who dropped off with a heart attack, etc.

Dick[20] is wrong on one or two minor points. Riccardo degli Uberti

I dont know if there is any way to reach him/ the letter he wrote to the Merlo is very fine, but?? misprint "raramente"[21] makes it less useful. Whether he wrote 'veramente' or simply (being in army) didn't know how often I spoke. but the "raramente" cd/ be used to weaken force of the rest of defence. (Merlo Giallo No. 127/ 7 Sept.) I wonder if they are still at ~~18~~ 16 via Domenico Chelini (if

IF that was the address, out by Barca di Remembranza unfinished church.

//

re/ guilds, O.K. but let 'em read Mommsen,[22] and understand that AUTARCHIA is right/ and that the liberi scambisti[23] are noodles. Ital/ agriculture ruin'd by dumping cheap grain from Egypt, even Antoninus P/[24] didn't stop that,// battaglia del grano,[25] also study the U,S, constitution, ALL it needs is enforcement, and yr/ guilds can be fitted in, need BOTH trade representation AND geographic as in [illegible deletion] 1800 here, when different states meant different [illegible deletion] agricultural interests, and shipping.

AND to learn neutrality from Svizzera{?}[26]

and so on benedictions.

thre is also a little NECESSARY history (data) in Cantos, if they cd/ ever get over their prejudice against poetry, or superstition that Walt Pater and aestheticism were the last word, and nowt but pickin dasies (OR celanDAMNdine) permitted.

What I mean re/ degli Ub/ is that "raramente" can be explained as printer's error, but Ub/ must know and not make the mistake again, even in conversation/ as it detracts from his authority. His father definitely knew the *nature* of my work. Mrs d/U/ may hv thought I only transmitted when in Rome or once each visit.

1. St. Paul.

2. **Ford Madox Ford.** EP frequently referred to him as "Fordie."

3. EP seems to think that Michel de Montaigne was Jewish, contrary to standard biographies.

4. The quotation appears in *Four Pages* 1 (Jan. 1948): 3 and is attributed to "Hyderabad paper 1897, quoted by Yeats."

5. Probably Winston Churchill.

6. John Bull, that is, England.

7. See cantos 49/245 and 51/251. EP also alludes to Geryon, the Dantean personification of usury, in cantos 88/583, 97/675, and 111/783.

8. It.: "undersigned"; the initials are of EP's 1933 pro-Fascist book, *Jefferson and/ or Mussolini.*

9. **Ford Madox Ford**'s family.

10. **Isabel Violet Hunt.**

11. Rapallo, where EP lived from 1924 to 1945.

12. A prison in Rome.

13. It.: "Hurrah for *Merlo Giallo.*"

14. It.: roughly, "cat scratches." EP is presumably denigrating the unknown Tobia's work in *Travaso*, a publication we have been unable to locate.

15. **Helen Rossetti Angeli.**

16. **Elkin Mathews.**

17. **Rémy de Gourmont.**

18. It.: "mental asylums."

19. Unidentified, but presumably a fellow inmate at St. Elizabeths.

20. **Riccardo M. degli Uberti.**

21. It.: "rarely." EP is complaining that Uberti erroneously characterized his speeches over Rome radio as rare, rather than regular events. He is anxious to cover this error lest it damage his hopes of release from the indictment of treason still hanging over him.

22. EP is presumably referring to Mommsen's *History of Rome.*

23. It.: literally, "loose or free railroad switchmen." EP apparently means "free traders." Perhaps this is an Italian idiom for that economic posture.

24. **Antoninus Pius.** EP approved of his grain laws.

25. It.: "cereal wars."

26. It.: "Switzerland."

1949

16. TLU-1   [ans. 16 January 1949]

O.R.A.

Might try in time to get some EP poetry to [illegible deletion] ORA.

When she sees Villari will she ask him if he has enough cash balance on hand to buy the [illegible deletion] Breglia "Punto di vista Monetaria"[1] and send it here. [in Dorothy Pound's hand:] {3211 10 Place—S.E.} (?Cagliostro)[2]

Has Callogero read ANY chinese philosophy or does he still mug roud in a world bounded on the East by Tigris and Euphrates.?? If he has a job he probably does NOT want to face any N matter not already chewed in undergrad/ days. Is he worth sending a copy of Pivot[3] to?

S.Johns and nearly all american beaneries ham ignorant of the orient,[4] and mean to stay so.

And Chinese philosophy outside the Confucian school just as useless and occidental or mesopotamian.[5] LaoTse, acc all versions yet seen, just as slithery as the yidds. Sheer subversive.

V.[6] much like to get Nicoletti's[7] address. dont know Capitani[8] but may have met him and not caught name.

NO american printed matter can be considered as statement of fact/ certain{ly} NO periodical reports of Europe/ that stuff was sent to inform V/ what sort of trype was current here.

I suppose the perlite way to putt it to Cagliostro is: Does he WANT his mind to stay bounded on the East by the Tigris and Euphrates?

I note in Harry-stop-her-knees {διὰ τ' ἀργύριον πολεμοῦμεν γάρ;}[9] with several other current rubs and ribs, including operation on acquisitiveness.

[marginal note in Dorothy Pound's hand:]{(Written later than Xmas Day.)}

---

1. In her letter of 19 December 1948 ORA praises EP by calling him a "fighter against usury" and goes on to mention that Breglia, professor of monetary science at the University of Rome, is rumored to share EP's opinion that the root of the economic problems is to be sought in the monetary system. She has his lessons on economy from "Punto di Vista Monetaria" (Monetary point of view) but has not had time to read it. This is what probably prompts EP, who is on the lookout for monetary allies. In her letter of 16 January 1949 ORA mentions that Villari has phoned her to say that he has sent Breglia's work to EP.

2. **Guido Calogero,** who was preparing for a three-year appointment at McGill University, Montreal, by taking English lessons with ORA.

3. EP's *Confucius: The Unwobbling Pivot and the Great Digest.* EP sent it to ORA on 3 April 1947, but two months later she still had not read it.

4. EP probably means St. John's College in Annapolis, Maryland, which had a curriculum focusing on the classics of Western Culture, as did other American universities ("beaneries"), and not those of the East.

5. EP's euphemism for the Semitic peoples.

6. **Luigi Villari.**

7. **Giaccino Nicoletti.** In her letter of 19 December 1948 ORA had reported that she had asked Calogero for news of Nicoletti and had learned that he was working with a publishing house in Milan but she had been unsuccessful in her attempt to find his address. Nicoletti avoided persecution following the war and ORA was "very glad that he was not one of the many victims of the Red Terror."

8. EP's comment is in response to ORA's reference (in her letter of 19 December 1953) to **Aldo Capitini,** "who it seems is now prominent as a worker for world federation and is also a vegetarian and the advocate of some new form of pantheistic religion!"

9. EP is quoting l. 489 of Aristophanes' *Lysistrata:* "Do we fight for money?"

17. TLU-1 [ans. 22 Feb. 1949]

O.R.A.

Saturnalian benedictions and buon anno.[1] Still think many of yr/ friends are "dumb", probably impossible to get new ideas in Varé and co/ but you might drive 'em to reread Mommsen's fifth vol/ chaps viii and xi.[2]

Anybody who cant connect the remarks on Caesar's econ/ reforms with Gesell is ossified from the 10th vertebra upward.[3] Shan't apologize for not reading M/ sooner, as no one can read everything first. Has any copy of Beard's introduction[4] to new edtn/ of Brooks Adams reached the ancient seat?

There must be some books that can be read without police interference in the liberated zones. Great need of cheap edtn of good trans/ of Mencius[5] in italian. I thought my s-i-l's kid brother[6] had sense enough to do one but he is wasting time. Someone ignorant of chinese cd/ at least trans/ from Pauthier and Legge,[7] with a few revisions from my more lively terminology. The serious (gawdhellupuz)[8] writers use 100 pages where ten wd/ serve IF they started with definitions, and by asking WHAT IS money FOR? what are Banks FOR? what is Law FOR?

Kid here asked prof/ in econ class/ for definition of money, prof sd/ wanted time to think,/ week later said he had lost his note book.

Roosenstein's america. lable on new pants "Sports goods, do not wash, dry clean only.".

The world wd. be brighter and happier if MORE people wd/ read my products/ those few who do, are.

I see the dirty dog Bullitt[9] is now admitting facts, but hasn{'}t manhood enough to admit that others stated them in TIME, while he was a sycophanting about the knees of the great he-sow.[10]

and so forth. augurii a tutti,[11] esp/ Maru,[12] and even to Signora Varé. who won't relish 'em. What ever became of the Gertosio?[13] ~~Ole~~ Old Ub/[14] said he was sorry for for De C/[15] during the worst days.

I dont suppose Villari cd/ be jailed for procuring a new and cheap edtn of Mommsen. I suppose Italy's worst enemies are the publishers. not the hired assassins and gunmen. Why don't Varé do a Mencius, even his slickest and dirtiest old schooltie friends cdn't call that unrefined. Surely Villari could contact Ungaro/[16] very able, and should be brought into action, not let set and rot. doubtless disgusted at the wholly disgustable, but an energy not to be lost.

    1. It.: "Happy New Year."

    2. Mommsen's *The History of Rome*, vol. 5, chapter 8 ("The Joint Rule of Pompeius and Caesar") and chapter 11 ("The Old Republic and the New Monarchy").

    3. ORA replied that Villari had phoned her after consulting Mommsen and had found, in contradiction of EP, "that Caesar took away the right of issuing money from the Senate and made it over to the State" (22 Feb. 1949).

    4. Charles A. Beard's introduction to **Brooks Adams's** *The Law of Civilization and Decay*.

    5. **Mencius** is the Latin form of Meng-tzu.

    6. My son-in-law's kid brother. His first name is unknown, but his last name would be Baratti, **Boris de Rachewiltz's** name when he met Mary.

    7. EP is referring to the following works in his possession: M. G. Pauthier's *Confucius et Mencius* and James Legge's *The Chinese Classics* and *The Four Books*.

    8. God help us.

    9. **William C. Bullitt.**

    10. These events remain obscure to us, but the "he-sow" is probably Roosevelt.

    11. It.: "greetings to everyone."

    12. **Malù.**

    13. **Maria Luisa Giartosio de Courten.** ORA responded to EP's inquiry by saying that Giartosio de Courten, a friend of ORA whom EP had visited in Rome, reported that she still had his books and was keeping them until he asked for them (9 June 1949). There are additional references to Giartosio de Courten in the correspondence, including the following response in ORA's letter of 19 January 1957: "I have found a copy of the volume containing the full three parts of the 'Beatrice di Dante' [illegible deletion] by Sigra. Giartosio, with preface by Balbino Giuliano. It was mailed to you from Imola on 17th so should reach within a month. It contains much matter that will interest you."

    14. **Ubaldo degli Uberti.**

    15. Possibly **Carlo DelCroix.**

    16. It is not clear whether EP has **Andriano Ungaro** or **Filippo Ungaro** in mind.

18. TLU-2   [ans. 15 May 1949]

O.R.A.

If she receives a packet of Stud/Integrale,[1] and of Oro and Lav.[2] can she get copies to Ramperti,[3] and to Vittorio Ambrosini.?[4]

ORA seems to lack someone to run errands. BUT. etc. Ambros/ seems to know what he wants, BUT socialism has been failing for 100 years because they want to socialize all the gadgets BEFORE getting national money (the latter better than social credit, credit being the future of money, far from despicable, but less solid.)

Even Eliot[5] seemed to have understood the folly of trying to control a locomotive from UNDER the wheels instead of from throttle.

I like Ambrosini's TONE. But someone ought to have learned from the ERRORS of the Regime. Apart, from swindles, they were:

1. monetary.

2. mistaking control for advice. as in ammassi,[6] which OUGHT to be voluntary, not compulsory. vide the Mantua Fondego[7] in about the year 1400, quoted in Cantos[8] (from Rivista di Diritto Commerciale.)[9]

Does Villari see these two men? DOES he understand the main points in Oro e Lav/? I forget whether you have seen it. You have seen the Confucius, at least the Studio Integ/ (?have you seen the Pivot?) Italy had first chance at 'em. But looks as if three other countries[10] will circulate them first before the ital/ versions circulate.

responsible VS irresponsible government.

homestead VS kolchos.[11]

EVEN collective or communal farming O.K. IF voluntary. IF anyone will do it on advice in particular conditions where it is advantageous.

"Meridiano" wd/ be improved if someone, ANYone wd/ put in an informative column per issue re/ acero, arachidi, or ANY specific agric/ measures

They cd/ or shd/ be able to get correspondents from outside italy to write on these subjects/ one intelligent [illegible deletion] translator and correlator in Rome who wd/ WRITE to "[illegible deletion] cranks" abroad, or read the specialist papers, wd/ improve Meridiano no end.

They are perfectly welcome to crib/ "steal" plagarize any of my old stuff, without saying WHERE it comes from. and there is some of it which has NOT yet sunk in.

Whether anyone save yourself has ever understood six words of it is unknown to the undersigned. Mebbe a few dead men did.

Aytano, playin{'} the good old tunes. Has he anyone with him who THINKS?

Lack of imagination bad/ but lack of CURIOSITY an equal or worse curse.

Fordie{,} wrong in much, dead right that TRANSLATION of that tur-gid mass of bloodthirsty rhetoric[12] ruin{'}d english style.[13] It prevented thought. Boobs chained to cliches/ cant think.

This ~~big~~ bug house FULL of 'em. Nigger in locked room STILL in Geth-saminie,[14] warning me in interrupted sing song: .

"for he is JU-
das.

Look out! Looo KOUT!

Blood, vengeance, hate. LOOK at the damn hymns/ seas of blood.

Hypnotic effect/ pre-radio/ tribal fury/ mass hysteria very "fine" à la Hitler. and less decorative than the thirty-foot long narrow banners.

Crusades/ to get usurers into power/

"Pawn yr/ castles " y.v.t. Bertrans de Born.[15]

"renieu"/[16] presumably the [illegible deletion] renewal of a not{e}, prob/ at higher interest/ given simply as "interest" in dud/ glossaries.

nigger incident very interesting/ sub-liminal.

it is the POISON in the mixture/ naturally with nice top dressing. Lao-tse ~~near~~ subversive, but not infuriating hashish. next most dangerous soothing-syrop.

Look at the evasion propaganda in the Xtn part of Chronache Nuove.[17]

How much russian infamy method in jesuit organization centuries ago?

monopoly on god/ on any god, stinks.

let us admit a humane touch in Micah.[18] and a little clean ethics more or less isolated in scheme to get {in the} dues for the taxing levites.

Has anyone noticed the persistent boost of chemical fertilizers in "Il vero Sesto Cajo Baccelli" guida (or giuda) dell' agricoltore.[19] almanach/ praps not much sold in metropolis, pub/Rufill Firenze.[20]

Firenze porca, Behrenson's bug-wash,

anima di Placci, non anima placida.[21]

The Church of Rome decayed, got steadily stupider pari passu[22] as the jew books were put into circulation, and stupidities engrafted on the clean greek and roman ideas of the early Church.

The New Test is ANTI the old, or anti all but a very few pages of it./ a few good ideas, and much and increasing corruption. "a beaucoup plus corrompu les esprits que les moeurs"??[23] I dunno as Remy[24] is right on THAT, but for centuries it did corrompre les esprits,[25] every time a theo-logian cited other than gk/ or lat. authors.

polit/ bearing of Jim. Ists/ version.??[26] ending with Ed/ vii[27] as bishop.

Enquiring re/ Lubin vol/[28] SO were Montaigne and Spinoza, BOTH misleaders. M. a corrupter, S/ an abstracter/ headed for Mohammet.

1. EP's *Confucio Ta S'eu Dai Gaku Studio Integrale.*
2. EP's *Oro e Lavoro.* For the first English edition, see *Gold and Labour.*
3. **Mario Ramperti.**

4. **Vittorio Ambrosio Ambrosini.** Villari describes Ambrosini as "bitterly anti-German" and "a soldier of very limited abilities" (*Italian Foreign Policy under Mussolini* 300). According to Villari, while Ambrosini was serving Mussolini in the Salò Republic, he "protested against the overbearing conduct of the German commands in Italy, saying that Italians were hardly masters in their own house" (340). Perhaps it is this act of independence to which EP is responding in this letter.

5. T. S. Eliot.

6. These are the stockpiles of agricultural produce that the Fascist government established in an effort to manage agricultural production. The scheme was similar to the contemporary Canadian Wheat Board, which still buys and sells all wheat grown in western Canada. EP frequently refers to this policy as wise management. See *Guide to Kulchur,* 167–68, 274, and 277.

7. Mantua Warehouse.

8. See canto 76/460.

9. EP's source.

10. The United States, England, and India. The Indian edition was published in Bombay in 1949 by Orient Longmans.

11. The American homestead, or family farm, versus the Soviet *kolkhov,* or collective farm. The comparison appears in the correspondence several times, especially in 1953 and 1954. See also cantos 99, 103, and 104 and letter 28.

12. The Bible.

13. EP is responding to ORA's remark on the Elizabethan and Euphuistic English style cultivated by Italian teachers of English in her letter of 19 April (Easter Sunday) 1948.

14. Gethsemane.

15. The epistolary salutation: "yours very truly"; EP is attributing the advice to **Bertrand de Born.** See "Sestina: Altaforte" (*Personae* 28) and "Near Perigord" (*Personae* 151–57).

16. Fr.: "redeem a debt."

17. New Testament.

18. The biblical prophet, mentioned also in canto 84/540.

19. It.: "'The true sixth Cajo Baccelli' guide (or Judas) of the agriculturist." Baccelli and the book remain unidentified, but presumably EP is referring to a current agricultural almanac.

20. Presumably Rufill is a publisher located in Florence.

21. It.: "Florence's pig, Behrenson's bug-wash/ the soul of Placci, not the soul of calm." "Behrenson" is presumably **Bernhard Berenson** but Placci is unidentified. The witticism remains obscure to us. EP repeats it in a 1950 letter ORA answered on 4 April 1950 but is not included here.

22. Lt.: "At the same time."

23. A French tag that occurs several times throughout this correspondence. In letter 53 EP translates it: "has ruined minds more than morals."

24. **Rémy de Gourmont,** the author of the French tag.

25. Fr.: "corrupt the souls."

26. James First version: the King James Bible.

27. Edward VII, king of England.

28. ORA's *David Lubin.*

19. TLS-2   [1949]

ORA/

Thanks for the chinoiserie.[1] YES, they wd/ pick a bit of bricabrac, a Chinese Mallarmé, rather than a chink who had thought of anything pertinent.

Are there ANY serious characters left in the stricken peninsula?

Were Corti's[2] books on the Rothschild translated and published in Italy? Absolutely the first serious prose work on XIXth century history.

I know this is belated news m̶ as they had great publicity at the time, 1928.

One got the general results, but {not} the mas{s} of useful detail, and the indication of mental squalor then raging (unless, of course, all the intelligent opposition has been snowed under by the infamy of controlled "free" press, intervening.)

ANYHOW, disgusting spectacle, and NO efficient curiosity was aroused [illegible deletion] with vigour to last on thru, and, shall we say, preventing̶ Lubin's from supposing that a price in an indefinite medium wd/ curse curse cure the trouble.

The stink associated with Metternich's[3] name, perfect{ly} just, but Browning and the rest got only the ө romantic swish{;} Byron having been got by the Mann act[4]

At any rate a reprint of the Corti is due, the work is not anti-yitt, as the worst slime were catholics, Gentz,[5] the elector of Hesse etc./ all Cortis I know are yidds and the bk/ published by the squirmy Gollancz,[6] so that [illegible deletion] a tactful wop cd/ approach it without thinking of the last remaining phrase in the Good Friday service.

When you think that some British slov slob did a 2 vol. Life of Cavour[7] with only two bits of history, one about i/3 page and one 2/3rds, shows where tolerance had been debased to. and the utterly vomitorious befuzzlement of "education". historiography, etc.

Again ask: any news of Notari?

D. says Varé's english bk/ is fluff,[8] but non-poisonous, am waiting to see it.

Stability of great chinese dynasties due to low tax rate. about 12% maximum, at least in theory. I dont spose the s{c}hool of Oriental bugwash, or prof/ Whatzis Mallarmé wd/ condescend to THOUGHT on that level.

The term honour completely eliminated from american scene, and "courage" idem from the halls of learning. braghe molle,[9] the bricabrac lot of 'em.

Low tax (no need to delegate power to high-tax) automatic protection against swelling of bugocracy. The "ins" wd/ not want to share with newly created offices.

Anyhow, as proper Carbonaro,[10] one can thank Corti for spectacle of Vienna borrowing herself out of existence. And Neapolitan royalty got its due.

I knew one Bourbon,[11] who hadn't learned YET: saw only inconvenience of not being able to "get money".

Some serious writing in Ecrits de Paris/ glad to know if any of yr/ friends have seen any elsewhere.

The U.S. as great a damned idiot today as Austria in 1820.

dirty press FULL of ads/ for loan offices. the people to follow ex-royal example.

{Ezra Pound}

1. Obviously some work on a Chinese subject that ORA had sent EP, but we have not identified it.

2. **Egon Caesar Count Corti.**

3. **Klemens Wenzel Nepomuk Lothar von Metternich.**

4. Robert James Mann (1865–1922), a Republican member of the U.S. House of Representatives, was the author of the Mann Act (1910), which forbade the transportation of women from one state to another for immoral purposes. The "stink" EP has in mind may be linked to some trouble Byron may have had in taking a woman across a border. In addition, EP is also thinking of **Klemens Wenzel Nepomuk Lothar von Metternich's** invitation of the Rothschilds to Vienna, where he obtained for them titles of nobility. Presumably "Browning and the rest" remained in the dark about the Semitic/banker's plot to control the world and Byron was silenced by the fuss over his sex scandals.

5. Probably **Friedrich von Gentz.** EP seems to include him among the Catholic "slime."

6. **Victor Gollancz.**

7. EP means Thayer's *The Life and Times of Cavour.*

8. A reference in a postscript by Dorothy Pound in letter 26 regarding this remark helps us date this letter as mid-1949 or as late as early 1950.

9. A variant of *brago molle,* It.: "soft mud." "Muck" is a favorite epithet of EP's for opinions with which he disagrees.

10. A member of the Italian secret society plotting to establish Italian unity and independence by means of agitation, conspiracy, and revolution. It is the most famous of several such societies that sprang up in Italy after the 1815 Congress of Vienna and which were largely supplanted by the leadership of **Giuseppe Mazzini.**

11. We do not know if EP met any member of the French royal house of Bourbon.

20. TLU-2   [ans. 29 June 1949]

Dear ORA

strictly anonymous communique

It's Borris and Mary[1] who are providin' the stage set. All I did was to
bring up my child with a few decent and highfalutin ideas. Such as having a centro culturale. Cant keep ALL the poets in jug.[2] etc. Yes, I remember the Giartosio.[3] As their politics were all wrong they ought to {be}
applyin their talent for intrigue to the useful purpose of gettin me out of
quod. (or mebbe their faction is just as OUT?) Anyhow, what my friends
lack is coordination. Soddy[4] very dull, rather tangled, and not I think clear
all thru. Co{u}ghlin[5] long silenced. Not infallible, but a useful noise
ONCE. at least, for whatever good an ineffective noise ever is. Must have
partially educated several. The son of gt/ corrupter seems to have just
bought a seat in the House of Rep/ for quarter of million $/ and that horse
faced bitch his maw been down to see him perjure himself, as runs in the
family.[6] (i.e. I spose even Congmen/ take some sort of oat{h} on being let
in to jaw-house. Enc/ cheerful note for yr/ sister Helen. Please forward
to O.R. (yes, not to confuse initials Olga Rudge,[7] Accademia Chigiana,
Siena.) Yes, as you see I have read the book (as well as having recd/ it.)
Mrs Ware[8] still alive?? no, have not seen Lubin's bk/[9] and hv/ forgot title. Remember I cannot make the least EFFORT. As I notice in other lu-
natics, things will come OUT of 'em, but nowt goes in.

Yes, I HAVE seen the Pelizzi.[10] Best thing going is the Duke of Bedford's
12xpoint program.[11] Being a Duke and an Englander perhaps Villari will
listen to it, as it is apparently useless to try to get anything into him via
EZ. Ploots[12] will never THINK till you tax the living guts out of 'em. and
prob/ not then.

Three big spy trials IN the papers,[13] also a big case vs/ big banks re/
which NO papers say anything, save one communist fly-by-night, start-
ed{,} I spose{,} fer that purpose.

I dare say old Serao[14] was right in assenting when I sd/ I had had more
freedom to print what I thought, in Italy, than elsewhere "probably because no one understood what I was saying." Mebbe when the english
translations have appeared some gol dratted wop will get round to looking at the original ital/ text.

I have managed to print ~~come~~ some Confucius in three other countries.
Josée Laval's open letter to Churchill[15] is the high spot of the week.

Einaudi's prize howler{:} "somebody has to put money into a bank before you can take it out." (Get him a wet nurse.)

I think, by a fluke, Ford's book on Rossetti[16] is in Rapallo/ {vide H.R.
Ang.}[17] not that F/ ever did any harm to Dante Gabe's glory, but that he

adored Christina's way of writing/ and was furious with the greater attention given the jewels and velvet. In fact the lucidity and clarity of english verse today (when it has any) comes very largely from Ford's ranting about Christina [illegible deletion] and the kind of simplicity of language he found in some of her verse, which did NOT hit the front page in the Swinburne plus '90 furores, or twilit Celts.

time when there was no where to print a poem by Hardy/[18] Ford's poetry unnoticed, but now readable when 200 Georgians etc. are NOT.

Returning to Einaudi's hat trick/ fer benefit of wop boob, and Miss Whoosis, of the dirty "Economist".[19] Magari[20] IF you did, i.e. if banks cd/ not "discount" as Sammy Lloyd[21] said "atall {bills} [illegible deletion] arising from legitamate operations of commerce (and possibly a lot that DON'T) all trade wd/ stop or wd. hv/ been cut down past bearing,

Waaaal, ef there was any sign that ANYone in Italy (except O.R.A.) had learned anything from my labours (mebbe a few still in jug, or under the hatches and still scared into prudence.()} one cd/ contemplate the imbecilities elsewhere with greater equan/etc/

Study of the classics the ONLY barrier vs/ mind-conditioning by the Luces,[22] Louses and Brit/ slopagandists.

The Mercure de France shd/ be thought about, edtr/ of the race chosen by JHV,[23] and confirmed by O.R.A. and ergo mistrusted by Camelot du Roi,[24] precursor, but A. Billy's[25] letter two years ago indicated a decent program, and a good italian correspondent for it would be, or COULD be, of use to civilization in general. If anybody ever met or spoke to anyone else, Pelizzi might have idea WHO cd/ do it. a bloke named Lanza {(}with most of the wrong ideas) writes perfect french with ease but gornoze[26] what he would send.

1. **Boris de Rachewiltz** and **Mary de Rachewiltz.**
2. Jail.
3. **Maria Luisa Giartosio de Courten.**
4. **Frederick Soddy.**
5. **Father Charles Edward Coughlin.**
6. Although EP's slur is unclear, he probably means James Roosevelt (1901–91), son of Franklin Delano and Eleanor Roosevelt. He ran for governor of California in 1950 and did serve in the House of Representatives but was not elected until 1955.
7. **Olga Rudge.**
8. A woman ORA met on one of her tours of the United States. She had written: "I think Mrs. Ware was Tinkham's cousin. She was connected with many of the old time Boston families; a very fine woman, capable of single-minded, disinterested devotion to an idea and an ideal, and a wonderful friend. She was always very poor but gave most generously of her time and intelligence" (9 June 1949).

9. In her letter of 29 June 1949, ORA mentioned that the Italian chamber of commerce was planning a commemoration of the centenary of **David Lubin's** birth and she was invited to take part. She also mentioned her biography of Lubin, without indicating that she was the author—hence EP's surprise (see letter 22) when he eventually begins to read *David Lubin*.

10. Pellizzi's *Una rivoluzione mancata*, which ORA was reading. She said it was "about the Corporate State [the Fascist state] and why it failed" (9 June 1949).

11. Probably the statement on the war from the British People's party, founded in 1939 by, among others, William Sackville Russell, who later became the **Twelfth Duke of Bedford,** and John Beckett, who had helped form the National Socialist League and was editor of *Action* (1936–37), in which EP published several pieces.

12. Plutocrats.

13. Probably the "trial of 11 Reds" (members of the Communist party's American Politburo) for conspiracy to teach and advocate the overthrow of the U.S. government by force and violence; the espionage trial of Judith Coplon, a twenty-eight-year-old former Justice Department analyst accused of stealing government secrets with intent to aid a foreign power; and the trial of **Alger Hiss,** former State Department official, for giving State Department documents to Whittaker Chambers for transmission to a Soviet spy ring in 1937 and 1938.

14. **Matilde Serao.**

15. EP is referring to an open letter from José Laval, also known as Comtesse de Chambrun, on the subject of her father, Pierre Laval (1883–1945), premier of France (1931–32 and 1935–36) and later premier of Vichy France (1942–44), executed by firing squad on 15 October 1945. ORA wrote that she "was much interested in Mme Laval Chambrun's letter about her murdered father, and sent it on to Pellizzi" (3 Aug. 1949). We have been unable to locate Laval's letter.

16. Ford's *Rossetti*. For EP's views on Ford's estimation of **Christina Rossetti's** and **Dante Gabriel Rossetti's** work, see "The Prose Tradition in Verse," *Polite Essays* 57–66.

17. EP is referring to Helen Rossetti Angeli's *Dante Gabriel Rossetti: His Friends and Enemies*.

18. Thomas Hardy (1840–1928).

19. A contributor identified only as Special Correspondent who wrote a column in "The World Overseas" section of the London *Economist*.

20. It.: "wouldn't it be nice."

21. **Samuel Jones Loyd.**

22. **Henry Robinson Luce** and **Clare Boothe Luce.**

23. Jehovah, that is, the Jews.

24. The Camelot du Roi was a French royalist group supported by the Ligue d' Action Française, a conservative political movement in France led by Charles Maurras.

25. **André Billy.**

26. God knows.

21. TLU-3 [post–1 July 1949][1]

The following letter is stimulated for the most part by EP's reading of ORA's biography of Lubin.

O.R.A.

Agenda/ did yr/ Lubin breed men or only kikes?[2] i.e. any of his family any good, or have they any filial respect?

I hv/ got as far as his wantin to stabilize price, and smelling the stink of the curse of Woodie and Frankie,[3] i.e. oedemitous pustulent burocracy. Is the Insteroot[4] still alive enough to note that there is no damn use in stabilizing price IN fluctuating monetary units. The corn hog being under the money hog?

There are known to be say half a dozen thinking men in England/ the two or three in america over the age of 24 are scared underground and work only under most elaborate self-protective longwindedness, NECESSARY under the stinking circs/ to maintain "position" and be consulted by the fogies and apes. Who is there in Italy now capable and courageous enough to keep up correspondence with the few sane foreigners. EVEN on indirect lines, such as classic studies. You will note that the first thing the barbarians do when the{y} get to Shanghai is to decree exclusion of the classics from the schools. Lubin seems to have found the bits of scripture (yitt) that I quote in the Pisans. and NOT to have been much bogged in the dirty morass that surrounds them, and that has made Xtianity a 77% curse for 1900 years. Glad to note that he spots the PAGAN influx, that being nearly all that is good (BUT not the bed rock). Leviticus XIX and Micah.[5] which Pacelli[6] probably loathes as much as Sieff.[7]

I forget the name of the pleasant but more or less limp blokes I once met at 34 v. Menot./[8] also lost addresses of Paolillo,[9] and the Ubs/[10]

As far as ascertainable there is more life in the three or four clean wop weeklies than in eng/ frog or yank press. BUT almost NO elucidation of essential program. sic: deliberative bodies to be radio-trasmessi; inviolable homestead. ammassi voluntary NOT obligatory, AND the sane tax (i.e. the gesellite tithe on the money-tickets themselves.) Europe no longer centre of money market, but cd/ continue to exist IF correlation of thought be continued. Too bad Italy has that god awful boil on her neck, Mons Vaticanus.[11] Offering blighted humanity the choice between two sets of lies, their ~~one~~ {own} and the barbarian. And even you bigot that you are, cant claim that the Osservatore[12] wd/ ever, print the truth any more than the Slimes[13] would.

Lub/ a bit blind to the danger of giving power to a dirty barbarian nation like Rhoosia. What matters is the cultural level, and control ought
to stay inside civilization not be thrust onto the over-lords of the mujik.
The mass imbecility, augmented by Luce[14] and co/ the press of London
etc. constitutes a peril.

Nacherly "democracy" based on presupposition that the electorate is
educatable and that the overlords will educate a week or so before giving the franchise, which of course dont happen. Drive here is to create a
slave state WITHOUT educating the overseers. At the moment I can find
NO journal of ideas, where even eight or ten serious men can intercom-
municate. Can, let us say, Villari report on the ideas Bedford is advertising? Do the four or five clean wop peprs TRY to exchange with the small
circulation weeklies in U.S. and Eng/ and NIF nawt WHY not?

Have just noted the isolated provincialism of Ortega y Gasset.[15] someone shd/ at least try to find out if S. American span/ exiles think. There's
that good swiss who might organize some sort of sheet for idea-exchange.
or definition. Gentizon.[16] The neo [illegible deletion] silent or worrying
about power. When out of power, clarify ideas.

Lub at least sound re/ socialist pestilence, but it grows out of looking
at work and product (even staples) and NOT at monetary units. Lub/
preceded, but that no reason not to PROcede to Doug/[17] and Gesell

yes. O.K. p 246/ Lub/ gets to purchas/pow of $. but still naively sup-
poses that it rests on supply of staples (as it MIGHT in a sane financial
system) whereas it depends on the skunks who control issue of money,
as long as there is ANYTHING whatsodamn ever to buy.

O.K. also that market in skunk-run countries is affected by press lies.
But basic mesopotamian error is presupposto that you need a world in
order to have a civilization. Autarchy saner. quando tutti saremo forti.[18]
Sane money inside any fairly adequate area and that area can have a civilization. Lub/ coloured by his Calif/[19] background. Nacherly cant see the
back of his own neck.

Not a case of saying "not" so, but of adding the necessary element.
Grain supply depends on work and nature/ money supply on the issuers.

as nearly all Lub's ideas HAVE gone into effect, and the results are what
they have been/ you can judge that there was a lacuna. Well [illegible
deletion] no, I suppose he did think that press lies might diminish??? or
was he sufficiently realist to know that they wd/ NOT be. anzi....[20]

whether having been the forerunner of the Leg of Nations and the UN[21]
is a title of merit is NOW dubious. ought to be a black border and a few
pails of tears added as footnote...

admitted that there ought to be international communication/ but that
monopoly is the devil's best pitchfork..

My GAWD. dear Lydia {Bariatinsk}[22] turning up after all these years.
p. 253

Institute useful almost SOLELY in as far as information can conduce to autarchy IN one or more decently governed areas. As per discovery no peanuts. The further the control from the field that grows the wheat the more skunks will insert themselves and the great{er} the chance that Roosevelts and Churchillss will be regarded a human beings and not sacks of pus. This no reason for destroying the institute.

Now be serious/ QUOTE/ "I come not to bring peace but a sword" How true. Israel the world's curse. The messianic letch which makes for the admirable in Lubin, or leads to individual crucifixion, i.e. frothy incoherence/ mixing up nice truths with inebriated rhetoric, makes the mass a curse. Lubin plus corrective, O.K. But like the socialists he works on branch not on the root. There is NO reason for the local market price to depend on world price save the falsities of the press and the faking of money.// I mean that is how it is wangled. If thinking ABOUT price formation leads to thinking about the assay of the money (whether metal or estimate stated on paper) that is useful. Lubin/ sound re/ need of honesty. But that is not new. Kung[23] or Herbert of Cherbury as winner over Macchiavel). The whole idea of cursing is Messopotamian/ not a trace of it in Confucius or Mencius. A dirty barren country deserts etc. or contrast between desert and milk and cocacola.

explain as you like. Interruption of exchange between Rome and China from beginning of time. Anyhow, curse idea non-existent in Confucian thought. What moral in Xt cursing the figtree?

Lub as bad as Marx with his non sequiturs, and as far behind as that viper Perkins.[24] all this migratory farm labour is NOT each own vine and fig. Manchine potential now gornoze[25] what but was ages ago 9000 times that of man. Let the farm labour set on its OWN vine and fig/ that is ALL the _needed_ work.

The utter idiocy of yelling more work. as {if} the ratio of needed work were unaltered by a century and more of mechanic invention. That is filth. and few in pubk/[26] life have washed their feet. Have the goddam wops even translated C.H.D's earlier work?

Lub/ slips on a juggling with words. {"}Democracy{"} does NOT mean {"}justice.{"} No point and gt/ chance of mess by asserting that one word ~~mans~~ means what another and different word {means}.

This is more than a quibble. Marx may have had good intentions, but he accepted ambiguous terminology, and his consequence stinks.

Coincidence in Pisan and Lub/ quotes from the great garbage heap. Admitting, in fact asserting{,} that there are gems in said miscuglio[27] and fanfare of bloated rhetoric, buncomb, bestiality. Probably if Lev. XIX, and Micah were printed separately, they wd/ have been publicly burnt. B.C. 213 they tried to annihilate Kung. I spose the same dhirty tartars that later got converted to Yittery. Nobody ever tried to burn the hebe[28] scriptures because they were an inconvenience to tyranny. In fact the devil's {'}appy

{'}unting ground. And the blood-flow in Xtn/ hymns. If inflamed metaphor ever cd/ excite to mob idiocy. {'}Is blood red banner etc.

Having had Prot/ upbringing, I naturally loathe the old testament and
hebraized Xtianity. [illegible deletion] The kike salesman from Tarsus
"St" Saul[29] taught the catholics to lie. i.e. sign on the dotted line and
profess to believe a rigamarole whether they understood it or not. So that
no prot/ expect{s} a convent to produce truth telling. Lub/ clear sighted
enough to see that catholicism stems from pagan sources (ergo a force for
civilization). cf/ Zielinsky[30] "La Sibylle". fer Cat/ theology.

Xtianity overswamped barbarian countries?? like Moammed, cause it
fits with violence and bellicosity. St.Francis a minority voice? Interesting to see how little of the o.t. you connect with Lub/ that I have not
quoted in Pisans. (nacherly with approval) {apart his letter to Yids.}

VERY sad end/ a man with decent intentions pre-begat the league of
nations, the cocatrice, the hell hole, the usurer's stinkery. Not the Czar
but the the damn barbarians, the mongol, the tartar. Geneva the sub-Franz
Joseph,[31] mother of the second and may we hope NOT the third war.

Apart from the idiocy of L/ and Wells[32] theologizing, Lub is just ignorant. Nine of the Mosaic commandments are in the Egyptian negative
confession (the tenth is re/ images... political cleverness on part of Mose.,
and destructive to most of the best in culture, everything that cant be
recorded in abstract statement, which {latter} tells little to the man who
dont know OBJECTS, generalized from,

Also the "{Biblic} law" is not ethics, it is a wheeze for collecting fees
for a privileged class, priests and levites. Lub/ a bit excited by Balfour
declaration,[33] as fishy a bit of prose as ever penned by yitt or brit. or scot,
I spose Balf was the abolition of all law, or civic sense, re introduction of
ex post facto [illegible deletion] laws, etc. sad comment/ on messianic
excitement. [illegible deletion] "yoke," {u fergiv us}, give away _words._

P.S. as prolog: take running comment with reservations, parts of it
modified by further reading in Dav. L// BUTT, all now past and academic. Wish at least ONE or two of our friends wd/ think of AGENDA as from
now; and get out of retrospect, and horse and buggy socialism, long since
out of date. Learn from Lub's errors, or error.

1. This letter is placed here because it includes the following note in **Dorothy
Pound**'s hand: "just received a line from Mary Baratti saying you were there in
castle. child. ok. so glad." There is an 11 July 1949 letter from ORA to EP from
"Schloos Brunenburg," which establishes ORA's stay at the castle (9–14 July) and
her leaving of **Rosamaria** there for the summer holidays.

2. ORA responded to this offensive query: "Yes, Lubin had a large family: 3
sons, Simon, Jesse, Theodore, the first a gutless idealist, the 2nd an unsuccessful business man, the 3rd has changed his name to Silverston and is a British
broker! He had also 4 daughters, Ruth (whom I never met), Laura, Eva, Dorothy

and Grace, all nice, particularly so Laura and Dorothy, now Mrs. George Heller" (3 Aug. 1949).

3. Woodrow Wilson and Franklin Delano Roosevelt.

4. The International Institute of Agriculture (IIA), founded by Lubin in Rome in 1906.

5. "And there is also the XIXth Leviticus./ 'Thou shalt purchase the field with money.'/ signed Jeremiah" (canto 74/440) and "Saith Micah:/ 'Each in the name of . . .' [his gods]" (canto 84/540).

6. **Eugenio Pacelli.**

7. **Baron Israel Moses Sieff.**

8. An inaccurate version of ORA's address: Via Ciro Menotti, 36.

9. Unidentified, but ORA wrote later: "Paolillo, I learn, is still with the Bank of Italy but has been transferred to Turin for the present, when Boris' 'E.P. Society' is going we must get in touch with him" (2 Feb. 1954).

10. **Ubaldo degli Uberti** and **Riccardo M. degli Uberti.**

11. EP means the Vatican with this pun on "mons veneris."

12. Presumably *Osservatore Romano*, a Vatican journal.

13. The *London Times*.

14. **Henry Robinson Luce.**

15. **José Ortega y Gasset.**

16. Presumably the "good Swiss" mentioned in the same paragraph.

17. **Major Clifford Hugh Douglas,** also mentioned below by his initials, C.H.D.

18. It.: "when all will be strong."

19. Lubin was a Californian.

20. It.: "on the contrary."

21. League of Nations and the United Nations.

22. Lydia Bariatinski. On page 253 of *David Lubin* ORA quotes a note written by Lubin to the effect that Russian indifference to the IIA was overcome following "an afternoon's chat in Rome with two Russian ladies, the Princess Bariatinsky and the Princess Narischkin." These women made arrangements for Lubin's meeting with Nicholas Mourawieff, who later served as ambassador in Rome, and thus Russia finally joined the Institute around 1910. Bariatinsky is mentioned in canto 79/488.

23. Kung Fu Tseu or Confucius (551–479 B.C.).

24. **Frances Perkins.**

25. God knows.

26. Public.

27. It.: "mixture, hodgepodge."

28. Hebrew.

29. St. Paul.

30. **Tadeusz Zielinski.**

31. **Franz Joseph.**

32. H. G. Wells (1866–1946); his letters to Lubin are cited in ORA's *David Lubin* 334–38.

33. The famous declaration contained in a letter of 2 November 1917 from Arthur James Balfour, British foreign secretary, to Lionel Walter Rothschild, promising the establishment of a Jewish homeland in Palestine.

22. TLU-3

O.R.A.

I see by th' paipers that DelCroix[1] is not only alive but speaking at Trieste in ~~April~~ June. (Meridiano June 12) pays to read the small print. Now THERE is a president fer yr/ wretched country and be it remembered that when I told him about Gesell, he beat on his head with his little wooden hands, shouting "Che magnifica idea"/ grabbed the phone and called to Bottai[2] to come "over here" (Veteran's building). Onforchoonately B/ was just leaving office to catch train to Napoli. DelC/ said on his own: Two evils: legalization of usury in banks, and of theft in Soc/ Anon/. Dane who paid for printing "Oro e Lavoro" also se{e}ms to be or to have still been alive, vide Gray's[3] art/1 in same issue. CONfound this habit people have of never meeting or speaking to each other. DelC/ ought to GET the idea into Pellizzi's cloudy noddle, and into Pettinato's. Nobody runs ANY errands or rubs two peoples' heads together.

Order out to chase that Lubin book/[4] still no idea (as you never were very precise) what virtues he had other than messopotamian origin. score two fer Nazareth? However, patiently awaiting light from printed page, if it hasn't been burried. Guerriero[5] had heard of him, after some reflection said: Practical Idealist?

Wd/ be almost BUT NOT QUITE worth a muscovite invasion to get rid of the Vatican, and the Pacelli gang/ as it is you hv/ had a barbarian invasion and NOT got rid of the vatican.

interesting note in a dhirty paper called Mondo, re/ Ricasoli[6] and the lesser clergy (as vs/ the stinkers) if using ideas in conversation, DONT fer garzake[7] indicate the whence.

You cant expect me to be serious ALL the time in the lesser manicomio.[8]

N.B. there seem to be TWO Guerriero/ the one here is NOT the one in Italy, at least the name is not the same. both initial A. cant find name of the one in italy at the moment.

GolDRAT it/ CIRCULATION/ Gesell stamp the only clear solution/ with that, what goes OUT must come back. CIR—CU—LATION. nobody seems to be clear about that in ANY other system.

PE/rusin' "D.Lubin" by ORA. (sfar as remember sd/ authoress never stated clearly that SHE writ a bloomink bk/ on the subject/ arrived at p 85. Dave seems to have got to some sane conclusions by a murky route/ but no matter. Mommsen or 4000 years of China wd/ have served.

//However the four clean pages of the O.T. functioned in that case.

Has ORA seen recent thesis that democracy (in decencet sense) entered the occidental mind when the Jesuits began translating Confucius, and flowered in the XVIII when C/ became more accessible.?

The particular types D.L. loathed seem rather to have riz in the interim.

This habit of NO ONE ever speaking to anyone else. ORA ignorant of Doug and Gesell, and they of Dave L/ WHEN a little communication wd/ have been useful.

The devil{'}s two horns and STINK emerge on p. 120/ in the single phrase. "world's importing centre." There shd be no importing or exporting centre? that is the filth/ that is the crevice thru which all the hells of monopoly get their grip. Ghandi much saner. autarchy much saner.

All this chance to manage, by dirty bugrocrats. Dave put one over on you. All this drift to control imposed from above by irresponsible IGNORAMUSES. The further {vid infra}[9] they get from the growing spot the less they know. Nobody got brains enough to legislate for the ends of the earth. [illegible deletion]

The curse of Geneva. Civilization moves outward from a nucleus. Peripheric location (Calif) gives rise to peripheric state of mind. No inutition of damage this universalism contained for civilization of centres.

naturally there is "something to be said for" desire of California to DUMP. Vide end of Anatole France's "Penguin"[10]

Liverpool the centre/ Messopotamian brigands holding up communication between China and the Mediterranean..

PRICES (world or anywhere else, above what you can reach by barter on the spot) or at least NOW are measured in MONEY, and as long as that is faked Mr Dave L/ can whistle.

up to page 120 he hasn't spotted the chief Geryon.

"price formation" conjurer's black handkerchief. Price is formed on the field/ deformed by finance.

all L's though{t} re/ transport very valuable. O.K. oh yuss. interception of exchange by traffic monopoly no worse nor better than by money monopoly,

but this hooey about "all" is buncomb. The messopotamian Machtreligion. Mohammedans tainted. Nothing clean save from China or, let us to say AFTER Sophokles.

incidentally I heard the "Grange" has gone rotten.

No doubt L's ideas have flooded this lunatic and devastated country. whereby their limitation is indicated. All part of the ~~mai~~ mania of outer space,

His sanity consisted in working FROM Sacramento. That is proper, and his desire for just measure/ but up to p. 120 ~~just PRICE dont figure as~~ no indication that dollar is not a fixed length or weight.

"tarif a local issue". Did he ever mention Kitson? OR consider tax problem? (am not trying to minimize his work/ but one can't stop at 1916).

Did Lubin really think Wanamaker[11] fit to sit on a committee to decide????

Awaiting book on Medici bank.[12] re/Lub/ the Este[13] probably had the answer. there is dead fish in wanting world wide etc/etc/ before you get sanity in any given area.

How long did Ferrara go without war? Borso seems to have got somewhere near reign of abundance?

DAMN the man, why the hell shdn't Europe or any country produce its own grain? The mesopotamian fallacy, curse of humanity. Have you YET got my Chinese dynasty cantos? 52/61? AND machines make no manure.

30% wallawalla,[14] as long as he boycotts question of monetary issue.

Until the producers/ FARMERS, say farmers, start controlling the issue of their own money....gosh.....evil not public issue of public money, but private issue of public money. private issue of private money...wangled by banks, but at least some weight against central tyranny IF any govt. ever touched the real issue.

Injustice, imbecility INSIDE every area/ if you cd/ (as was done in Worgl)[15] get justice inside ANY area it wd/ be a start and model.

WHY shd/ a farmer sell at world price? habit, or idiocy. autarchy much saner. Import what NOT produced at home. China B.C. natural NOT artificial price of transport favour the LOCAL product.

Lubin; story of a search. conditioned (as you admit) by ignorance, and insensitivity traditional.. but not going back to Moses cleverness in ruling out images, cause L/ didn't know what egyptians used 'em FOR. Also of course lack of catholic confessional, repentance, contrition etc. Nothing like Xtianity to keep alive resentment (as per/ nigger lunatic warning ME against Judas.) force of myth. I don't suppose you cd/ do additional chapter, and a reissue, showing evils of planning. God curse the Fabians. "ta 'ihna ta dhina."[16] etc. No. that is unconfucian we will not kuss the damn nuisances, they punish themselves.

This DAMNED habit of nobody meeting anyone else. No sign L/ ever heard of Kitson or Brooks Adams/ any italian edtn/ of yr/ book?

captans annonam maledictus in plebe sit.[17]

St Amb/ also Ari/ on Thales.

Have the bloody swine of UNO and Unesco done ANYTHING to continue work L/ started. (probably have to be boiled in oil and reborn in a caul, before that).

very skeptical re/ world price being fixed by ANY reality other than the swinishness of saboteurs in finance and transport.

ad interim {p. 194}

still stinking with the assumption: lavoro un merce.[18] perfume of the time (1904). Not L's fault. And of course immense retrogression toward it, with Woodrow[19] the filthy out in front.

1. **Carlo DelCroix.**
2. **Giuseppe Bottai.**
3. EP's nickname for **Luigi Villari.**
4. EP is still reading ORA's biography of **David Lubin.**
5. EP also mentions in this letter "TWO Guerriero." They are, perhaps, **Augusto Guerriero** and Aniello Guerriero. ORA had written of an Aniello Guerriero, whom she thought she might have met while traveling in the United States (9 June 1949).
6. Probably Bettino Ricasoli (1809–80), the scion of an ancient and distinguished partician family who had two brief stints as prime minister (as Cavour's successor, 1861–62, 1866–67). He was interested in religious reform and in reconciliation between the Vatican and the state.
7. God's sake.
8. It.: "mental hospital."
9. Lt.: "see below."
10. *L'Île des pingouins*, a satirical animal fable on French history by Anatole France (1844–1924).
11. No doubt a member of the Wanamaker family, which owns a well-known Philadelphia department store bearing the family name.
12. EP is referring to the Medici family of Florence and their bank. Cosimo de' Medici (1389–1464) and his descendants ruled through the influence of their wealth and political skills. EP tells the history of the Medici family in the early cantos, especially canto 21. We have no information about a book on the Medici Bank expected by EP at this time.
13. Niccolò d'Este (1393–1441), lord of Ferrara, is praised by EP in *The Cantos* for Ferrara's long history of peace. During his rule, and especially that of his successor, Borso d'Este, Ferrara was known as *la terra della pace* (the domain of peace). EP mentions Borso later in the letter and several times in *The Cantos* and ascribes to him the phrase "keep the peace." It was this history that led Pope Eugenius IV to choose Ferrara as the site of a council convened in hopes of healing the schism between the churches of Rome and Constantinople—even though the council had to be moved to Florence following an outbreak of the plague in Ferrara.
14. Thirty percent bullshit.
15. See letter 14.
16. Possibly Gk.: "τά ἴχνη τά δεινά," "the terrible footsteps" or "clues."
17. Lt.: "the hoggers of harvest are cursed among the people." This remark, attributed to **St. Ambrose,** is a Poundian touchstone, cited in canto 88/581 in which **Carlos DelCroix** is also invoked. Thales is also mentioned in *The Cantos* (77/468 and 88/580) in connection with monopoly and twice in *Guide to Kulchur* (117 and 224) in connection with the view, which Aristotle attributed to Thales, that the world not only originates in water but returns to it.
18. It.: "labor and goods."
19. Woodrow Wilson.

23. TLU-2   [late 1949 or early 1950]

O.R.A.

re/ the dirty bit of work from Tarsus[1] (not denying his merits). The Xtn (Christian) is basicly dishonest from the minute he starts professing belief in a formula which he either does not believe, or does not understand. This dates from Tarsus. And is why no beastly prot/ ever expects trusth from a catholic.

J.C. indubitably had a good chunk of the true tradition,[2] BUT the yidd already had Leviticus XIX/ so there is no use pretending those pious sentimengs differentiate the Christer from the yitt/

The bulk of jewish law is nothing but a wheeze, however, to jerk fines out of the populace for the benefit of the cohens and levis.

Zielinsky has neatly shown that all the dogma worth a damn came from greek mysteries etc/ everything that built the cathedrals.

Yr friend Lubin notes this tother way on/ i.e. that the Christers lugged in pagan elements. (Thank gawd fer that.)

Now the root of hell may be double/ I. signing statements in incomprehensible language, or that the signer believes to be bunk (for political reasons, faut de mieux.[3] Pacelli as the ONLY alternative to Moscow, or any other shortsighted expediency.

and second/ the idiocy which places gawd in outer space/ eyes on ends of the cosmos/

panta hrei/[4] but not as water down a dran/

anyone not an ape or green anarch or atheist shd/ be able to see EVIDENCE in the pattern of the first leaf he picks off a willow or any other damn tree.

Decent religion respects heaven AND earth/ and the fanatical imbecility of the Xtns/ leaves out the mustard seed. substituting after the dumb ox Aquinas[5] an abstraction. Paganism, Roman Impero[6] etc/ was based on slavery and buggary and ergo unsatisfactory/ Xtianity, with all its lies and forgeries, brought a bit of civilization into barbarian continents/

Kung gives what a man can believe without kidding himself.

and Pacelli cant represent divinity, at least not to anyone who hasn't pulled wool autarchicly over their own peepers.

T{he} good wop is Ghibbeline/[7] and the vatican is the enemy of a good part of civilization, tho preferable to sher savagery/ tartar hordes, Roosevelts, Churchills and other forms of decomposition.

mi spiego?[8]

and universal money controlled by swine at greatest remove is only the worst form of planning. The further from the field/ and starting when the ammasso[9] is compulsory the nearer the usurer's nest egg.

It seems likely that a bloke named Albert Schweitzer has got on the track of the truth, playing Bach, and being a medical missionary 20 years in Africa. Haven't yet had his text. naturally as he is an HONEST xtn/ various ecclesiasts are annoyed. (this opinion not yet documented, but he seems to have got a sane angle. {as [Chinese character]}[10]

trying to git down to bedROCK and STAY there. 99% of all planners are either deliberate crooks, or hired dupes of same. Granted that Lubin was fighting a swindle/ it amounts to false news/ NO use stabilizing or getting a "just" price in faked monetary units. The planners are [illegible deletion] nearly all up to one very old swindle/ namely restriction of output/ as per centuries usage, since the Portagoose uprooted spice trees after getting to Goa. to keep up price on restricted market.

Lubin is PRE Douglas, pre Gesell/ ~~bother~~ both the latter go on from where the sainted (but also hallucinated by outer space Lubin, left off). I [illegible deletion] await yr/ strafe with interest.

Por[11] fell for the planners/ And less danger of local famine EVEN with autarchy, than when price, via money is juggled by usurers situated at 10000 miles distance, where the farmer cant kill 'em. And where they by nature ignore local conditions, but almost NEVER care a damn what they are.

The mortgage holder (bond holder) dont care if the company or farm fails. He forecloses and "reorganizes" at pleasure. and the goddam goy falls for it.

Heaven AND earth/ nothing cd/ be more idiotic than a religion that has put corsets on the holy mystery of fecundity. In fact Xtianity is one of the worst hoaxes. No hoax ever ~~worth~~{k}ed without enough truth in it to be plausible.

difficult, of course, for a local bishop whose claim to world tyranny is based on a forged document,[12] to exercise SIMPLE honesty. Suspect the church been on the down grade since ~~Abrose~~ Ambrose/[13] occasionally kicked into temporary decency by refinement or rise of general standard of manners (concordat or zummat.) But any religion however dirty is better than none at all. mi spiego?

Protestantism ABSOLUTELY anti-religious/ a yell for honesty vs/ the vatican's lies. Ever{y} injection of {O.T.} bible (anthology of conflicting views that has imbecillito the yidd for 2500 years) has pejorated christianity. As long as there was proper ceremony and hocuspocus (as in funeral show even now) there was chance of xtianity and religion cohabiting. Practically nothing authentic but a few gestures, which fortunately Pacelli and co/ dont understand or they wd abolish 'em. mi spiego?

Ovid nearer the ~~trust~~ truth than that squirt Aquinas.

But fer garzache[14] let em go on being catholic, with their tiddledeewiddldies/ and even their theo-cannibalism/[15] ANYthing rather than a half educated lout in a bare barn ergotizing about theology, into which he has had no proper initiation. Anybody who has looked at a maple-leaf can do without further demonstration that Marx didn't make the world, and that mud is an unlikely origin.

ONLy what a blessing it wd/ be for Italy if the Vatican cd/ be planted in Patagonia,[16] or even Tel Aviv.

Question of method/ the Lubins will ~AW~ ALWAYS be used and exploited by scoundrels Roosevelts Sieffs who do NOT want honesty or bonifica[17] in home district and who USE world schemes to disguise and cover local dishonesty/ pie in sky or in the FUTURE, never the now and the here. Autarchy was functioning/ one SLIP. war. does not invalidate benefits of autarchic drive.

1. St. Paul.

2. The "wisdom or mystery tradition," which EP sometimes calls simply "Eleusis."

3. Fr.: "for want of better."

4. Gk.: "all things flow"; an aphorism attributed to Heraclitus.

5. An allusive canard. In Aquinian hagiography, as a young neophyte the robust Thomas Aquinas (ca. 1225–74) was regarded as slow and was called "the dumb ox."

6. It.: "empire."

7. An ultramontanist, one who, in Medieval times, favored the emperor over the papacy. Those who took the papacy's side were called Guelfs.

8. It.: "Do I make myself clear?"

9. It.: "stockpile."

10. EP has written the character used in canto 88/581: "ching: To reverence; to respect; to honour" (Terrell 2:505).

11. **Odon Por.**

12. Presumably an allusion to the Donation of Constantine, a document in which the Emperor Constantine I granted to Sylvester I, bishop of Rome (314–335), and his successors spiritual supremacy over all other patriarchates and secular supremacy over the Western Empire. It is now universally admitted to be a forgery written between 750 and 800 A.D. Lorenzo Valla exposed it in 1440, launching a controversy that lasted until the end of the eighteenth century. See also letter 110.

13. **St. Ambrose.**

14. God's sake.

15. A reference to transubstantiation, the Catholic communion in which the body and blood of Christ is believed to be eaten and drunk in the apparent form of bread and wine.

16. Southernmost province of Argentina, a metonym for "far away."

17. It.: "land reclamation." This was made into a national crusade by the Fascist regime and the most touted project was the drainage of the Pontine marshes. EP refers to land reclamation several times in the correspondence (see letters 24, 34, 50, 72, 74, 105, and 120).

24. TLU-2   [late December 1949]

ORA

VERY pleased to hear fr/yu on Xmas eve. Inclined to think yr/ sister[1]
lucky (from all I hear fr/ London) to be druv. out of England, even if it
needed an earthquake to hoist her. Dont think the Rossettis responsible
for contemporary filth. In fact no one struggled with more prevoyance[2]
than yr/ unappreciated cousin Cassandra, F.M. Hueffer Ford./ consider
NOW, (rise, you always do to this bait)/ Were I rabid anti-cawflik I wd/
be givin thanks for Pacelli. Note how different an animal you wd/ hv/
had at the head of yr/ coagulate if de G/[3] had been brought up on the respectable classics/ as per yesterdays find in Pausanias[4] about some dhirrty greek receiving from Philip and Alex (Macedon) "the most invidious
of all gifts: to be made tyrant in his own patria by a foreign power." Acha-
ia, xxvii.8

mebbe considerin the season, I better lay off teasin you about Pacelli's
last stumer.[5]

The BASIC problem is not belief but conduct. That is where the dhirrty
christians from Saul of Tar-slop[6] onward have perverted the occident,
whatever bits of truth or decency they carried with them. The Old Test.
contains mebbe 5 pages. Lev. XIX,[7] per es/[8] in a mash of epileptic rhetoric
and levantine eroticism. The decent Christers left out a lot. In fact primi-
tiv. Xtn/ ANTI-old "law". gradually submerged, till as the archivesc/[9] sez:
only one line left in the gd/Fried-day show.[10]

Pup, or anyone else gets so excited re/ some idea that they hv/ to back
it up with lies and forgery. Religion/ pullet-ticks[11] alle-samee. Filth of BBC
puppygander[12] OR the fatty-can.[13] Last Soc. Cr/ australian[14] anti-mason-
ic puppygander contains fallacy, jesuits and illuminati, encyclopedists etc.
Einstein demoralizing Euclid{'}s discipline. and gets to yr/ weed-killer.[15]
Greeks got to considerin conduct on Athenian stage, and civilized in so
far as wild animals of the occident are capable of reciving civilization,
the savages of of the north. Plop, aestheticism, etc. all slobbered by questions of BELIEF. sign on the dotted etc. and from thens descensus like
down a greased pole. Forget whether you met Beatrice Abbot[16] when in
{this} awful ½sphere?

DeGourmont rather mild re/Xtianity, saying it has "beaucoup plus
corrumpu les esprits que les moeurs.{"}[17] The hellenic elements IN Xtianity have corrupted no one. Meaning elements common to greeks and to
some american indians. BUT bless the old whore fer conserving some of
the ceremonies (Easter show in Siena for example. or even local funeral
rites. as in Rapallo.)

LOCAL control of local purchasing power, not more than one tenth or
one seventh shd/ be controlled from a distance (a centre of coordination).

There ought to be someone with more spare time than O.R.A. to keep in touch with THOUGHT outside the blinking peninsula. Good man named Ritter[18] writes me in despair but ALSO without correlating his thought to what has been thought outside Italy. Nobody ever meets anyone else.

Who is Paolo Pavolini?[19] ANY sign of thought in socialist messers? what percent???// 80% neofascist kids complete idiots? the various weeklies seem to get WEAKER and less thoughtful each month. all personal quibbling. NO sense of history, that is of any before?? I wonder what date.

P.S. Why the DEVIL nobody ever knows anyone else, for example, NOTARI, possibly most intelligent living wop, and NOBODY ever speaks to, or of him. Also he knows how to WRITE. Wonder if L.V.[20] shares papers with his friends. Various subjects that he doesn't touch. Does he understand ANY of 'em? what ever became of Paolillo? dozens of questions to ask, and O.R.A. ought not to be bothered with them. But SHOULD, and how, have a deputy capable of doing so.

the worst enemies of any program are its supporters/ per es/ Gesellites who cant understand stamp as tax/ which wshould NEVER exceed 1% monthly. as to reports of neo-fascists, evidently nearly all brainless. No reports on actual govt appear valid/ either the stench of the Cor d.Ser[21] or just attacks. NOT looking for possible constructivity. ALL of which wd/ be based on the ventennio,[22] unless someone has noticed Torlonia's pre-1922 bonifica.[23]

Yrs/ post Petrus/[24] I never met the Panther skin/ Ruspoli[25] harangued me for 1½ hours in Rapallo one day, ceasing to be society knut, an thazz all I kno about plowing, but believe I cd/ have drawn proper diagrams after F.R. finished. Glad you are sending P.R. to him.

fer the rest YU peePull make me tried. The way OUT of taxes is stamp-scrip/ moneta prescrittibile,[26] 1% monthly never more. and the rest is people NEVER meeting or collaborating. Before the church lost its ben dell intelletto,[27] it distinguished between usura and partaggio.[28] You want yr/ ½% blood back from the leech without enquiring whether the God damn bank or stank is USING yr/ deposit for fruit or for corrosive. If 20 or 40 of you wd/ MEET and decide to putt yr/ two pences fardings together and buy stone or a printing press, or PRODUCE something. you cd/ thumb yr noses at the banks. Vide Monte dei Paschi[29] centuries ago.

fer three months NO sign of ANY intelligence reached here fr/ woptalia.[30] Cheered by news that a Texas drunk in a California bar was telling the kawlidg boys he knew more than they ever wd/ he not having been to a UniWORSEity, but having heard it at Pisa.

unfortunately these be but 2 in 150 million robots/ all being mineralized.

Brooks Adams right in saying frogs had got mentally fixed. wops evidently getting frenchified.

1. ORA had written that her sister, **Helen Rossetti Angeli,** would be leaving London, "where the Rossetti family have lived for the last 127 years or so," and would be settling in Rome (18 Dec. 1949).

2. Fr.: "prudence."

3. **Rémy de Gourmont,** also mentioned below.

4. Pausanias of Lydia. EP has been reading his *Description of Greece,* probably in J. G. Frazer's translation of 1898.

5. Pope Pius XII's last stupidity (Gm.: *Stumm,* "dumb"). EP's letters to ORA contain several disapproving references to this Pope; this particular aside probably refers to Pope Pius XII's 1949 decree that threatened with excommunication those Catholics who knowingly and voluntarily elected to join the Communist party. See also letter 46.

6. Saul of Tarsus, or St. Paul.

7. Leviticus 19. See letter 21.

8. *Per esempio,* It.: "for example."

9. Probably *arcivéscovo,* It.: archbishop.

10. Christ's passion and crucifixion.

11. Politics.

12. Propaganda.

13. The Vatican.

14. An unidentified Australian Social Credit publication apparently commented on the putative link between Jesuits, Illuminati, and Encyclopedists commonly asserted in secret histories following the Abbè Barruel. The error is unclear.

15. ORA had mentioned that one of the young men to whom she is teaching English told her of a weed killer originally developed by the American military to destroy crops in enemy territory. She was appalled (18 Dec. 1949).

16. **Beatrice Abbott.**

17. EP cites the same phrase by **Rémy de Gourmont** in letter 18.

18. Probably Karl Ritter, a diplomat.

19. **Paolo Pavolini.**

20. **Luigi Villari.**

21. *Corriere della Sera,* an Italian daily.

22. It.: "twenty years," that is, the Fascist era in Italy, 1922–43.

23. Prince Alessandro Torlonia supervised Swiss and French engineers in draining Lake Fucino in 1854–75 and took proprietorship of the land. The land was divided into numerous small farms by the Italian Land Reforms Acts of 1952–53. See letter 23.

24. Lt.: "after Peter," probably a pun on *post scriptum.*

25. Presumably **Father Francesco Ruspoli,** also referred to as "F.R." below.

26. It.: "stamp-scrip money," that is, Gesellist money.

27. A reference to Dante; when people lose this, something akin to discernment or good sense, they fall into sin.

28. In "Gold and Work" EP explains that "the distinction between production and corrosion has been lost; and so has the distinction between the sharing-out of the fruits of work done in collaboration (a true and just dividend, called *partaggio* in the Middle Ages) and the corrosive interest that represents no increase in useful and material production of any sort" (*Selected Prose* 351).

29. EP devotes canto 43 to celebration of this Sienese bank established in 1622.

30. EP's name for Italy.

1950

25. TLS-1   [early 1950][1]

O.R.A.

Mary hopes Malu will be well enough to go to the castle next summer, so that's O.K., last summer arrangement seems to have been satisfac/ to both sides.

The REASON why Cato[2] shd/ not stop etc/ is that the young are so gawd/n IGGURUNT, and only their seniors remember anything of importance. Cavour[3] busting a gut to teach the wops to have a jaw-house BUT wops like yanks so damn silly they never meet. Vicari too diffident to come to via Menotti,[4] Ungaro disgusted and NOT teaching Vic/ WHAT a constitution IS. Thus Vic/ (hope you saw his noble effort in Oggi??[5] if not ask Olga about it.) Gets as far a Rummy Rolle'em, but can't understand fight for constitution.

Q. interesting note in Mercure de Frog fer Sept/,[6] travel diary of 1819, some dutch skirt, noting the bloody massacres in France 1814 or '15. cats an prots,[7] like in Spain in our time, cats and reds. Apparently Mirabeau[8] got to idiocy of nation renting* its own credit/ hence I spose HIS obit, and bad press. As per Gesell, the rotten reds, shooting the good [illegible deletion] reds the minute currency is brought into question. Someone ought to burn the moral ignominy of the Shaw-Upton Sinclair[9] pinkies, who will NOT face monetary issue.

IGNorance, ignorance, ignorance. Italian neo papers still the liveliest, BUT provincial. Takes a rotten paper like Mondo[10] to rotocalco[11] the brit/ Hussif's Leg (pardohn, League) Housewifes' League.

According to reports only a millionaire can invite friends to tea in Demi-Xtiania. If the tea and buns were provided has ORA time to invite a few of the less idiotic infesters of RRRoma to tea, say once a month, and put a dent in their ignorance of the outer world? System practiced by that rough-neck Jack London on his friends in N.York, while he in Rocky Mts. not to mention the endowed banquets of ancient Egypt and the Subura,

*paying rent FOR its own etc.

"who learn first, teach those who follow"/ trouble Villari, Varé etc. is they do NOT meet the next generation, let alone the young. Wot ever become of ole Picchio?[12] obit? and Paolillo? AND Dick degli U's[13] address?

DID I send you that Arrian qt/ re/ Alexander Gt. paying soldiers debts.[14] None of this stink about "loans TO ~~ven~~ veterans, from private punks, guaranteed by the state."

Being a author long dead praps Varé cd/ recognize THAT.

What about this guy IgnatZZ Silone?[15] of course the idiocy of taxing production and increasing the money tax as the production increases is fit only for a sub-anthropoid society.

{Cordiali}

{D.P.}

1. This letter was written later than ORA's visit to Brunnenburg Castle in mid-July 1949 and before the summer of 1950; although it was written by EP, it was signed by **Dorothy Pound.**

2. Probably Marcus Porcius Cato the elder (234–149 B.C.), Roman politician and general and author of *Origenes*, the first history of Rome, which does not survive. His only surviving work is a treatise on agriculture, *De agri cultura*, ca. 160 B.C.

3. **Camillo Benso di Cavour.**

4. ORA lived at Via Ciro Menotti, 36.

5. Probably *Oggi e Domani*, an anti-Fascist periodical.

6. EP is referring to an excerpt from Maurice Garçon's "Voyage d'une Holland-aise en France" that deals with a Dutch girl's visit to a Roman site in the south of France where she meets Olivier, an old minister, who recounts the horrors of the "White Terror" in the year 1815. The minister's account includes the follow-ing: "In 1815 protestants were tortured and killed. Women were shot to death after suffering outrageous atrocities. Protestant men were forced to wear a type of fan-cy ornament around their necks (in imitation of a Catholic cross) as a sign of their mocking of the Holy Spirit. The ornament was heated in fire and then stuck or branded onto the unfortunate victims of Catholic fanaticism. One monster, rev-elling in how he had slain forty protestants with his own hand, gave himself the name 'Tretallion' which in the local slang meant triple killer, and another improv-ing on the first called himself 'Quartallion' (quadruple killer)" (50). The minister goes on to describe the massacre of 220 soldiers of the imperial army and the pitiful measures taken by the royal government to restore order. The trouble did not end until the Protestants, taught by the trouble of 1815, assembled their own army and, during a face-off between the warring parties, a deputation arriving from Cevennes (where all the inhabitants were Protestants) convinced the Catholics that, were the events of 1815 to be repeated, 30,000 highlanders and farmers would come to the aid of their oppressed brothers. Once this threat was made the rebels dispersed and order was reestablished

7. Catholics and Protestants.

8. Probably Marquis De Victor Riquetti Mirabeau (1715–89), who in a publica-tion known as "L'ami des hommes" (1756) anticipated Quesnay's system by fo-cusing on the dependence of all aspects of the state on agriculture and proposing the kind of reforms that could help revive both agriculture and, in turn, the state. His son, Honore Gabriel, also wrote on economic matters.

9. George Bernard Shaw, whose name is associated with the Socialist Fabian Society, and Upton Sinclair are mentioned here as representatives of those with left-wing political affiliations.

10. Probably *Il Mondo,* a Rome-based liberal and anti-Fascist newspaper, suppressed in the mid-1920s.

11. *Rotocàlco,* It.: "rotogravure."

12. Probably **Ruggero Pier Piccio.**

13. **Riccardo M. degli Uberti.**

14. The following passage about Alexander the Great is likely the one EP has in mind: "Arriving at Ecbatana, Alexander sent back to the sea the Thessalian cavalry and the rest of the allies, paying each the agreed pay in full, and himself making a largess of two thousand talents; but anyone who would continue to serve him for pay on his own account he ordered to be enlisted, and a great number were so enrolled." Arrian 1:19, 289. See also letter 36.

15. **Ignazio Silone.**

26. TLU-2   [ans. 4 April 1950]

ORA/

Egon Corti's "House of Rothschild", "Reign of House of Rothschild"[1] created consid/ stir 20 years ago. Belatedly reading 'em. [illegible deletion] WERE they translated into wop? Need several Lubinss to balance THAT milking. "Ve vandt qviet to milk our goys." Not Meyer Anselm's[2] fault. The imbecile infantilism of all the goddam figures on scene of that era, except Cavour, irresistible. In fact intellectual jew couldn't possibly have seen ANY use for the animals except milk or ~~beff~~ beef. Nathan[3] "came to despise humanity"/ seeing it from London bourse, Natural focus of all the vilest in England. ANYhow, when you think that some Brit/ punk managed to print a fat 2 vol/ Life of Cavour[4] with only 3/4 th of one page on econ/ you can gauge the created ignorance of the mutts/ and the foetor of the so called press. This is merely query as to whether the almost SOLE history of the period is in print in Italian. Got library copy, and wondering if copy bought in Britain will get thru the holy post. London efforts to suppress Calcutta edtn/ of "Unwobbling Pivot" VERY, shall we say, entertaining. Have also ordered Varé's vol/[5] with deep mistrust. Tho interested to see what he has managed to get by the brit/ pub/g gang IF he had good intentions.

Didn't realize the Pup[6] kept 'em in the ghetto till 1850. Trouble not that they got OUT of the ghetto, but that they carried the ghetto ~~into w~~ everywhere they got into. with all that is worst in it. And no refuge for communities that wd/ like to have a little territory to themselves.

Amusing NOW to see ruin of real estate values by infusion of negro population, which swarms 8 families into a house. Pathos for elderly whites who had sunk their small capital in homes in certain areas. An nobody likes blacks better than I do. In fact I prefer some of 'em to most whites. In France you can still see towns 10 miles apart with the racial characteristis of early almost pre-mediaeval migrations.

To show the necessity of black leven. Dick told his black cook that the
H. bomb had been exploded, and instead of shocking sideways it had
shocked in profondita, splitting the earth in two like an apple. Respon-
sus est: "Ah [illegible deletion] knew dey's do somthin' ~~lak&~~ lak' that.
Foolin roun' too much with dem things." Great chase on for small spies
here at moment.

re/ The Corti sewer/ Europe distinctly behind the horse-sense of
J.Adams, Jackson etc.[7] at that time. Really bestial ignorance of money
problem.

Anybody opposing either Marx's mudwash or Roth's[8] cynical dishonesty, is of course branded anti-yitt. {goy expected to agree to both simultaneously & unconditionally.} It is AMAZING given the fact and the
number of people who were mixed in them that the slime of ignorance
re/ monetary issue shd/ have grown steadily deeper, or at least NO general education occurred, so that my generation began in densest most
infantile ignorance of things that every school boy of 16 ought to know
like his multiplication table. AND that the past 30 years struggle of a
handful of men has been utterly unable to penetrate. Sane college student writes me that a class mate is not interested in economics because
it leaves out the human element. and sh/ c-mate utterly impervious to
question: is housekeeping inhuman. Praps. use of unintelligible greek
long words helps maintain darkness.

The BASIC lie is on p/ 190. the idea that "financiers have the opportunity of rendering service to the country."[9]

The whole XIX siecle swallowed that imbecility or that plausibility or
whatever you call it.

Has anyone ever gone into question of sterilization of Rossini.[10] I used
to think he stopped because he saw music going the wrong way, cdn't stop
it, and quit. Now I find ~~in~~ him in bad company. Just as ~~Fe~~ Freudian filth
paralyzes its victims, alle samee grub that is stung by wasp to provide
food for wasp-egg.

//

more marvelous signs of jewish reign of terror in N.Y. elderly ~~sho~~ school
teachers etc/ fear for their jobs.

//

quote fr/ student's letter: cant imagine Christ hurrying anywhere, can't
imagine S.Paul doing anything else.

//

Ask Villari if Poumie's de la Siboutie's Memoirs[11] have been translated into italian. English trans/ to hand. As it deal{s} with France 1800–1863,
couldn't get V/ on "nostalgia".

very nice lot of actualities.

Very little sign of mental life in Italy showing in current papers recd.

1. Count Egon Caesar Corti's *The Rise of the House of Rothschild* and *The Reign of the House of Rothschild* were published in 1928.

2. **Mayer Amschel Rothschild.**

3. Probably Lord Nathan (Nathaniel) Meyer Rothschild (1840–1915), until his death the head of the English house of the Rothschilds. A Liberal, he sat in Parliament (1865–85) and was the first Jew to sit in the House of Lords; he also served as governor of the Bank of England (hence perhaps EP's "London bourse," that is, the London stock exchange), and was a member of the Royal Commission on Alien Immigration (1902).

4. Thayer's *The Life and Times of Cavour.*

5. Varè's *The Two Imposters.* EP read and commented on this book at considerable length in three letters to ORA not included here, one written on 13 February 1950 and the other two answered by ORA on 4 April 1950.

6. Pope Pius IX sought a loan from the Rothschilds in 1849. Corti commented: "Carl [Meyer Rothschild (1788–1855), head of the Naples Bank] made it a condition for granting the loan that the gates and walls of the ghetto should be abolished, that Jews should be allowed to live where they pleased in the Papal States, and that all special taxes and separate forms of procedure for dealing with Jews in the courts should be abolished." *Reign* 273; see also 272–76.

7. Presidents John Adams and Andrew Jackson. EP documents the struggle between Jackson and **Nicholas Biddle** in *Eleven New Cantos.*

8. **Mayer Amschel Rothschild.**

9. EP is quoting here from a letter of 12 October 1840 by James Meyer Rothschild (1792–1868), head of the Paris Bank. The letter marked the conclusion of an attempt to influence French foreign policy. See Corti, *Reign* 189–90.

10. Giaocchino Antonio Rossini (1792–1868).

11. François Louis's *Recollections of a Parisian.*

---

27. TLS-2   [ans. 16 April 1950]

ORA

despite Varé's legal technicalities[1] I cant call you a OAR.

I have a long standing debt to yr/ unkle Dan Gabe,[2] and if anything wd/ persuade you to take a short vacation or an hour off per day, I shd/ hv/ NO comDamPunction whatsodam of paying off $100 of it with D's money.[3]

I believe some other subversive attempt was made, unsuccessfully.

Mary says she hopes for visitors, so I hope that means that you will at any rate get to Merano with one or more young.

YES. the anagraphic augment, they named {it} Patricia[4] and her hair turned RED, BUT I hear it is getting paler.

You dodged one question/ re V's parentela with Manin???[5]

Don{'}t accuse ME. I have already said the only word of sense in Italian print, recently, was by Scarfoglio/[6] down on the nail re/ the South's bank deposits.

As for the Giartosio/ it is writ in the great bugiotologia[7] that the {"}heathen rage.{"}

Of course it is the dam Xtians who rage, especially about poetic lucidity. Scotus Erigena[8] and Dante both wrote clear verses. The holy crusaders dug up the one several centuries post mortem, and wd/ have done Dante the same only someone hid the os/ in a small packing case, now, or at least recently, on view in Ravenna. Marked *Dantis ossa*,[9] only it's empty.

I propose TRYING to use the Vare Impost{s}/ to EDUCATE etc. it ought to do SOME good.

If Mary is clever enough to lure T.S.Elephant[10] to Brunnenburg, she shd/ plant him with a contract for your Memoirs.[11] which shd/ "render" more than berlitzing.[12]

He has recently taken refuge in a voyage to the Cap Gd. Hop/[13] but as Doc. Johnson sd/ "no man wd/ go on board a ship who cd/ break into a prison."[14]

and while YOU are educating...you might as well put in a few licks nearer the top. There is a lot that man does NOT know.

Tho I dare say V's narsty fir friends cd/ land you as lucrative a firm, which wd/ lack only my name on its list of authors (published contra voglia)[15]

very difficult to be intelligible in a milieu that hasn't the FOGGGdamniEST idea of the American Constitution, and that has never heard of the Leopoldine Reforms.[16] Whereas on this side of Columbus error, the ignorance of Europe is blacker than the heart of Pacelli. The first Vol/ of Corti has been shipped to Merano, so if you get there, you cd/ wile away an hour learning what REAL swine Mr Meternich{'s} gang[17] were/ the Roth/[18] being quite justified in ruining THEM. Gentz for example. in fact the wholeDamLot. with the elector of Hesse[19] no better than any [illegible deletion].

CAN you look in yr/ phone book and see if Ian Monro[20] is at his old address, whatever that was/ somewhere along the Margutta, but i forget the number if it was Margut/ at any rate the information is desired. As per the request for yr/ autograph in the Div/ Com/[21] YOU ought to know mieux que[22] that the murkn peepulus[23] is NOT thoroughly informed re/ italian history. Let alone ANY facts of the past trentennio.[24] Not after Luce and the lesser Lice have been stuffing 'em for 30 Or [illegible deletion] 40 years.

Has V/ an american publisher? or one in view. My copy of 2 Imp/ was from Lunnon.[25]

Yes, of course I agree that the book should do some good. Ignorance being TOTAL even a few data help.

AND without fantasticating re/ Eliot, if you wd/ jot down a few recollections I *think* I cd/ place 'em.. can't guarantee it.

But as a granDad I want a more EDUCATED world for Walt/ and Patricia. No scruples as to how I obtain it. I suppose Lubin was too IGNORANT to have heard of Del Mar.[26] The filth of the American Univs/ in ignoring him is even thicker and dirtier than that of their less specific occultation of 98% of all history. Alexander Del Mar? what do the pseudoeruditi of Italy know about him??

Too bad honest econ/ been left so largely to illiterates.

By the way, if you want a little clean decent piety OUTside of China, have a look into Louis Agassiz,[27] or von Humbol{d}t.[28] And now to be serious for a moment. What about Malu's medical expenses? Qui non si scherza.[29] May say that Mary found ole Doc Wms/[30] {s}imple measure, namely swobbing the chest with cold water (NOT cold bath, just swobbing the FRONT, thorax, with cold water was more use for Walter's cold than the fancy medicines, penicillin etc. kind of simple thing one knows and forgets. May be no use vs/ bugs, but clears off the lung-moss they nest in. Treatment first thing [illegible deletion] when one gets up in morning. Malu may be too weak? but doubt it.

[in Dorothy Pound's hand:] {EP put in that word fluffy[31] when I had read only 3 pages. I found it all most interesting, though painful. Entirely apart from E's arabesques—I want the enclosed[32] to go towards Malù's medical expenses.}

{Saluti cordiali}
{Dorothy Pound}

1. Varè's *The Two Imposters*. See letter 26.

2. **Dante Gabriel Rossetti.**

3. **Dorothy Pound**'s money left to her by her parents; for details see *Ezra Pound/ Dorothy Shakespear.*

4. Mary's second child, Patrizia Barbara Cinzia Flavia de Rachewiltz, recently born (1950).

5. **Daniele Manin.** ORA responded to EP's question as follows: "Manin was not a relation of Varè's father, but a friend, and Varè père took part with him in the defence of the Venetian republic in 1848 or some such date" (16 April 1950).

6. **Carlo Scarfoglio.**

7. It.: *bugia*, "lie" + Gk.: *logos*, "word": EP's play on *Patrologia*, two collections by J. P. Migne of the "words" (*logoi*) of the church fathers (*pateres*)—one of the Greek fathers (*Patrologia Graeca*), the other of the Latin fathers (*Patrologia Latina*).

8. There is no record of **Johannes Scotus Erigena** being exhumed; however, as he does in *The Cantos* (36/90 and 83/538), EP is probably confusing Erigena with the thirteenth-century pantheist heretic Amaury de Bene.

9. It.: "Dante's bones."

10. T. S. Eliot.

11. EP encouraged ORA to write her memoirs and, as later letters attest, she did. A section appeared as "Pages of Memoir" in *Edge*.

12. A reference to ORA's teaching of English as a second language.

13. **Mary de Rachewiltz** visited Eliot in London in the spring of 1948. See Matthews, *Great Tom* 163. In a letter of 3 January 1950 Eliot discusses leaving by boat for a six-week holiday to South Africa. See Levy and Scherle, *Affectionately T. S. Eliot* 17–18.

14. This is Samuel Johnson's comment recorded by James Boswell in *The Journal of a Tour to the Hebrides with Samuel Johnson*, 31 August 1759: "No man will be a sailor who has contrivance enough to get himself into a jail; for being on a ship is being in a jail with the chance of being drowned. . . . A man in a jail has more room, better food, and commonly enough better company" (84).

15. It.: "against [my] wishes."

16. The **Leopoldine Reforms** and the Constitution are frequent motifs in EP's work; his "paideuma" includes praise for both; for example, see *The Fifth Decad of Cantos*.

17. EP is responding to ORA's remarks about Metternich in a letter of 4 April 1950; ORA had written that she had read, some time before, "Harold Nicholson's history of the Treaty of Vienna I was struck by the 'enlightment' of Metternich and all his tribe (Castlereagh included) when compared to the incredible criminals who govern the world today."

18. The Rothschild family.

19. The elector in question is William II, elector 1821–31. His forebear is William I, elector 1803–21.

20. **Ian Smeaton Munro.** ORA replied that she had "looked in the telephone directory, there is no Monro and only one Monroe, who sells calculating machines in the Via Nazionale" (16 Apr. 1950).

21. Though probably first mentioned in a missing ORA letter to which EP is responding here, this refers to a reminiscence from a visit to Chicago in the 1930s recounted in a letter of 24 August 1958. ORA received a request by an American young lady who "brought a copy of Dante's Commedia" and asked her to sign it, since "Dante Gabriel Rossetti [and] Dante Alighieri were evidently all the same to her."

22. Fr.: "better than."

23. American populace. EP frequently uses "murkn" and variants for "American."

24. It.: "period of thirty years."

25. London.

26. **Alexander Del Mar.**

27. **Louis Agassiz.**

28. **Alexander von Humboldt.**

29. It.: "Here one cannot joke."

30. William Carlos Williams.

31. A reference to EP's observation in letter 19 that "D. says Varè's english bk/ is fluff, but non-poisonous, am waiting to see it."

32. Money.

28. TLU-1   [post–27 October 1950]

ORAg

Douglas on Perversion.[1] or loose terminology, or not-understood. by anarchy of her youth she means (and defines) community-ism

Communism[2] has lost all sense of commune, or community as organic. in sense of anarchy?? "without PERSONAL arXon"[3] or governor, is possible where there is a strong feeling for law or custom more MOS (custom) than LEX (law) and this got Italy thru the interregnum, when there was little or no government.

and the x priests at once tried to exploit it advocating nothing but priest rule, first locally but tending.....

where all sense of custom (say English) has been covered with swill of polyglot flux[.] anarchy comes to Capone[4] and Rosenstein. mere banditry and corruption. not the least order4d communities swapping with each other.

No freedom (locally) without local control of money OR local control of exchange value in some form issued against locally produced food.

1. In "Antitheses," a page-long anonymous advertisement for the **Square $ Series** printed on the inside cover of *Nine* 9 (Summer–Autumn 1952), mention is made of an essay by C. H. Douglas on "perversion." Two perversions are mentioned here: the first pertains to the "homestead versus the kolchosz" and the second is said to obscure "the ideas of both democrats and monarchists" (293).

2. In a letter dated 27 October 1950, ORA had written that she was sending for EP's perusal "what is practically the autobiography of my adolescence 'A Girl among the Anarchists' published in 1903, which probably never came your way." **A Girl among the Anarchists** was written by ORA and her sister Helen under the pseudonym Isabel Meredith. The rest of the letter deals with ORA's book and her early life as an Anarchist.

3. Gk.: "ruler."

4. Al Capone (1899–1947).

29. TLU-1   [October or November 1950][1]

O.R.A.

Two desideria. circumstances: shall be sending by slow post (air too costly) a vol/ vurry cleverly compacted.[2] in short Mr Paige OUGHT to show you that one can avoid spilling friends dhirrrty laundry and yet etc. contribute to generl kulChar.

anyhow, when you get it, and find time fer perusal, mebbe you can tone down some local prejudice vs/ the worthy editor.

SECONDLY, to hell with this ten hours a day business. in view of what the Hudson[3] pays per page. You may not [illegible deletion] hv/ been drunk with as many indians as de Angulo,[4] but you have moved amid more savage scenes, as per that btch/ in the Leg of Nations.

Yr/ letters contain marrow, fer wich a MARket eggzists.

Fordie died too soon, and without an editorial chair or one wd/ have set him to purr-suading you.

Write the stuff as letters to ME if it rePUGns you to think of the greasy and mush-headed public.

Why not a li'l ease.

You don't suffer from aphasia OR from lack of memory/ tho you havent yet got the name of the s.o.b. who came to see yu in N.Yok re the SIN-emma.

One Nurseries ready to send maples saplings/[5] think they can arrange all formalities as this end/ certificates of health of trees.etc.

Dept. of Ag/[6] also invites D/[7] to come down fer jaw. which cd/ be done if there are hitches. But oughtn't to necessary if Boris[8] exhibits letter from the Whoosis and Whazzis Nurseries, of somewhere in N.England. ONLY they say shipment shd/ be made inNOVember, otherwise too late to dig saps/ fr/ fruz ground. 2̶0̶0̶ 200 saps/ can go the minute B/ clears at Rome end.

anyhow, Mary[9] d̶ shd/ have the letter by now but dont know if B/ still in Rome or who can deal with matter.

1. D. D. Paige's volume of EP's letters (*Selected Letters*) was published on 26 October 1950; a copy was in ORA's hands by 10 December 1950, the date of a letter in which she acknowledges having received it.

2. Paige's collection of EP's letters.

3. The *Hudson Review*, the New York journal which in 1950 started publishing and promoting EP's work and of others promoted by him. EP constantly encouraged ORA to write her memoirs, but the chapter she sent to the *Hudson Review* was not accepted for publication. For EP's remarks on her memoirs, see letters 109, 111, 112, 116, 119, 120, 122, and 123.

4. Jaime de Angulo, an anthropologist whose work EP admired; at EP's instigation de Angulo's "Indians in Overalls," an account of the language and manners of the Pit River Indians, was published in the *Hudson Review*.

5. EP's plan to grow maple trees at Brunnenburg did not work out; of those planted, only one survives.

6. Presumably the U.S. Department of Agriculture.

7. **Dorothy Pound.**

8. **Boris de Rachewiltz.**

9. **Mary de Rachewiltz.**

1951

30. TLU-2   [ans. 4 February 1951]

O.R.A.

in search of a little LIGHT from Italia tradita.[1] Drummond's rectification in Fiera Letteraria 7th Jan.[2] very interesting, only one phrase I want
light on. "detto certamente in malafede dai funzionari della radio."[3] Now
I do NOT believe for ten seconds that it was given in malafede. Question academic in so far as the funzonari are out of jug, and it dont matter
whether they were in or out of fede, pink, pblue or whatever. and Ez/ is
in jug and wishes his friends wd/ if they choose assassinate each other
AFTER getting [illegible deletion] him OUT, rather than feuding before
hand. But as NEWS on the state of the peninsula, it wd/ ENlighten to
know if J.D. wrote the sentence, and if so, whether from british pt/ of view
or dummyspeudo pt/ of view, or whether the Fiera had to defame t{he}
"tyranny" even now in order to go on being printed. Drummond article
or letter ought to be useful. And IF there were any life in the MINDS of
the goddam Romani (which he incidentally sez there is NOT...in note
appended to the article) it might be timely to start in on EZ'z DIFFER-
ENCES with the "tyranny" and the points he was trying to git into the
woptalian "mind" from 1923–3343. Incidentally Leahy[4] sez Petain wanted fer the Frog-gerry something between the U.S.Consterooshun and
Muss'[5] first plan fer woptalia. (The Admiral also show{s} what utter swine
the allies have been in abandoning Petain to the sewage of what used to
be France. At any rate JD's pp/ third from last wd/ give Studer[6] or someone di buona volontaaaa.[7] a chance to go on re/ Brooks Adams, Kitson
AND Gesell. Under at least the working assumption that the Peninsula
wont be wholly destroyed by Einstein's dirty mathematics. News needed HERE is which of the ROmani is capable of an orderly exposition of
ANY useful historic data. Nice note by Piero Rebora[8] in Mattino dell Ital
Centrale, for the 5th Jan. Any dat{a} on Rebora? (article on Dante fern-
inst the angry-saxons,[9] mentioning the ROsetter fambly az well. Also any
chances of wop/trans of Impact,[10] of which hv/ already seen proofs, so it
must be or hv/ been on way to pub/ctn in Britain la perfide.

Current Hudson has first boost of Fordie[11] that wdn't hv/ turned his stom-
ach. The boom has been goin' strong (in the olfactory sense{)} but at any
rate his stuff getting back into print. and a few people getting at what he
was really worth, which was CONsiderable. Kenner[12] underestimates cause
he hasn't seen some of the stuff that is still unobtainable. People COULD
hv/ learned from J.Adams letters to Waterhouse, but they weren't published
till 1927.[13] centennial dopo mor{t}e J.Ad. Also in notes of B. Rush[14] proof,
VESTIGIA of civilization in this overwhelmed continent.

re/ the Fiera/ someone COULD reply on basis of note in last American edtn/ of SELECTED poems, which states this agreement sic: "which promise was faithfully observed by the Italian government"/

whatever fede may hv/ been in the "funzionari della radio" whose names incidentally wd/ show that they d/n well were NOT in malafede. BUT until I know more of the A'MMosphere in Roma of the first year after the jew-bulleeee, I can't tell if they wd/ want to be dragged into the disKUSShion.

where there was so much dishonour, it might be worth while to affirm what honour there WAS. IF yu (blastitall) people wd/ only show some sign of being aware of the existence of each other......

anyhow the year starts with two good lick{s} of work pro-anonimo[15] in woptalia. Did Paige send you Anceschi's study[16] in whatever that highbrow wopgazeen was?

Just heard that Stancioff[17] got out of Bulgaria alive. Mrs S/ here lecturing on agrarianism as alternative to atombump.

Linder[18] advising Georgia farmers to make each farm as autonomous as possible. MIXed crop, not dependence on market and stinkulations.

1. It.: "Italy betrayed."

2. **John Drummond's** "La verita sul caso Pound."

3. It.: "said, certainly in bad faith, by radio officials." To EP's query ORA responded: "You are quite right, I think there was no 'bad faith' on the part of Propaganda people, and I agree that a note to that effect should be published for it is their due; and I do not think any bad results would follow for the writers" (4 Feb. 1951).

4. **William D. Leahy's** I Was There contains many references to **General Philippe Pétain** and one to EP (464).

5. Benito Mussolini. EP often refers to him as "Muss" or simply "M."

6. Unidentified EP friend.

7. It.: "with good will."

8. Probably Piero Rebora, who later wrote "Ezra Pound: Canto Pisani" on the Pisan Cantos.

9. EP probably means "amongst the Anglo-Saxons," that is, he is thinking of Dante's reception in England. Dante did not visit England.

10. An Italian translation of Impact; we have no information about the publication of such a translation.

11. **Hugh Kenner's** "Remember That I Have Remembered," a review of Ford's Parade's End.

12. **Hugh Kenner.**

13. See John Adams, Statesman and Friend.

14. **Benjamin Rush.** The Spur of Fame, ed. Schultz and Adair, contains conversations between John Adams and Rush.

15. It.: "anonymous." EP is presumably thinking about two of his works he published anonymously.

16. Luciano Anceschi wrote a number of articles on EP (see Ricks 123); the article in question is "Palinsesti del protoumanesimo poetico americano."

17. **Anna Stancioff's** husband, Dimitri Stancioff.

18. **Tom Linder.**

31. TLU-3   14 February 1951

O.R.A.

J.Drummond, Lungotevere Mellini 17. re/ Count of Pantzdown must be relative Mollie Panter-Downs[1] who writes brit. news in N.Yorker. Paige address Casella Postale 30, Rapallo. Seriously as soon as someone CAN safely stand UP and hammer on civilization of the handful or at least one or two Cavourians who tried to keep open a forum for honest debate, the better. Admiral Leahy, ventriloquist's dummy in "I was there", sez Petain wanted something between U.S.Constitution and Muss' first proposals. Trust new bill of rights will reach you from Pg/[2] curiosity might be aroused re possible inducements to recant. Not to be dogmaticly stated. question of someone with courage. J.D. ran mimeographed weekly bulletin in 1938, {(|Italian news(|)} trying to combat jewzfeld lies, and had quite a bad time, don{'}t know details, but jailed, and perfidy at every pore ALWAYS. The honest englander makes news. Tower Hill etc. suitable take-off. Nobody on yr/ list ready for honest ~~moeny.~~ money. Billion $ propaganda now as for 2000 years vs/ usury, monopoly, altering the value of the integer of account, and suppressing history. esp/ re the AT LEAST twelve epochal uses of token coin. I *had* got to three of 'em. Sparta (everyone knows of) Carthage, China. Money [illegible deletion] ALWAYS an instrument of policy. TWO founts of light, mediterranean, and Middle Kingdom. yr/ xtianity messes, from trying to hitch old.test epilepsy (and a few bits of sense) to ideas the old kikes never intended to have 'em hitched to. LEAVE the festas to the Madonna delle Salame,[3] but don{'}t have flat chested mutts pretending that they MEAN this or that piece of hoakum. and DAMN yr Pacelli.[4] (also look up yr/ {"}Inferno{"} fer a few of his dhirrrty precursors and precurseds,

AND the blinkin fascists TRIED to get the below to come UP. and it wdn't. wasn't there case in Turin of some bloke up'd to vice Prefetto, but not the brain to get any further. HONESTÀ at top, wd. solve most of the mess. Moulton[5] name vaguely familiar fer some time. Probably ignores the Federal Reserve altogether in his vapours, but will try to see book. FORD very useful in spotting the DAMAGE K.James version had done to eng/ lang/, also Wordsworth "so intent on common word he ~~nvr~~ never thought of mot juste.{"} J.Adams letters to Waterhouse HAD already got the answer. naturally slicks, and the pewk of curent periodicals stink

to heaven. Luce lower that Roosenbelly. Glad to hear re/ Convito.[6] even
after 40 years. Mary getting useful perspective on english rural life.[7] hope
you can talk with her when she gets back. Saluti to Helen, glad you have
that much good company. as well as etc/etc/ Ford was blinkin catholic,
it was the damage done by the TRANSLATION, the language of it{,}
impeding exact statement that he spotted. I dont know who had noticed
it before him. tho Gourmont saw the muddle of ideas. that not same as
pompous and affected mode of speech. Of course got the fat man into the
dog house with all the geese{,} Gosses e tutti quanti.[8] In fact he had NO
ONE to play with till Wyndham L/[9] and my generation riz up. Glad he
coming into his own, tho only the chosen people will reap his royalties
as he named one literary eggs-secutor and Julie[10] is married to another.
However that may remove obstacles to publication and circulation. They
e sure got a national home. Whether the goys are to have one, I dunno.
Honduras and/or British Guiana have been suggested as possible sites for
the remnants of [illegible deletion] Americans of european and british
origin.

re yr/ from the bottom.[11] The franchise shd/ be extended a LITTLE faster than people are fit to use it/ WITH clear understanding AT the top. that
the TOP will be wrecked if they do not educate the bottom fast enough.
i.e. fast enough to prevent the avalanche of sewage that has with accel-
eration engulphed the U.S. from day Lincoln was shot for bankers' con-
venience/ next phase in the 1870s/ and final massacre under Woodrow[12]
the vile, the pimp, the instrument of infamy and precursor of his infinitely
more filthy successor.

1. **Mollie Panter-Downes.**

2. D. D. Paige. See letter 29.

3. It.: "salami." EP is mocking Catholic feasts as occasions for food rather than
procreation.

4. In her reply ORA addressed their disagreement on the subject of the Catholic Church and Pope Pius XII (**Eugenio Pacelli**) in particular: "it is of course quite
understood that I totally disagree with you on the subject of Pius XII. You have a
total misapprehension of his personality and heroic work. On that as on a few
other points we must agree to differ....unti{l} you see the light!" (19 Mar. 1951).

5. **Harold G. Moulton.**

6. ORA had written: "By the way, my father's translation of the Convito with
the alternative meanings given by Dante for the terms used there, which you
recommended for publication, was published, much to the dear Fofus's (his family pet name) satisfaction" (4 Feb. 1951).

7. Presumably Mary was visiting **Henry S. Swabey** in England.

8. It.: "and all amounts."

9. **Wyndham Lewis.**

10. Ford's sister.

11. This is EP's response to ORA's comments about Mussolini's "corporate state," which "if it had been properly carried out and not corrupted by nominating all the leaders from above instead of having them selected from below and if the whole system had not been undermined by time-serving toad-eaters, would have provided the solution, together with vocational representation instead of geographical representation" (4 Feb. 1951). See also letters 54 and 55.

12. Wilson's successor was Warren G. Harding, but EP may have Roosevelt in mind here.

32. TLU-2   3 May 1951

O.R.A.

HOW (longOCATaline)[1] haz the Banc/Nz/Lav[2] been printing in yenglisch? Never envied BADoglio but he sure had a flair for the voc/del pad/.[3] Now can't Sapori[4] (who t{h}rice notes loans to Sovereigns) have ALSO noted that they were prob/ loans for armaments, or at least non-productive activity? Thammy Lloyd[5] etc/ re/ (vid Brooks Adams)[6] legit/ operations of commerce/ O.K. AND not Lorenzo's interest in civilized activity but LACK of *one* clear distinctions/ i.e. productive and non productive basis of loans. Interest due teleologically to increase in domestic animals and plants (probably that can be extended with modern chemical productivity of beni commerciabili.)[7] Princeton Univ/ shd/ send Sap/ a copy of their UNsatisfactory trans/ of the Han Shu "Food and Money in Ancient China"/[8] some though{t} has been given to terminology. what they call money might hv/ been called "commerciabili beni" in opening section. but at any rate "means of exchange" shows translator was trying to think. Princeton Univ. Press, Princeton N.J. they wd/ prob/ send rev/ cop. very badly arranged for consultation of chinese orig/ Rouvere's[9] naivete in supposing no discount MERELY because it warnt writ down on the books. Will Sap/ rev/ the Del M/?? in the ¼ly? The LOUSY name of Keynes.[10] ANY chance of noticing wail of Fed/ Reserve sharks over RFC competition (however crooked)? Keynes spirochetic son of Pigou?[11] or what breed of cockroach? well I'm damnd if I read even yr/ trans/ of a discussion. I take it there is no lie K/ wdn't hv/ told. And what bunk to "rank below" instead of DEFINING the ONE CLEAR gesellite idea. esp/ as MARX was NOT a monetary economist at all. At any rate no one has told grampaw of existence of ANY statement of Moarx on problem of ISSUE. why cant the prof/s be serious. Keynes gave de jure recog/? when{?} AFTER it existed in more civilized countries? Whether the slimer knew of Del Mar and helped conceal him or was just ham iggurunt, I dunno. DARE Lab/ or Sap/ face the single line: some of the non-interest-bearing nat/ debt in circ/ as currency?

THIS strictly private and anonymous communique. BUT no copyright on the questions enclosed. use of gold or other "precious" commodity as med/ of ex/[12] is ~~BARTR~~ BARTER and the barrators will ALWAYS be against numisma,[13] i.e. any honest government and WANT their absolute monopoly either via shortage (created or real) of actual, or of tickets allegedly based on.

Idea of money as certificate of work done, WORKED in Brazilian coffee plantations (the "little Tags". vid/ Agassiz {'}Voyage in Brazil.{'}[14] Wish I knew WHO ever speaks viva voc[15] to whom. Europa Nazione dont arouse naive enthusiasm and total confidence. Any side light on suppression of Rome American which seemed the rump end of Stars and Swipes, a dhirty propga/ orgn/ in contrast to the honest "Infantry Journal" which latter was hard to get. Can ANYone get Banc Naz Lav ¼ly except members of gang. Americn. Univ. libraries shd/ subscribe but it carries no sign that it is on sale. Sapori's name vaguely familiar, wonder hv/ I met him?

of course ALL pub/ housing schemes shd/ be self liquidating as per familiar Guernsey market house/[16] U.S. colonies etc. system. and GESELL shows way and Marx does NOT. Has even ORA considered the bank side of Gesell/[17] i.e. banks accept the script on deposit at 2% discount. (that gets away, i,e, improves on EP's idea of using the prescriptbl as merely auxiliary currency/ contemporary with old fashioned fixed notes. What Trucco[18] is in print? at what price? O.P. only had one little pamphlet of Avigliano,[19] used as salve to local vanity rather than lighthouse. any second hand Feder[20] available? ANY of yr/ highbrow friends capable of serious private correspondence?

1. EP is quoting the opening phrase of Cicero's *First Oration against Catiline*. See also letter 36.

2. *National Bank of Lavoro Quarterly*, which ORA seems to have sent to EP; in a letter dated 24 May 1951, ORA responded to some of EP's queries: "The Banca Nazionale del Lavoro has been publishing that Review in English for 2 years; it is sent to a free mailing list; I sent you the other day an extract of another art. by Sapori on the earlier Italian bankers who made loans to the English Kings with which he conducted their wars to suppress Scotch freedom and also the French wars. [. . .] Del Mar is I think practically unknown over here. The little pamphlet I got is very important; if I could have another copy I would get it to Sapori whom I do not know but can get at." In another letter, dated 8 June 1951, she wrote that she did not know Sapori personally, but was told that he was a professor at the University of Florence.

3. Perhaps *voce del padrone*, It.: "a boss's voice" or "a boss's word."

4. **Armando Sapori.**

5. **Samuel Jones Loyd.**

6. In a 1950 letter in which he lists **Alexander Del Mar**'s books and provides commentary on Del Mar's economic insights (answered by ORA on 8 July 1950,

but not included here), EP had written that "Brooks Ad/ on Sammy LLoyd gets
to equivalent racket. CONTROLL of monetary issue, the lever of sovereignty."
EP has in mind here *The Law of Civilization and Decay* (1943), in which Brooks
Adams writes that Samuel Loyd was responsible for the Bank Act of 1844 in Great
Britain. Loyd was a strong advocate of the gold standard, and his act's basic tenet
was that all gold available should be equal to the amount of paper money issued,
and more specifically, any bank notes issued in excess of £14,000,000 "must have
direct reference to corresponding fluctuations in the amount of gold" (314).

7. It.: "marketable goods."

8. Han Shu's *Food and Money in Ancient China*.

9. Probably French critic, writer, and draftsman André Louis Guillaume Rouveyre
(1879–1962). He was acquainted with many influential artists of his time, including the poets Apollinaire and **Rémy de Gourmont** (whose work he illustrated) and
the painters Albert Marquet and Matisse (who illustrated his novel *Repli*).

10. **John Maynard Keynes.**

11. **Arthur Cecil Pigou.**

12. Medium of exchange.

13. Gk.: "currency." Here EP means a "nummulary" as opposed to a commodity or labor theory of monetary value. EP refers to this concept in a letter answered
by ORA on 8 July 1950 but not included here in which he alludes to **Alexander
Del Mar**'s discussion of *nomisma* or *numisma*, that is, metallic money, in *History of Money in Ancient Countries*. In his introduction (1), Del Mar points out that
the value of money is conventional and a function of the quantity of money in
circulation and the quantity of goods and services deliverable. This theory of
monetary value Del Mar calls "nummulary."

14. Agassiz and Agassiz, *A Journey to Brazil*.

15. *Viva voce*, Lt.: "by word of mouth."

16. Probably a reference to the Channel Island, which had, at one point, its own
coinage.

17. EP's fullest discussion of Gesell is found in "The Individual in his Milieu:
A Study of Relations and Gesell" in *Selected Prose* 272–83.

18. Probably Angelo Francesco Trucco, an Italian writer.

19. O.P. is probably **Odon Por**. Avigliano is perhaps the town of Avigliana.

20. **Gottfried Feder's** *Das Programm der N.S.D.A.P. und seine weltanschaulichen Grundgedanken*.

33. TLU-3   24 May 1951

O.R.A.

Just heard fr/ Gius Maranini,[1] address il Preside, Univ. deg/ Stud/ Firenze, plus some indication of soc/pol/ dept. Probably only because his dam-
wife wants to send a bk/ of poems, prob/ 7th. rate. BUT still praps time
they began to consider Ez real donation to econ/ that wd/ prb/ go on ½
page. BUT note that at Econ/ Cong/ Pisa, both Coppola d'A/ and Arena[2]
listened when I sd/ MUST hv/ precise terminology IF any wish to have
ANY SCIENCE of econ/ their pale eyes wandered when I got to Gesell,

but re/ terminology they listened. Now, lacking Remy de Gourmont on Dissociation d' Idees,[3] cd/ at least note the following. Doug/[4] failed to emphasize.

Difference between DEBT and interest bearing debt. Naturally all money is a claim or a diritto[5] to a cert/ amt/ of goods or services.

Del Mar/ {interest} teleologically due to increase in domestic animals and plants. Possibly NOW some augment due to synthetic but useful products, fibres etc.

Also if homo economicus dont exist, some are more defiled than others, traditional "avare"[6] etc.

Increase of volume of nation's money to keep step with increased quantity of goods {WHEN there is any is not inflation. Locke, to Del M/ and Volpe's[7] "misurata" inflazione.[8] Del M's computed about right at 3% in the [illegible deletion] 1880s/

As yet no general examination of Gesellite mode of TAXATION in proportion to other kinds (almost all infamous and idiotic) Waaal some pale shadow like Maranini MIGHT touch gingerly.

Did yu see Cherchi in Popolo Nuovo? I hear the econ part was cut, and then. [illegible deletion] dumm Xtn apes,[9] wdn't mention the secular Cavour. That damn hump on Mons V/[10] is a curse and murrain[11] and a marasmus[12] (may be something else as well, but certainly spreads mental rot/ "beaucoup plus corrumpu les esprits, que les moeurs."[13]

Waal Mme Stancioff STILL bogged by Aquinas, Ez at least hammers on canonist DIFFERENCE between usura and partaggio/[14] nothing new. Del M/ approached differently, Ez/ from canonist, as when the Church was being virtuous (whether in RARE moments, etc. yu can compute)/ difference between a fixed charge regardless of whether the crop had grown, and a share of whatever had been produced. and these differences shd/ be hammered in IN the first half hour of ANY economics course in anydam Univ/

The Banc/ Lav/ ¼ly/ useful in impressing barbarians,/ and the language ergo useful{,} tho shameful to all latinity.

The other item re/ yr/ fambly. Note that the people who most respected pore ole Fordie were the ones who knew him best. As per Stella's autobiography,[15] after having been conjunct for fairly long term of years. And the superficial others were those who noted absurdities PLAINLY observable without any difficulty. of which there were enough. but they weren't the rock bottom. And his value proportionate value BOTH as man and as writer keeps coming up stronger with the flow of time.

Incidentally hv/ just started rereading Browning, or bits that I never got thru before. inversions, tangles and ABSTRACTIONS, but gt/ abundance. passed on to Hardy,[16] POLLON D'ANTHROPON IDEN[17] or at least cogitated and got a good deal into his underbrush.

If any americans turn up on yr/ doorstep CURSE 'em{,} lambast 'em for NOT communicating with each other until at least a few A B: abs get into their _mutual_ comprehension.

Thoreau rotting their sense of cooperation/ Pascal[18] a spirochete among frawgs/ As Br/ Ad/[19] noted their fixity/ blighted parisians, all sewed up in a bag/ unaware of any thought save that in their arrondissement.[20]

benedictions.

HUDSON[21] enquiring re/ yr/ memoirs.

1. **Giuseppe Maranini.**

2. **Coppola d'Anna** and **Arena** (unidentified) are mentioned together several times in the correspondence; see letters 59, 71, and 81.

3. Fr.: "dissociation of ideas," a Gourmontian notion that discrimination was a rarer and more precious capacity than the recognition of resemblance—at least with respect to abstractions.

4. **Major Clifford Hugh Douglas.**

5. It.: "right, claim."

6. Probably _avarizia_, It.: "avarice."

7. Probably Gioacchimo Volpe (1876–1971), historian of modern Italy, director of the Institute of Contemporary Italian History at the University of Rome, Fascist deputy (1924–29), and author of the partisan _Storia del movimento fascista_ and the more objective _L'Italia moderna._ He broke with Mussolini and remained loyal to the king and Badoglio.

8. It.: "moderate inflation."

9. The Christian Democratic party of Italy.

10. The Vatican.

11. In canto 45/229 EP writes that "Usura is a murrain."

12. "Progressive emaciation."

13. See letter 18.

14. It.: "a share" as opposed to a "fixed charge," that is, interest.

15. **Stella Bowen's** _Drawn from Life_ contains many portraits of contemporary personalities, including those of EP and Max Beerbohm.

16. Thomas Hardy (1840–1928).

17. This is EP's transliteration of the first four words of the third line of Homer's _The Odyssey:_ "πολλῶν δ' ἀνθρώπων ἴδεν ἄστεα καὶ νόον ἔγνω": "The cities of many men he saw, and their thoughts he knew" (editors' trans.).

18. Pierre Pascal, who is mentioned in letter 43.

19. **Brooks Adams.**

20. A ward in Paris.

21. _Hudson Review._

34. TLU-2   14 June 1951

ORA

Reflek/shines on "L'Agricultura Ital" evidently open to Papi & "Zeitschrift fur Europaesche DENKEN".[1] DNK me foot so long as they take seriously Ortaggi y Gasses[2] and other mutts who deal in general phrases without specific DATA. About fed up with wops/ and prob/ not my job to watch 'em/ sabotage of import of useful seed etc/ and worse/ artificial scarcities, and no attention to dissociations of econ/ terms. As yet NO proper sense of Gourmont's services in emphasizing "DISsociation d'idees" may not hav/ been gtst/ frog writer of his time but cert one of most intelligent. Whether Agric/ Ital/ can say simply that the present sub-fascismus plus slop WILL or shd/ import useful but non-habituated vegetation, I dunno. Wd/ like to git Papi to come clear on it. Remembering that the goddam Portagoose started digging up spice trees as soon as he got into Goa/[3] gornoze when but centuries ago.

If any DENKERS on the loose, why dont they start thinking what is law FOR? what the idea back of custom of jury trial? WHY no useful condensation of Blackstone[4] for general reader? i.e. parts that every freshman OUGHT to know? Is there ANYTHING in "Agric/ Ital" that is not due to fascist or prefasc/ initiatives? O.K.Torlonia started bonifica?[5] is anything made of THAT ~~bu~~ by the dummycrats? ANY local correlations with Abbot's data re/ fluorine and other mineral poisons?[6]

ANY consideration of the four point bill of rights printed in England,[7] OR of any ONE of the 4 points? ANY attempt to dissociate interest-bearing from non-interest-bearing debt?? OR to expose falsifications of PAST history, where the pore mutts dont dare mention current falsifications? ANYone who has heard of Tallyrand?[8] or the Leopoldine Reforms? or of economic thought printed in England BUT not in the large british press?

Gt/ mistake not to separate the CONSTRUCTIVE parts of heretical or innovative writers from their fantasies. thus with Frobenius (to keep on plugging) where BEFORE F/ does one find what he had to say/ mebbe it cd/ be got onto half a page, apart from necessary but specific data. Loss of Agassiz i.e. snowed under because of his sanity. Also dark ages very probably NOT before 1400 but between 1527 and von Humboldt.[9] Loss of catholic clarity, and not yet got to Aristotelian use of PARTICULARS before wallowing in generalities which latter habit ~~to~~ rots all the so called DENK (dank, stank etc.) of the lecturers boosted in the heavy reviews. First question re any of these palookas is: what are they writing it FOR?

OF course any man or femelle who wont face problems of monetary issue OR difference between share of what has been produced, and fixed charge or penalty levied on the producer, is not worth consideration outside a few perfumed idiot salons.

1. *Zeitschrift für Europäische Denken.*

2. José **Ortega y Gasset.**

3. Portuguese colony on west coast of India from 1510; mentioned in cantos 97 and 104; see letter 48.

4. EP planned to publish the essential sections of **Sir William Blackstone's** *Commentaries on the Laws of England* in a **Square $ Series** pamphlet, but never did so.

5. See letter 24.

6. In 1947 **Beatrice Abbott** had written to EP that "fluoride in the water supply was causing deformed Children, and that there was cobalt in milk and grains" (quoted in Tytell 299).

7. Not clear, although this may be the same point made in canto 85/547: "III.6.xi. Rights refers to the Bill of Rights."

8. Charles Maurice de Talleyrand-Périgord (1754–1838).

9. **Alexander von Humboldt.**

35. TLU-1   22 June 1951

ORA/

thank Helen for amusin note on Persia/ O.P.[1] has a scholarship for Teheran, starting Sept/ and of course watching anxiously to see whether it will work at that date. I have no address for Sapori/ interested to know whether Banc Naz ¼ly cd/ print him in Italian or if only safe in language of the conquering cads. How far can he go? is Maranini any use? WILL any of 'em review Del Mar? or consider Gesellite system AS TAX. Every kid of 15 ought to have difference between interest-bearing and NON-interest-bearing debt lammed into his head with a meat ax/ tho perhsaps the bright xtiani wd/ all be fer getting on the credit side of the usury swindle. {"}TWO pillars of Xtndom{"}/ thazza good one. I cdn't hv/ done better in satirizing the churrrrch. Hence the decline of italian literature after the death of Dante/ a few partial revivals/ down, down into baroc-co, roccoco, and I hear that in S.america they have even "plasteresco".

Walt/ Raleigh[2] v. diffuse, but occasional sentences/ mercantilist as vs/ usurers/ and lost his physical head. Anyhow, interesting when opposing import duties, and showing their ill effects. sez Genova wuz druv to money lending when she blocked trade. The SANE tax is on stagnant money. Perjurers in high places do their countries no lasting good. As to Karma, the U.S. pays in Korea for destruction of Europe/ how far this can be balanced by naive innocence of gt/ part of iggurent fluff-headed ma-jority of gentle denizens of this ¼sphere gornoze. BUT foreign press not v. helpful in destroying the "build-up" of the late infamy. tho they are abusing some minor vermin, [illegible deletion] lice, luces and roaches. Some furriner ought to note the SQUALID IGNORANCE of the altilo-

cati/[3] not matter of the character of the stinkers, alone, but of the UNI-
VERSAL ignorance of the snobs and mutts in high places/ damblastadors,
embassy staffs, etc/ loss of all sense of language/ not question of one or
two very LARG{E} swine, but of loss of sense of words. Perjury expect-
able from crooks, but should have been NOTICED by the allegedly literate, not taken as matter of course, of curse, of politics. as matter of fact
it was NOT noticed as part of CURSE, but taken as "of course", merely
politics, as if no mosquito ever carried malarial germs, and the germs
innocuous. AS sheer question of STYLE, of literature, or language/ the
literary cakeaters no use AS LITERATES, AND it is time one had a little
outside help in cursing the Universities, foundations, bribers, dazzlers.
SOME perspective as from outside looking in on the OOze, dispassion-
ate/ of course gt/ joke on grampaw that he shd/ hav/ {been} publicizing
constitution while the ooze was intent on destroying it. BUT one did live
to see Jeff/[4] quoted on fascist posters, mebbe not in the [illegible deletion]
south?? I forget the date? but was not alone in being able to attest that
he was quoted, in print ON [illegible deletion] posters. This was NEWS
tother day to [illegible deletion] Chilean wife of a Kansas purrfezzer.

Do yu see Sapori? what he got to say about SABOTAGE by present
rulers of yr/ disgraziata?[5] Yu dont answer my WHY is B.Naz Lav ¼ly[6]
printed in eng?

is there any LITERATE participation in MSI?[7] Any estimate of General Juin?[8] this an aside, very vague about him, and any frawg presumed a
swine till one has positive data.

Shdn't Sapori see Ecrits de Paris? cdn't be get some facts into them, re/
things that matter. What about periodical exchanges with B.Naz Lav/
¼ly? Have yu recd/ yr Del Mar? {"Barbara Villiers."}[9]

1. **Omar Pound.**

2. Sir Walter Raleigh (1552?–1618). EP is probably reading *The Works of Sir
Walter Raleigh.*

3. It.: "high places."

4. Thomas Jefferson.

5. It.: "the unfortunate, unlucky."

6. *National Bank of Lavoro Quarterly.* See letter 32. ORA does not seem to have
responded to this specific question.

7. **Movimento Sociale Italiano.**

8. **Alphonse Juin.**

9. Del Mar's *Barbara Villiers,* one of his shorter works, was originally published
under the pseudonym Barbara Villiers. Parts of it were later reprinted in the **Square
$ Series.**

36. TLU-1   [ans. 5 July 1951]

ORA

Sapori hopeful/ been kussing Cione[1] to Villari/ HOW long, oh KitKat-a-line//[2] the goddam bubblers printing tosh re/ economia, as if it cd/ be discussed in total iggurunce of monetary issue/ purchasing power/ circulation. And surely time name of Marx was marked OFF. stultifier of ten decades. Despite a few facts cribbed from brit/ factory inspectors. Do keep at some of 'em to get DelMar translated into wop/Brooks-Ad/ also still useful, and KULCHURD, mebbe they have to have a little refinement before they will learn the simple dissociations of ideas/ started [illegible deletion] on before Mencius and Ari/[3] took note of 'em.

Ratio of gold to silver in antiquity/ why do they still wobble with Mommsen and Rostovtzeff.[4]

Sap/ or some wop MIGHT be persuaded to read CHD[5] and/or G.Dobbs[6] (recent and ultimate brit/) wd also be useful IF someone ELSE wd/ try to see if Doug/ has opened his mind to ANY of the points I hv/ been hammering at him fer 30 years. HOW much he approaches "corporate" idea. And{,} as ideal{,} WHY liv/ on credit save in emergency. plenty of work has BEEN done by the dead; invention design etc/ Obviously not an immediate possibility, but if a man is making blueprint of ideal why not hope to get out of need of using credit at all. Save in sense that the state or organized producers shd/ let issue certificates of work done even before the product is deliverable. I wish SOMEONE wd/ think. this is probably an academic distinction, BUT econ/ist ought to be able to think it. Also some damWop OUGHT to be able to estimate my additions, however small, to Doug/ and Gesell, and my correlations c/ Wd/ Sap. read my Oro et Lav? hav yu any spare copies? or did yu evr receive the ital/ summary of Kitson? Uberti's trans/ of Overholser[7] has come to light, but Ovr/ not so thorough as Del M/

Has anyone considered that four point program/ re/ limit of taxation and LOCAL control of local purchasing power. (i.e. SOME control left to areas smaller than the nation) Wd/ Sap/ note Alex/ the Gt/ paying his sojers' debts/? think it is in Appian.[8] I mean IF he has to play round with something safely antique in order to git printed in that ¼ly. Do yr/ students appreciate Remy de Gourmont/ important for emphasis on DISsociation of ideas?

Wish yu cd/ meet Gabriela Mistral[9] if she stops off in Roma.

Del Mar no stylist (save at moments), no knowledg of medieval terminology. v. valuable in insisting on what amounts to saying: Money is an articulation. Prosody is an articulation of the sound of a poem. Money an artic/ of/ say NAtional money is articulation of total purchasing power of the nation. somebody ELSE ought to tell Doug/ that a tax of stagnant money is better than a tax on sales. the supreme foulness is to penalize a man for building a house OR for improving his property, or in fact for any kind of production.

[in Dorothy Pound's hand:] {I hope to send off another copy of "Barbara Villiers" to you tomorrow. for Sapori—or who ever—D.P. Have also ordered copies for you & Sap: of Planning the Earth.}[10]

1. EP is probably reading Cione's *Storia della republica sociale italiana*, in which he deals with the Fascist Saló Republic (1943–45) or *Tra croce e Mussolini*.

2. EP is combining the opening phrase of Cicero's *First Oration against Catiline* with his nickname for **Kitasono Katue.** See also letter 32.

3. Aristotle.

4. Probably Michael Ivanovitch Rostovzeff (1870–1952), author of *The Social and Economic History of the Roman Empire.*

5. **Major Clifford Hugh Douglas.**

6. Probably Geoffrey Dobbs's *Planning the Earth.*

7. **Willis A. Overholser.**

8. "Appian" is a mistake for "Arrian." See letter 25.

9. **Gabriela Mistral.**

10. In a letter dated 11 November 1951 ORA had mentioned this work by Geoffrey Dobbs.

37. TLU-3 21 July 1951

ORA

Re/ Alexis Cairel,[1] is he still alive? Very interesting quote, BUT all those foundations are dead set against any sensibility whatsoever. I.E. against the perceptive faculties. I dont know that current attack, finally 40 years late{,} running in that dumb cluck McCormick's[2] papers wd/ interest yu. The fact of my having put over some of the best writer{s} wd/ carry no weight with Cairel if he is still alive. despite his general statement I cannot conceive ANY of the committees of these gangs doing anything good. ~~save~~ they fight perceptive capacity. {Am} perfectly willing to be convinced that an honest man might etc....but know of no case where it happens. Burocracy and mental cowardice. Rhodes,[3] the ape, inf/ cx/[4] as not educated, admired Oxford kulchur?? or the cultured gent/ gents./ mostly killed off in first three months after Aug/ 1914/ which followed Federal Reserve act, signed by Woodie Wilson the damned, Dec 23, 1913,[5] so that the bankers wd/ lose nothing by THAT war, Stimson,[6] the stuffy (E.M.[7] just plowed thru his vol.) sez: must let business make money out of war or business wont WORK.{"} Anyhow {"}acceptances on N.Y." nicely [illegible deletion] fixed for internat/ gombeen[8] men. BEFORE Aug/ 1914. And all these "endowments" financed out of usury.

Gold, equiv/ to barter/ no need of "intrinsic" value of currency, where
yu hv/ LAW that works, hence all goldbugs are against ANY orderly govt/
and push for chaos and disorder, so that they can have their antient and
stinkingk monopoly. Intelligentizia in this country isolated itself into
impotence/ silly snobbism after the civil war/ place poisoned FOR my
generation. Lavender and kid gloves, too refeened fer politics. Dave's[9] ma
here two days ago murmuring equiv/ to parody/ "I didn't raise my boy
to go to congress" (quite naive, unthought, but symptomatic of degeneration and lack of civic sense. which had got to work. Quite a lot, or at
least some{,} decent education now on radio/ BUT (Orage{'s}[10] formula for
recession of power) a little clear opposition to bank-usury on the air, and
the swine put on television to hogswoggle and befuddle the mutts. I doubt
if one yank in a MILLION yet understands need of communication between the intelligent. Quite good young poet yesterday instinctively
moving to leave at sight of highly cultured couple of enthusiasts fer kulchur and greek drama. I mean he hadn't met 'em, and instinctively shrank
from doing so.

"Europa Nazione"??[11] at least a few adults/ would they print any REAL
history? I suppose Villari told 'em to send it. What about ethics? do they
think honesty has A̶Y̶ ANY historic role? Guicciardini did. BUT Di Marzio only man I ever knew who had noticed this kink of Guicciardini's.

that damn Thoreau...retire to wilderness Anschauung.[12] Yes, vurry
noble ONCE, but now a nuisance.

when are the SWINE going to admit that the destruction of Italy by the
cads, was a serious error?? geographic expression// upset of balance of
power, Vil's friend SAW that. ignorance/ OOzenstink IGGURUNT, apart
from being a skunk.

AND Cornelio[13] was bumped off, unless I hv/ been misinformed. I have
managed to get the quote printed here and in India/ but gt/ resistance even
to importing such doctrine into England. Whether Pete[14] HAS actually
got 25 copies into the degraded Isle, I kno not. "l'honore assai."[15] If there
is any truth in the rumour that the DUMBenicans[16] are taking up Marx,
it wd/ show original rot in Xtianity. Which religion has done some good
among barbarians t̶o̶ tho repellent to the civilized mind. The bits of it that
agree with Kung cd/ be salvaged and codified. How ANY literate man or
female can fall for the hoax of orig. sin, has me beat, OBvious con game
to get fines and profits fer priests and levites.

I wonder if Dinklespiel ever reached Europe. murkn humour of ½ century ago: It iss a goot thing that Eve wass in deh garten, unn̶derwise
Adtam wd/ haff blamed it on the kat, und dat wd/ be ridiKulus."

waal/ perfect accord: Kung, Dante, Agassiz. apart from a few gothic
trimmings.

A home washing machine (or a plow) NOT at work all the time. one
of worst idiocies of Perkins or the OOze or any of these swine is mania

for "full-employment" plant (9000 times one man potential) supposed NOT to lie idle. Rockdrills, dynamite/ now yu gettUM to think? ANd 'Del M/ emphasis: the so called monetary unit, really a FRACTION. Doug/{:} money an INStrument of policy rather than (an accurate) measure. AND so on. I spose railway fare v. high in Italy now.

1. **Alexis Carrel.** In a letter dated 15 July 1951, ORA had written about a long talk she had in New York years before with Carrel, then director of the Rockefeller Research Institute, who told her that "he was very anxious for America because this standardisation was leading to mental instability." ORA opined that "standardised mechanical work gradually dehumanises man, and he loses his balance, and Carrel was of the opinion that this made the U.S. particularly open to mass panic, mass hysteria."
2. **Robert Rutherford McCormick.**
3. **Cecil Rhodes.**
4. Inferiority complex.
5. The Owen-Glass Act of 23 December 1913, which created the U.S. Federal Reserve System.
6. Probably Henry L. Stimson (1867–1950), American politician appointed secretary of war in Roosevelt's government in 1940. He generally favored aggressive policies such as the repeal of the Neutrality Act and the deployment of the atom bomb.
7. **Eustace Mullins.**
8. Irish slang. Here it probably means "loan shark."
9. Probably **David M. Gordon** or perhaps **Thomas David Horton.**
10. **A. R. Orage.**
11. Presumably an Italian newspaper sent to EP.
12. Gm.: "Perception, view, outlook."
13. Probably **Cornelio di Marzio.**
14. **Peter Russell.**
15. It.: "enough honor."
16. The monastic order of the Dominicans.

38. TLU-3   13 August 1951

{Ag. 51}

O.R.A.

please pass on to Villari.

Leto's "OVRA"[1] seems most estimable vol/ {1st part} bit dull because taken from possibly least interesting pt/ of view free from pettegolezze[2] (as V/ offers in book by narsty little necktie.) but equanimo/[3] and in accord with what I saw from so different angle. Only variant so far is that (circa p. 150) he starts the rot. *after* African campaign. I am waker on dates than anything else, and had put it simply after the decennio celebration.[4] Of course L/ was in position to see many more details than isolated furriner in seaside watering place.[5] Cappelli[6] serious publisher. What else do yu or V/ recommend in that series? Am of course RABIDLY pro-autarchia/ but L/ seems to be most certainly right re/ perversion of it. The filth comes from socialism, Marx, Hen George/[7] etc/ all those lumps who avoid monetary problem or fail to START with sovereignty IN power of issue, and start blowing peoples' noses for 'em. Ten cents reward for notice of ANY marxist, or anyone who started in that morass and ever learned ANYthing. Imbecility of present tax system/ brute blindness re/ Gesell and the SANEST mode of keeping money in circulation and bringing it back into the fisc. Old Impero ruin'd by cheap grain from Egypt. Damn food poisoning, chemicals and the rest of the usurer's monekeyshines. Apart from honest retrospect such as Leto's/ Italy seems falling back into provincialism/ no sign of contemporary thought AFTER leading large part of it during the ventennio. BUT, no{,} can{'}t say that, Gesell had as much or rather a good deal MORE publicity than elsewhere, apart from Fack's[8] printing the books/. Recent from north of alps: "Nobody in Germany thinks Gesell was a crack-pot." Very lucid note by D.H.[9] re/ Coxey,[10] in local Ohio paper/ will try to get you spare copy, or at least mimeographed copy. Apart from Sapori's retrospect, safe because FAR enough back/ is there ANY serious discussion of monetary system in woptalia? As fer the pink tea and blue china trash. A subject which interested Locke, Hume, Berkeley[11] AND Cleaopatra is not below the notice of these punks who run licherary choinuls.

e.e.c[12] occasionally erupts re/ canaille litteraire.[13]

I wonder if Leto reads english? OR if Cappelli is in strong enough position to use my Jeff/Mus.[14] I suppose the translation V/ once had has been lost? but L/ if he knows eng/ might be interested in concordance of several views. If nubian attendant (10.30 p.m. ~~know~~ knocks at my dorr to approve of my more lyric utterance, and to say it "makes me feel good" {i.e.} made him the n.a.[15] feel good to bring me a quote in a low grade but costly Luce abberation. mebbe the cultured wop is ready for more specific text/ or perhaps NOT. considering who some of yr/ present hierarcha are and *have* been. I doubt if fake mentioned on Leto's p. 154 was a patch on american swindles/ wonder wd/ anyone pub/ trans of Dobbs? Certain filths are NOT confined by national frontiers/ and same symptoms appear in Russia, U.S. and {in} civilized nations. Wd/ be glad of loan of a copy of my translation of Por,[16] IF anyone can get hold of one. the infamy of roosevelts and Winstons owners stinks and will stink. Imperial Roosevelt dead and turned to s...[17]

The stink you stank, is stinking with us yet. Put that in arabic over the door of yr/ nearest mosque.

comment of remaining part of Leto, by next epizl. IF any.

1. In response to EP's queries about Guido Leto's *Ovra*, ORA wrote that Villari, who was away on holiday, had spoken to her of Leto's book but that she had not read it. She continued: "I think Leto right in ascribing the after African campaign [illegible deletion] as date [1935–36] when rot sets in; there had of course been many instances of toadyism and local tyranny before; but until then M. had kept a fairly level head. After that he lost touch with realities. [. . .] To suppress all open expression of opposition as was done by the Fascist régime is fatal to that regime itself. Personally I dislike very much a demagogic press but under present conditions see no alternative. The Fascist agricultural and to a large extent autarchic policy, and above all the syndical and guild system seem to me the only alternative to the 'servile State', the 'slave state' of the Marxians. But I think there again the system once started should be from the bottom up; not from the apex to the base as it worked out in the Fascist State" (16 Aug. 1951).

2. It.: "gossip, chatter."

3. It.: "impartial."

4. The celebration of the tenth anniversary of the Fascist era (1932).

5. Rapallo on the Riviera di Levante, where the Pounds maintained a residence from 1924 to 1945.

6. Italian publisher of Leto's book.

7. **Henry George.**

8. **Hugo R. Fack.**

9. **Thomas David Horton.**

10. Probably Jacob Sechler Coxey (1854–1951), an American reformer mentioned by EP in canto 84.

11. In addition to philosophy George Berkeley (1685–1753) wrote widely on economics, credit, and eighteenth-century banking and currency problems.

12. E. E. Cummings.

13. Fr.: "literary riff-raff."

14. EP's *Jefferson and/or Mussolini*.

15. The "nubian attendant" mentioned earlier in the paragraph.

16. Por's *Italy's Policy of Social Economics, 1930–40*.

17. Shit.

39. TLU-3   16 August 1951

{15 Ag}

O.R.A.

please pass to L.V.[1]

Leto's bk/[2] up to p/ 206. Apart from Roose being a swill-pail and Churchill a sow/ Leto certainly convalidates Ez opinion, and judgment of the facts IN Italy/ and shd/ ultimately emphasize Pellizzi's groan "IF he only WOULD see you, or someone like you. He sees all the wrong people."[3] Lack of ethical nose bitched the regime. Somewhere in the Four books[4] it is writ: only men of a certain degree of culture will stay honest

WITHOUT an assured income. Do yr/ wypers carry note that red china
has now banned Kung from private schools, already banned from public.
The people who objected to Muss' tolerance of moral skunks did NOT
do so from ethical but simply from snobistic reasons. Did NOT connect
rot of the state with tolerance of corruption. The groans, save for a few
people, did NOT see connection/ in fact had NOT the Studio Integrale[5]
till I gave it to them. Essentially all the needed distinctions are made in
the four books. And of course the fatt-y-can does preach or at any rate
does not instil honesty/ it wants mystic bugwash, and an obliteration of
dissociations. "always deal in things whose value is unknown" sd/ Frank
Harr[6] the observant rastaquouere.[7] Yes, the scholastic philosophy did
attempt definitions/ but all washed up in 1527. ~~Go~~ Green,[8] who starts
lying after 1694{,} observed "no longer gt/ political power, remained non-
dimeno[9] a gt/ financial power." Some damwop ought someday to give Ez
credit fer attempt to ~~tell the~~ tell 'em what they needed damwell to
KNOW. also of course the year long endeavour to get at least some of the
truth re/ italy (positive sides) into furrin countries, and bust the BBC
Oooze-Eden[10] misrepresentation.

Leto read as one of the most honest books I know. also instructions p.
188 circa/ much needed as ~~LITR~~ LITERARY instruction. fr/ Stendhal[11]
to Galdos,[12] that is how books are written. Mebbe if L/ ever had see{n}
the little skunk (C.)[13] he wd/ have avoided so mild a judgement as he may
hv/ had. A trivial balloon or inflated bladder. perhaps not so stinking mean
as Eden/ but neither of 'em with ANY of the instincts of the galantuo-
mo.[14] A sloppier mess, probably less eaten with personal rancour and with
a childish rather than senile (prematurely senile) vanity. Anyhow, if anyone know{s} L/ shd/ be glad to present my compliments and confirma-
tions (as from a so different post of observation.)

———

If wops were{n't} so nearly ALL dead from neck up, a few of them wd/
connect banning of Confucius in red chinese schools with what Ez/ told
the damwops years ago. Of course squirrilheaded idiocy here sees NO
significance in TIME. 2½ years delay in essential publications.

AND apart from ban/ an attempt to vulgarize contemporary chinese
verse/ drag it down to level of New Masses[15] (N.York trash of the 1920s.)

a "swift perception of relations" sd/ Aristotl/ these mutts aint GOT
ANY sense of relations.

Truman whining about smear campaigns. with NO reflection on lies
poured out by Ooozenstink{'}s gang for years zgainst Italy, against the
constitution and anyone who defended it. Sample: the commie swine
yapping about MY hate campaign vs/ the blacks. AND so on.

Mary expresses wish you cd/ get up to Meran, mebbe can discuss that
in next epizl.

1. **Luigi Villari.**
2. See letter 38.
3. Presumably Mussolini is seeing all the wrong people.
4. The four classics of Confucianism: Confucius's *Unwobbling Pivot, The Great Digest*, and *The Analects*, and Mencius's *On the Mind*. See Legge, *The Chinese Classics*.
5. EP's *Confucio Ta S'eu Dai Gaku Studio Integrale.*
6. **Frank Harris.**
7. Fr.: "someone who makes a great show but has no visible means of support."
8. **John Richard Green.**
9. It.: "however."
10. **Anthony Eden.**
11. Stendhal (Marie-Henri Beyle) (1783–1842).
12. **Benito Pérez Galdós.**
13. **Galeazzo Ciano.**
14. It.: "gentleman, man of integrity."
15. New York–based Communist journal.

40. TLU-2 [20 August 1951]

O.R.A.

Welcome reminiscence. Mind of a editer is a darker forest than of other men, dunno if sufficiently highbrow for Mgn/[1] but certainly printable, Mene[2] while assure v. high quality of readers from the typescript. Of course the least interesting part fer me, BUT the part that will get it past edt/ office and interest the purr/fazzers of licherchoor as mostly know it/ BUT glad to get a few SOLID data, to see whence the Mad Ox (known also as 40 Mad dogs Hueffer)[3] took off ffrom. As usual when he was most suspect of damnd lies etc/ there WAS a basis.[4]

The Lubin era yu hv/ done, and bk/ cd/ be referred to BUTT might I suggest yu put in more DEtail when yu get to the Dictat and the architects of infamy at Versailles.[5] How far yu knew or now know the setting? Tindarus/[6] acceptances on N.York signed by cod-face the damned on 23 Dec/ 1913/[7] or whether the story will be in print in time for you to correlate. I dunno. possibly mimeographed copies will exist.

Nice news story broke yester re/ the refeend nature of Frankie's assassins and Winstein's[8] partisan pals.

If Mgn don{'}t take the ms/ must see where it can fetch maximum $ exchange. and wait its hour/ also Mg/ may want to see the whole ms/ before committing himself. However HIGHEST grade perusers in limited number, assured.

I don{'}t mean yu need scamp the Lubin, merely that as yu hv/ writ what I take to be most of it, yu needn't force yrself to repeat. Definite impressions of the slobs 1919 wd/ be of interest, as very few witnesses are convincing. I for example cd/ merely boil with disgust at the lot of 'em. Tho

in cf/ with their still more foul successors, hv/ no doubt some were night-
ingales.

The INTelligent population appears to hv/ an increase of one/ i/e/
mary's brother "in-row" i.e. Boris' kid brother. suitable acquaintance for
you/ so am telling him to look in if he comes up from Ischia. Mary says
she wd/ like you to come back to Merano/ and as I can't offer hospitality
in normal modes, and as I want her to have more intelligent conversation than she gets from the Meranini,[9] or whatever yu call 'em. I shd/ be
delighted to "cover the transport" if you can be persuaded to take a week's
mountain air. The servant had so many emotions, etc/ that M/ is now
running the place senza,[10] so I cant suggest more than one guest at a time/
unless Rosamaria wants to turn in and WORRK while attending you.

If I were modern enough and......wd/ of course stop by in an Isotta (or
Baillila)[11] and transport yu/ no questions asked.

Wonder have we the germ of H.James' "Brooksmith"[12] in the female
retainer of FMBr/[13] who cdn't stand trashy pictures.

You wrote of that Whitman letter before/[14] for strictly practical pur-
poses/ subjugation of editors etc/ it wd/ be useful to have text of it as footnote (or insertion)

1. EP had received a section of ORA's memoir, provisionally entitled "The
Anecdotage of an Interpreter," written at his suggestion and with his encouragement and intended for magazine ("Mgn") publication. The complete memoir is
not extant; only a few chapters are available in the Ezra Pound Papers.

2. Meanwhile.

3. **Ford Madox Ford.**

4. In her memoir ORA discusses her years of growing up with her cousins; ORA
believed that Ford tended to lie about or "romanticize" the events of his life.

5. The period ORA spent at Versailles as **David Lubin's** translator.

6. EP probably has in mind Tyndareus, King of Sparta, husband of Leda, and
father of the Dioscuri, Clytemnestra, and Helen.

7. The Owen-Glass Act, which created the U.S. Federal Reserve System, signed
into law by Woodrow Wilson on this date. It is also mentioned in letter 37.

8. Another of EP's names for Churchill.

9. The citizens of Merano.

10. It.: "without."

11. A gallant advance on EP's part. He is imitating Italian automobile makers'
slogans and commercials.

12. In Henry James's "Brooksmith," an impeccable servant presiding over a
London salon disappears after his employer's death (*Complete Tales* 8:13–31).

13. **Ford Madox Brown.**

14. ORA had recently sold "the sheets of Whitman's Leaves of Grass and Two
Rivulets" to Scribner's of New York, for $300.00. They contained "a few scrib-
bled notes on the margin and the directions in his own handwriting to the Printer, the whole set [was given] to my Father when he was getting out an English
edition" (19 Nov. 1950).

41. TLS-2 29 September 1951

We include the following excerpt from ORA's letter for the light it sheds on her political posture. She thanks EP for his "interesting letter of 13th" of September, which is not extant.

[...] I heartily agree with what you say about amnesty. When one sees the hideous and now acknowledged mess that the "democracies" got the world into in 1939 one can but be amazed that the successors of these "Powers" have the cheek to hold up their heads and claim a right to condemn those who foresaw what it would all lead to. I am always astonished that people in high office could not see what was apparent to people of very ordinary intelligence, such as myself; i.e. that the destruction of Germany meant the destruction of the one barrier between the advance of Genghis Kahn and his hordes into the Western world. I have no *a priori* liking for the Germans (rather the contrary, anti-Teutonism was hereditary in my family and 1914–18 did not ~~work in~~ make me like them any better) I remember the "Maggio raioso" the last flare up of romanticism in Italy, and perhaps in Europe. I look upon Hitler as a raving homicidal lunatic and am simply filled with disgust at the wholesale massacres of Jews under the most horrible circumstances, though I am far from being inclined to believe in every tale of "atrocities" served up by propaganda. But it was criminal for the British Government to pledge Poland their word that she should be restored to her 1919 frontiers, and then leave her to be overrun by Russia, the Baltic Republic wiped out, and that at a time when energetic action {could have been taken, for} ~~when~~ they had ~~their~~ armies of the Allies in the field {and} could have compelled Stalin to retire into his own very ample frontiers. I suppose the fact is that one phase of universal history has worked itself out to the bitter end, and {a} new phase will arise, of which we can but dimly see a few of the coming outlines. You and your school, are I believe, on the right track on the currency question and on that of money as a whole. It is monstrous that production and distribution should be conditioned by money—mere tickets, as you rightly say—when it obviously ought to be the other way round. Another of the outlines is, I believe, a right organisation and working of the corporative system.[1] In that Mussolini was in line with the real needs, and I believe that his ideas on that matter offer the only solution to the relations between [illegible deletion] workers, managers, technicians, capital and consumers. I am much interested in noting that after the spate of cowardice and stupidity which marked the first realisation of utter defeat and impotency, the Italians{,} ~~are~~ or rather a small élite, are beginning to realise this. I am sending you a little review, Studi Gentiliani, of which the first two numbers have appeared. Most of the names of contributors are unknown

to me, but they seem to be on the right tack. Read "Mussolini a scritto
due volte la prefazione alla nuova poesia".[2] In philosophy, the Satanic
conceit of the XIXth and 1st half of the XXth centuries has received a blow
from which it will not recover, and we shall probably see (not you or me
but our grandchildren) a return to the theology of Dante in a world once
again decentralised, (this top-heavy centralised bureaucracy will collapse
under its own weight) religious and imaginative. The only alternative
seems to me "1984", the authe(n)tic reign of the Devil on earth. [. . .]

    1. Corporativism; see letters 54 and 55.
    2. It.: "Mussolini has doubly written the preface to the new poetry." This is the
title of a piece (unknown to us) in *Studi Gentiliani*.

42. TLU-3   [5 October 1951]

O.R.A.

substitute psychosis for character, and in 20 years you get Roosevelt,
which is to say FILTH enthroned. No I do not rise to {')Il Borghese{'}.[1] I
dont think any of that gang will ever make a 100% honest statement/
never sufficient exactitude to tell the reader anything of importance. I
think it was Pellizzi years ago point(ed) out that Corriere[2] NEVER wanted the exact statement. Frank Harris on yr/ BEloved kikes "they always
deal in things the value of which is unknown"//
    this with language/ the sewage of the press, simply the sewage of in-
exact language so that nothing ever really believed.
    By the way just learned that Tom Watson[3] (possibly the last literate
american senator) wrote a Story of France. which contains some good stuff
re taxes. "Taxation is, after all, confiscation." and more re/ sidetracking
of proposals in States Gen/ of 1484. [illegible deletion] pubd/ 1899.
    no not the last literate Senator/ there was Cutting[4] who listed eleven
of 'em in the 1930s/ Col/ Lhouse[5] and Wilstein[6] did NOT believe in either democracy or representative government/ they plugged for IRRE-
SPONSIBLE hidden oligarchy/ and their fruit was rotten. Must hv/ been
LHouse quoting Radek[7] or someone re/ NOT a democracy, it aint no
democ/ its plut/
    did yu see Muss' diary writ, during captivity before the huns got him
out? Europeo Feb 5 1950 and 2 following issues.[8]
    If Soskice[9] is out of job/ mebbe time to consider reprint of Blackstone
or some REAL reasons for law. Am not the least sure that old Jennie's
miscarriage will get back into Downy St/[10]
    The KEEN mind of yr/ admired etc/ was responsible for that gem: Ajh
all I'm interested in is BUNK, seein' what yu can putt over." that was
the third item or milestone or lever in my revolt against current amurikun
legal thought.

The morals of the canaille litteraire/ as in current art/1 by Tate.[11] "If yu see a child about to fall into an open well, do not make an unseemly noise to prevent it."

american aestheticism, as among the minor slitterati in woptalia before 1939/ A dark confrère writes me from American Academy {ROMA} having sized up the salon celebrities of present Caput or ex-caput mundi.[12]

The theology of Dante. all that matters was quite alive in Agassiz without needing archaic trimmings. Trust yu will notice blurb on back cover of Analects when yu get it.

await the Stud/ Gentil/[13] DID I alert yu to ANOTHER vol/ of Brooks Adams, pb/ 1913/ Theory of Social Revolutions?[14]

anonimussimo/ devmo[15]

might fergit J.Iscariot after this lapse of time/ but WHAT adequate reparations shd/ be asked for damage from this centuries wave of corrosive from Vienna/ S.Freud's backwash?

1. *Il Borghese*, a right-wing journal founded in 1950. In her letter of 29 September 1951, ORA had inquired about a "paper I sent some weeks ago: 'Il Borghese'? I think it is very clever, and does not seem afraid to speak freely."

2. *Corriere della Sera*, an Italian daily.

3. **Tom Watson.**

4. New Mexico Senator Bronson Cutting (1888–1935). When EP asked Cutting how many literate senators there were, Cutting supplied nine names, adding, "and I suppose Dwight L. Morrow" (*Guide to Kulchur* 260). By adding Morrow's and Cutting's names to the nine Cutting sent, EP gets eleven. Cutting is mentioned in canto 98. For EP and Cutting see also *EP and Senator Bronson Cutting*.

5. **Colonel Edward Mandell House.**

6. Probably Woodrow Wilson.

7. Probably **Karl Radek.**

8. The journal is probably *Europa Fascista*. EP is discussing the publication of Mussolini's diary supposedly kept during his captivity in August 1943, but there is some doubt about its authenticity. Although EP probably translated the diary into English, he presumably did not wish to be seen as advancing the Fascist cause while incarcerated since the piece was published anonymously in *Edge* as "In Captivity: Notebook of Thoughts in Ponza and La Maddalena." See letter 119.

9. In a letter dated 5 September 1951, ORA had written: "By the way, I suppose you know that Ford's nephew, Sir Frank Soskice, the son of his sister Juliet who married a penniless and very nice Russian Jew, David Soskice, is now Attorney General under the Labour Government and considered the most brilliant legal mind of the day? So does the wheel of Fortune go round."

10. EP means Churchill, whose mother's name was Jennie and who would become prime minister again following an election later in the month.

11. **Allen Tate.**

12. Lt.: "capital or ex-capital of the world," that is, Rome.

13. *Studi Gentiliani*, mentioned by ORA in letter 41.

14. Adams's *The Theory of Social Revolutions*.

15. It.: "most devotedly."

43. TLU-2   14, 23 October [1951]
14 Oct

O.R.A.

a number of resignations, indictments etc/ for minor muck/ petty lar-
ceny in high places etc/ This merely to say hv/ read Col/ House's[1] "Intimate Papers" dont know what weight he still carries/ time-lag etc. BUT
vol. [illegible deletion] II, p/ 291 he does say Trieste 2/3 italian, inhabitants. and uses phrase re/ what Italy "is entitled to". Apart from his participation in the great betrayal,[2] he [illegible deletion] seems to hv/ been more
intelligent than most of his contemporary MUTTS. Whether ANY ethos
has lasted thru Ooozefelt reign difficult to say/ but politics stirring the mud.
AND if any lesson re/ Lhouse and other memoirs it is that a VERY little
truth takes a lot of beating. Radek re/ the U.S. being a plutocracy, has out-
lasted billions of pages of news tosh. etc. and Woodrow Codfyce's honesty
re/ Panama[3] tolls made him into a little Jesu. "Il più scaltro non esiste"[4]
    Yr. little sardine tin REX, said at least that.

NEWS/ an econ/ prof/ not an absoloot ass. In fact Edward S.Shaw econ.
Prof. Leland Stanford Univ. California "Money, Income and Monetary
Policy"/[5] considerable advance on text permitted in univ/ courses. HE
thinks, BUT alas stops thinking when he gets to "full employment"
wangle/ which needs constant war/[6] BUT the bk/ shd/ be reviewed in
Italy. pub/ 1950 Richard Irving IRVING Inc. Chicago/ can't someone write
to Shaw for a review copy/ Leland Stanford shd/ be sufficient address.
Families with washing machines do NOT keep 'em working 8 hours a
day 6 days per week. And Anatole France wrote *L'Isle des Pinguins*[7] nigh
½ century ago. Idiocy of keeping "plant" at work TOO much/ and needing sales for profit/ only war bottomless pit for sales. And gold swine will
always want disorder/ cause with ORDER no need of metalic barter,

    23 Oct/ at last seen page-proofs of Stone Classics/[8] but point of this p.s.
is that Pierre Pascal has writ/ very nice letter/ wanting collaborazione
illimitata/[9] for Euridice, via Gius. Sacconi[10] 19/b can you advise me/? or
can any of yr/ frequenters? wd/ it be useful to print some of the econ/ etc./
I shd/ think the Ital/ version of Confucius[11] the best they cd/ do, for me
and for them. I dont want to send anonymous communiques to indiscreti
at that particular time.

    After all there is a political etc/etc/ Mr Jones (Jesse)[12] spilling a good
deal. etc. I believe Pascal is O.K. as to heart/ but want some indications
of ambience etc/

1. See letter 42.
2. The overthrow of Mussolini by **Marshall Pietro Badoglio** on 25 July 1943.
3. Following the 1912 exemption of American ships from Panama Canal tolls,
Wilson refused to change his mind about what he regarded as a violation of the

terms of the 1901 Hay-Pauneforte Treaty according to which the United States had promised that the canal would be open on "terms of entire equality" to "vessels of all nations."

4. It.: "Nothing worse exists."

5. EP is referring to Edward Stone Shaw's *Money, Income, and Monetary Policy.*

6. The notion that only warfare could gurantee full employment is one the Fascists adopted from Syndicalism.

7. France published *L'Île des pingouins* in 1908. See also letter 22.

8. EP's *Confucian Analects*, which was published later that autumn.

9. It.: "general contributions," that is, journal contributions on any topic.

10. On page two of EP's letter ORA wrote: "Dear Villari, perhaps you know something about that Pierre Pascal and Euridice to whom E.P. refers. I have never heard of them. [. . .] Please let me have the letter back as I will see if the Banca Naz. Luvoro will write you for the book that E.P. says shld be reviewed." In a letter of 11 November 1951, ORA added that "Villari tells me that Pascal is living at Via Francesco crispi, No. 23, and is a very intelligent political refugee from the post-war persecutions in France." The Pierre Pascal in question is probably the French author (b. 1908) whose books deal with the Russian Revolution (1917–21). Nothing else about him is mentioned in the correspondence.

11. EP's *Confucio Ta S'eu Dai Gaku Studio Integrale.*

12. EP is referring to Jesse Holman Jones's *Fifty Billion Dollars.*

44. TLU-2   [1951][1]

ORA/

Gawd bless my soUL; does Helen know that "deah VIolet"[2] was for the last ten years, at least, of her life, rumbling round about doing a book on HOWell??[3] must be masses of material somewhere. Write to Douglas Goldring,[4] Stone House{,} Middle St. Deal, Kent. in my name asking what has become of the material. V/ named three lit/ exectrs/,[5] other two died I believe, at any rate Ethel Mayne did.// Very little doubt Howell was a scamp/ but amused Whistler.[6] Only item I recall was old Luke Ionides[7] re/ Howell (pirate) lamenting that there wasn't a port left in Europe where a man cd/ take a prize.[8]

Lukie once sacked a turkish pasha/[9] when as a young man his pa had [illegible deletion] great prestige, due to richness as merchant.

The mud always does take the shape marked for it. And the mud, like Winston, always damn{s} the men who make the necessary ideas. All the grimy little bugwashee in the U.S. now benefit by Lenin's decree on banks guaranteed accounts up to given "small" figure. When last I heard it was $10,000. "rights of the small depositors" and all that is true in Sowbelly's Stewd deal,[10] is taken from CH Douglas. consumer credit. Naturally perverted to the level of.... Enc/ a clip re/ DGR[11] that has been on ice since whenevr.

Ronnie[12] quoted Beaverbrook[13] re/ Smirchill or Atlee[14] program "No cow without its own typist."[15]

Greasy hypocrisy today re/ atrocities in Korea, "surprise" AFTER
Katyn.[16] And no wops/ making esprit re/ Churchill///
Note evidently started last August/ lost in turmoil.

Buon anno[17]

1. In a letter dated 23 June 1951, Louis Dudek reports that around this time EP
sent a 26 June 1951 clipping from the *Washington Times-Herald* about the Katyn
massacre (*DK* 70). This would suggest that the letter was written in late summer
or early fall 1951.

2. **Isabel Violet Hunt.**

3. **Helen Rossetti Angeli** had been working on a book on Charles Augustus
Howell but **Isabel Violet Hunt** had begun a biography of William Dean Howell
that remained unfinished at her death. EP is confusing the two Howells.

4. **Douglas Goldring.**

5. The "three literary executors" were Ethel Colburn Mayne, Gerald Henderson, and **Douglas Goldring.**

6. James McNeil Whistler (1834–1903).

7. **Luke Ionides.**

8. This is William Dean Howell, not Charles Augustus. EP is recalling Ionides'
memoir: "In those days there was a man of the name of Howell, who used to help
Whistler in printing his etchings, and Howell was suspected of keeping for himself a large number of the proofs which were taken" ("Memories I" 45). Later Ionides relates a scam Howell perpetrated in which he took money for drawings that
Burne-Jones had asked him to present to the Ionides clan as gifts ("Memories VIII"
409–10). The remark about ports attributed to Howell is not found in "Memories."

9. This is from Ionides' "Memories." Working as an agent for his father's firm,
Ionides was refused a permit for the departure of his ships (loaded with grain) from
the port of Kustendji (in present day Rumania). He wrote to George Zrifi, a banker at Constantinople, and he got this reply: "The dismissal of the Pasha and the
custom-house officers is placed in your hands." Luke dismissed the Pasha but
retained the custom officer at Kustendji ("Memories VI" 150–51).

10. Roosevelt's New Deal.

11. **Dante Gabriel Rossetti.** The clipping has not survived.

12. **Ronald Duncan.**

13. **First Baron William Maxwell Aitken Beaverbrook.**

14. **Clement Richard Attlee.**

15. Parody of interwar British electioneering slogan: "No pot without a chick-
en."

16. Katyn is a forest near Smolensk, Russia, where the Russians massacred
thousands of Polish officers and soldiers in 1940. The mass grave was discovered
by the Germans in 1943 and the atrocity was reported over Berlin radio. The
Russians countercharged that the massacre had been committed by the Germans.
The allies failed to pursue an investigation after the war because of Russian opposition, causing much bitterness. EP seems to regard it as a *cause célèbre* for Axis
sympathizers like himself.

17. It.: "Happy New Year."

1952

45. TLU-3 7 January 1952

{7 Jn 52}

ORA

NO, the fault is not with the advertisers and go-getters, it is with the silly little snobs who wont use the means at their disposal. [illegible deletion] microfilm saved a lot of Vivaldi.[1] Fault at the "top" alleged top. Voice vs/ print. Present politics COULD get back to Athens/ range of voice then the market place.

Now larger/ and telvis[2] cuts yet another chance of fake. BUT the dirty snobs/ dont USE means/ word in Roma that radio wasn't refined. etc/ alibi of the yellow who were afraid. Eden's snobbism vs/ son of blacksmith.[3] Maria Theresa[4] LOST in historic shuffle/ aristos[5] stink with Gentz and Metternich (Rothschild{'}s INFERIORS by a vast gulf.) Failure of correlation/ Universities lost by default. Idiocy of tax system, Aug. Boeckh[6] not used in classics/ greek-lat. Silliness of univ/ courses in "philosophy" omitting Kung fu tseu.

same old gramophone Ari-vs/ Plato etc. And what my old friend Vy-Oler[7] just wrote of as "that nit-wit in the vatican."

Yr/ beloved paper "Borghese" very rancid. amusing enfantillages[8] re/ Hemingway (hv/ lost date, but must by now be couple of months back.)

Not to minimize the danger of cocacola'd minds, BUT to kick the pussilanimous who do NOT observe the symptoms (ideogram often translated "omens.")[9]

A little professional honour wd/ force correction of lies, esp/ the kind that contain enough truth to fool the iggurunt.

ONE review that wd/ really print corrections cd/ serve as focal point/ but it don{'}t exist. That is the fault of 300 people who do NOT communicate with each other.

Obviously the filth of the age is out to destroy the vita contemplativa[10] altogether/ but there is no reason to surrender to filth. OU TAUTA PROS KAKOISI DEILIAN EXEI.[11] Kindly kick Monotti in the jaw as a new year's greeting. the world{'}s worst correspondent. phone him I said so.

Now in this defiled country not ALL the radio commentators are swine/ BUT the ones with decent impulses are IGNORANT. as was the chief foulness Oozesmelt. BUT people on college faculties, and even those who cd/ swing a tea-urn DO NOT associate with or get near enough to the commentators to TELL them the few necessary facts. AND that silliness came in after the Civil War, Hen James lavender gloves etc. Friend yester quoted some kid re/ Hemingway: always has a ~~violent~~ violet on his boxing glove.

cummings retreats into Thoreauvian wilderness. AND the ~~balme~~ blame rests on the beau-monde az wuz.[12]

Count the people in the "literary" (gawd save the world) news/ who will NOT think of particular problems.

over 50 years/ european youtng fed on dog-biscuit (politics without knowledge of probleme monnetaire)[13] Eng/ and American young fed on cream-puffs, post-Paterine aesthetic approach with no ballast.

Get Aug. Boeckh/ Public Economy of Athens,[14] into Sapori esp/ two chapters near end. German 1817/ 2nd. eng. trans 1842. Aug/ prejudiced, BUT gives facts/ a lot of Douglas went into making Periclean civilization. etc.

appy new year. delayed note for Helen finally posted yester.

1. Microfilm of Antonio Vivaldi's manuscripts at the Sächsische Landesbibliothek in Dresden, Germany, that EP had had made in the 1930s. The claim that EP and **Olga Rudge** were responsible for saving these manuscripts from destruction resulting from the bombing of Dresden in World War II is not entirely true, since only one of these manuscripts was damaged and none of them destroyed. For details see Schafer 329.

2. It.: "television."

3. Mussolini.

4. Maria Theresa, empress of Austria (1717–80); she is mentioned in canto 103/ 733.

5. Aristocrats.

6. August Böckh, who is mentioned later in the letter.

7. **Viola Baxter.**

8. From *enfant*, Fr.: "child," hence "childishness."

9. This is the ideogram used in canto 99/709.

10. Lt.: "contemplative way."

11. EP's translation ("but there is no reason to surrender to filth") comes close to the spirit of Sophocles' Greek in *Electra*: οὐ ταῦτα πρὸς κακοῖσι δειλίαν ἔχειν: "Shall we to all our ills add cowardice?" (l. 351; Loeb edition, 151). This tag is used in cantos 85, 86, 109, 116, and at the end of EP's translation of Sophocles' *Women of Trachis* (50).

12. Fr. + En.: "high society of the past."

13. Fr.: "the problem of money."

14. EP is referring to Böckh's *Public Economy of Athens*, in which he deals with money and coinage in classical times.

46. TLU-3   [19 February 1952]

O.R.A.

NO, maa'aaam/ YU europewns will NEBBER unnerstan' deh KullUD race/ marse blackman will most ᵥ certainly NOT return to africa to infect what the dirty brits have left there/ with any more occidental hogwash/ He will stay here (incidentally D's[1] one comfort) being human and refusing to be poured into a mould and cut to the stinckging patter{n} on the slicks and the weakly papers. An occasional upsurge of African agricultural heritage as in G.W.Carver,[2] O.KAY but also marse Blakman him LAZY/ lazy as Lin Yu Tang.[3] thank god for it/ AS a humanizing element most needed here/ tho yr/ beloved kikes try to utilize him for purposes of demoralization/ hell/ he ain' nebber been moralized/ thank God. The pleasantness of the animal kingdom unbitched by Calvin, and the ruck end of that unfortunate drift "qui a beaucoup plus corrumpu les esprits que les moeurs."[4]

Possibly some bleat about Eng/ hist/ on radio/ Westminster Hall etc/ as contrast to the defilement of Italy by the muck that collaborated with Ooozenstink/ and the pig Wwinstein Kirchberg//[5] Glorious Italian history for for a century/ and then diliquescence/ what I am mumbling toward is/ that the Fascist error may have been (feel it was) the denial of the Risorgimento/[6] instead of hammering on the M/M the first M/ being Mazzini. They shd/ have hammered the continuity///// too late by time the Verona manifest.[7] AND that omitted TWO points/ grampaw ha sempre ragione[8] (?). At any rate Kung had.

I can sympathize with hating (I mean the italian hating political opponents// CONsidering that the "opposition{"} has cert/ enlisted some of the lousiest crablice gawd ever let crawl/ I dunno about their being internationals. CAN _NOT_ recall a single instance to back up yr/ theory.[9] they hate the frogs/ they failed to collaborate with the teutons/ the{y} loathe the aussstrians/ and they paid NO attention to anything that went on OUTside of Italy. they fawn traditionally on the Milorrd/ and condone the perfidy of Albion, synonym for La Perfide/ They have a loathsome carbuncle on the back of the peninsular neck/ which helped Ooozenstink and the snooty ploots[10] help rhoosia/ as against the more organized parts of europe// and of course a provincial canaille litteraire is the same any where/ dross/ and the smaller the rincon,[11] the drossier.

Let us ask whether sanity did not desert the rump of the Church in 1870/ and Pacelli's last fantastic imbecilities[12] make it impossible for any to do more than evade intellectual responsibility when discussing the mass of hoakum offered in place of the better canon of the tradition. for 80 years a drive precisely to ELIMinate anything universal universally

acceptable (from Mencius thru Dante to Agassiz.) lot of gimcrack orna-
mentation/ plus celibates (or pseudocellibates) telling us all about how
to be married. NUTS. and 19 centuries time lag on the Maories ANYhow.

IF ora cd/ hv/ heard pseudo-Cambridge voice of ambass/ fr Isssrael on
radio a few moments ago/ even she wd/ hv/ howled for a pogrom.

A policy of degradation common to Roosevelt and the Fattycan/ always
going LOWER for his support/ the Fatcan driving out the intelligent/ and
trying to enforce mind conditioning BEFORE Luce and Co/ that slug
Spellman,[13] going to Mohamed for cannon fodder rather that to the higher
~~Bhug~~ Bhud or Confucio. French put logic in place of organic mind/ also
verkik'd,[14] steady jewish penetration since??? 1200 or whenever. wops
only people who will face a distinction in ideas. taken six years and still
impossible to get anyone in U.S. or Britain to NOTICE a definition of any
idea not ballyhoo{'}d in the press. (these are exaggerated statements but
no room left on this air letter to work out percentages. take it that you
COULD in Italy before the dirtyXtns{)} time to get a few people to think.

4 P.S.of course exceptions to ALL these yawps, Agassiz was a swiss
presumably violating ANY possible genera{liz}tion one cd/ make on tab-
ulated statistics, re/ nature of Svizzeri.

5 large blackman won't organize on scale/ hasn't like damfrog, the genie
de la mauvais organization.[15]

6/ won't go to large scale africa to be damn burocrat bossing aborigi-
nes the dirty fabian idea: to every cow a typist, is NOT colourd man's
idea.

1. **Dorothy Pound.**

2. George Washington Carver (?1860–1943).

3. Chinese emperor of the Tang dynasty proverbial for his indolence.

4. See letter 18.

5. Winston Churchill.

6. It.: "Revival," the name given to Mazzini's nineteenth-century revolutionary and nationalist movement.

7. A reference to Mussolini's Program of Verona for the Salò Republic, around
23 September 1943. Mentioned in cantos 86 and 108.

8. It.: "is always right."

9. ORA had claimed that Italians were not nationalists ("they are as factious
today as in the days of Dante") but internationalists. She had also opined that the
Asians would be followed by the Africans in ridding themselves of their European masters (10 Feb. 1952). EP disagreed on both counts.

10. Plutocrats.

11. *Rincón,* Sp: "corner, nook."

12. Presumably this is a reference to Pope Pius XII's proclamation on All Saints'
Day 1950 of the dogma of the bodily Assumption of the Blessed Virgin into heav-
en. See also letter 24.

13. Probably Cardinal Francis Joseph Spellman (1889–1967), the influential Roman Catholic American (New York) prelate; in 1953 he defended Senator Joseph McCarthy's House Un-American Activities Committee.

14. Semitized.

15. Fr.: "genius for malevolent organization."

47. TLU-3 [13 June 1952]

ORA

No idea WHAT the AGIP[1] is, but the argot "gip" pronounced as with a J, signifies cheat the eyeteeth out of, and is prob/ proper semantic source of most govt/ organisms. The s.o.b. who block import of agricultural advantages/ seed or sapling/[2] seem pretty well representative of the post Piazza Loreto/ etc. hell rot the lot of 'em.

Caraffa[3] is historic name/ but thought it was associated with project of digging up Dant's bones// Do you know the present C. d. A. well enough to introduce Omar to him? said O.P. still is, or was at last bulletin, still in Teheran, on persian govt/ scholarship/ ergo untainted by U.S. or Brit/ connection/ and amused by persians/ contemplating coming round via Singapore etc. to the Rocky Mts/ He spik french, not woptalian. and I suppose some persian, as he was working on project of dictionary of "az she iz spoke". Anyhow, some means of communication with C.d A/ might exist.

Drew Pearson[4] on radio sez Gaspers[5] on way out and Graziani[6] the next. Beaverbrook headlining revival of decency at Predappio[7].....both sources suspect and evidently whooping for wrong reasons, and hoping that only the worst will revive.

Have had no news from Italy since the municipal elections/ and no idea which municips/ were in question.

London Slimes in tears for expulsion of Bunting/[8] as if ANY foreign nation still naive enough to consider a Slimes correspondent other than instrument of as much infamy as his employers cd/ induce him to commit. Not of course that Basil is the type the Slimes wd naturally WANT to represent 'em, or as if he warn't likely to send as much of the truth as they wd/ stand for.

Above suggestion dependent on how well you know C/d/A. O.P.'s address will be added, if you think it any use to write to him.

Police continue to be had up for burglary in the Holy City of Wash/ D.C. and general effect of Sow-Belly's long reign, plus epigons continues to bear similar fruit in all frutiness. at various levels.

[address in Dorothy Pound's hand:]

(Omar S. Pound)

{c/o American Embassy}
{Teheran. Iran.}

let us not be narrow/ some dirty siriote[9] greek?? or natural byzantine, nacherly plugged for a monopoly of transit facilities to the next world. As Ari's sez, a common business practice by the time of Demosthenes.[10]

Of course I don't know C d/A's background/ shd/ think if yu know him well enough to send O.P. introd/ letter/ better simply say "son of a friend"/ let him speculate re/ nomenclature if so disposed.

P.S. to return to discussion of infant piety and idees recues/[11] it was the damKike who divorced the idea of divinity from agriculture/ got it into manger after the grain had been cut/ Hou Chi[12] had to be content (or discontent) with alley outside.

And the agriculturalist Cain, the villain in mystery Ersat'z by the butchers of lesser cattle.[13]

OR may be we shd/ blame this on the christers/ the yidd having ignored the divinity of grain altogether ~~unti~~ until some exotic cult mentioned the presepio.[14]

1. Azienda Generale Italiana Petroli, a public corporation established in 1926 to regulate the exploration and production of domestic and foreign oil.

2. A reference to EP's efforts to have maple trees planted in Brunnenburg.

3. Carrafa d'Andria, otherwise unidentified.

4. **Drew Pearson.**

5. **Alcide De Gasperi.**

6. **Rodolfo Graziani.**

7. Mussolini's birthplace.

8. **Basil Bunting.**

9. EP probably means "Syrian."

10. **Demosthenes** lived during the third century B.C.

11. *Idees reçuès*, Fr.: "received opinion."

12. Mentioned in canto 85/747, Hou Chi was "the minister of agriculture under Shun [Chinese emperor 2255–2205 B.C.] later worshipped as the god of agriculture" (Terrell 2:684).

13. This is a tag that occurs several times in the correspondence and twice in *The Cantos* (87/573 and 93/623). Terrell explains that "Pound divided primitive men into four categories: (1) hunters, (2) killers of bulls, (3) killers of lesser cattle, and (4) articulturists" and thought that "ethics begins with agriculture" (2:496). See also letters 67, 71, and 103.

14. It.: "crib."

48. TLU-3

30 June [1952]

30 Giugn

I dont kno that ORA ever saw "Benedetta's" GARRARÀ/[1] in which it is finally discovered that what was queer about the protagonists was that they didn't hv/ any HEADS. Whether wops/ too myopic to TELL the outer world anything during their brief glory, have learned ANYthing yet, I dunno. it OUGHT to be up to them to resent confusion of the terms re/ italy/ fascism{,} nazism{,} communism CONTinually linked to slopaganda by the rump of the rooseve{l}tees.

Even without programs and recorded acts/ swine like OOze and Winston wd/ ALWAYS hold human rights, justice, honesty in a contempt that fascist italy wd/ not have tolerated/ BUT somebody in the ingenius peninsula ought NOW to object to muddling of these terms/

an intelligentzia or professoriate COULD without sticking out its neck or getting itself suppressed on party lines (real or alledged) COULD object to continual falsification of terminology/ naturally the christians/ mistranslating the pentatuch/ falsifying the meaning of genesis and in general betraying the greek sources of all their clean ideas have given a background for this sort of muddle/

"ont beaucoup plus corrumpu les esprits que les moeurs".[2]

BUT note/ that the swine say {"}fascism{"}/ and NEVER mention the corporate state OR vocational representation/ i.e. all the constructive elements of the ventennio tra are trascurati/[3] with the yell from that pipsqueak D.Pearson "to make DUMMMocracy liVVV"/

a cry for honest news and unfalsified history COULD start in Italy/ then after 30 years the damFROGS wd/ hear about it. and it might even reach Sodom on Thames[4] and thence the incult amurikun hinterland.

Still impos/ apparently get permission to grow food or import necessary seed etc/ dam Danes uprooting apple trees. {Trees} as Portagoose in Goa {pepper trees} 300 years ago/ Naturally no one know mentions Portugal, blessed by a hrooshun veto/ and NOT internally interfered with by UN. Saviotti[5] reported prof/ of aesthetics in the{ir} muzik school.

Any of yr/ circle read Dutch/ thing called Critisch Bulletin seems to be open to horse sense/ nice cover wood block/ Chronos looking Pegassus in the teeth. If ORA looking fer text book/ might try the english translations of my late italian efforts/ Carta da Visita and Oro e Lavoro have got past the barrage/ two fires etc/ I think I askeDum to send yu copies {fer class use, or not}

I did ask about Sturzo[6] and Spampanato[7] of course the vital issue{s} NOW are not partisan/ but seems impos/ get 3 literates to to recognize that fact/ and focus controversy onto questions that are THERE{,} and will be{,} under whatever lables the controllers use for the moment.

terminology/ news/ history/ when the swine swallow their own lies
they muddle.

Pinay[8] froggering re/ european assembly/ it wd/ stink like any other
UNLESS provision made for representation BY TRADES. and I did note
in Carta d/v/that Mazzini[9] had already provided (in idea) for local control of local purchasing power/ though I might have hammered it in more
emphaticly.

yez, ma'am, than Q/ fer lending me that cawpy of I Doveri.[10]

Dave[11] dug up copy of McNair Wilson's "Monarchy or Money Power"/
quite good for [illegible deletion] 1932/ lot of interesting hist/ items/ as
to why they shd/ have wanted to crwuth Napoleon/ bit of trimmings re/
gawd an the crown tend to confuse his argymints/ but useful author/
   and so on

saluti {Helen} a Rosamaria e
tutti

1. EP is referring to Benedetta's *Viaggio di Gararà*.
2. See letter 18.
3. It.: "neglected."
4. London.
5. **Gino Saviotti.** An exchange of letters between EP and Saviotti was published
as "Appunti. XV. Nunc dimittis" in *L'Indice*.
6. **Father Luigi Sturzo.**
7. **Bruno Spampanato.**
8. Probably **Jose V. de Piña Martins.**
9. EP is thinking of his comments in *Carta da visita* about Mazzini's economic thought. EP includes the following quotation from Mazzini's *Duties of Man:*
"'The distribution of this *credit,*' Mazzini continues, 'should not be undertaken
by the Government, nor by a National Central Bank; but, with a vigilant eye on
the National Power, *by local Banks administered by elective Local Councils*" ("A
Visiting Card," *Selected Prose* 312).
10. An Italian journal.
11. Probably **Thomas David Horton.**

49. TLU-3   15 August 1952

ORA/

Thebiade/ farraGosto[1]/ 15 Ag/ '52. TheBlade, with concrete mixer or
whatnot adding to noise of goDDam jet planes HELL-yKopters etc/ Glad
to cheer Pelo Pardi[2] at 3rd/ remove/ wonder what ever became of Ruspoli (who first surprisingly lectured me on the Pelo/ think it was Pr/
Francesco R/[3] who also dragged out Mons/ Pisani's[4] to his ma's drawing
room, to get me straight re/ canonist cleanliness/ as of WHEN the church
had some decency/

can HE be mobilized/ he once had some land//

"Kulch"[5] is out again at last/ also contains a few words re/ taxes and Rossoni's[6] sanity/ Einaudi probably bitched by britisch bloomsbury/ Cambridge yitticulture etc/

brits/ cant even BLEAT/ and no controversial writers capable of slamming the Slimes for confusing interest with usury/

tell Labino to be damned re/Views/ there are historic FACTS/ it is IGNORANCE that blocks the decent/ and the UNignorant can always scare the hypocrites out of immediate drawing rooms/ and add a note of gloom to the lies they print in the hired pressMess.

No/ I approve the order in Contini's vol/[7] is the preface pseudonymous? and stile trentennio/[8] sprouting unobserved/ ORA prob/ not ready to believe the degadation of cimici lett/i letto/ letterato etc/[9]

Very useful to have the Barker art/l[10] translated/ AND it gets past the sabotage of the larger pubrs/ Mondadori and co/ people who try to get RIGHTS in order to NOT print.

One practical friend tho't it wd/ help industria turistica to have literate resident in Rapallo as of pre-war but found Am/ Exp/ Crook (Thos/ and Son)[11] uncomprehending and unearthed INTERESTING item/ that yr/ dear Gasperi's BRUVVER in Lawx is head of Italian Tourism/ so I dare say Coca shall COLE where the bum/ dont keeps his wopscalions on the hum. Incidentally I find in KULCH a few curses vs/ deturpage del paisaggio/[12] meaning the orangeade 20 ft/ bottles on the Genova Rd/

Did I also qt/ yu Santayana/ that "Muss had done more for Rome than three Napoleons."

As for the remains of ang/sax or ang/frog culture/ I dont suppose Aldington[13] will budge out of France/ but if he ever does come to Romaaaa, you and Helen might gather a l few echos de Londres d' Antan.[14]

A Polish view of same as of now/ prob/ not fill yu with optimism.

Two points in Spamp/ one his perception of money as sign of sovereignty/ 2/ that M/ mentioned the U.S. Constitution

sorry not to hv/ met him/ 20 years ago. AND of course plenty for him to DO/ IF he can focus on real issues as of anno XXX/ Alberi e Cisterni/[15] Mazzini's NEGLECTED page/(yes 'm that yu lent me.) imbecility of tax SYSTEM.

Have yu a spare Del Mar for him/ if not give him yr/ copy and I will have another sent yu. ALSO/ IF any wop sufficiently LARGE to see that rise in cultural level ANYwhere/ even here in Baruchistan/[16] MIGHT be useful EVEN in woptaly/ some wop SHOULD protest the idiotic term "nazi-fascist"/ chicken-footed-goat that never existed or shall we couple some other monstrous elements, and while all the brit/am slimers are howling totalitarian/ even Pegler.[17] with his eye on trade union tyranny, has never heard of vocational representation/ "sarà fascista"/[18] they are HAM iggurint of ALL the constructive ideas re/ corporate state/ a topic never mentioned/ like honour, it is not that they are consciously opposed to same/ but have NEVER heard it MENtioned/ prof/ here last week/ never encountered a demand for DEFINITION of words/ honest and thoughtful/ had govt definition expanded onto 2 ½ pages without hitting bullseye.

of usury

1. *Ferragosto*, It.: "feast of the Assumption," a major Italian holiday celebrated on 15 August.

2. **Giulio Del Pelo Pardi.**

3. **Father Francesco Ruspoli.**

4. **Monsignor Piero Pisani.**

5. A new edition of *Guide to Kulchur* was published on 29 August 1952 by New Directions; the English edition by Peter Owen was published on 15 October 1952.

6. For EP's comments on **Edmondo Rossoni** see *Guide to Kulchur* 166–67.

7. This is in response to ORA's letter of 10 August 1952, in which she had written that she had received a copy of *L'Alleluja: Poesie di Ennio Contini e la prima decade dei cantos di Ezra Pound* but thought the title all wrong: "It shld surely be *Ezra Pound e Ennio Contini;* the one of world-wide reputation, the other so far a nonentity."

8. It.: "style of the thirty years." EP commonly refers to the Fascist era (1922–42) as the "ventennio." We are not sure exactly what he means by "trentennio," perhaps high modernism, 1912–42.

9. It.: literally, "bedbugs bed/s bed/ man of letters etc." EP is presumably punning on the two meanings of *lètto*, "bed" and "read," and the English word *letter* as well as his status as a "bug" and a man of letters in the "bughouse."

10. We have been unable to locate this article; it is likely an essay by George Barker, the British poet.

11. Presumably American Express and Thomas Cook and Son, both corporations heavily involved in the tourist business.

12. *Deturpage del passaggio*, It.: "defacement of the passage way," i.e. billboards along the highway. Apparently he complained of large bottle-shaped advertisements in *Guide to Kulchur*, but we have not located the passage.

13. **Richard Aldington.**

14. Fr.: "London of yesteryear."

15. It: "trees and cisterns."

16. EP's derisive name for the United States, after **Bernard Mannes Baruch.**

17. **Westbrook Pegler.**

18. It.: "[it] will be Fascist."

50. TLU-3   22 September 1952

22 Sep 52

O.R.A.

that beingthe case/[1] why cant you get Spampanato and PeloPs/[2] to meet/ especially as ~~Br~~ Boris seems to have the gift of the gab/ but no steady job/ but certainly capable of communicating etc/ AND start a party to be called AGRARI[3] having *NO institutional program*/ NOTHING that could connect them with any political -ism/

laying aside{,} for the present{,} all discussion of the dirtiest of all swindles/ that nested in issuing all purchasing power as interest-bearing DEBT.

starting with slogan: alberi e cisterni.[4] then proceeding to include aqueducts/ bonifica/ and specific augments/ soja/ arachidi, acero, kadzu/ AND these new soil treatments/ tiny quantities in sprays/ and of course retaining Pelop)s plow technique.

There wd/ be nothing neo in that. If the present jibberals, jabberalls etc/ wanted to shout for private enterprise they wd/ yell for Torlonia's prefascist private bonifica.//[5] but they haveN~~8~~t even sense to do that.

The only activity that the sons of hell and sewage cd/ call subversive [illegible deletion] would be a desire for definite terminology/ I note Tallyrand calling down crooks at Vienna, for changing the meaning of words from one session to another/ At which shell game he seems to have stopped 'em. However, no program can go too far into detail let the Agrari stop simply with the part of this page outlined in red.[6]

The rest of the activity cd/ proceed quietly in private conversation/ and serve as stimulus to social intercourse or the amelioration of conversation.

Eden's soaping up Tito[7] dont seem, for the moment, to have got him anywhere. AND his fotos look more and more like Charlie Chaplin/ whom our justice dept has finally noticed/ too bad the brits/ couldn't have kept him for exclusive use of their foreign office/ had he been a pervert instead of merely a rather stingy letcher, he might not have incurred the present slight inconvenience.[8]

AND so on/ pardon frivolity after a serious opening.

Pelo/ and Spamp ought to be able to think of a few other honest men/ Ungaro[9] has a level head and wd/ be useful IF mobilizable. I dont know whether Tasca[10] has still any land/ his relatives weren't paupers ten years ago. I think B/[11] knows a Torlonia/ and it was Fr Ruspoli who first told me about Pelops/ being very enthusiastic.

AM I clear in the opening/ *NO institutional* program whatsoever. And no immediate mention of trying to educate people re/ nature of money.

Social Credit landslide in British Columbia/ that is second Canadian province/ Soc/ Credit leader being branded a fascist. ~~bb~~ by disappointed swine/[12]

And prob/ the brit/ soc/crs/ will fuss re/ about his heterodoxy/ but at
{any} rate/ *si muove*/[13] it need{s} extra effort to write in italian.

Do Pel/ and Spamp read english easily/

1. In a letter of 18 September 1952 ORA reported that, according to a young
agronomist who was taking English lessons from her, the European Community
Association had given a grant of 6,000,000 lire for large-scale experiments in South
Italy with Del Pelo Pardo's agricultural methods. The experiments had been successful, but she expressed doubt about the methods' continued success because
chemical fertilizer and agricultural machinery manufacturers were too powerful.

2. **Giulio Del Pelo Pardi.**

3. *Agrario*, It.: "agrarian."

4. It.: "trees and cisterns," a tag also used in letter 49 and repeated a number of
other times in these letters.

5. See letter 24.

6. The paragraph beginning with "starting with slogan" is "outlined in red" ink.

7. Marshall Tito (1892–1980).

8. Chaplin was suspected of having Communist affiliations and in September
1952, when he was at sea on his way to England, Attorney General James P.
McGrawny rescinded his entry permit without which he could not return to the
United States.

9. Either **Andriano Ungaro** or **Filippo Ungaro.**

10. **Angelo Tasca.**

11. **Boris de Rachelwiltz.**

12. The first Canadian province was Alberta. William Bennett (b. 1900) won an
election in August 1952 to form the second provincial government in Canada by
a Social Credit party; he and his party remained in power until 1972. The first
Social Credit government had been formed by **William Aberhart** in Alberta in
1935.

13. It.: "move yourself."

51. TLU-1   24 October [1952]

24 Oc

O.R.A.

CANT get any serious correspondence from Italy/ NO promptitude in
either reviewing or translating the few eng/ or americ/ books worth a
damn. NOTE C.C.Tansill[1] (prof. at Catholic University, in Wash) "Back
Door to War." (Regnery 1952). Spampanato too long for americ/ pubr/
ought not to be beyond scope of human imagination to publish CON-
DENSATIONS of these big documentary books/ like the Tansill/ translating the parts that dont duplicate what is known locally. At last got
name of the brit/ damnblastador/ Ron. Graham/[2] mucker. No real pool-
ing of imagination. CHDouglas dead,[3] as yu may hv/ heard/ probably

NOT due to shock of a little literacy getting into the Social Crediter/ Gilling-Smith[4] reviewing Sapori at length, with promise of Del Mar and Mullins/

Yu may remember an article on China in Merid/ d Rom/ anyhow anything touched by Ciano/ Eden/ Bullet,[5] bound to rot. Yr/ arab velleity/ remember the arabs in Rome were so disgusted with arab stupidity that they thought might as well let the kikes have it. Despite being an Italian Ciano (the younger) was a punk, no better than FDR/ Churchill or Eden//// and I doubt if yu can blame it all on his grandma// YOU misinterpret my dislike of certain qualities/ but races have 'em.

Glad to see some small recognition (gold laurel leaf) given to Saturno Montanari[6] (young Rav~~ven~~(n)ate killed in war at tender age). benefitted by the STYLE of the era.

Did I ask you for data re/ damn/ fergit the blokes name/ on some wop kulchurl wangle?

Other point/ McNair Wilson's books ought to be known in Italy/ his Napoleonic stuff[7] (esp one on Gipsy Queen/ Cabarus('} daughter) might entertain Helen.

I sent on her translation[8] to the Hudson/

I imagine Tansill or his pubr/ wd/ send review copy to Roma IF any damWOP had enough virility to guarantee to review it. He mentions yr/ friend Aug Rosso.[9]

1. In *Back Door to War* **Charles Callan Tansill** suggested that the responsibility for the entry into World War II rested in great measure upon Roosevelt. ORA reported that Villari had just published in *Il Secolo d'Italia* "a very long review (2 whole pages of the paper) on Charles Callan Tansill's book" (5 Nov. 1952). In a letter dated 10 November 1952 but not included here, EP requested a copy of this review.

2. Sir Ronald Graham was the British ambassador to Rome around 1925.

3. **Major Clifford Hugh Douglas** died on 29 September 1952.

4. Although Dryden Gilling-Smith was a British Social Credit writer, we have been unable to find such reviews. Gilling-Smith may have been working on a review of Sapori's *Le marchand italian au moyen age* and may have shown interest in reviewing one or more of Del Mar's books and **Eustace Mullins's** *The Secrets of the Federal Reserve*.

5. **William C. Bullitt.**

6. **Saturno Montanari.**

7. The book EP has in mind is *Napoleonic Wars*.

8. A reference to **Helen Rossetti Angeli's** translation of "Linno alla Matematica," a poem by Giorgio Cicogna, and forwarded to EP. In an earlier letter ORA had described Cicogna as "a really remarkable writer and poet, who was also an airman in World War I, an engineer, and an inventor" (20 July 1952).

9. Augustus Rosso, unidentified but mentioned in a letter of 14 August 1943 not included here.

52. TLS-2   5 November 1952

In this letter from which we quote a brief section, ORA thanks EP for
sending her Guide to Kulchur; *the book elicits a long and rather typical*
retrospect from her.

[. . .] It is indeed a {"}challenging{"} book, especially for me as many of
the references ~~to people~~ are to people I do not know. All that period of
literary innovations in England and Paris, the period in which my cousin Ford played a prominent part and of which you were one of the main
exponents, I never came into contact with. In the '90's I was all wrapped
up with such people as Prince Kropotkin,[1] and Stepniak[2] and many who
shared their views but were totally unknown to fame, Errico Malatesta,[3]
Alexandre Cohen, Saverio Merlino,[4] with at times a glimpse of Louise
Michel{;}[5] and there was Antonio Agresti whom I married and came to
Italy, and was {there} soon absorbed with David Lubin and his work{,}
which brought me in touch with prominent economists such as Maffeo:
Pantaleoni,[6] and Luzzatti;[7] and then there were a few survivors from a
previous age, the Painter Giovanni Costa[8] who had fought with Garibaldi[9] at the siege of Rome in 1949.[10] And ~~then~~ there was a group of artists
and art-critics and poets and philosophers, but none of them in touch with
Blast or Vortex or any of those movements. Of one thing I am glad, and
that is that Marx and his doctrines were always repulsive to me; human
personality, the right of the individual to express himself, the distrust of
bureaucracy and of stifling and interfering governments. Then the Great
war and its great enthusiasms, and then the great disappointment; and
then the hope that corporativism might bring a solution of the social
question outside the dragooning shibboleths of Social Democracy and
then the disappointment of seeing [illegible deletion] "les nains sapant
sans cesse l'ouvrage des géants",[11] and all the little Jacks in office using
their little brief authority to hasten the world on to ruin. And now in my
78th year I see how utterly hollow was the faith in "PROGRESS", "EN-
LIGHTENMENT" and all the other shibboleths. I had worked hard and
honestly to promote international relations, I had hoped that something
would come of Conferences, Congresses, etc. etc. that were to bring about
peace and justice, and I have seen that they were used by rascals to de-
ceive fools. I agree with you that the only hope would be in ~~such~~ work
for "alberi e cisterni", aqueducts, bonifica, soja, arachidi, acero, and Pelo-
pardi's soil cultivation. But my active days are over. I have all I can manage {to do} in helping this little adopted family of mine to keep afloat, and
from morning to night I am busy with lessons—teaching young people
who want to take university degrees in English literature, and who have

to read the Elizabethan dramatists, and John Donne, and Pope, and then Swift and the Satirists—of whom it seems to me that Aldous Huxley with Ape and Essence is one of the finest—and the Romantics {and I do a lot of translations but none of this remotely literary}. I am a great lover of Blake. [. . .]

1. **Prince Peter Kropotkin.**
2. Stepnyak, or **Sergei Michailovich Kravchinski.**
3. **Errico Malatesta.**
4. **Francesco Salverio Merlino.**
5. **Louise Michel.**
6. **Maffeo Pantaleoni.**
7. **Luigi Luzzatti.**
8. **Giovanni Costa.**
9. **Giuseppe Garibaldi.**
10. An error for 1849.
11. Fr.: "Dwarfs constantly undermining the work of giants."

53. TLU-3   8 November 1952

8 Nov.

ORA

DANM it, NObody ever thinks. Note that Visconti-Venosta[1] 1897 noticed that the roads outside Homburg were bordered with fruit trees/[2] 55 years later the idea has NOT reached Italy, where a bit of shade wd/ do no harm. And UNFRUIT tress do border an occasional road.

Gourmont certainly right that Xtianity has ruined minds more than morals/ and the Vatican in 1900 years hasn't either propagated a definition of usury/ i.e. not got it into the general mind/ OR bust the stinginess that wd/ shudder at the thought of PUBLIC fruit pickable by whomsoever. Miserum hum/ gen/[3] etc.

And as for the literati (who ought to be spelled with a different prefix) The habit of commentary which tries to define and IMPROVE meanings/ has been chucked into the pozzo nero of terza pagina/[4] yatter about yatter about yatter/ always expanding.

I hear Belloc[5] is gaga/ but apparently he did define usury/ distinct from interest, in 1925 and in {'}32. Also Del Mar got to definition of origin of interest.

all of which can be simplified into def: Usury a charge for the use of purchasing power levied without regard to production, and often without regard even to the possibilities of production.

Some blind cawflik has TRANSLATED the decrees of the church councils/ WOT a field day for a Voltaire.

As Confucian I shall let 'em set/ AND as the hierarchy of the old'Ore is licking psychiatric boots/ yu might note that the Hroosun savages prohibit party members from being touched by psycho{aNAL}ists/ but when they want (verbatim) to DEVISER (unhing{e}, unscrew, ruin) a man they put one of these kike-leeches on him.

Pegler has got round to depicting the filth and corruption (not simple lechery but mental) of the cocktailparty level. AND [illegible deletion] no one bothers to fight Moscow IN the drawing rooms of the damploots. I hv/ in mind partic/ case reported from Roma/ she cobra/

Haven't you ANY visitors who can ASSURE reviews of books like Tansill's/ and at least try to get useful texts translated into wop/ ten years here, ten there. on time lag/ {TIMELAG} a few week-old recordings/ which might keep at least some of the minor protags/ awake.

Did I mention McNair Wilson's books to you/ very readable/ and the ole man still on the hoof/ now that one has again found his address.

Beastly kristers ROTTED with rhetoric/ take kids that like to knock something down/ and then sing the Magnificat/ total inebriety/ exalted them of low degree (to hell with the results/ no worry about disorder/. NO sense of responsibility/ mess and hysteria/ and yu sure ought to hv/ heard the black parson on the radio/ all about GAWWWW/[6] not Stev/[7] or Ike GAW was going to electUm.

1. Probably Giovanni Visconti-Venosta (1831–96), a man of letters who was politically active as a youth in the Risorgimento in Lombardy; his memoir *Ricordi di gioventu* focuses on the Risorgimento.

2. In a letter dated 15 December 1952 ORA said that EP's plan for increasing food supplies would never work in Italy because, unlike the Germans, Italians have "contempt for public property."

3. *Miserium humanum genum*, Lt.: "the suffering of humankind."

4. It.: "cesspool" of "the third page," that is, the page in Italian newspapers devoted to cultural matters.

5. **Hilaire Belloc.**

6. God.

7. **Adlai Ewing Stevenson.**

54. TLS-2   15 December 1952

We include the following segment from ORA's letter not only because it deals with corporativism, one of the constant threads in the correspondence, but also because it shows that ORA was not blind to the deficiencies of Mussolini's regime. She begins by saying that she has seen Giuseppe Bottai's "Verve il Corporativisomo Democratico o verve una democrazia corporativa!" which she finds very important; she has asked

Bottai for another copy of the article and plans to send it to EP, but the copy is not extant. Later in the same letter she mentions another study dealing with some of the issues mentioned here, Camillo Pellizzi's Una rivoluzione mancata.

[. . .] The fact is that the parliamentary systems have all broken down on the European Continent and if Europe is not to fall into hopeless decadence a new system must be found, and I firmly believe that the new system must be based on vocational representation and not on geographical. Mussolini had got hold of a need which the syndicalist Enrico Leone,[1] Trevisonne, and others of that school who were anti-Marxist socialist-anarchists ~~were~~ had perceived. But the Fascist attempt to set up the guild State failed because it was made [illegible deletion] subordinate to the One Party. Criticism was banned; the system which under the law of April 1926 was to have worked from the base upwards, was instead transformed into a system of appointees from above; the "gerarchi{,}" who often became petty local tyrants, had too big a finger in the pie. But these are all defects from which lessons may be learnt, but the fundamental idea of the system is the right one, I believe. It would work for decentralisation and for the removal of the professional politician (one of the most noxious features of modern political life). If worked properly{,} the workers should not be represented as they often were by lawyers and such like who knew nothing of the matter they were supposed to represent, but by the actual men engaged in the several lines of work. [. . .]

1. **Enrico Leone.**

55. TLU-3   19 December 1952

19 Dec 52

PREcisely, my deah O.R.A.[1]
PREcisely/ and if these out in fronters wd/ lay off the boycott/ and not like that louse of a louse/ and in general all vermin/ try to pass off E.P.'s writing as senile diliquescence/ it might therefrom be drug/ that VOcational rep/ is constitutional in this defiled country/ every state could choose its representatives on a VOcational basis/ anything from 2 to whatever congressmen/ cd/ be apportioned/ to farm/ labour/ farm professions management, workers/ on up or down as far as the fragmentation [illegible deletion] might/ be desired.
      AND if someone had the gutz to enquire: IF Göring instead of sending 24 vols/ of Nietczzsch to Mus/[2] had been capable of sending him two fasciculae of Confucio/ etc.

Iggurunce/ and incommunication between DIFFERENT circles/

Of course the plain dishonesty ditched a lot of good effort/ tho the simple minded uscieri[3] were rank amateurs in cf/ the mayors and pros/atts/[4] of our gangster organization/

AND there was infinitely MORE chance of criticism in Italy of the deplorato[5] than in Eng/ or the JSA.

Until the decentralizers/ or a few of 'em/ have sense to yell: "local control of local *PURchasing Power*"/ they will stew in the old socio/ Marxist sewage.

Del Mar/ control of monetary issue. notes sane politic division/ Rome/ gold under Pontifex Max (power usurped by Caesars)/silver/ farmed out to nobles and favorites/ bronze to privileged town{s}.

AND the industrialists go on having their pockets picked by Lazard freres,[6] in the delusion that they are mastering the workers, by allying themselves with crablice.

delighted to come in in vBülow/[7] re some cardinal that he did not get elected pup/ because mit Das Bankhaus Pacelli kompromettiert.[8]

The damage done by [illegible deletion] xtianity and xtn igornace is not yet equanimously contemplated by them that see a false dilemma/ i.e. xt or plain stupid denial of Dante, Mencius and Agassiz.

If a young female Stancioff ever gets to Rome, tell her where to find a few decent artists.

yes/ hv/ seen the Pellizzi vol/ anodyne.[9]

as to wayside fruit/[10] I used to watch wops blow their tops when I told 'em germans were good for 'em.

that they (the huns) humanized the (rationalistic) wops.

the sabotage of Confucian studies/ I note that Tucci[11] hasn't got round to noticing Stone Classics edtn/ either/ who pays HIS printing bill for barbaric tongue in Roma antique?

but more idiotic here/ as basic opposition in the last and greatest not marxist country is confucian/ only a little xtn icing in minority wobblers at the edges/

the homestead vs/ kolchosz/[12] and the apes yelling for contributions to voice of america/ some of whose crooks are being suspen{d}ed, sacked and/or indicted AT LAST

What about Contini/[13] [illegible deletion] I see by the lousy Lett/ It/ that he is in jug/ but no indic/ as to pubk/ or private excentricity.

best for X mas/ to you, Helen, and young.

Have Vertès' caricatures[14] reached Roma ex-caput? dealing with one of the minor, but pestilent, byproducts of xtianity?

I don't spose that Bot/[15] KNOWS how the dif/ states of the U.S. could legally elect their congressmen. Could yu TELL him? nobuddy knows or does ANYthing whatsodam until TOLD.

1. EP is referring to ORA's account of "corporativism" in letter 54. Corporativism is a form of sociopolitical organization based on institutional arrangements whereby capital and labor are integrated into obligatory, hierarchical, and functional occupational units that may control power in a state or be controlled by a political authority that exists independently of them. Corporativism claims to offer an alternative to parliamentary liberalism. Fascist Corporativism grew out of syndicalism and nationalism. Fascism began to commit itself to Corporativism in 1925, with the system's high point coming between 1929 and 1935. The beginning of the Ethiopian war in 1935 signaled an end to Corporativism's period of innovation, even though in 1939 a Chamber of Fasci and Corporations replaced the old system of the Chamber of Deputies. Since Mussolini lacked confidence in it, Corporativism and its organs never really enjoyed broad powers.

2. We have found no information regarding the twenty-four volumes of Nietzsche Hermann Göring (1893–1946) is said to have sent to Mussolini. Perhaps this story, repeated elsewhere in this correspondence, is apocryphal.

3. It.: "those who have come out." EP seems to mean individuals who took dishonest advantage of their position.

4. Perhaps "professional attorneys."

5. It.: "the deplored."

6. Fr.: "Lazard brothers," EP's generic Jewish law firm.

7. **Prince Bernhard Heinrich von Bülow.** EP appears to be reading Bülow's *Memoirs.*

8. Gm.: "compromised with the Pacelli bank." EP seems to think that Pope Pius XII's office was bought for him by banker relatives.

9. EP is referring to ORA's mention of Pellizzi's *Una rivoluzione mancata* in her letter of 5 December 1952.

10. See letter 53.

11. In a letter dated 24 May 1952, ORA mentioned *East and West,* a review that Tucci, a Tibetan scholar, published in English as an organ for Italian contacts with the Far East. Tucci is also mentioned in a letter dated 22 May 1952 but not included here.

12. See letter 18.

13. See letter 49.

14. These caricatures are not extant.

15. **Giuseppe Bottai.**

1953

56. TLU-3   14 January 1953
14 Jan 53

ORA
found WANTING

No the U.S. senate cd/ not be vocational rep/[1] without emending constitution/ and wd/ be clumsy, given the past tradition and organization/ But the house of representatives could, and would I think be better place to begin/ each state can select its reps/ as it likes/ no need to stick to geographic division/ of districts./

AND the senate the remaining bulwark against centralization in the hands of internat/ finance/ apolid,[2] and partly in the hands of a curious people. Of course the reps/ from some states (farm block) are fairly near vocational reps/ but in state having a dozen or more cong/men and various sources of production/ any state cd/ make the start/ AFTER the idea got to 'em. Judging from the bestial imbecility re/ monetary issue, that might mean a "geological epoch"/ but its is their mudheadedness not the constitution that wd/ cause the delay.

Bloke from Ceylon just left/ may give him yr/ address/ Padmanabha. Dare say a suitable acquaint for any eng/speaking, well who does? does Spampanato? In short the occident beling[3] the bloody mess the Times and other Slimes hv/ made it no reason for a decent oriental not to take back a few memories of the reliques of our civilization, the occasional dabs of culture Ooozenstink and Wwinstein haven't effaced.

Do yu see Social Crediter?[4] Gilling-Smith on Stilwelk,[5] Dec 20 to Jan 3/ three issues.

P.S. re/ Pac/[6] if he weren't a mutt he cd/ have perfo5med some better function during the last 7 years of the ventennio/ or from concordat onward.

OBviously there are pious mottos to be found in Xtn writings. buttt......

Alzo/ what is the connect with Das Bankhaus Pacelli "kompromittiert"[7] when they took Sart instead of some forgotten puppet.

P.S.2/ continuing/ I think if you took off his petticoats and theatrical costumery you'd find a stincking social snob like Eden. Remember Rennel Rodd[8] treated Mus/ decently, like a human being and a little real inner decency wd/ have done a lot to moderate and counteract the dirt pulling the wrong way with M.

seriously re/ Pacelli/ an institution that blocks/ and has for centuries 98% of all mental life, naturally selects as its head an atavism/ a damned nuisance/

The role of the Church since 1900 is NOT a credit to humanity. It is not as vile in aim as the universal conspiracy to plant one tyranny without mitigations, or as low as the usururs etc. Dare say 1870 was last gasp

And not enough force inside the institution to undo that job/ Hv. got to emend line re Cecco Beppe NEVER having done ANYthing good/ just found in Bülow that the old whishers did at least veto Rampolla.[9]

must allow for environment brot up as he prob was/ cdn't be much better.

benedictions and best to
Helen

1. EP's commentary is pursuant to ORA's championing of syndical style vocational representation as opposed to geographical representation—the standard in British-derived representative democracies.

2. Probably *apolide*, It.: "stateless."

3. Being.

4. *Social Creditor*, published in Liverpool, England, since 1938.

5. Probably John Stilwell (1886–1963), a business executive and brother of **General Joseph Warren Stilwell.**

6. **Eugenio Pacelli.** ORA has defended him against EP's censure in letter 55.

7. See letter 55.

8. **Rennel Rodd.** It is not clear which of his works EP has in mind here.

9. **Mariano Rampolla, Marchese del Tindaro.** During the conclave of 1903 it appeared that Rampolla might be elected Pope, but Cardinal Puscyna of Austria-Hungary blocked Rampolla's election. EP apparently found the account of this incident in Bülow's *Memoirs* (606–11).

57. TLU-3   25 January 1953

25 Ja

ORA/

Bottai's style very heavy/ but good sign that he is able to print anything at all/ as to WHY his style is heavy/ no need to go into that. Nothing new/ I hv/ two memories/ one DelCroix grabbing phone and yelling to Bot/ to come hear about Gesell, "che MAGnifica idea.!" B/ just leaving office to catch train for Napoliiiii.

Alzo Bot/ with almost equal promptitude, if without equal elan/ phoning to Turin to tell the dambliotecario[1] to get on job/ re/ Vivaldi.[2]

Bublarian OUT at the moment, but something ultimately got done.

Given time lag of decade/ do you spose Bot/ wd/ NOW read any of my writings? He did read Por, or at least print him.

I think yu know, and Spanp/[3] or someone might get it into some edtrs/ head (or whatso top(s) vertb/colm/) that I did NOT do my Jef/Mus[4] FOR woptaly in '32 but DID translate it after the crash.[5] Drummond don{'}t like {the} translation/ BUT it ought to be resurrected, without or without corrections of "style" so called.

IF they wd/ state the basic antithesis/ wd/ save a lot of printing composition.

Representative or UNrepresentative govt/ responsible OR irresponsible idem. free expression of opinion on the part of those QUALIFIED r to have an opinion.

NOdambody whatso has NOTICED that there was an IDEA inside that phrase.

One Dutchman Hollander noticed the joke in Patria Mia re/ the Easter islands.[6] that was 37 year time lag/ {IKE} included ONE Confucian principle in his nine points/ dunno if anyone noticed that.

And if Mrs Chinaboy Luce joins Lucky Luciano,[7] it will be wot the dummpy-Xtns have asked for. And Our Charley[8] wont be snoopin round for small change, or collecting his pay from the back doors of village brothels.

BUTT....the dogma in the manger...Oh well, taint even the dogma, its the habits.

Yes, remember Bot/ another time/ poker face trying to get XXth century notions into XVth century Sienese {audience's} head{s}. Do tell him about the Leopoldine Reforms if he hasn't yet heard of 'em? IN FACT if people wd/ read my works (verse, so called, included) they wd/ waste less of their time on protective argument.

How old it is Bot/? young enough to listen to gaffir?

OR if not, to discover that Pegler has been writing about trade unions, and shd/ be about ripe to learn MORE about 'em. What come of Rossoni? and Bevione?[9] (doubt if either will go without ucelletti).[10] That was gt/ argument in Brescia restaurant, cisalpine burocracy: COULD one eat POlenta[11] without 'em{?} (the auzeletz)??[12] Taint my dish either way/ but I wd/ like to cite {sight} some canneloni or una mozarella in carozza.[13] Pizza HAS been brought and used on a Central american damblastador, of aesthetic leanings. BUTT he has since faded.

1. Like "Bublarian" below, this is EP's variation on *bibliotecario*, It.: "librarian."

2. See letter 45.

3. **Bruno Spampanato.**

4. *Jefferson and/or Mussolini* was published by Nott in London in 1935. EP translated it into Italian and had it printed in December 1944, but the edition was destroyed because its pro-Fascist posture was no longer acceptable in Italy.

5. After Mussolini's overthrow on 25 July 1943.

6. Perhaps the "joke" EP is referring to here is a tale told by the "sultan of Zammbuk or some such place [who] was in London"; this "tale from the southern pacific [which] is of universal application" addresses the need for the state to subsidize artists (*Patria Mia* 71–72).

7. After listening to various pleas for EP's release, **Clare Boothe Luce** took up EP's case with the State Department; as well, on 6 February 1956, *Life*, a magazine owned by her husband, ran an editorial that drew attention to EP's strange legal status. EP may have selected the epithet "Mrs Chinaboy" because of her husband's highly publicized visit to China in 1945 during which he was the only foreigner at a dinner Chiang Kai-shek held in honor of Mao Tse-tung. Her connection with the mafioso Lucky Luciano is presumably her anticipated appointment as American ambassador to Italy (1953–56). Luciano was released from prison in 1953 and deported to his native Italy.

8. Unidentified, but perhaps merely a term for the stereotypical gangster.

9. **Giuseppe Bevione.** ORA responded: "I have an idea that Rossoni was murdered, but am not sure, will try to find out. Bevione, I think, is living unmolested, but have not heard of him recently" (16 Feb. 1953). **Edmondo Rossoni** was condemned to death in the Verona trials (1944) but was not executed.

10. *Uccèlletti*, It.: "little birds," that is, "inducements."

11. Mush made usually with cornmeal.

12. Presumably a semi-phonetic rendition of *uccèlletti*.

13. Mozzarella en carrozza is a fried mozzarella sandwich.

58. TLU-3   3 March 1953
3 Marzo

ORA
    lack, goddamit LACK of communications/, cant expect ME to be a Fuhrer of wops/ ought to be at least one wop/ to kill such lice as E.L.Morrow,[1] who yaps of "totalitarian" as if Mus/ and not FDR, sowbelly the damned, had brot Stalin into Berlin.[2]

    ALSO, swine talking of nazis as "fascists"/[3] there were no gas ovens in Italy/ it is for an ITALIAN to say it and say it with a sting. There WAS a laboratory for ideas in papers run by Rossoni, Bottai, Farinacci/[4] BUT your dear sheenies, Sulzberger,[5] Meyer,[6] and the brit/ pimps did NOT transmit this fact to their populace/ and the stinking insularity and monopolism of the eng/ and am/ univs/ boycotted Frobenius and Del Mar/

    It is time for Spamp/ or someone to READ a few foreign stinkers, stinking in the year of misery and false religion 1953/

    just got what I hear is serious vol/ History of Crusades by Steven Runciman/[7] seems serious/ wonder if he is son or relative of the "invisible man"/[8] the slider. if so/ ought to know a bit about infamies.

    AND someone in Rome ought to MAINTAIN correspondence with the few honest english (or scotch) who have survived the Boozy Buffoon and the tailor(')s dummy.

    Isn't there ANY one in Rome who wd/ write at least once a fortnight to Wykes-Joyce,[9] or Yorke Crompton/[10] or even to some of the busier and harder heads now trying to educate the goddam insular britons?

burden on yr/ anonymous correspondent is too heavy/ some of the correlation shd/ be done by someone else.

I hear Begnac[11] includes a quote/ expect D/[12] to bring me his vol/ this week sometime.

Two brit/ mags/[13] apparently opening to sanity. a bit late, but better than never.

yes, contents of yr/ last noted[14]

Tansil{l}[15] and Runciman shd/ be noted/ perhaps even that highly shifty and suspect {"}Borghese{"} cd/ have guts to review the Runciman, if not Tansill's work.

newsstand tosh all the same/ BUT can be, to some degree USED/ never to stand on or rely on, but for familiarizing apes with a few names.

P.S. some of the blokes who Badogliated,[16] p{o}st fascismo think the new corrupters will employ 'em cause they are clever. FATAL wop weakness.

One good line in some rubbish attributed to Aristotl/ that I dipped into last night/ i.e. that the CHARACTER of the speaker had a lot to do with his effect on audience. fact OBvious on television, when a McCarthy[17] gets up against a lying skunk like Spivak.[18]

any of yr/ erudites know where ANY serious study been made as to why Aristotle used to get chucked out of medieval universities. Might have been for good motive

/P.S. continu/ because of his messing with general terms/ or might have been because of usual xtian messiness when faced with some of Ari's lucid moments.

P.S.SS/ as for the boycott of DelMar and Frobenius your HORRIBLE xtians smell a bit of truth a mile off and run from it like the devil from howly whather. wie Teufil um Taufstein.[19]

1. Probably Edward R. Murrow, head of the CBS foreign news staff around 1953.

2. Berlin surrendered to the Soviet army on 2 May 1945. EP's accusation that the allies were responsible for Soviet gains in the East was common among Fascists.

3. ORA, too, insists on the distinction between fascism and Nazism: "But I can assure you there is in Italy a revival from the supine immediate post-war condition; a revision of much that was embodied in the original fascist movement, before B.M. [Benito Mussolini] became the succubus of A.H. [Adolf Hitler]. Parliamentary institutions are working so badly here that they are becoming a derision, and the only alternative between a bloody communist tyranny and a degraded servile demagogy will be a revised and improved corporative State based on vocational representation" (29 Mar. 1953).

4. **Roberto Farinacci.**

5. **Cyrus Leo Sulzberger II.**

6. **Eugene Meyer.**

7. Stephen Runciman's *A History of the Crusades.*

8. Probably Walter Runciman (1870–1949), a British statesman who visited the United States in January 1937 and held trade talks with Roosevelt.

9. Max Wykes-Joyce, author of *Triad of Genius.*

10. Unidentified. In a letter received by Louis Dudek on 4 April 1953, EP wrote: "I dunno what you and Oiks, or Crompton wd/ make of each other. I have never met either of them." Dudek is just as puzzled by Crompton as we are; in his notes he writes that "'Oiks' and Crompton were people in EP's mind, their identity was not conveyed to me" (*DK* 100).

11. EP is probably referring to Begnac's *Palazzo Venezia.*

12. **Dorothy Pound.**

13. Most likely EP has in mind *Nine* and *The European*, mentioned in letter 59.

14. ORA's letter of 16 February 1953, which consists mostly of her grievances about the Italian political system and the need for reform of the Montecitori (Parliament).

15. See letter 51.

16. An allusion to **Marshal Pietro Badoglio's** overthrow of Mussolini.

17. Senator Joseph McCarthy (1908–57).

18. **Lawrence Edmund Spivak.**

19. *Wie Teufel um Taufstein*, Gm.: "like the devil in the baptismal fount."

59. TLU-3   5 April [1953]

5 Ap/

ORA

Yes, Mary a gt/ comfort..[1] Reading Begnac, Palazzo Venez.[2]

Mightn't it be time for some of 'em to consider what I SAID/

the dirt, residue of pink-pork-parlour Rooseveltian stinckg/ makes very difficult to get ANY exact facts into print.

Did you see Pellizzi's note in Tempo. 20 March. It will take a LONG time to get THOSE facts into this desert.

and of course some sort of correlation in Rome wd/ be USEFUL.

as to whether ANYone ~~inp~~ in Roma is likely to think that I could or would be useful to ~~TE~~ THEM, that is another kettle of onions/ Begnac re/ Augusto Turati,[3] re/ before I knew details/ seem{s} however to corroborate my view/ TEN years construction/ then ten years undermining and going wrong.

Wd/ be useful to emphasize my role as OBSERVER, and 30 year effort to get clean and real news from Italy to the U.S.

in fact as simbolo of Italo-American amity, I might even be USED.

And as to the present smear in snotty-smart papers like the New Yorker (cultural level of Mickey-Rooney and Eleanor)[4]

There is of course not a line in support of ANY kind of totalitarianism anywhere in my writing. And the level of Montale[5] calling my econ: bimetalism/[6] is NOT below that of the peprs here which are still dominated by New Deal refuse.

The LACK of DeGourmont in Italy// that is{,} has any damwop ana-
lyzed the ROOT of party idiocy/ socialist, liberaloid or other/ {?}

i.e. failure to DISSOCIATE. All these idiots put up PACKETS of ideas/
never a SINGLE idea to be voted on/ clots of ideas which there is NO need
of treating together.

party system/ 40 parties, ALL with jockers in their hand/ and ALL
avoiding the problem of monetary issue.

The irony of my talking about the U.S.Constitution while it was being subverted. had in fact been nullified by the codfaced cockroach Wilson the Woodrow, the damned.

I note{,} in the {chapter re/} Turati, the drive toward swollen executive/
IMpertinently rampant HERE till Judge Pine's decision.[7] {last fall}

Keep an eye on the number of crooks let OUT before Truman left/ and
those now going IN (to jail)

BUT also the very slight notice given to lowering the amount of cov-
erage for speculation on stock exchange and even some spew re/ return
to gold.

which MIGHT seem almost incredible/ BUTTTTT....

Did I say, or did anyone note the Observer's[8] quote re/ freedom of speech
on radio.

There are several matters of principle/ as well as of law/ that might
serve italian essayists.

Freedom for expression of opinion on the part of those qualified to have
an opinion.

use of general lables/ even "fascist" might be avoided as far as possi-
ble/ It only serves to make noise/ for the piazza, yes, but NOT before/ or
at any rate not ten years or ten months before/

It appears that the present ital/ govt. approaches "fascism" uninterrupt-
edly.

But until you define the term, the sentence is meaningless.

the sons of hell/ continue to try to lump italian fascism of tTurati (Aug),
of Starace,[9] Hitler, Moscow under one lable/

You will have seen Spamp/ in Ecrits de Paris, blasted ole Seur Latine
reduced to discovering Italy 30 years late.

Is Helen's book[10] being sent to the DECENT magazines for review?
Nine, European, Shenendoah, for example?

Do you remember name of secretary to Banco d Italia who got me to
see Arena/[11] a friend of the Uberti, been trying remember name for some
time/

shd/ also like know who sees WHOM/ Por ought to be writing in VOI,[12]
or not?

1. **Mary de Rachewiltz** visited EP at St. Elizabeths for the first time in March 1953.
2. See letter 58.
3. EP is referring to Augusto Turati's *Una rivoluzione e un capo,* translated and published as *A Revolution and Its Leader (Benito Mussolini).*
4. Eleanor Roosevelt.
5. **Eugenio Montale.**
6. The view that the value of money derives from gold and silver, rather than just gold. It is one variety of a commodity theory of money. Social Credit monetary theory was a quantity theory.
7. A reference to the 29 April 1952 decision by U.S. District Court Judge David Andrew Pine (1891–1970) that President Truman had acted unconstitutionally in nationalizing the steel mills on 8 April 1952, a ruling later upheld by the Supreme Court.
8. *The Observer,* a British newspaper.
9. **Achille Starace.**
10. In a letter dated 29 March 1953, ORA had written that "Helen's book on [Charles Augustus] Howell has been taken by a publisher and will appear in the autumn."
11. Arena is mentioned several times in the correspondence together with **Coppola d'Anna.**
12. Probably *Voice,* a Social Credit paper started in England by **Henry S. Swabey** that EP contributed to frequently.

60. TLU-2   21 April 1953

21 Ap/

O.R.A.

What ever became of Paolillo[1] (not enquired before cause cdn't remember his name)? IS de Begnac[2] capable of writing MORE history correlating the ideas in the riviste clandestine[3] which he did NOT see/ with some of the good ideas mentioned in his Palazzo Venezia/ apparently from contacts with an almost completely different set of wops?

Carta del Carnaro,[4] per es/?[5] never heard of it.

Is there enough coordinative sense among a dozen romans to meet once a fortnight/ and discuss the foreign periodicals that are NOT reported in the local rotocalco?[6]

Por embedded in garlic etc/ MIGHT correlate/ but probably wont

Spampanato's set got ANY members who read english?

Florentines ever come to Rome now? Marainini?[7] Luchini?[8]

anyone see Jenks Rural Economy?[9] some Roman paper ought to try exchange copies. Pelo Pardi mentioned inside back cover of current "NINE." Agriculture the basis/ but not safe IF the s.o.b. can tax it to hell. Gesell only way out of THAT.

M/[10] met german prof/ who thot Gesell party very good/ i.e. Y.M.C.A.
and boyscout organization so far as he knew/ did NOT know it had anything to do with monetary issue...

Ron Duncan in Everybody's March 14/ tax unused land popular mag/
I dont know whom else can reach large circ/ Ignorance in Sunday Observ-
er/ but Conolly evidently done first useful act of his life/ in bk/ on Burgess and Maclean.[11]

Cant get ANY roman correspondents to indicate any THOUGHT re/
ideas NOW useful. such as tax on stagnant money

or Jefferson's objection[12] to ALL pubk/ debt not repayable in 19 years/
i.e. taxation without REPresentation of unborn and minorenni.[13]

America populated with squirrils/ London ~~to~~ 1908–{20} at least FOUR
centres, weekly meetings, for serious discussion. N.Ages/ Yeats, Fordie,
Steed[14] with minor encounters less regular.

AND so on.

1. In response ORA wrote that "Dr. Paolillo is still at the Banca d'Italia" and
provided his address (27 Apr. 1953).

2. See letter 58.

3. It.: "clandestine reviews."

4. Begnac refers to *La Carta del Carnaro*, edited by Renzo De Felice.

5. *Per esempio*, It.: "for example."

6. *Rotocàlco*, It.: "rotogravure."

7. Probably **Giuseppe Maranini.**

8. **Alberto Luchini.**

9. Jenks's *From the Ground Up.*

10. **Mary de Rachewiltz.**

11. **Cyril Connolly's** *The Missing Diplomats* is a book on Guy Francis de Moncy Burgess and Donald Duart MacLean, the so-called Foreign Office Spies.

12. "He thought that a nation had no right to contract debts that couldn't be
reasonably paid within the lifetime of the parties contracting" (*Jefferson and/or
Mussolini* 115).

13. It.: "those under age, minors."

14. EP was in London between 1908 and 1920. *The New Age* is a weekly paper
run by **A. R. Orage** with offices on Cursitor Street—its circle also met at the A.B.C.
restaurant in Chancery Lane. Yeats's circle met during the poet's Monday evening
"at homes" in Woburn Buildings. Ford's circle met at South Lodge, where Ford
was living with **Isabel Violet Hunt. Harry Wickham Steed** had a flat close to Holland Park Road when EP lived at Holland Place Chambers.

61. TLU-3   30 April 1953
30 Ap.

O.R.A.
precisely "L'Europa sarà fascista"[1] in the sense a few used that word.
Roosevelt was a moral leper and perjurer and everything near him stank/
thank god Ike's gang is getting rid of some of the worst filth, but is still
obtuse. Of course there was never a word in favour of dictatorship in my
writing, save as interim necessity, and M/[2] never suggested it as universal system where incompatible with local Anschauung (or if so/ not in
anything I had heard of.) Begnac turns up some unpleasing items that I
did NOT know of/ as for Italy transmitter of Greece/ etc. I cert/ never
neglected that note/ and add CIVIC sense m{,} legal sense. la politica to
yr/ list. Cantos emphasize Leopoldine reforms. which seem unduly ab-
sent from a good deal of current historiography/ and the Grnovese Mazzini circle or whatever rejected the double M/M monogram.[3] which I sent
'em. Error of the Ventennio as I saw it/ the neglect of Risorgimento/
whose Laureate unwreathed was R.Browning more effective than local
wop/bards. The goddam cake-eaters and aesthetes/ Bot/ {e.g.} Obs{cu}[4] etc/
idiotis re/monetary issue. Paolillo had sense to define money as certificate of debt. (and need NOT be interest-bearing.) Naturally I cd/ be use-
ful/ if the Ooozenstinks had had sense to put me back on the air I might
have saved a certain amount of useless slaughter/ AND if they had not
blocked information, cd/ have indicated at least some of the honest men
(and at least one female)[5] fit to have advised 'em in cleaning up/ Of course
Roose betrayed the world to Moscow/ there was one war on/ and the dirty
work aimed at ~~causgn~~ making sure of a third/ with the U.S. and the occident in weak position and the kiko-russ on top/ god rot the lot of 'em/
includinge Weinstein Kirchberg/ and the barber{'}s block/. Winston of
Clowning St/ the Barclay Gammon[6] of the political night club/
    The air here still stinks with Roose's backwash/ decent radio stuff the
exception/ but at least a few howls from senilities trying to tell the Republicans they need invective talent (available but apparently not wanted YET.) Mebbe Claire[7] cd/ grasp that point.
    The right road/ Leopoldine reforms/ a later Habsburg Emperor ploughed
his ceremonial furrow/ some connection of Maria Theresa.[8] bilFF[9] has
read J.Webster/ did any of yr/ charmed circle round the fambly vault note
the Confucian preface to one of W's plays/ bilFF's theory is that the Possum never read it or the play, but merely Lamb's selections.[10]
    Emend yr/ note to Bottai/ not denigrare se stessi but denigrare altri
woptaliani/[11] the advance from the [illegible deletion] M/M was *toward*

the U.S. Constitution/ {shd be} noting Italy's advantage in guild tradition, which American had NOT.

Pegler is aware of trade unions/ and abuses of same/ someone NOT in bug'Ouze[12] shd/ contact him. praps/ the young Pelopardo[13] can do it when he gets here, BUT I hear he dun't kno the murkn languages, and I dont spose Peg/ knows more wop than Bella Napoli and vino rosso.[14] Bot/ and Paolillo ought to be able to get me out of here/ Bot's trouble is he is vurry Dull on the page/ Mus/ renovated Italian prose/ and nobody but Farinacci learned enough from him AS WRITER.

incidentally yu shd/ by slow post receive a mag/ with three good artl/s on ole Fordie. who DID know more ~~ou~~ about what ~~x~~ eng/ writing OUGHT to be, than any of his contemporaries/ tho he didn't always get what he knew onto the page. (his excess was however aimed the right way and that may now show over the debris of Joyce and the Anglican worthy.[15] U.S.system and guild tradition ought to converge in act, not merely in one lunatic{'}s fantasy.

ABC the first serious wop paper that has reached me/ I am NOT falling for Il Bug/easy/[16] journalist's slither.

ABC cd/ serve useful function IF it wd/ get clear not long-winded reviews of the REAL books printed in english and boycotted by the jew press/ Washington Post/ London Zlimes and N.Y.Slimes.

Wd/ it be useful re/ yr/ sane suggestion re/ Senate from Guilds in Italy/ that acc/ U.S.Constr/ it wd/ have to be opposite here/ Senate from geog/ area (i.e. the States) and congressmen chose{N} as representatives of different productive activities. Reuther[17] shd/ be noticed/

And as the way to GET noticed by him is to note his merits/ Bot/ shd/ try that line/ approaching both Pegler and Reuther/ also shd/ star Senator Mundt/[18] and watch the more prudent Senators who have some decency. And not swallow smear ~~of~~ {against} McCarthy.

Lubin was an ass about money/ what's use of uniform {wobbling} or just price if measured in fake money. Yu hv/ noted another Canadia province[19] has gone what is alleged to be Social Credit/ and isn't quite that/ but at least uses the name. Mary sd a german prof in Meran approved Gesellite party/ but did not kno it had anything to do with monetary issue/ (thought it just boy-scouts, virtue etc.)

Bottai ought ALSO to get my Confucius into print/ per{F}ectly welcome to serialize it in ABC senza pagare/[20] OR to foster ital/ trans/ of my Analects. He jumped to phone and yelled to Torino re/ the Vivaldi, but the bib/ario was out/ so it was delayed a bit/ but he might remember the incident/ does he send exchange copies of ABC to the dozen foreign reviews that ought to see it/ or will he if list is supplied him?

believe upper house by region and lower by trades is better/ BUT the approach to such reform [illegible deletion] wd/ depend on local tastes and habit.

best to Helen

1. It. "Europe will be Fascist." ORA had expressed the confidence that the best of fascism would be adopted in Europe in a letter to Bottai (18 Apr. 1953).

2. Mussolini.

3. Presumably representing Mazzini and Mussolini.

4. Obscure.

5. ORA, no doubt.

6. Some proverbial clownish figure of whom we are ignorant.

7. **Clare Boothe Luce.**

8. EP means Joseph II, emperor of Austria (1765–90), son of Maria Theresa. Terrell explains that in eighteenth-century Europe there was a vogue for Chinese customs. In this case, the ceremonial plowing of a furrow, one of the Chinese rites of spring, is acted out literally by Joseph, who in 1769 "took a real plow and plowed some real land to show [his peasants] he meant business" (2:487). The incident is related in cantos 86 and 100.

9. **William French.**

10. French has read a play by John Webster (1580–1625), probably *The Duchess of Malfi*, on which T. S. Eliot commented in "Four Elizabethan Dramatists: A Preface to an Unwritten Book" (*Selected Essays* 109–17). French maliciously speculates that Eliot read only Charles Lamb's prose version of Webster's play, presumably in *Specimens of Early Dramatic Poets Who Lived about the Time of Shakespeare*. In his essay Eliot mentions this work and blames Lamb for reinforcing "the distinction between drama and literature." For the Confucian preface see letter 71, in which EP speaks of a Confucian "passage" in Webster.

11. It.: "denigrate themselves," "other Italians."

12. The bug house.

13. Tomasso Del Pelo Pardi, who, together with **Boris de Rachewiltz,** edited **Giulio Del Pelo Pardi**'s *Agricoltura e civiltà*.

14. It.: "Beautiful Napoli" and "red wine."

15. T. S. Eliot.

16. *Il Borghese.*

17. **Walter Reuther.**

18. **Karl E. Mundt.**

19. British Columbia.

20. It.: "without paying."

62. TLU-1   27 June 1953
{27 giugn}

ORA

idea of petition[1] O.K. but NOT a petition as in their idiotic or perfidi-
ous draft/ looked as if composed by pink or "Partisan review"

all the dirtiest insinuations accepted/ A proper petition cd/ start with
Pellizi's article/ and then according to temper or signers/ point out. what
they dont know/

i.e. fight against usurpation of power and profanation of U.S.Consti-
tution/ ran from Cod Face[2] in 1913/ down to Judge Pine's decision/ FIRST
CLEAN act

and one doesn't know if he wd/ have been upheld if he hadn't had ~~th~~
the whole Steel Trust[3] behind him/

RECENT editorial, note the *word RECENT.* says ex post facto law is
out of fashion/

Then there is the geo politik/ resistance to bringing red savages into
Berlin/[4] that might be better line with C.L.[5] I dunno where that sect stands
re/ the constitution. Anyhow. a petition shd/ NOT have a joker (or several jokers) in it.

NO news and no one has sent me papers from Italy since the election/
today I get Aspects de la France with a little attention to Italy i,e. a front
page art/l.

Also WHOM will C.L. meet{?} There is the silly cocktail element in
Roma that did NOT like regeneration or bonifica, or bat/ del grano/[6] or
civilization of the quarta sponda.[7]

And was it Talleyrand who said "Their interests ARE their principles"?

Germany more respected at this moment/ lot of hoorahs for the E.Ger/
rioters.

France (that is the Ecrits and Aspects, Royalist etc. segment) seems to
be discovering Italy ~~333~~ 30 year time lag,

Did I say that Truman was cursing Ike during electoral wind, for NOT
telling him what I had been trying to TELL 'em over Rome, radio/ nacherly he didn't KNOW that's what he was doing.

There is at last some disfavour of Potsdam[8] and Yalta[9] printed in the
minority or so called "republican" or capitalist press.

and so on/

saluti a Helen,

---

1. This is one of several references in the correspondence to efforts to secure
EP's release from St. Elizabeths. ORA's letter of 5 June 1953 apparently included
a draft of the petition, but it is not extant. She was trying to get an introduction
to **Clare Boothe Luce.** She wrote that **John Drummond** had plans to get "a good

many prominent Italians to sign a paper expressing their hope that the U.S. Government would set free the most outstanding American poet and leader in the new trend literature has taken in the last twenty years." On 3 August 1953 ORA reported that she had written to Mary "asking her to inquire of T.S. Eliot if he would send me a copy inscribed by him to the Ambassador with a note asking me, as of the immediate family of the other great translator of Early Italian Poets, to present it to her. I think this would give me the opportunity I want for getting on the subject."

2. Woodrow Wilson; see also letters 37 and 40.

3. See letter 59.

4. Berlin was still under divided Allied occupation because it was surrounded by Communist East Germany. The Soviets were applying pressure in the hope of forcing the British, American, and French to abandon their zones within Berlin. In 1948, they had severed land communication, to which the West responded with an airlift to supply Berlin.

5. **Clare Boothe Luce.**

6. *Battitura del grano*, It.: "threshing of grain."

7. We do not know what EP means here, since *sponda* is Italian for "bank" or "edge."

8. The site of a conference of the leaders of the "Big Three" Allied Forces from 17 July to 2 August 1945. Earlier agreements on occupation zones and administration of Germany were confirmed and the British and the Americans drew up an ultimatum to be communicated to the Japanese.

9. A seaport in Southern Ukraine on the Black Sea, the site of the wartime conference of Roosevelt, Churchill, and Stalin that took place from 4 to 12 February 1945.

63. TLU-1   29 June 1953

O.R.A.

having got to p/ 164. and reflecting, it comes over me that I hv/ never read a book where the author appears to be telling the exact truth with such, as is in/ i/e. putting it down more exactly than F.H. no fuss, no feathers, no curleycues. Which must be a with DIStinction. Fritz Hesse "Das Spiel um Deutschland"/[1] Paul List Verlag. MUNCHEN 15 Goethe Str 43 there is something like a 13b/ on another part of the address. anyhow very important account, from press chief ♭ german embassy, London. Seems young Ed/[2] gave us three years peace from '36 to 39/ whatever his intellect etc/

cert/ a bk/ Bot/ OUGHT to notice in ABC. I keep hammering that some ital/ paper OUGHT to show awareness to real books printed outside Italy/ not merely the trype that gets most advertisement. Seems Portugal knows more about me than Italy and Japan further along in translating me/ also Germany.

well, let us not be personal/ but it wd/ be a sign of intelligence on part of some wop edtr/ to gain prestige by at least some show of awareness to foreign better books.

I note also in less serious dept. That Vlaminck has had "Paysages et Personnages" pubd/ by Flammarion, Paris.[3]

What do yu kno of Sir Horace Wilson? still alive or not? FH gives credit both to him and to Chamberlain/ ~~np~~ no dolling up anyone.[4]

1. Although an English translation by F. A Voigt was published by Allan Wingate in 1954, EP must have been reading the German text, sent to him by Hesse's daughter, EP scholar Eva Hesse.

2. Edward VIII (1894–1972), king of England, 20 January–11 December 1936. Fritz Hesse quotes Edward as saying over the phone to Leopold von Hoesch: "I sent for the Prime Minister and gave him a piece of my mind. I told the old so-and-so that I would abdicate if he made war. There was a frightful scene. But you needn't worry. There won't be a war" (22). This incident took place when Germany occupied the Rhineland in 1936. Hesse rejects the notion that Edward's abdication had anything to do with politics or foreign policy—in contrast to **Joachim von Ribbentrop,** who shared EP's suspicions (31–32).

3. The book was published in 1953.

4. Sir Horace Wilson, Chamberlain's confidential adviser, delivered a proposal to Hitler's foreign minister, Ribbentrop. **Fritz Hesse** does not give the precise date, but the negotiations probably took place in Salzburg sometime after the Munich agreement of 15 September 1938. Wilson returned to Berlin on 26 September 1939 with some sort of offer. EP is accepting Hesse's general argument that war with Britain was avoidable and that Wilson and Chamberlain wished to avoid it. A corollary of this view is that Germany should have been permitted to absorb Eastern European countries such as Czechoslovakia and Poland. "Giving credit" means, then, that Wilson and Chamberlain wished to avoid war and let Nazi Germany do as it wished in Eastern Europe.

64. TLU-3   7 August 1953

7 Ag

O R A

IF yu get at theLuce,[1] yu might point out what god DAMN fools they were not to make use of me/ supposing (hypocritically) that they had any decent intentions. IF they had put me back on the air,[2] various p[illegible deletion] resisters wd/ have believed me/ in preference to brit/ swine yelling for assassination of Gentile[3] etc. They made no use of the knowledge I had gathered during the 600 days/[4] and are still coddling Hiss' friends/[5] What I cd/ have done for quicker tranquility wd/ have been to put 'em in touch with q a few honest italians/

instead of forcing the worst skunks into high place. etc/ alZo/ judge in Boston affirmed: no treason without evil intention. Nobody but swine like Thos Mann,[6] or Rose Benet[7] wd/ accuse me of evil intention/ whatever technical bugwash a shyster lawyer cd/ trump up. Yu do NOT strengthen a country by having double-x-ers back of the lines.

IGGURUNCE still teeming. Quite decent bloke calling bolchevism "red-fascism" on the air. this STINKS. even Hitler wasn't pro-moscow. Two parties: We will enslave you/ and B. let us pick yr/ pockets. Frank Edwards[8] on the air for 8 million trade unionists/ at least anti-bank. BUT iggurunt. Sen. Bridges[9] calling for gold. Moscow pouring gold and platinum into Switzerland. Canada got so much iron, oil, alumin, and power/ that NO conceivable bestiality can break her for 50 years. BUT the old racket of rent on nation's credit, ramps like that bloody lion in Milton,[10] and dandles the kid only in hope of dining on cutlets.

Ike wd/ do right IF somebuddy wd/ tell him. (at least I think his intentions are good). I see Pellegrini is back in Roma. Not such a good head as Bevione (if one may judge from single encounter). BUT not an idiot. At least I spose it is the Pelleg/ whom I met ONCE.

"God has need of every individual soul."[11] and to hell with Haegel.[12] whom I hv/ not read, but suspect of being source of gt. amt of buncomb. WHY did they mislay Agassiz?

fango fango riman.[13]

Nobody has translated the Paradiso with any respect to technical terms/ someone shd/ go ON from my edtn/ of Guido (not the Faber reprint, but the Genova edtn/ and essays in Make it New.[14] VII th Canto, cf/ Donna mi Prega.

anybody ever suspect Ganges, Canto XI was a hint re/ Bhuddaaaa?[15]

Fordie got OFF the progress bunk long ago/ BUT held yu got to eggzert to prevent its gettin WUSS. He was also soundly ᵱ opposed to encirclement. In fact a valuable enlightener, 10 years my elder, and having been on the spot in the middle from early age/ And when I NOW encounter the horrible crudity of the incult yanks, I begin to estimate the amount of his patience and better understand his horrified gasps of exhaustion in the face of my jejune transponaneity.[16] Kid in Aberdeen sez his prof/ verbat/ re Eliot": Huh, the man's an american. Can't write english. Doesn't know the language." end/ qt.

1. Manage to get the ear of **Clare Boothe Luce** with a petition for EP's release.
2. EP's "American Hour" broadcasts over Rome Radio.
3. **Giovanni Gentile.**
4. Mussolini's Salò Republic.
5. **Alger Hiss's** friends would be Communists.
6. Thomas Mann (1875–1955).
7. **William Rose Benét.**
8. **Frank Allyn Edwards.**

9. **Henry Styles Bridges.**

10. EP is referring to this passage in John Milton's *Paradise Lost:*

> About them [Adam and Eve] frisking played
> All beasts of th' earth, since wild, and of all chase
> In wood or wilderness, forest or den.
> Sporting the lion ramped, and in his paw
> Dandled the kid; bears, Tigers, ounces, pards
> Gamboled before them.
>
> (4:340–45)

11. This is in response to ORA's claim that she is "a Christian because Christianity proclaims and insists on the importance of human personality" (3 Aug. 1953).

12. Georg Wilhem Friedrich Hegel (1800–1893). ORA had written: "Stariolatry, derived I believe from Hegel's doctrines (which I have never read) is the modern Moloch to which everything must be sacrificed" (3 Aug. 1953). EP apparently agrees, and on the same grounds.

13. It.: "[humans were made of] mud [and] mud remains."

14. Not *The Translations of Ezra Pound,* but *Guido Cavalcanti Rime* and his essays in *Make It New.*

15. This is a reference to Dante's *Paradiso* 11.49–51: "Di questa costa, là dov'ella frange/ più sua rattezza, nacque al mondo un sole,/ come fa questo tal volta di Gange" ("From this slope, where it most breaks its steepness, a sun rose on the world, as this does sometimes from the Ganges"; translation by John D. Sinclair). EP's point, presumably, is that the mention of Ganges suggests that Dante was thinking of the Buddha in this passage. ORA replied: "[Dante's] lines are always running in my head. [. . .] sometime ago there was an article in East and West, about Dante and the Buddha, showing that Dante knew of the Indian philosophy and was referring to the B. when he enquires of the fate of the just man (I cannot here recall the lines but you know them)" (21 Sept. 1953).

16. EP claimed that Ford's "roll" on the floor upon being shown *Canzoni* in progress "saved me at least two years, perhaps more" (*Pound/Ford* 172).

---

65. TLU-3   7 August 1953

{7 Ag}

O.R.A.

CONtinuing/

You wd/ in any case not write anything idiotic/ and (B) it wd/ be extremely useful to have several facts in print set down by someone who had been in position to know.[1]

Gt/ struggle with people absolutely without circle of reference/ i.e. totally IGnorant/ still calling russians "red fascists"/

The young too young to remember Romain Rolland[2] up in Svizzera during other war, bleating about being above the conflict.

I said (radio) that I was NOT above but down under with it going on over me/ material interests in England/ no one in Ital/ forces as near me as young Angold.[3]

I was in fact working on translation into italian of a prose book of his when the partigiani[4] came to door with tommy-gun/ not at precice moment/ at that partic/ moment I was working on Mencius.

The false picture of Italy/ SMEAR so heavy that takes rock drill to get it into anyone that a FASCIST govt/ had given me freedom of microphone/ as per statement in Mercure de France.[5] (You have a copy? if not will send at once).

Dick degli Uberti wrote a good note in Merlo Giallo[6] years ago/ but one note in Merlo dont hold up against avalanche of yid lies/ note Thos. Mann STILL lying in a pocket vol/ "Seven Arts"/ and Rose Benet with THREE straight lies in a book of reference/ which Paige has spotted. (Chapter and verse if you can use 'em).

If you have freedom to print and B/[7] nerve to print it/ wd/ cert/ be useful to state exactly what I was doing/ having virtually kidnapped a microphone/

{yesterday a} young man with good intentions, getting garbled "monitorings" of discorsi,[8] starts after Pearl Harbour/ inexact/ plus lapse of time and no knowledge of what preceded, makes 'em a bit incomprehensible/ also I seem to have been more severe BEFORE the war started but in papers of small circulation or stray interviews.

The Fr Hesse bk/ wd/ give chance to mention men who tried to PREvent the war. Hesse, v. Hoesch. Edward {VIII}[9] DID stave it off for three years. Include Ian Monro[10] (M.Post corresp/ in Rome) and I think R.Packhard.[11]

at least a few tried to get the real news into the U.S.

As to being RIGHT, there is now a faint perception that Roose was NOT a blessing to the U.S./ Churchill{,} god damn him, has admitted the war was unnecessary, and wanted at the end to attack thru the Balkans. The IF they had listened to E.P. is at least proper subject for speculation/ and the NON-use of E.P.'s knowledge AFTER the 600 days is mentionable.

If you think feasable and WANT any particular details, they can be sent you. Monotti and Pellizzi and Vicari can fill in a few more/ I dont know whether v.Hoesch is remembered by ANYone. Even a man in Hesse{'s} position did not know about gas ovens till Sept. _1944_ and they were not particularly german, I mean not spirito del popolo/[12] _and_ there were _none_ in ITALY tho I have only seen ONE statement of that fact, forget if in Begnac[13] or Spampanato/ also my geo-politik to use a large word was NOT germanic/

[in margin:](read oggi)[14] Marvine H/ [illegible addition] having got out of Morocco says her opinion of same is "sobered" "tussel from crossing Libya and Cirenaica & countries where a dream was ~~in process of~~ actually being crystaliz~~ation~~ed, then someone tore up the mould and we were left a half imaginary civilization. It'll take more than a race of fonctionaires in pijamas and chemises de nuit to fulfill birthright of N.Africa.

there is a young new eye/ coming out of french sphere.

what else(?)/ La vera storia[15] will get writ sometime. The Hesse manifestly a straight statement. very much NOT in Papen[16] class. H/ saw it over Ribbentrop's[17] shoulder. von P/ considered very light (but that is not in the Spiel um D/ld).[18] We ought to have known more about Feder[19] (again a different compartment, haven't found him mentioned in the Hesse as far as I hv/ read.

Sigura in Barcelona shd/ send his t stuff to ABC./ he has translated some of it into english, but I suppose the spanish wd/ be more useful in Roma? or not?

The struggle to prevent the 2nd/ war from making a third/ ...well Korea is a police action...etc. anyhow, apparently Edward and v. Hoesch save(d) Europe three years of hell/ and v.H. died of the strain.[20] Hesse takes pains to say he saw the body and that Hoesch hadnn't been poisoned. They say, or rather bedside physician said Boris of Bulgaria[21] WAS.

Any of yr/ friends know a man named Robin Saunderson?[22] (I dont(,) but have heard him well spoken of)/ also does yr/ or any's memory touch Richatson-Hat (VERY suspicious sound) connected with the still more louche name of Reuter.??[23]

Returning to opening sentence. I shd/ think you could be about as good a witness to my INtentions from 1939 onward as anyone. Whether it shd/ go back to first meeting I dont know. or rather I dont know that it wd/ be helpful to use that chapter at this moment. Though it might. all depends on treatment. No use creating such panic and dither as THOUGHT did at that time in little Suvitch[24] (if that was his name). dd. d. d.dinamite, s-si sI, dinamite. the overall picture, possibly less timely now that the robin red-breast line.[25]

banZAI

1. ORA had written that Bottai had asked her to write "an occasional sketch of some of the people I have known, on the lines of that one on Lubin which he published"; she wanted to do one on EP, but feared "it would be stupid, as I am feeling old and tired and worn out" (3 Aug. 1953). In her next letter (28 Aug. 1953) she reported that she was doing such a sketch for *ABC*.

2. **Romain Rolland.**

3. **J. P. Angold.** As he recounts here, EP translated Angold's unpublished "Work and Privilege" into Italian, but it was never published.

4. It.: "partisans."

5. Probably "Letters from Dorothy Pound and Shakespear and Parkyn," which appeared in *Mercure de France*. This piece also included letters from the anti-Fascist journalist **Carlo Scarfoglio** and two other Italians friends of EP.

6. Weekly satirical magazine opposed to fascism; it was founded in Rome in 1924 by Alberto Giannini but suppressed in 1926. Later it began to be reprinted in France and was renamed *Becco Giallo*.

7. Bottai.

8. It.: "speeches."

9. See letter 63.

10. **Ian Smeaton Munro.**

11. **Reynolds Packard.**

12. It.: "spirit of the people."

13. See letter 58.

14. It.: "today."

15. It.: "the real story."

16. **Franz von Papen.**

17. **Joachim von Ribbentrop.**

18. Hesse's *Das Spiel um Deutschland*. After the outbreak of war with Britain, Hesse was recalled from London, fired by Göbbels, and attached to Ribbentrop's Foreign Office as an "adviser on English affairs" (89). Hence he saw the war "over Ribbentrop's shoulder." He retained this position until 1945.

19. Perhaps **Gottfried Feder.**

20. Hesse takes pains to say he saw the body and that Hoesch had not been poisoned: "von Hoesch died forty-eight hours after Ribbentrop left England. I saw him hardly an hour before his death and know from the doctor who was treating him that he was not poisoned and did not commit suicide. He died of heart failure. He had suffered from angina pectoris for years and the tremendous excitement of the past few weeks had so overstrained him that he did not survive the crisis" (24).

21. Boris III (1894–1943), king of Bulgaria, 1918–43.

22. Unidentified; in letter 70 EP mentions a Colin Saunderson, but strikes out the first name.

23. The international news agency founded by Baron de Paul Julius.

24. **Fulvio Suvich.** See also Terrell 2:571–72.

25. A reference to ORA's observation: "When I think of you in Washington I think of Blake's lines 'A robin redbreast (read poet) in a cage—puts all Heaven in a rage'. Such stupidity is unpardonable" (3 Aug. 1953).

66. TLU-3   2 September 1953

Sep 2

O.R.A.

good GOD, O.R.A.

have I got to start on YOU, to keep even YOU from swallowing the god damned lies of the same god damned liars who lied re/ Mus and Adolph. There is no witch hunt[1]

They lie about McCarthy, the press in the hands of dirty jews and worse goyim does NOT mention Jenner[2] and the quieter men who AT LAST, after 30 years are so/ smoking out some of the lesser vermin/ and within the last ten days have even got to the larger swine/ noticing that U.N. was founded in treason. Pegler runs a lone hopeless BITCH-hunt, still swatting at Eleanor horse-fyce/ BUT the liberal pewk who never mentioned freedom of expression during the twenty years from Sowbelly's entrance into the HiteWhouse/[3] howl when one looks into THEIR treason/ black and slimy.

No credit YET to the men who saw Moscow a quarter of a century ago/ no spot light on the fools and worse who sold out the occident in lust ~~from~~ for world power and the abolition of the heritage of the charters.

One bother is that Luce[4] was among the boosters of FDR/ Boy I trusted to get some spare copies of T.Herald[5] got absorbed in his own troubles and didn't. However leading art/l telling truth re U.N. saying Truman not a traiter (merely product of small town crime), but too stupid to see what was going on/ and Ike idem.

charity etc/ The little squirt from Mo/[6] set off the atom bomb AFTER Japan was ready to quit/ but at any rate he is OUT. And let us hope Churchill will get a bloodclot and Eden die of leprosy or some physical manifestation of soul's putridity. Any how dont YOU start swallowing press howls.

AND when someone starts gathering honest men/ they may have an Italy. quia impossibile est.[7]

Seems that I did a lot of needless work/ as apparently the blasted huns had got an even clearer idea of money than I had heard of their having. New bk/ labled Hit's private conversations/[8] but seems that some Feder was also translated in 1932/ but one didn't heard of it in our little provincial circles.

As to south wop's I remember a voice in Milan: "Why shd/ we be under those niggers?"[9] Di dolor Albergo di Lusso.[10] P/a cat/[11]

As to Gregory/[12] probably a repentant pink/ now scared and going with the current/ Marvelous scene here a few years ago/ repentant ex-edtr/ New Masses[13] with half empty quart cylinder of whisky and his taxi driver, a charrming jew who merely threw up his hands during interview saying: "No, one will ever believe it."/ yes, yes, the VERY pink who had shut free discussion out of the "organ" of marxism.

I am still waiting for you to catch me a serious adult who will turn his mind to a few BASIC issues. Can Bot/ YET mention the folly of paying rent on the nation's OWN credit. OR face some of my notes on tax SYSTEM. OR print definitions of USURY. You might start on that, giving it as my definition.

A charge for the use of purchasing power, levied without regard to production, often without regard even to the possibilities of production.

Did yu see Rouver on the Medici Bank? got it past one of the damn ENdowments/ but they later denied knowledge of any book on the Medici Bank/

Alzo it wd/ save time, when treating of Moscow betrayal of labor/ to keep the issue to antithesis of Homestead and Kolschoz.[14] If true that Lenin was nauseated by way things were going in Russia, cd/ emphasize that Moscow did NOT attack capital. but merely attacked the homestead.

Pella[15] got better face than old Gaspers.[16] I never cd/ swallow that caricature of DeValera's[17] ugly phiz. AND I wonder when some of the lowest slime will be putt OUT.

General, whazzis name TOLD FDR there was treason and FDR did NOT bother/ he then told Truman with equally negative result. Lubin's virtues have blinded you to the possibility of their being less virtuous jews/ at least a few. AND it took nigh onto 40 years to make a bullseye re/ Woodrow/ also damn him. Tho less leprous than Frankie DR

The sane tax is on stagnant money/ it is unavoidable via Gesell/ it is the fairest, it costs least to levt, it does not make crimes out of simple and normal actions, transport etc/ and thence lead to expensive police to STOP transport of say diamond{s}, or put up the price of booze.

Some of yr/ bright entourage OUGHT to get news from north of the alps re/ what the Gesellites are doing.

Manning[18] was boycotted by brit/ press at coronation BUT Amery[19] seems to have presided at some meeting/ so that perfumes Canadian air, and no Coty/[20] one must get further detail/ tho some parody of Social Credit, or even some half measures bearing Doug/ite lable continue/ McCormack[21] calls it "funny Money". AND so on.

{of} course if either Bot/ or Pella want to USE my immodest talents all they need to do is to ASK for 'em/ and manage the transport?

P.S. Did I mention the Scotch mohamedan's impractical suggestion

---

1. EP is upset at ORA's characterization of the activities of Senator Joseph McCarthy's House Committee on Un-American Activities as a "witch hunt" (28 Aug. 1953). Obviously EP enthusiastically approves of McCarthy's motives and tolerates his tactics.

2. **William E. Jenner.**

3. Roosevelt's inauguration day was Saturday, 4 March 1933.

4. **Henry Robinson Luce.**

5. *Washington Times-Herald;* presumably Luce supported Roosevelt, whom EP liked even less than he liked Woodrow Wilson.

6. Missouri.

7. Lt.: "which is impossible."

8. EP means *Hitler's Secret Conversations.*

9. ORA had written, "the South Italians are the best" (28 Aug. 1953).

10. It.: "The sorrow of a luxury hotel." Apparently the prejudicial statement was heard in a luxury hotel.

11. Presumably "Pegler is a Catholic."

12. Professor Gregory, an American who visited ORA in Rome with his wife and who commented unfavorably on the McCarthy Committee, something she had reported in a letter of 28 August 1953.

13. We do not know which editor of *New Masses* is meant here.

14. See letter 18.

15. **Giuseppe Pella.** ORA had written, "I rather like the Pella ministry" (28 Aug. 1953).

16. **Alcide De Gasperi.**

17. **Éamon De Valera.**

18. **Ernest Charles Manning.** EP thought he should have received more attention from the British press during his attendance at the coronation of Queen Elizabeth II in 1952.

19. Probably Leopold Charles Maurice Amery (1873–1955), Conservative British statesman and author of *Thoughts on the British Constitution* and *My Political Life.* He is also mentioned in letter 71 and in a letter dated 31 December 1953 but not included here.

20. Not a perfume made by François Coty (1874–1934).

21. **Robert Rutherford McCormick.**

67. TLU-3   8 September 1953
8 Sp/

ORA

Any means of communicating with Rob. Paribeni who in "Il Nazionale {9 Ag}" shows awake to bestiality in attempt to eliminate study of greek and lat/{.}[1] DRIVE going on all over/ usury gang subsidizing study of languages WITHOUT literature/ oriental etc/ the{y} abolish the classics/ teach the young that environment is everything/ i.e. all decent example hidden/ no stimulus to doing anything of interesting/ slave morale driven in/ Paribeni O.K. but shd/ correlate/ no attempt visible anywhere to estab/ communication between honest men in the DIFFERENT countries.

You cling to yr/ rotten vatican from lack of seeing nature of corruption/ worsening ever since bible fad set in. Old test/ almost without decent examples/ men no good get whores to assassinate etc/ cf/ Kumasaka.[2]

All of which started when I intended (I mean the above pp/ started) when I meant to write hammering on AMOUNT of Cavalcanti in the Divina Com/ which I hadn't reread carefully since editing Guido/[3] in which action I found intelligence when a mediaeval theolog based himself on greek and lat/ and mess whenever he dragged in jewsih confusion.

Renaissance from Gemisto Plethon[4] at council of Ferrara/ next uplift from Intorcetta's trans/ Confucio/[5] via Leibnitz, Voltaire.[6] AND mess, Miltonic hogwash etc/ whenever they got to jew book/ fervid eroticism and african rhetoric/ NO order, beaucoup plus corrompu les esprits que les moeurs.[7] Cybelle, sex fad/ and decay of language/ bible reading inculcates barbarism/ and Zielinsky[8] finally shows that all decent catholic DOGMA is from greek not from kike. Chas. ~~LL~~ II. sd/ to hv/ tried to RESTORE the language after the Cromwello-miltonik mess.[9] Think it is Mme Genlis[10] who mentions that. dunno what her source.

If they had read Dante and Sophokles they wd/ NOT tolerate filth at the top like Roose and Winston. Anyhow, more power to Paribeni. Am still trying to find another serious correspondent in Italy. Adolf's table talk now in english.[11] He and Feder MUCH clearer re/ money than were the woptalians of the ~~Decennio~~ Ventennio. Might have saved me time had I know it/ but some advantage in having DelMar. me and them all working without collusion. May be was the ONLY subject on which Adolf WAS clear-headed.[12] Anyhow Hesse[13] notes his hysteria/ and Hesse deaf and dumb re/ econ/

AGAIN, is there anyone in Bot's gang capable of watching, quoting, translating the small amount of intelligent writing that gets printed (or writ) outside the geographic expression.

Yes, jew/ no ethics/ leviticus[14] as racket to collect fines for priests and levis/ trade mystery of butchers of lesser cattle/[15] neither discipline of hunting tribes (courage needed)/ not splendour of Mithra,[16] also bull ring daring/ the villain of the piece the agriculturalist Cain/ really a rotten root. I know people don('}t know where to go from thaaar, and as Geo/ Washington sd/ the benevolent effect. Yes, I HAD noted Don Camillo[17] in Candido or whichever weekly, and was about to agitate for translation when I found someone had already transd/ and was publishing a vol/ of Don C.

OBviously, if yu dont define usury/ and don't see opposition of homestead and kolschoz.[18] And let the skunks get away with discovering muscovite character NOW, with no ref/ to people who have been mentioning the dirty subject for 30 years. NO good polemical writing drat. it.

One point up, Moscow now calling Adenaur[19] a fascist. and the term progressive given with stink re/ pinks in Korea. "Why are all usurers liberals?"

Do hammer the DEFINITION into yr/ pupils, muddle thru 18 years of church councils, TRYING to get to border line: Usury a charge for use of purchasing power levied without regard to production, often without regard even to the possibilities of production.

Young French[20] dug into Plutarch's Moralia/ better than Cato but NOT included in Loeb library/[21] (in which XREIA,[22] demand{,} is mistranslated, lest Aristotle's good sense on that point shd/ reach the under-grad. Gibbon[23] just story book. Mommsen did note that Rome more durabl than Assyria because settled veterans in homesteads/ but all historiography now outof date until it recognizes Alex DelMar. Western heritage: Blackstone and Agassiz. And damn nuissance I cant sit on head of some minister of education yu might mention this to Monotti, it is nonpolitical and he not a TOTAL damphool. somewhere amid the wreckage/ 8 years damned interruption. (or not). Eng/ Institute making an effort. will try to get program for you.

Saluti to the young/ when is Malu going to nuptuate? and so forth.

The Cavalcanti in Dante subject wd/ be VERY good for some y.m.'s[24] thesis. IN fact there is plenty of work to be done, live jobs instead of bunk. Emery has translated La Sibylle,[25] and Davenport[26] says he WILL trans/ Erlebte Erdteile.[27] BUT there could be a LOT more intercommunication, and more concentration on the FIRST rate authors. as distinct from fads and parrochial celebrities. Both Yeats and Santayana had perception of this need for a canon, a *basis* of study/ not an attempt to limit curiosity, let 'em read whatever trash they like/ but hammer in a few authors that matter. Didn't Dante FUNCTION in the Risorgimento?[28] or am I in error on that pt/?

1. ORA replied that **Boris de Rachewiltz** would be bringing **Roberto Paribeni** to see her. She, too, deplored the neglect of classical studies and wanted to establish an "Italo-American Committee for the promotion of classical studies," which stemmed from EP's 1953 declaration to correct the neglect of classical studies that was signed by several equally alarmed American professors (2 Feb. 1954). ORA planned to ask Paribeni to get "the Ministry of Education here to take the initiative in founding an Italian Vergilian Society to match the American one my friend Mary Raiola (Swiss American in spite of her Italian name) was instrumental in founding in the U.S." (21 Sept. 1953). In a letter of 18 November 1953 ORA reported that Boris had met with Paribeni and Professor Magnoni, of the Ministry of Education, and Professor Morey, formerly the cultural attaché to the American embassy. ORA eventually helped organize the Committee for the Defence of Classical Culture, which was "a section of the Comitato internazionale per l'Unità e la Universalità della Cultura, founded some years ago. [. . .] The president is Prof. Paribeni, the famous archaeologist, for Italy, and Prof. Morey for U.S.A." (2 Feb.

1954). ORA later wrote EP that her committee was designed to "support the effort made by Mrs. Raiola at Cumae (Villa Virgiliana) and by yourself in the U.S." (14 Feb. 1954).

2. In the Noh play Kumasaka's "spirit returns to do justice to the glory of Ushiwaka and to tell of his own defeat" (*Translations of Ezra Pound* 248). As EP explains in *Guide to Kulchur*: "The ghost of Kamasaka returns not from a grudge and not to gain anything; but to state clearly that the very young man who had killed him had not done so by a fluke or slip, but that he had out fenced him" (81).

3. *Guido Cavalcanti Rime.*

4. **Gemisthus Plethon.**

5. EP presumably has in mind Prospero Intorcetta's *Sinarum Scientia Politico-Moralis.*

6. Gottfried Wilhelm von Leibniz (1646–1716) and Voltaire are invoked presumably as celebrated "atheists" or debunkers of Christianity.

7. See letter 18.

8. **Tadeusz Zielinski.**

9. This is not only a reference to John Milton's role in the government of Oliver Cromwell but also to Milton's language, which EP despised for being Latinate and "unnatural." Charles II was restored to the British throne in 1660, eleven years after his father's execution by Cromwell.

10. **Comtesse de Genlis.**

11. *Hitler's Secret Conversations* was published in London as *Hitler's Table Talk.*

12. ORA responds thus: "I suspect Hitler's intelligence about currency was due to [Hjalmar] Schacht who was a kind of financial genius" (21 Sept. 1953).

13. EP is referring to Hesse's *Das Spiel um Deutschland.*

14. EP refers approvingly to Leviticus 19.35–36 in cantos 74 and 76. See also letter 21.

15. See letters 47 and 71.

16. Mithraism was a Persian cult that spread through the Roman legions in the second century A.D. when Christianity was making inroads amongst slaves and servants. Mithraic ritual involved the slaughter of bulls, as opposed to the sheep, or "lesser cattle," slaughtered in Hebrew ritual. Mithras is invoked in cantos 23 and 76.

17. ORA had recommended **Giovanni Guareschi's** *The Little World of Don Camillo* as "a very good and true" book (28 Aug. 1953).

18. See letter 18.

19. Konrad Adenauer (1876–1967).

20. **William French.**

21. The first of the fourteen volumes of *Plutarch's Moralia* with an English translation by Frank Cole Babbitt appeared in the Loeb series in 1927; the series was not completed until the late 1960s. The Loeb volume *Marcus Porcius Cato on Agriculture and Marcus Terentius Varro on Agriculture*, translated by William Davis Hooper, appeared in 1934.

22. Gk.: "use." According to EP, the word is used by Aristotle to mean "use" rather than "demand"; he therefore challenges H. Rackham's use of the term "demand" in his translation of Aristotle's *Nicomachean Ethics* (*Guide to Kulchur*

324)—this, of course, is another example of EP's insistence on the importance of correct terminology. Here is the passage EP has in mind: "And this standard is in reality demand, which is what holds everything together, since if men cease to have wants or if their wants alter, exchange will go on no longer, or will be on different lines. But demand has come to be conventionally represented by money; this is why money is called *nomisma* (customary currency), because it does not exist by nature but by custom (*nomos*), and can be altered and rendered useless at will" (5.5.11).

23. Gibbon's *History of the Decline and Fall of the Roman Empire*.

24. Young man's.

25. A translation of Zielinski's *La Sibylle* was published in English in *Edge*. The translator is not credited, but apparently it was Clark Emery.

26. **Guy Davenport.**

27. This proposed translation of **Leo Frobenius**'s *Erlebte Erdteile* never appeared.

28. ORA responded: "Certainly Dante 'functioned' in the Risorgimento. Mazzini was based on Dante" (21 Sept. 1953).

68. TLU-2   20 October 1953
20 Ott

O.R.A.

O.K. Vergilian soc/ (with an e for an i[1] etc.)

IS yr/ friend[2] capable of considering the USE I *might* have been to, say, the American Academy in roMA IF the goddam ploots weren't sewed up in a bag.

Does she belong to the kind of latin prof who is HAM iggurnent of everything else but the ACADEMIC list of roman authors OMITTING, say, the prose which gives away something, and fearing confronto[3] with the greeks?

Virgil a 2nd/ rater in cf/ with Homer. Dante a FIRST rate writer in confronto with whomsodam.

Not that I wd/ raise this point to blight the Virg/ Soc/

With a little imagination/ ORA consider what I COULD hv/ done, re/ bringing actual american and other talent to roma/ while the Am/ Acad/ was being merely a centre of ignorance, utterly unaware of CONSTRUC-TIVE work of the ventennio/ and still worse of the first decennio[4] of it.

Yu may hv/ to re-adjust in face of DEFINITE words uttered by Adolf/. Schacht[5] a squirmy character, friend of Montague Norman[6] etc/ MAY have revealed some his knowledge of fact and real econ/ only because Adolf was behinf him with a red hot poker/ I.E.Adolf saw thru the swindle and drove Schacht into honesty for a while/

Of course Adolf an hysterik/ and Wagnerian BUT acc/ current vol (of which I have as yet seen only quotes, BUT GOOD quotes), (he saw.)

IGGURUNCE/ arty circles neglecting Aristotle. Ever hear of Franklin

Pierce (not the president pre-Lincoln) wrote "Federal Usurpation," Appleton 19~~10~~08.[7] putt it on yr/ reading list.

as to banks/ NO book on econ that I hv/ seen has noted what one waited to see in Ripley's daily caricature "Believe it or not.{"}}[8] question IF yu borrow at 4% and lend at 6% what is yr/ rate of profit. {i.e. 50%} {of course it is an annual rate, BUTTTTTT why not face it) and the Bunks multiply it by TEN/ and for centuries education does NOT "struggle" against or even mention it.

Did I mention Tasso's vol/ on econ/ (naturally he went to bughouse.)[9]

Yes, the brit/ crits are purrLight re/ translations NOW. [illegible deletion] All but a few pages of the vol/ are 30 years old).

Star sez: Duke of Bedford's death "almost certainly" accidental/ sez he interested in socialism (the opposite of Social Credit) and then sez Soc/ Credit is acc/ their definition Gesellite (Doug/ hvg allus opposed Gesell, and the silly Soc/ Cr/ papers in Eng/ almost boycotting all gesellite thought, though Aberhart[10] applied exaggerate{d} form of stamp scrip, which OUGHT to disgust anyone, but didn't{,} as the first stamp-scribes were too IGGURUNT to see error of weekly stamp (sometimes at 2%, 104% for use of money, nearly as outrageous as ordinary bank infamies).

IF they had read Dante and Sophokles they would NOT have tolerated filth at the top.

Does M.Raiola[11] MEET anyone?

yes/ Dante re/Bhudd. O.K. and yr/ ~~next~~ third quote[12] SO applicable to the present ambas/e

"the Dean of radio commentators"[13] here suspected no irony or humour in Stockholm red comment that Nobel to Winston was snub to Ike "who had also written a book".[14]

I dare say the banderlog will be too bashful to comment. At any rate Shaw and Gide make a nice trinity with W.C.[15] {'}Oly, ole, Ole.

1. EP is correcting his spelling of **Mary Raiola's** society and, of course, punning on "an eye for an eye."

2. **Mary Raiola;** see letter 67.

3. It.: "comparison."

4. It.: "decade," that is, 1922–32.

5. **Hjalmar Horace Greeley Schacht.**

6. Montague Collet Norman (1871–1950), president of the Bank of England, 1920–44.

7. In his book Pierce pleas for the sacredness of the U.S. Constitution.

8. "Ripley's Believe It or Not," a syndicated cartoon featuring hard to believe facts. Apparently EP found the bank profit quiz in the cartoon.

9. Torquato Tasso (1544–95), Italian epic poet who suffered from mental instability that resulted in two separate confinements. We do not know of a volume on economics.

10. **William Aberhart.**

11. **Mary Raiola.**

12. ORA's third quotation is "Luce intellettual piena d'amore": "Intellectual light full of love" (21 Sept. 1953).

13. **Westbrook Pegler.**

14. Churchill won the 1953 Nobel Prize for literature for his six-volume *The Second World War*; Dwight D. Eisenhower's book was *Crusade in Europe*.

15. George Bernard Shaw won the Nobel Prize for literature in 1925 and André Gide (1869–1951) won in 1947.

69. TLU-1   31 October 1953
31 Ott 52

ORA

Are you getting an italian edtn/ of Hitler's Table Talk (title here, H's Secret Conversations")?[1]

Crazy as a coot, as Mus/ noted on first me{e}ting him. BUT with extraordinary flashes of lucidity. He smelled the idiocy of judeo-xtianity, but had no basis either in Aristotle or Confucius.

first impressions of quick perception/ Justification of germans who tried to bump him off/ AND of those who saw need of strong Italy to balance the Neitzsche-Wagner teuto-bobble wobble.

On the whole, NO ethical basis. Not to say that Italy didn't produce a punk named Macchiavelli. Lucidity without clarity. Churchill just the same [illegible deletion] kind of grabber and without any extenuating charm.

Admiral D/: "our obese dove of peace"[2]

If there isn't a wop edtn/ I shall probably have to send you the american one, which wd/ probably be a waste of a few bucks, as an ital/ vol/ wd/ cost less. Whether anyone will have the guts to print Mullins' reviewm which contains the gist of H's monetary sanity, remains to be seen.

The Hesse vol/ is presumably to be trans/d into eng/[3] (Not Hess, as Swabey mis-spells it in his note)[4]

I 'haven't Picchio's address,[5] but he must be in phone bk/ Can you phone him to get the Hesse, and review it. I was glad to learn re/Venice beano, that Pic/ hadn't been liquidated by your Gasping demi-doodlers.

also my saluti, which I cant send him without an indirizz[6] (or for that matter a prenom, at least I dont seem to remember anything but his patronymic.)

Brit/ reviewers being purr-light re/ collected translations/ and what causes that it is largely that it is all 30 years old, save a few pages.

Adolf had alzo a lucid moment re/ soja. plus some disordered profundities/ a quick or sharp mind rather than a powerful one.

desire for truth, NOT hitched to e{t}hics. Hold on, most of the above not definitive judgement. Got to finish the book and hunt for more exact expression of my estimates.

Mus/ cd/ never have gone off vol-plane into unreality and illusion, in that manner.

a watch if it loses balance wheel, buzzes. wd/ not sporadicly recover and then lose the cog. etc. ad interim as if inebriated with Napoleon's remark "A little bit of imagination re rules the world." which he hasn't yet quoted and prob/y never read.

defective sense of specific gravity {gravities plural}. Mus/{,} I shd say{,} erred from blindness re/ human character in specific instances NOT from failure to compute relative weight{s} of what he had actually thought of.

1. For ORA's response, see letter 70.
2. Domville's description of Churchill in *From Admiral to Cabin Boy*.
3. Hesse's book was translated by F. A. Voigt; see letter 63.
4. EP is presumably referring to a short article by **Henry S. Swabey** enclosed with the letter; it is not extant.
5. ORA does not know this person (18 Nov. 1953). This is EP's second reference to Picchio, previously referred to as "ole Picchio" (letter 25). He is probably **Ruggero Pier Piccio**.
6. *Indirizzo*, It.: address."

70. TLU-3   5 November 1953
5 Nv

ORA

Verg/ with an e/ a damn fad of 50 years ago/ HOWEVER that is nothing to boggle over.[1] The thing for la Raiola to do is to WEEP on the steps of one of these lousy foundations. To conceal any clean idea she may have UNTIL she has got in/ they are dripping with usurious gains/ now people are beginning to see that they play into hands of Moscow/ so they wd/ prob/ like something in the way of non-russian facade.

Why don't she try sobstuff on INTERCULTURAL Relations, 655 Madison Av. New York 21. don't mention me or anything clean/ but sob over Vergil/ Frazer's Golden BowWow[2] etc.

Flood the Int/Kulch/ with whatever printed or personal matter she can lay hold of.

Too bad yu dont remember names of any ADULTS left in the U.S./ what the sons of hell gain is VIA keeping decent men relatively incommunicado.

* * as to Italy/ WHEN will anyone get round to reprinting selection from my Meridiano di Roma stuff. The Hitler Conversations[3] very lucid re/ money/ unfortunately he was bit by dirty jew mania for World DOmin-

ion, as yu used to point out/ this WORST of German diseases was got from yr/ idiolized and filthy biblical bastards. Adolf clear on the baccillus of kikism/ that is on nearly all the other poisons. but failed to get a vaccine against that.

As to the juggyslaves/[4] Colin (or Robin) something or other was present when the lousy Randolph C/[5] was selling the idea of betraying Mihaelovitch[6] to his greasy Nobel prized progenitor/ and was nauseated. At any rate that is one of the definite bits of history that I have at close range from the lady to whom ~~Colin~~ Saunderson[7] related it.

Believe that is his name, but dont repeat it/ as I may not be supposed to know where the news leaked from. He has since got out of Parleymoot.[8]

Good luck to Malú and her Gigante.[9] She has copped one several inches larger than the original.

The Gesell has a LONG past/ Jesuits in Paraguai Guernsey Market House/ american colonial currencies. Jefferson's note to Crawford.[10] Gesell and Rossoni's remark which ADDED (whether he realized it or not). Cosi lo stato fa il suo affare.[11]

If I had known enough about Feder and Adolf I might have convinced more wops/ Del Crox got the id{e}a INSTANTLY/ you might remind Bottai, that DelCrox AT ONCE, beat on his head with his artificial hands, shouting "Che MAGnifica idea!"[12] Grabbed phone and told Bottai: "Come over here, I got a man I want you to meet."

UNfortunately, destino, Bot/ was that moment leaving his uff/o[13] to catch train for Naples.

Does he remember telephoning to Turin Library re/ Vivaldi/ librarian was out then. but the Vivaldi matter proceeded. Just recd/ Michigan program/ 7 or more Vivaldi items, in program of 10 or 11 pieces.

Nuisance that yu have NO american reliques with nome/ cogn/ and indirizz/[14] It is slow work making contact with INDividual adults.

Will Helen's pubrs/[15] send review copies to american mags/ At least to Hudson Rev/

any hope re/ Riccardo Luzzatto? who is being married by an excitable red-head of my acquaintance?

QUEER company. as he has worked for the vermin.

BUT....several dupes have seen a little light during the past 8 years.. no idea whether R.L. is among them.

A little iron{y} MIGHT spread, even in Longanesi's[16] wobb{l}y, re/ awful horror of american press re/ russians STILL practicing habits of Katin/[17] other ox gored this time. some sort of rat poison for the men STILL in power who suppressed information re/ real nature of Moscow and the eternal squalor of russians.

One rabbi AT last calling Eleanor a liar// are you going to use THAT as argument re/ holiness of high kikery? what about TIMING?

I dont see why Ford and Fullbright shd/ shy away from Virgil (a harm-
less and anodyne subject)[18] at least it wdn't be direct support of Moscow/
STIMULATE study of American history (avoiding everything sent
during Sowbelly's reign) but asking about Franklin Pierce:[19] "Federal
Encroachment {Usurpation}", 1908 and [illegible deletion] H.R. Fraser's
"Democracy in the Making" 1938[20]
Aren't any of yr/ hopefuls capable of reviewing the real american au-
thors/ or reading DelMar/ AND reviewing old Domvile.[21]
benedictions
Fraser note{s} that Biddle[22] embezzled $400,000 and in 1831. Randolph
of Roanoke[23] seeing idiocy of nation borrowing its own money.
WHY nobody objects to being diddled out of the USEFUL parts of
knowledge beats ~~ne~~ me.

1. Another indication of EP's concern for exactitude in speech.
2. Frazer's *The Golden Bough*.
3. ORA's response to EP's inquiries is direct, terse, and uncompromising: "I have
not read Hitler's Table Talk and do not know whether an Italian translation is
being published. But do not trouble to send it to me. [. . .] I look upon ~~as~~ Hitler as
a madman, and a dangerous one; it is all very well to speak in a more or less flip-
pant way of 'better deads', but when from such talk one sets down to really kill-
ing off all those belonging to such categories as one can lay hands on, it is a case
of criminal lunacy. Besides, as articles in the Ecrits de Paris, reviewing books by
some of the German Generals, show, he was a megalomaniac and ruined his own
plans by his idiotic behaviour" (18 Nov. 1953).
4. Yugoslavs.
5. Randolph Churchill, Winston's son.
6. **General Draza Mihailovitch.**
7. See letter 65.
8. Parliament.
9. It.: "gigantic." **Malù** had used the term to refer to EP, but here EP applies it
to **Malù**'s fiancee.
10. Cited in canto 89/593: "'And if bills be bottomed . . .' sd/ Mr Jefferson/ loc
cit to Crawford 1816." "Loc cit" is **Thomas Hart Benton's** *Thirty Years' View*.
William Harris Crawford (1772–1834), a native of Virginia, was elected to the
Georgia senate in 1802 and then to the U.S. Senate in 1807 and 1811. In his letter
to Crawford Jefferson calls for the issue of paper money by the government to
replace gold and silver. To this day, U.S. currency is issued by the Federal Reserve,
a government consortium of private banks. The failure of successive U.S. administrations either to issue money directly or to establish a government bank is a
standing grievance of EP and other monetary reformers. See also letter 118.
11. It.: "thus the state makes his business."
12. It.: "What a magnificent idea!"
13. *Ufficio*, It.: "office."
14. *Nome, cognome,* and *indirizzo*, It.: "name," "surname," and "address."
15. The Richards Press, publishers of **Helen Rossetti Angeli's** *Pre-Raphaelite
Twilight*.

16. **Leo Longanesi.**

17. Katyn. See letter 44.

18. EP is suggesting the Ford Foundation and Fulbright fellowships as possible funding sources for **Mary Raiola's** society. The Ford Foundation was established with gifts from Henry Ford and Edsel Ford and at this time funded work on international affairs, communications, humanities, and the arts. EP would have been familiar with it through **James Laughlin,** who worked for the foundation for five years during the 1950s and edited its magazine, *Perspectives.* The Fulbright fellowships were conceived by J. William Fulbright and instituted in 1946 to promote better understanding between the people of the United States and those of other countries.

19. See letter 68.

20. Fraser's *Democracy in the Making.*

21. **Sir Barry Domville.**

22. **Nicholas Biddle.**

23. **John Randolph.**

71. TLU-2   1 December 1953

1 Dec 53

Yes, my Dear O.R.A. BUTTT[1] we shd/ ask WHAT kind of a bloody lunatic, and what druv him/ and NOT allow *ourselves* to be intoxicated by the very filth of propaganda[2] which you so rightly deplore. The POSITIVE lucidities which revived the whole of germany by enthusiasm/ the 6 months blind in hospital[3] knowing no one/ NO high connections/ the mass of kraut stupidity opposed to him/ now, even the sowbellied ape FDR must hv/ had some knack to get hold of the unfortunate americans/ some opposed imbecility, and republican idiocy, such as double x/d 'em into nomination of Wilkie[4] (to the surprise of a official, out-in-front republicans.) AND one must place pore Adolf in proportion to the two loathsome tops/ FDR and W.C. neither of whom EVER was under hammer of necessity, or in ANY misery, or suffered five minutes from sympathy with the multitude. NEVER five minute agony for the state of the people. Chakravarty[5] two days ago, said re/ feeling in Germany after the other war/ YES, Tagore[6] felt that. He was there. The misery after that defeat, the effect of blockade famine on the children. The "Conversations" are a totally unknown Adolf, A/ NOT in public. From internal evidence I opined that he went off his head in the last six months, when he was OFF german soil. Then looked at rather narsty introd/ where this was confirmed.[7] In general, believe one shd/ always read/ introds AFTER reading a text. Extra precautiob against being lead by propaganda-lice. Thank gorr. N.Pork[8] is without newspapers, if only for ONE day. even a strike CAN be useful. As for Amery,[9] it is with difficulty that I attribute good motive to the old hawg. BUT he has biblic/ precedent (or di Abe get stopped in mid figliocide?)/[10] As for your chosen/[11] they seem by statistic to hv/ been chosen to supply about 90% of the moscow agents highly placed in the Goosen-stein govt. to sell civilization down the road. AND of course, the one valid myth in Xtianity, is that the kikes crucified, same old mass hysteria. And by "myth" I mean a relation that recurrus, time and again/ the true myth is something that repeats/ and is figured by a great metaphor. Nacherly yr/ kikery crucifies. Age old opposition of butchers of lesser cattle[12] to the growers of grain. The agriculturalist the villain in their fable. And none of the skill needed to bull-kill for Mithra. Or the bravery of the hunting tribes. Tone of Adolf's talk nearer that of Gourmont's notes in the Mer-cure de France years ago. Franchement ecrire ce qu'on pense.[13]

I didn't think the stuff in Virgil as clear as some of the straight Gesell writing. I dont know whether you have even had Gesell's own book??? Which did NOT get round to looking at the stamp scrip from STATAL[14] pt/ of view. One flash of Rossoni's, to COMPLETE Gesell's system. or rather G/ hardly got to a system. Was still working on land question, and left it unfinished. Doug/[15] SAW the tax element, but wanted to sell his own brand of medicine, and failed to perceive the amelioration of all tax-ation methods inherent in G/ Adolf notes price of bread stable 500 {as against fluctuating metallic component of coins.} years under Hanse/[16] 400 in Venetian republic. A man's going nuts does not free one from re-sponsibility to his preceding lucidities// AND then, look at all that Wag-nerian Nietzschean morass/ Goring sending 24 vol/ of Nietzc/ to Mus/[17] ahj/// Did I say bilFF dug up passage in a Webster play, showing Wb/ had presumably seen Intorcetta's trans/ of Confucius?[18] Alzo/ cf/ the Hindoo blither (I was irritated into looking at some last week/ and they were murmuring about the Qho'ran[19] on the air. ALL of which is simply low-er savagery in cf/ China. Young man/ here thinking of entering Inst/ Orient. studies in Roma/ I have passed on the E.West/[20] {their bulletin} Have you their address, so that I can tell him where to write.

returning to Krauts/ Wyndham Lewis in 1914 wrote approx: the ger-man is now so stuffed with rhetoric that he never knows whether he is one of Attila's horde or Diesel engine. TIME Bottai and the rest of 'em began to assert function of those who ~~stopped~~ started RESISTING the jew-N.Pork-Moscow octopus back in the 1920s/ Despite yr/ sainted Lubin/ there have been too MANY of 'em, from Berlin to N.York, to MosKu. And Lubin, even on yr/ evidence did NOT see the need of stabilizing grain price in terms of SOMETHING STABLE. Re/ the Venice, and Hansa/

Coppola[21] might start speculating as to whether a stable ratio between wheat and Barley AGAINST the government ticket (i.e. monetary inte-ger of account) wdn't free one from need of ANY other regulations.

That is not a declaration, it is a query.

One of the few honest starts of the Spew Deal, was Doc. Warren's[22] commodity dollar/ price index complicated.

and Warren died, and the pewks took over. Development credit is fairly Hitlerian/ but there was Paraguai and the Guernsey market house/ And american colonial paper. and abe Lincoln/ however name doesn't matter if they will chew on the Dantescan line re/ QUIDITIES, knowledge of same (as opposed to mere nomenclature).

Virgilian[23] is a nice tame label/ let 'em take on some of the more pertinent classics as well/ Cato/ Varro/ Demosthenes on rascality/ and Aristotl (being ware of mistranslations in the "Loeb" edtn.

1. EP is responding to ORA's opinion of Hitler.

2. ORA had written that it is the mind-conditioning techniques of the modern world (radio, television, the cinema, advertising) that are destroying modern people (18 Nov. 1953).

3. This is an exaggeration; Hitler was badly gassed in October 1918 and rendered blind for several days; he recuperated in a military hospital at Pasewalk.

4. **Wendell Lewis Wilkie.**

5. **Amiya Chakravarty.**

6. **Rabindrinath Tagore.**

7. EP is referring to comments about Hitler's state of mind after Stalingrad in H. R. Trevor-Roper's introduction, entitled "The Mind of Adolf Hitler," in *Hitler's Secret Conversations* (esp. xiv–xv).

8. New York.

9. See letter 66.

10. EP refers to Abraham, whom God tested by asking him to kill his son (see Genesis 22).

11. ORA's "chosen" are presumably the Jews.

12. See letters 47 and 67.

13. Fr.: "Write frankly what one thinks."

14. *Statale*, It.: "state's."

15. **Major Clifford Hugh Douglas.**

16. EP is referring to the following remarks in *Hitler's Secret Conversations:* "The example of the Hanse inspired all commercial and industrial activity of the Middle Ages. That's how the price of bread could be kept the same for four hundred years, that of barley—and, consequently, that of beer—for more than five hundred years; and this in spite of all the changes of money" (374).

17. See letter 55.

18. See letters 61 and 67.

19. The Koran.

20. *East and West*, a journal mentioned several times in the correspondence.

21. **Coppola d'Anna** had recently published a negative review of an enquiry into unemployment in the south of Italy by a Parliamentary committee. ORA suggested that agricultural reforms along the lines of those recommended by **Giulio Del Pelo Pardi** would do the trick. See letters 33, 59, and 81.

22. **George F. Warren.**

23. A reference to **Mary Raiola's** Vergilian Society.

1954

72. TLU-2   21 January 1954
21 Jan 54

ORA

Have got back yr/ Girl among Anarchs/ from the only clean pair of anarchists I know of in this defiled country.[1] They at least reject the fruits of capitalism/ do own farm work and printing, I spose their offspring is headed to make trio/ tho Dachine thinks Holley is a bit afraid I will turn him into a Jeffersonian democrat.

I dont know whether the foulest mess in U.S. has spread his unclean Pulitzer prizes aroma to Italy/ prob/ no jew (well that is t extreme statement) let us say few jews are likely to sink to the subMontale level of P.Viereck./ son of an unruly father something (Sylvester) or other Viereck/[2] The younger has treated his father badly/ and no need to go into origins/ but he is as foul a liar as Orwell/[3] and a sycophant/

Yeats sound (on) danger of contamination from attacking filth. War vs/ militant socialism/ eng/ gets socialism and U.S. militar-ism etc.

Now as far as I remember I never mentioned germany on Rome radio/[4] can't of course remember every word of 600 and more discorsi/ But I doubt if anyone [illegible deletion] save a Spew-Dealer can twist anything I said into praise of gas ovens.

AND the lie to that effect is the very soul of Rooseveltism and the party line. Whether anyone in Italy yet dares tell the truth re/ Roose and Mussolini I dont know. But certainly the sillies(t) smear is that which calls Mus anti-kike. Cant someone do a vol/ on the role of jews in the Fascist revolution/doing it as praise and constitution.

Terminology/ and yet again TERminology/ antithesis of homestead and kulschoz.[5] Fake of Moscow, pretending to attack LeihKapital[6] and really attacking the homestead.

Watch the Times Lit/ Slop for a review of Fritz Hesse.[7] I dont know that it will ever appear. BUT keep an eye out for it, and get it translated or commented in ABC (if ABC still exists.)

Also you may not have seen Jefferson quoted on Fascist posters/ I DID. and if it was not propter it was at least POST.

To my mind one gt/ mistake of Ventennio was cutting loose from Risorgimento/ la rivoluzione continua/ in sense of continuing revolution.

Leopoldine/ 1776, Risorgimento. And the Pe(s)ce-Gorini or someone shd/ take up that line of my defence.

The free enterprisers are silly not to stress Torlonia pre-fascist bonifica/ that is the process, from the time of Crassus(') fire companies in RomAAAAA antikaaaa.[8]

Somebuddy might stretch a hand to the honest few in England/ not that Washington or London has or would ever look for honest italians. that wd/ be too much to expect/ However at least one good brit naval man refers to Mr Churchill by the more general interpretation of his initials.[9] ORA

Yes/ re Dachine/ I distinguish these real ones, from the larger anarchis{t} sheet run on capitalist money. Scott[10] died and some Single Tax idiot[11] has got hold of his paper. The illiteracy of monetary reformers almost justifies the stand-pat-ers.

Kenner has done nice mopping up operation on Blackmur,[12] but we need still MORE criticism, even in purely licherary domain. The pompous presumption of apes, and the custom of inexact rapportage/ Vierick ~~as~~ worse than Montale/ ~~another~~ A quite decent jew has done a blurb full of inexactitudes. but not malicious (tho of course he was let in NOT as an interviewer..) AND these half educated blokes do NOT hear what is said to 'em.

Fack even worse, I think I reported, I wrote him from town jail mentioning [illegible deletion] Tremaine (comptroller of N.Y. in 1939)/ and he prints it TRUMAN

which alters the sense, and attributes to the haberdasher much greater awareness of reality than ANY god damn Spew Dealer will ever attain to. Possibly helps the lunacy idea. But still there ARE historic facts NOT dependent on my incarceration.

Ike going toward corporate state[13] etc/ quite unaware/ in fact the influence of C.H.Douglas and Benito is most entertaining.

Shift to govt. by radio instead of by press is all to the good/ but Fuhrer Prinzip[14] moving by leaps and bounds. Fult. Lewis[15] perceiving that the electorate is NOT sufficiently informed to vote on all issues. etc.

People like Pellizzi better go CULTURAL/ revival of Dante studien, and Mazzini. for at least 3 years/

Has Edwards[16] sent you his bulletin{?} I dont want to be connected with it in any way/ but other people shd/ support it. Sent free, quarterly. Incidentally the jew psychiatrist (I think it is plural) at any rate one assured me he hadn't learned anything new about Cantos from recent talks by Berryman and Flemming/[17] and another puzzled as to how anybody cd/ find 'em antisemitic. Certainly the synagogue in Gibraltar and the Old Levy in Freiburg[18] give the ebreo[19] a fair chance.

BUT the effect of old testament etc/ ~~a fake religion/ or~~ something that shd/ be relegated to anthropological research NOT considered a path for 1954. Lower than African ~~leged~~ legend/ and used to corrupt filthily the greek ideas in Xtian mythology. Muddle on Muddle. [illegible deletion] Did I say I startled the gt/ Marianne M/[20] into admission that: Christians are NOT interested in truth. Pity that ~~the~~ so large a % of the literate christers and tied up to Fattycan. Prot/ism alzo impossible, tho presbyterians give lip service to honesty, re/ let us say everything but money. You have or haven't read Brooks Adams?

Best to Helen. When did you say Malu was to git spliced?[21]

1. EP had lent **A Girl among the Anarchists** to **Dachine Ranier** and **Holley Cantine**. The book was returned from California with a note on letterhead of the Catholic University of America, San Rafael, Calif.

2. **Peter Viereck** and his father, Sylvester. EP is probably reacting to Peter Viereck's appointment (beginning in 1955) to the newly founded chair in American poetry and civilization at the University of Florence. In a letter to **Boris de Rachewiltz**, dated 18 August 1954 (NYPL) EP wrote: "Just read that Peter Vierick is going to lecture at Univ. of Florence/ warn Pellizz and EVERYbody that he is one of the vilest bits of meRRda produced in Baruchistan. and treated his own father like a dog. Total nastiness and shd/ be ostracIced."

3. George Orwell.

4. In fact, he did.

5. See letter 18.

6. Gm.: "loan capital."

7. It was reviewed anonymously in the *Times Literary Supplement* (see "German Onlooker"); also see the response in a letter to the editor by M. H. Fischer (12 Feb. 1954): 105, and letter 74. ORA had already promised to get Bottai to review the book in *ABC*.

8. *Roma antica*, ancient Rome. EP is referring to **Marcus Licinius Crassus'** so-called protection racket, reported in *Plutarch's Lives* (2.4).

9. EP, of course, means "W.C."

10. Probably Howard Scott (b. 1890), American engineer and founder, with Thorstein Veblen, of the technocracy movement, which advocated an "Energy Certificate" to replace currency. He and Veblen formed the Technical Alliance, a group of engineers, scientists, and technicians based in New York in 1919. That movement disbanded by the midtwenties. In 1932, Scott formed the Continental Committee on Technocracy with Walter Rautenstrauch, chairman of Columbia's Department of Industrial Engineering. The movement attracted a great deal of attention. Among its recruits were Harold Loeb and Charles A. Beard. Scott then formed Technocracy Inc., which was widely accused of Fascist tendencies. Although suffering from schism and adverse publicity, Technocracy survives in pockets to this day.

11. A follower of **Henry George**.

12. **Hugh Kenner** defended EP against R. P. Blackmur's strictures as found in "An Adjunct to the Muses Diadem."

13. For information on the Corporate State, see letters 54 and 55.

14. "Führer Principle," the totalitarian idea that all authority derives from the leader.

15. **Fulton Lewis**.

16. John Hamilton Edwards, editor of the *Pound Newsletter* and coeditor, with William V. Vasse, of *The Annotated Index to the Cantos of Ezra Pound.*

17. John Berryman (1914–72) and **William Fleming.** For a report on Fleming's EP activities in Melbourne from 1953 to 1957, see Fleming's "The Melbourne Vortex."

18. In canto 20/89–90 EP relates his visit to the Provençal scholar Emile Lévy in Freiburg. Apparently Lévy was Jewish. In canto 22/104–6 he recounts a visit to a synagogue in Gibraltar. That this last anecdote could easily give offense underlines EP's obtuseness about his racism.

19. It.: "Hebrew."

20. Marianne Moore (1887–1972).

21. ORA had written on 26 June 1954 that **Malù** was to be married in October. On 12 August 1954 she clarified that Malù's marriage to Aldo Mingoli would take place on 7 October 1954. On 25 September 1954 ORA wrote to thank the Pounds for their wedding present.

73. TLU-2   6 February 1954

6 Feb 54

ORA

RICORDI has brought out Pietro Berri's "Indice Discografico VIVAL-DIANO," and this COULD be USED. He pays proper attention to Olga's work/[1] but there are other points which he does not know. To credit both of yr/ anon correspondent and to the Regime. I don't know if ABC is the place to print 'em. But at least gli amici[2] shd/ bear 'em in mind, and FIRE when opportune. After O.R.[3] had been to Torino, Luchini[4] took me to Bottai. I told him of the Turin collection[5] and he AT ONCE grabbed phone, for long distance. The Librarian was out/ so there was no instant effect. but the "deplorato regime" put up a mezzo milione[6] to publish the Viv/

The Regime, as you are aware, Flopped. I TOLD the republica cisalpina.[7] Mez/[8] said "buona iniziativa".[9] I indicated that Malipiero[10] was north of the dividing line and ~~had the~~ waas "indicato" (or -issimo).[11] The Republica Cisalp/ lasted long enough to get Malip/ started/ and the momentum carried him and his friends into glorious edition (I think it is now 150 concerti, but am sure they have done 75.)

You can probably vouch for part of the facts/ i.e. that I had NO contacts in Roma after Rapicavoli's untimely death.[12] Cam{e} down specificly to stimulate microfoto record of treasures in Italian archives/ musical/ literary/ historic. CULTURAL activity. Even Bot/ may know (or if not DiM[13] cd/ tell him) that my writings were certainly NOT dictated, I mean what I wrote in Meridiano, was as *you* know, in considerable contrast to les idées reçues.[14]

That is INFORMATION, and the sooner it can be jammed thru the punk curtain, the quicker. The spew-deal lies are no longer as popular as they were. Theheran and Yalta[15] are not spoken of *universally* with admiration/ THO the slime left by [illegible deletion] Sowjowl still covers a good deal of arable land.

Mr White's[16] bust has silently disappeared from the library of the Internal. Monetary Fund. And the Times-Herald suggests removal of FDR's messy mug from the dime. But there is a lot of strength still left in the sodomites.

Any of yr/ circle old enough to remember Benton's "Thirty Years View"/ shd/ be required in curricula. am finding it late.

W.H.Davis[17] "the super tramp" (poet) had another re/ Algernon[18] on putney heath/ indignant nurse-maid: "Narsty old man, 'e sharn't look at MY baby."

alzo. returning to kulch/ Vicari or Monotti might remember that I used several unparliamentary expressions re/ radio music/ and finally got 'em to use Vivaldi...[illegible deletion] all the discs they HAD..along with my discussions of Brooks Adams and other suitable topics.

50 years ago there were some Benton's in Rome, grandson I take it of the Senator, wonder if you encountered them? Think the pat/ famil/ had got connection with "Old England" (preSelfridge invasion of Roman market), that wd/ hv/ been about 1902.

Never heard of Morey/[19] the OLD profs/ in this defiled nation are still ANTI-/ definitely a GANG against the whole "movement"/ non-civic/ petrified/

The life went into the little reviews/ the old ones simply merchandise/ and vast bribes to those who will drift, oppose nothing, and clog. However the YOUNG (i.e. them about 50) are getting into the current.

Good article on poesia totale, in La Nazione, 22 Jan.[20] Hope Drummond can get some spare copies/ and let yu see one.

Die Tat 7/ Nov. Weltwoche, (Zurich) Jan 15 contain munitions.

how come yu got nevvy Named Dennis?[21]

best to Helen.

Long regretted I never got to Putney, but everyone I knew said Watts Dntn submerged it, [illegible deletion] etc. I didn't know he had broken in on Landor.[22]

1. **Olga Rudge's** work on preserving Vivaldi's manuscripts. See letter 45.
2. It.: "friends."
3. **Olga Rudge.**
4. Probably **Alberto Luchini.**
5. The Turin Collection of Vivaldi Manuscripts. See letter 45.
6. It.: "'deplorable regime,'" "half a million."

7. Probably a reference to the Salò Republic.

8. Probably Fernando Mezzassoma, minister of popular culture in the Fascist government.

9. It.: "good initiative."

10. Probably Gian Francesco Malipiero, a musician and composer.

11. It.: "manifest," "most manifest."

12. It is not clear which member of the noted Italian family EP has in mind here. The name also appears in canto 93/630.

13. **Cornelio di Marzio.** The writings were not dictated because the journal's editorial board declared that it did not agree with or condone EP's opinions.

14. Fr.: "received opinion."

15. Site of Allied conference in November 1943.

16. **Henry Dexter White.**

17. **W. H. Davies.**

18. Algernon Charles Swinburne (1837–1909) lived at Putney.

19. See letter 67.

20. EP refers to the same article on totalitarian poetry in letter 74, attributing it to M. Ris.

21. ORA had mentioned her great-nephew Emmanuel Dennis and his sister, Helen Dennis Guglielmini, children of **Helen Rossetti Angeli** (2 Feb. 1954).

22. **Walter Theodore Watts-Dunton** nursed Swinburne at Putney and encouraged him in his writing. Mollie Panter-Downes reports that Watts-Dunton's "beloved master" was **Walter Savage Landor,** "into whose confused ears he had poured the torment of his homage when he threw himself at the feet of the older poet in Florence in 1864, on the second of his visits to Italy" (*At the Pines* 36–37).

74. TLU-3 NYPL   23 February 1954
23 Fb 54/

ORA/

recd/ clipping.[1] Does ANYone who gets injected with Marx or {H}en. George EVERY return to lucidity? Possibly those who drop Marx IN-STANTLY when they meet something better. I see it is E*rne*sto di Marz-io/ so I suppose the news that Cornelio[2] had been bumped off was correct. Anyhow Ern/ does NOT look anything like C/ If you are meeting via the classics[3] ANY educative functionary{,} IS there ANY use of discussing THOUGHT with him? The basic objection to communism is that it is from Moscow/ originally hired by yr/ beloved goddam kikes in N.Y. or elsewhere. Anyhow it can now be treated under heading FUORI i barbari/[4] goddam hrusskys/. A fake, as bad any other kikery/ pretended to attack Leihkapi-tal and attacked the homestead. ANY any attempt to deMuskivize wop commies shd/ be based on that distinction. Geographic formation of Italy ruling out communal farming everywhere save in a chunk of flat land verso[5] Foggia etc. la tovagliera[6] {(}or whatever they call it). AND there ought to be enough latin logic even in the most arrabiati[7] to SEE that.

Of course yu hv that old ulcer on Monte Vat/[8] which will hold down on compleat sincerity/ IF it gets a whiff of it. Nevertheless if you have any logical friends, like Pari[9] and Scard/ It might be time to consider the basis of the Sq/$ [illegible deletion] series.[10] Next Item is a chapter from Benton. To keep Parib/ etc. from one track mindedness. Par/ to hammer on gk and lat/ YES/ but in conversation etc to suggest the use of historic studies/ even those of the U.S. (sanity in which can be sd/ to stem from Tuscany and the Leopoldine Reforms/ so far as I know no wops HAVE yet emphasized, or even acknowledged that connection. AND the force of the much vaunted local pride, cd/ be mobilized.

Idiocy of the IkeMinistration/ seems to steer 'em onto ALL the Roosevetian filth/ and away from the one decent idea smuggled past the "boys from St Louis". Evidently the Brannon plan[11] made sense, I haven't g yet got a copy, so dont take this hint as final/ but Bran/ SEEMS, acc/ report{,} to have "had something". and God bless McCarthy.

The foulness of ALL liberals is that so far as is nknown, none of the bank buzzards and bootlickers EVER advocated freedom to speak {for} from anything save whiggery in its worst forms. Alzo, as enquiry, have any of the alledged historians in europe YET got rid of de Toqueville,[12] the visiting fireman? A damn bore anyhow which prob/ renders him dear to the universitaires. Lot of waste wor unnecessary work done by honest men during past 60 years, because they had NOT read the Benton "Thirty Years View"/ I wonder if there are three copies in Italy? Seems when Clem vii (or some other of 'em) sent block of marble for Washington monument, the local fanatics bust it up and chucked it into the Potomac.[13] Does any wop listen to the socalled Voice of America, sd/ to be directed at victims back of the iron curtain? One needs 200 ears. Seriously{,} does Scard take an interest in education? Lot of yap here re "MORE", but no notice of quality, or selection of EDUCATIVE text books.

Do wops read the U.S.Constitution? any conversation re/ camera elected by trades, and senate by provinces.{?}

believe ALL {most} representative votes are {now} too large. but haven't examined state legislatures and state senates, here. Anyhow, a senate of 26 and camera of 120 wd/ probably be more useful. with articulation on down, so that everone cd/ know someone who can speak to someone further up in the hierarchy. I may have missed a sentence/ but the MSI[14] seems to avoid the BASIC issue, and skate round on the surface. Bonifica, Torlonia, plus the regime/ O.K. not a{n} MSI patent.

AND the idiots still quoting ma Perkins,[15] I suppose unconsciously, and she one of the worst Rooseveltian stenches.

they might at least catch up with 1930. or EIGHTEEN 30. Randolph of Roanoke, Calhoun already debunked some of the hogwash. As did, naturally, Jackson, Benton, VanBuren.

Manion[16] on air, a little excited, but on the right track, both he and Bricker[17] mention the CONSTitution.

Did I outline Dante revival? correlation with Mussato/[18] development of PRECICE terminology from Cavalcanti. Caval/ got to pensiero filosofico/[19] Dante to pensiero ~~CIVCCO~~ CIVICO.[20] However far Guido had got on that line we don't know, or at least I dont, never heard of any further available data. That art/l in La Nazione shd/ be USED.

Very amusin note in London Slobserver/[21] the snarling pup Conolly[22] beaten into his corner, still grumping. WATCH for Times Lit Sup/ review of Das Spiel um Deutschland.[23] Blgn[24] says they have printed one (i.e. Blg's). I wait to see what B/ has been able[illegible deletion] to get past ½Price, OR been himself able to grasp. NOBODY in Italy reviews the right books YET.

and so forth, best to Helen
and the young

1. ORA had included in her letter of 14 February 1954 introductory remarks written for the newly organizing Committee for the Defence of Classical Culture. See letter 67.

2. Ernesto di Marzio is unidentified. ORA wrote on 28 March 1954: "Villari who came round this afternoon tells me that Cornelio di Marzio was killed in some shooting affray."

3. ORA had reported that she would be attending a reception in Rome in connection with the Committee for the Defence of Classical Culture (14 Feb. 1954).

4. It.: "barbarians out!"

5. It.: "next to" or "across from."

6. It.: "the napkin."

7. It.: "angry."

8. The Vatican.

9. Probably **Roberto Paribeni.**

10. **Square $ Series.**

11. **Charles Brannan**'s plan, which called for direct government income assistance to farmers and limits on assistance to big farms, was brought to the House floor and incorporated into a high-supports bill sponsored by Representative Stephen Pace, but was defeated in the Senate by a more traditional plan sponsored by Representative Albert Gore.

12. Alexis, Comte de Tocqueville (1805–59). Apparently EP does not share the nearly universal admiration for his *De la démocratie en Amérique.*

13. According to Pamela Scott and Antoinette J. Lee, "Construction of the monument was halted at about 170 feet, in 1855, following the theft of a stone donated by the Vatican and the consequent reorganization of the [Washington National Monument Society]" (101). Since the pope at the time was Pius IX, EP was just guessing at the name.

14. **Movimento Sociale Italiano.**

15. EP is mixing a reference to **Frances Perkins** with one to Ma Perkins, the heroine of a radio soap opera of the day.

16. **Clarence Manion** presented "The Manion Report," a weekly radio broadcast, from Southbend, Indiana, presenting a conservative analysis of public affairs.

17. **John William Bricker.**

18. **Albertino Mussato.**

19. It.: "philosophical thought."

20. It.: "political thought."

21. *London Observer.*

22. Probably **Cyril Connolly.**

23. "German Onlooker." See also letter 72.

24. **Montgomery Belgion,** apparently the reviewer of Hesse's book, although his name does not appear with the review.

75. TLU-3 NYPL   3 April 1954

3 Ap 54

O.R.A.

Yes if somebody like yr Taylor[1] had the courage to enter these precincts, but the sheer terror of american adults/ PLUS what in Ruskin's day was called philistinism. beyond imagination UNTIL experience shows it. A few know ENOUGH to be frightened. The mass is brainwashed.

There is an H.J.Taylor[2] on the air, bien pensant.[3] IF some foreigner with a philosophic mind wd/ EXAMINE the american diseases/ which are now an universal peril/

one of 'em is the bloobheaded natr/ of the business man/ incapable of supposing a man of letters knows any history and is qualified to think about government. Plus the plutocrats inf/ cx/[4] and infantile jealousy of any gerarchia[5] based on mind and not on $.

Against this as plus value, the touching gratitude at level of bighouse attendant, for Square Dollar books. Of course an exceptional character, worried about a greek testament. Plus a black quoting the Analects. Monarchism, requiring CHARACTER who WILL do no wrong. Democracy on supposition of an INFORMED electorate/which should drive the informed to educate the BLOODY electors.

I dont suppose you cd/ drive YOUR Taylor into conversation? We NEED controversial writers/ who are not afraid to read DelMar, Frobenius or even Mullins. Bit of Benton now in press/ smear campaign, {100 years} silence re/ both B/ and VanBuren. Lack of knowledge of sequence/ Kung/ Intorcetta, Leibnitz, Voltaire, Leopoldine reforms, 1776. Geographic division {of U.S.} THEN having rough connection with DIFFERENT interests and knowledges.

Dulness of anti communist propaganda, which fails to set HOMESTEAD against kolschoz.[6] civilization is from the podere,[7] the homestead. Mary writes that yr/ slimy DeG/[8] is trying to break up fibre of the Tirol/ I never did like that bloke{'}s phiz, OR DeValera's.[9] The old whore seems to produce that [illegible deletion] type of profile. The baby face is another type that I am reluctant to believe in. Dear Violet[10] re/ Churchill at dinner table. "Looks as if he hadn't been properly BORN." Await the Howells[11] with interest.

A worried and bewildered prof/ complaining that politicians dont *represent* him/ dont know whether he had been started on that line by my writing.

They will {use} mental package p deals NEVER specific facts and dissociations.

Princeton Univ/ just done "Idea of Usury "/ Villari ought to write for a review copy/ I DOUBT if the bloke, B.N.Nelson[12] DEFINES the term "usury"/ but he has a long list of reference, that WOULD have been useful 20 years ago/ Del Mar only serious omission. It wd/ be useful to have the book reviewed/ and the omission (if it exists) correlated to my definition. Bk/ only came yester and I cant interrupt more useful reading. B.N.N. does mention Salmasius.[13] Ambrose,[14] Antonino.[15]

CONfound Vicari, he OUGHT to have called on you but he is jeune homme modeste,[16] that is to say he started with the refinement of the Exarchate, and hasn't got over that pleasing characteristic. Villari might write to Princeton Univ. Press, Princeton N.J. they wont be getting many foreign reviews/ AND it wd/ be a useful way of getting a toe hold. The bastards now accept me as a critic of LITERATURE i.e. the safe ground, based on stuff I wrote 30 years ago. which even pups like Conolly[17] on Sunday Times (London) cant go on pretending "ain't there".

Bottai MIGHT be driven to sneer at talk about fascism (communist-fascism) and such camouflage combined with silence re/ all specific points/ such as vocational representation. Has yr/ Taylor courage enough to face question of Federal Reserve/ and the infamy of Wilson and SowBelly? Benton died in 1858. so yu wont have any personal memories/ am not sure the homophones in Roma{, 1902,} were his nipots.[18] but surmise so.

One must ALSO provide for the contingency of NOT being hydrogen'd. Last night's radio optimism was a bit thin. They haven't yet material ENOUGH for a h. bomb that will annihilate the *whole* planet. BUT as they have already reduced NECESSARY expense from thousands $ per ounce, to a few bucks per lb/, that lact of fissionable material shd/ not be considered as permanent. proGGGressooo,

yr/ final Handschrift P.S.[19] is nearly indecipherable but have at last made out the first sentence. AND now the 2nd.

If I cd/ persuade you not to waste yr/ time on hack work UGH/ and IF either Eng/ or It/y cd/ organize a forum for REAL exchange of ideas, exchange of REAL ideas/ NOT ignoring Del Mar/ Frobenius, Zielinsky,/ quite a back log of stuff that OUGHT to be printed in english and that NO editor has mind enough to include.

A man like Taylor OUGHT to meet Pomeroy,[20] even if he dont dare look in on y.v.t. what is his address? I wont write to T/ but Pom/ could, without implication. Hesse reply to Fisher is admirable, but Belgion not sure he can get it printed. Has Villari reviewed Hesse? or will he or would Bottai/ wop prejudice vs/ Krauts is NOT constructive. Civilization comes from the Medit/basin and from the Middle Kingdom/[21] some of it did cross the Alps/ whether roman pride likes to admit it or not. AND caput mundi can only aspire to being head IF it draws knowledge (DETAILED knowledge) into it.

P.S. copy of yrs/ to Taylor just arrived/ question: to ask him stop here and collect news for whether yu think useful you on his way to Roma/ or more discrete to wait till you see him, and THEN mention the opprobrious name {& send news hither.}

1. **Henry C. Taylor.**

2. Probably **Henry Junior Taylor.**

3. Fr.: "sagacious."

4. Inferiority complex.

5. It.: "hierarchy." Fascist party officials were known as the "gerarchia," much as Communist officials were known as the "nomenclatura" in the Soviet bloc.

6. See letter 18.

7. It.: "farm, small holding."

8. Presumably **Alcide De Gasperi.**

9. **Éamon De Valera.**

10. **Isabel Violet Hunt.**

11. ORA had written EP that Helen's *Pre-Raphaelite Twilight* had just been published (28 Mar. 1954).

12. Nelson's *The Idea of Usury.*

13. Claude Salmasius or **Claude de Saumaise.**

14. **St. Ambrose.**

15. St. Antoninus (1389–1459), whom the Italians would call "St. Antonino." In an essay EP wrote, "There was a lot of hard mental work done in the millennium between St. Ambrogio and St. Antonino but I don't think our historiographers have yet given us a competent analysis of the period" (*Ezra Pound/Japan* 164).

16. Fr.: "a modest young man."

17. Probably **Cyril Connolly.**

18. The Bentons in Rome. EP surmises they might have been nephews ("nipots") of **Thomas Hart Benton.**

19. ORA's handwritten postscript reads: "P.S. re American hangers on of Preraphaelitism, someone sent it to Helen, so don't trouble to send me. Of course you are right. Geography makes Italy individualistic; communal farms impossible in a country where nothing but loving individual care can secure results. Am distressed over the turn things are taking in Egypt" (28 Mar. 1954).

20. **Eugene C. Pomeroy.**

21. China.

76. TLU-1 NYPL   23 April 1954
23 to ??th Ap 54

ORA.

Thank Hel[1] for How/l. Or in more decorous language more comprehensible to the patrons of the Richards Press. Be pleased to convey to your distinguished sister H.R.A. my thanks for her "Story of Charles Augustus"/ I wonder if she ever saw the memoirs of "old Lukie" Ionides, which my belle-mere extracted from him, by taking 'em down in long-hand?[2]

Pub'd in "transatlantic review" by Fordie? I saw quite a bit of old Ion/ along 1917–20. when he was in low fortune/ never met the opulent parts of his fambly. There is, or was, a set of transat/ in Rapallo. Heaven knows whether they can be dug up without personal intervention IF Helen wd/ be interested?

* * *

Nothr point/ a gang of Rosicrucians in Calif/ listing Dante as one of 'em. Hv/ yu any light on this.{?} alzo they claim Mazzini whom I tho't was a mason/ at least they know of some respectable authors and use a candle-stick with 3 (NOT 7) branches.

I don{'}t recall Valli[3] saying rosy-cross, but have v. hazy memory what he did say/ his theory seemed plausible UNTIL he gave illustrations. also they don't mention Yeats, their largest publicity agent for a number of decades/ must find out if he got expelled for OBstreperosity. All good poets prim/ sec/[4] Ghibbeline. (or do you demur?)

Any of yr/ PIOUS f{r}iends worried re/ a frog priest named Lubac[5] (I think is the name) playing round the bHHuDDist fringe or zummat. Henri de Lubac, or zummat.

DO get someone to encourage Jenks or Rural Economy for putting Guernsey on his front cover. (Market House)

Does someone/ Bot/ ABC or SOMEwop eggschange with Jenks? and IF not WHY not????

The U.S. being revived by a Tennessee lawyer named JenKINS.[6] first sign the old stock isn't extinct.

* * *

Frater Viennet[7] has just brot in an old copy of Blackfriars (Monthly Rev. of Eng. Dominicans, which yu may know) May 1951, I find Alan Neame doing laudatory article on E.P. BUT making most erroneous staements.[8] In view of which IF the Vatican radio talk by Martins IS translated, or when it is/ I think it would be useful to send a copy to the address apparently simply Editor, Blackfriars, Oxford.

with accompanying letter, mentioning the Neame article and saying that the economy is not stated with proper conformity to E.P.'s statements. This not out of any desire to mislead the reader either as to E.P.'s ideas or to economics. Mr Neame's statements could be made exact with alteration of a very few words. IF they are interested.

Neame also correct re "faith" but wd/ be clearer if he drew definition line between faith and dogma, the latter jeopardized by linguistic expression ANY how.

    1. **Helen Rossetti Angeli.** EP has received "How/l," Helen's book on Charles Augustus Howell.

    2. EP's mother-in-law, Olivia Shakespear (his "belle-mere"), took down Ionides' "Memories."

    3. **Luigi Valli.**

    4. Probably *primo cento*, Lt.: "the 1100s."

    5. **Henri de Lubac.** EP may be thinking of *Le drame de l'humanisme athée.*

    6. **Ray H. Jenkins.**

    7. In letter 77 EP calls him "Viannet." Although the spelling of his name is unclear, he is a Franciscan brother who taught at Siena College in upstate New York and brought books to EP at St. Elizabeths.

    8. EP is referring to **Alan Neame's** "Ezra Pound Reconsidered," a review of EP's Money Pamphlets. For more information on the Money Pamphlets, see Gallup, *Ezra Pound* A40b n., A46 n., A50b-c, A51b, A52b-c, 53b, and E2r.

77. TLU-3   13 May 1954

13 Maggio

O.R.A.

For the comfort of Mrs Raiola/[1] on the purely Utopian plane/ ONE Material solution re/ Cumae, might depend on mere question of visas/ D & I wd/ have to live somewhere and pay rent/ IF ever the grip of Dexter White's friends were loosened. I have long cursed the IMBECility of the American Academy in Roma, in NOT becoming a centro internaz/[2] Had they not been dominated by Boston fugg/[3] and ploot loathing of the arts/ etc. They wd/ YEARS, not say decades{,} ago have let me use one of their kennels. This not in disparagement of the Aldritches,[4] or VanBurens/. How much room is there at Cumae?? I wd/ want place for two, plus 2 guest rooms/

And rent on same cd/ go to the general upkeep. No need to rely on the stinking ploots/ IF the Ecclesiastic and Statal authorities can get round the strangle hold the kikes and hroosians still have on the yellowlivered yanks and pry yr/ tottering friend out of buGGhouz.

I am sufficiently catholic to swallow the lable/ Yester/ If found John Randolph (of Roanoke) re/Aeneas, the Sir Chas/ Grandison, prince of coxcombs.

BUT after Gavain Douglas[5] put him into scotch there is melody in it.
I wdn't need pay, perfectly willing to talk to a FEW humanizable students
re Sophokles, Dante, and the tripod leading to Dante, or Dant's immediate precursors/ [illegible deletion] R.StVictor (Bro/ Viannet[6] promise to
tote round a Migne vol/)[7] Mussato/ Guido/ etc.

Glad Bottai has showed up/ Three moments/ to refresh his memory/
phone call from DelCroix, he may not recall{,} as I dont think DelC/
mentioned name of "Hi, I got a man here I want yu to meet." That was
DelC/ re/ me/ and "/gh che Magnifica idea" (i.e. Gesell). B/ just leaving
office to catch train for Napoli. 2/ B's phone to Torino, re/ Vivaldi ms/
librarian out at moment/ BUT subsidy granted for printing Viv/ 3/ Bottai poker face [illegible deletion] presiding or at least holding down a
meeting in Siena/ the Ventennio BANG. vs/ eighth century (prima del
Mille)[8] or whatever it is that IS the Sienese state of mind.
        **

The manner in which all yr/ blasted Kropots.[9] (IF he does, I haven't read
him) but all the godDAMN'D liberal yappers except Mazzini (who is
something else yet again) AVOID the main disease/ and the MAIN po font
of sovereignty.
        et cetera/
Vocational representation the NEXT mechanism/ nemico, l'ignoranza.
directio voluntatis/[10] from Mencius thru Dante/
Nasty snarl from F.Edwards, {Frank not J.H.},[11] AFL/ air noise/ continual crab/ Clothing makers union apparently very sane union/ Pegler has
sense enough to know union corruption is a nuisance and NOT ignore
existence of unionism/ god knows what the Universities have done save
progressively ROT for past 50 years.

Yap about quantity of schools/ very little about WHAT shd/ be taught.
Freedom congress in I think it was Omaha/ various groups/ Minute
Women, etc. mentioning the Constitution/ and crablike sidle of a few
profs/ admitting existence of J.Adams, VanBuren, Jackson.

Met Sturzo at Wickham Steeds,[12] who cheerily introduced me as an
"ardent fascist"/ Sturz went away sorrowful and Madtame Hrose saidt:
{"}He iss a ferry hgreatt zoul."

Cant reproach him (Sturz) for being at Steed{'}s, I was there myself. In
fact one of my founts of education. OBservation post during, forget when
it started 1915 possibly. Steed got ONE artl/ of mine into the Slopliment/[13]
then Richmond[14] came home from vacation and plugged THAT spira-
glio.[15]

Mary says the acero[16] is growing/ at least those at the castle. Havent
yet seen "il Caffe".

recd/ Boris 2 Scarabei/ and typescript on "Istopatologia"/[17] let us by all means cultivatione ambition as well as maples and peanuts/ Riforma ecclesiastica/[18] a sane university a Napo'i.[19] The damBrits/ are bubbling re/ unpoisoned food etc. US Radio yelling for unbleached flour/ evidently to be ADDED to the recompensing chemicals as a top dressing in {"}bon bread{"} or "bond bread"/ loss of consonants in the yittomurkn langvitch[20] making it impos/ to tell exact name of that patent product.

I dont think McCarthy can take on much MORE at the moment. But ABC might add a cultural page, not question of amount of print, but to concentrate the AWARENESS.

Lore[21] says Cologne broadcast {Ez po'try} on the 9th. or thereabout. I dont know whether she was on Vanni's[22] list. She had hoped to do 40 cantos/ but has got thru 20/ along with short poems I dont know quite how many. Address at moment Lore Lenberg, bei Frau Luck

Steinackerstr/ 4, Freiburg i/Br/

ABC ought to be sent complimentary to Rev. Henry Swabey

The Rectory, Port-Perry, Ontario, Canada.

he will prob/ return to Eng/ in the summer, but no lo use Bot's losing a good possible correspondent. He reads Ital/ tho wd/ have to be translated/ Bot/ cdn't get better correspondent {his own stuff}

for Canada now/ and Eng/ later.

1. ORA had told EP how wonderful it would be for him to reside at Raiola's Cumae villa and act as a modern-day Socrates to her Vergilian Society (9 May 1954).

2. It.: "international center."

3. Probably "obfuscation."

4. **Chester Holmes Aldrich.**

5. **Gavin Douglas.**

6. See letter 76.

7. EP is thinking here of three texts, all originally edited by J. P. Migne and included in his *Patrologia Latina:* Richard of St. Victor's *Benjamin Minor* (vol. 196, cols. 1–64) and Paul the Deacon's *Ad Langobardicam Historiam* (vol. 95, cols. 419–32) and *Historia Miscella* (vol. 95, cols. 739–1144).

8. **Pierre Mille.**

9. In a letter of 9 May 1954, ORA recommended Leverdays's *Les assemlées parlantes* to EP, which **Prince Peter Kropotkin** had recommended to her as "a destructive criticism of the myth of popular representation."

10. It.: "inimical to ignorance."

11. **Frank Allyn Edwards.** "J.H." is John Hamilton Edwards, mentioned below as ORA's visitor. See also letter 72.

12. EP is probably referring to a meeting with **Father Luigi Sturzo** that took place at **Henry Wickham Steed**'s home in London.

13. EP's "The Poems of Cavalcanti."
14. Unidentified, but presumably Steed's superior at the *Times*, and no admirer of EP.
15. It.: "opening."
16. It.: "maple tree."
17. Works by **Boris de Rachewiltz.** "Scarabei" is *Scarabei dell'antico Egitto.* We do not have a record of "Istopatalogia."
18. It.: "ecclesiastic reform."
19. It.: "in Napoli."
20. "Yit-American language." EP is alleging that American English is heavily influenced by Jewish speech.
21. **Lore Marianne Lenbergis.** At this time Lenbergis would have been working on her Ph.D. thesis on the *Pisan Cantos* under Hugh Kenner. However, EP may be thinking of a translation of *The Cantos* into German. We do not have a record of such a translation.
22. **Vanni Scheiwiller.**

78. TLU-1   29 May 1954
29 Maggio/

ORA
recd/ copies yr/ translation Martins. Omaggi,[1] etc. Enc/[2] signs p.c.[3] of minority sanity/ Valle not yet nominated/ whether ANY use in getting wops to notice the several decent organizations now demanding clean govt. and the obliteration of Dexter White's friends/ incredible that Ooozenstink and Morgenthau shd/ not have collaborated with D/W. etc. Anyhow, the putridity is beginning to annoy several yanks/ and McCarthy increased {"}ventennio of treason{"} to "21 years of treason" in his phillipics. Gawd bless him/ and he has built well in so far as not the dirtiest s,o.b. in the HiteWhouse camorra[4] can pin the anti-yitt lable on him.
"Minute Women of U.S." gets out perhaps sanest paper/ some of the others fairly raw/ and wasting time on non essentials.
Keep forgetting (I do) name of admiral who has pried up the iron curtain of censorship. Mary sent {"}Patria{"} clip/ O.K. the gist of Lavoro ed Usura/ very good. What kind of monarchists are they.{?} I dont mind ANY exterior form of organization/ naturally a royal court is a focus of all sorts of STINK/ but probably more visible than a usurers{'} office/ where the same vermin wd/ and will congregate to poison the nation. Advantage of visibility.
AND as an american I have no right whatsodam to mention such local wop issues. Homini bonae voluntatis.[5]
No, Villari can't have an article BY me. Ideas, yes, but does he ever USE 'em? Possibly, now and again. BUT some wop/ pa{p}er OUGHT to give a couple of pages to information on CLEAN thought outside woptalia.

Vanni has had foolish impulse/ probably before he got clear idea of Cursus Ezraticus/[6] must keep series UNIFORM with Lav/ ed Usura/ Kung/ Mussato/ Richard St.Victor. A catholic biJAYzuss author whom a confucian CAN read, and whom Dante & Guido damn well DID read. Wd/ have improved my G.C.[7] notes if I had reread him in 1927/ CAN'T do everything all at once/ and probably better for ME, as me, to get round to him again in 1954.

Benton reviewed in Spewlitzer paper in S.Louis.[8] and new biog/ of Bent/ under weigh by a friend of Davenports. Idlet so damned american i.e. cunctative re/ Zielinksy trans. Believe have a ~~pollo{k}~~ pollok[9] to do eng/ version Benj. Minor of R. StV/

NO sense in wasting time/ No american have ANY perception of the idiocy of wasting time. dither and dodder.

As to how much dirty U.S. linen can be sent to wop laundry I dunno. Bloke named Brandt sd/ 40 years ago/ the further from the scene the more truth yu can print.

slobber over Halitosis salMolasses[10] NOW that they hv/ found uranium. some damWOP ought to do nice gentle li'l essay on abyssunian codes and customs/ where is old ROCKE?[11] He knows. My set of photos probably liberated in the destruction of Rapallo. Why dont YOU correspond with old Domvile?[12] It wd/ cheer yr/ idle moments. For the tenth time when is Malú gittin spliced? If I dont git a box of dragées,[13] I will retaliate viciously.

That summary in La Patria/[14] shows clear head. AND wipes the filth off the Italian pages of the Montale ambience.

vurry nice le'r from Gius. B.[15] BUT can't get any idea of his present position, weight, ambience other than on one occasion chez toi.[16] NOR any idea if any of the amusing papers reach italy/ Craigh-Scott{'}s book hasn't arrive{d} HERE. "Candour" MIGHT be cause of diversion/ I got enuff to do savin the U.S.A. and woptalia without trying to keep Britain from eating poison/ there are SEVERAL brit/ papers/ yellin for clean food/ and to hell with surrogati.[17]

Here they advertise unbleached flour PLUS "strengthenings"

other gleam via Australian radio/ re/ Petrov or whats his name putting finger on deputies. "Their names are NOT household words.{"}

ONE item on U.S. air/ Haile Sal "READS books on economics as other people read detective stories." ergo him UP on his feet and M/ up by the heels.

this OUGHT to be driven into the piffling italian aesthete{s}/ Fiera Lits/ and swine who never discovered the ventennio till it over.

{over} [page 2 of the letter starts with an address to "O.R.A.," but is clearly marked as {"note for Boris/"}]

1. It.: "respects."
2. Encouraging.
3. Percent.
4. It.: "racket."
5. Lt.: "Men of good will."
6. "Ezra's Course of Study."
7. EP's *Guido Cavalcanti Rime.*
8. **Charles Guenther** reviewed *Bank of the United States,* an extract from **Thomas Hart Benton's** *Thirty Years' View,* in the *St. Louis Post-Dispatch,* founded by Joseph Pulitzer, on 20 May 1954.
9. EP means **Stanislas V. Yankowski.**
10. Haile Selassie (1892–1975).
11. **Cyril Edmund Alan Spencer Rocke.**
12. **Sir Barry Domville.**
13. Fr.: "sugar-coated almonds."
14. The summary was of an article appearing in *Rassegna di libera polemicartico-letteraria,* a journal first published in Milan in 1949.
15. **Giusepppe Bottai.**
16. Fr.: "at your place."
17. It.: "substitutes."

79. TLU-3   22 June 1954
22 June 54

O.R.A.

Apropos interesting article in INCOM April 10th/

Olga writes me that the drug attack is evidently weaker in Italy than here. BUT it needs serious consideration/ AS a definite political weapon/. AND the more intelligent men shd/ not go to sleep on it/ N.York in very bad shape/ corruption seeping down thru 21 years/ they catch the pushers but do NOT get the main characters/ O.R. says veryl little among students/ knows of only one case in your ambiente/[1]

WAS any knowledge GAINED during that trouble? probably not though I want every detail possible/ both as to sources of supply, AND methods of treatment. The definite drive here is not only to produce violent irresponsibility at the bottom/ blacks used for the mass attack, supplied by friends of Dexter White and his coreligionists/ BUT everything done to get at the TOP sensibilities/

start with marijuana, which one jazz player said all of 'em tend to use, because it magnifies TIME, which means they can gain precision.

duration of an experience depending on the velocity of the mind during that experience. Same applies to sense of space/ vid/ canto whatever, but all I know anything about is opium[2] (not from use but from encounter with distinguished "hops"). Heroin is what I most want information oN. English case histories of another era not much use, in fact, almost no use re/ these new devilments.

"Incom" article said Italy had licked home ~~nanufacture~~ manufacture and was now trying to stop stuff in transit from near east. Present note is request that you talk of the subject and get yr/ contacts to bring in DATA.

It has historic value alzo re/ how much used and BY ~~WHIVH~~ WHICH prominent characters or non-characters in and before "liberation".

I suppose Villari is responsible for two interesting copies of Rivista Romana/ can you bring him up to date on D.P.[3] address [illegible deletion] (as those copies went to one she has not inhabited for 5 or 6 years). present address 3514 Brothers Place, Washington S.E. {D.C.}

One copy Kung's Odes[4] at last recd/ heaven knows when they will send you yours/ this is american (privately) April and publicly april is supposed to arrive on Sept. 10.

One gathers that in REAL life/ the Mafia has pretty well got top [illegible deletion] sides with any theories of govt/ in Baruchistan

in the 1920s/ all young men were supposed to write shapeless non-metric vers libre and have pink ideas/ in the 1950s/ from Botteghe Oscure, Encounter, New Ventures (imitation from Laughlins title).[5] ALL writers are supposed to eschew ALL civic thought/ and the old idiots, once my respected colleagues fall for it, and lend their names QUITE blindly, 100% per cent TOTALLY to those hoaxes, flattering approaches etc/ Epileptic fury of the Spivak gang interviewing Jenkins/

returning to first topic, Eugene O'Neil's[6] son among those giving tone/ little apes think it smart etc/ AND with FILTH enthroned for five administrations/ where are they to get any other shining summits to aim at.

Boris just sent great essay by Pelo Pardi/[7] which someone might have mentioned to me 20 years ago.

Several Confucian phrases/ quoted in it western classics/ Instruction vs/ education Kung: not a dish. etc.

Nother character dug up some sense from Blake: {"}destroy the arts if you'd mankind destroy.{"}

and FUNDS FUNDS FUNDS, and flatter for any writer who will maintain aesthetic NON-civic attitudes.

Revolt vs/ philistia was alive/ was humanist/ BUT it is out of date. PeloP's much needed.

THEME/ for G.B.[8] or whomso: the use of dope as POLITICAL instrument; those wanting sheer degeneration and destruction use it consciously/ to produce irresponsible violence/

the temptation of artists etc/ is the increased momentary power/ or feeling of it. "LIFE" printed photos of spiders' webs, under influence of

different drugs/ some MORE precise. some wholly disordered. The bastards give the stuff free to exceptional talents, to hook the lesser fringes.
And the word in N.Y. is, no need to go to Harlem, try any high
school.(which is equiv wop. liceo.)[9] AND they catch the small peddlers
but do NOT get to the main sources of flood.

Fool laws, fool restrictions making crimes of non criminal acts/ mere
imports of say diamonds, and games of chance. hence a criminal class
without sense of guilt{,} and sympathy for ~~them~~ {the members}.

22/{P.S} for Boris and ORA/ from W.F.[10] re/ Pelops/ "The pamphlet which
yu (EP) read in English on sunday (viv. voc trans)[11] must have copy/ outside Kung and Dante I've not been moved by such sheer intelligence. Practical so compactly assembled potency and range {on part of the populace}

   1. *Ambiènte*, It.: "environment." EP means "neighborhood."
   2. EP's personal knowledge of opium probably came from his friendship with
the poet **Ralph Cheever Dunning,** a neighbor during his Paris years, 1920–24. EP's
information on drugs among musicians probably came from **William French,** who
was a jazz bassist.
   3. **Dorothy Pound.**
   4. EP's *The Classic Anthology Defined by Confucius.*
   5. These are all journal titles; **James Laughlin** called his publishing house (on
EP's suggestion) New Directions.
   6. Eugene O'Neill.
   7. Probably **Giulio Del Pelo Pardi's** *Per la pace del mondo.* It is referred to frequently in subsequent letters.
   8. **Giuseppe Bottai.**
   9. *Licèo*, It.: "secondary school."
   10. Probably **William French.**
   11. *Viva voce*, It.: "orally transmitted."

80. TLU-3   1 July 1954
1 Lug/

dear O.R.A.

I dont know that I will grant you the rope and hangman cliche/[1] even
if V/ is one of the race chosen by one of the foulest concepts ever put over
as a hoax/ and labled Divinity/ namely JHV[2] the total swine and total
negation of all divine attributes/ and furthest remove from all light. love,
and other Splendours of the Mediaeval Church/ as per R. of St Victor/
Dante and the ghibbeline mystics/

It ought to be recognized that POISON is a political weapon/ used by
a gang of pimps. Roosevelts/ R.Churchills/ betrayers of all the Mihaelo-
vitch/[3] etc. AND a man who has suffered IN his own flesh and blood
OUGHTto have a curiosity as to the main sources of diffusion/ The In-

com article was interesting/ but being in rotocalco, it is suspect/ i.e. that they tossed 4 large hogs to the law/ and concealed the TOP level infamies. AND it is a point of concentration/ for clean men who want to act WITH the law/ without getting entangled in politics/ Ld Sandwich[4] and the early editions of the SCHEME called for race hatreds and were phrased precisely to CREATE race hatreds/

if the s.o.b. are merely destructive, they need no more staff work and correlation than spirochetes or other baccillae/ BUT an objection to syphilis bugs can with difficulty be openly prosecuted with LAW.

Yes, I know, the METHOD shd/ have been (as per ms/sent to B/)[5] rewritten LONG ago/ USURA should have been defined LONG ago/ the church bungled and bumbled thru 40 Church Councils/ etc. One cannot think of everything all at once.

I hope the ODES are on their way to you. KUNG's way of preventing confucians falling into wrangles over abstract formulae. 305 odes, and all come to one sentence: {"}NO twisty thoughts{"} (which is the three ideograms on the final page.)

Gt/ enthusiasm for the Pelo P/ pamphlet Boris sent on last week/ already on way to translation/ I HOPE except the godDAMN yanks are so slow.

club "snow" story,[6] quite up to date/ however that is top level/ society parasites/ NOT every high school/

Might be useful to have post cards or photo of Napoli villa/ centre/ classic studies etc.

I think Guenther cd/ carry an article on it. AND the more demand for proper PERSONNEL, the better.

The MINORU[7] (vide my Fenollosa NOH book, bringing the Jap plays (CLASSICAL) to Venice for theatre festival/

CONsiderable opportunity for E.P. propaganda/ which should be used to the FULL.

Brit/ monetary crank/ whose name I forget printed some VERY interesting remarks by Peron/[8] on MONEY/ naturally the Argentine is NOT getting much support in the LOUSE press.

BUT the whole of Argentine econ/ shd/ be kept CONSTANTLY in display in italian press/

News tonight that Germany is free/ and the dirty frogs flopping lower and lower/ For not reading Albert Londres[9] 35 years ago. AND for getting one of yr/ beloved spirochetes into the Premiership.[10]

Another copy of Mullins[11] being sent you/ new and cheaper edtn/ said to be going to 100 thousand copies/ NO pay to the author who is living on unemployment bonus/ having been sacked from his job when the 1st/ edtn/ appeared.

The Spewman housing regime etc/ coming out and out and out/ graft, Rooseveltism etc. banzai/ and whoopalallah/ 21 years treason/ and 40 years theft/

And Winston has removed his rump½like moog from this Capital.

AND I am in more ~~of~~ or less in an agony of anxious hope that ART has roosted for a few moments on this defiled hemisphere.

Am not give{n} normally to prayer/ but have put up a few during the last trimestre.

For 40 years the damn paint4rs have been unable to paint beauty because they had no beauty inside 'em.

VanderPyl on Vlaminck:[12] a great brute sweating paint/ everything taken from outside.

I suppose Moreau[13] wantedto paint some inside. Degas and Manet did make something beautiful/ BUT for 40 years....agh///

P.S. another idea/ rather than keep 'em shut up I wonder if D.P. might not send you the packet of Beatrice Abbot's[14] letters recd/ by her during past years// they cd/ then be given to Boris and deposited at Brunnenburg/ several items in them that may have escaped yr/ attention.

JHV/ figliocide demon who chose a foul race to do evil. AND the mediaeval church SAW this.

pere eternel vous avez tort, et ben devetz avoir vergogne vostre fils bien amis est mort, et vous dormez comme un ivrogne.[15]

1. A reference to the following in ORA's letter of 26 June 1954: "I cannot ask Varè [about drug use in Italy] for as you probably know, his eldest daughter Diana [. . .] is a victim of the drug habit [. . .] and, of course one must not talk of hemp in the family of one who has been hanged."

2. Jehovah.

3. **General Draza Mihailovitch.**

4. The Lord Sandwich EP has in mind is probably John Montague, the fourth Earl of Sandwich (1718–92) after whom the edible is named. Montague had a reputation for accepting bribes and for general political corruption.

5. Presumably EP had mailed a manuscript dealing with drug use to **Boris de Rachewiltz.**

6. In her letter of 26 June 1954 ORA had related an anecdote about a group of young people who ordered cocaine at an unnamed American night club and received it.

7. A reference to "Excerpts from Fenollosa's Records of His Conversations with Umewaka Minoru," in *'Noh' or Accomplishment.*

8. Juan Perón (1895–1976).

9. **Albert Londres.**

10. Doubtless a reference to Pierre Mendès France, who was invested as premier of France 17 June 1954. His government fell on 5 February 1955.

11. No doubt EP is referring to Mullins's *The Secrets of the Federal Reserve.*

12. **Fritz Vanderpyl.** EP is citing canto 74/435: "by paint immortal as no other age is immortal/ la France dixneuvième/ Degas Manet Guys unforgettable/ a great brute sweating paint said Vanderpyl 40 years later of Vlaminck." Vanderpyl is also memorialized in canto 7/25: "'Beer bottle on the statue's pediment!/ 'That, Fritz, is the era, to-day against the past,/ 'Contemporary.'"

13. **Gustave Moreau.**

14. **Beatrice Abbott.** Dorothy forwarded these letters to ORA on 8 July 1954 with instructions that they be given to **Mary de Rachewiltz** for safe keeping at Brunnenburg.

15. Med. Fr.: "Eternal father, you have made a mistake, and must have been drunk; your beloved son is dead, and you sleep like a drunkard."

81. TLU-3   21 July 1954

21 Lug 54.

O.R.A.

The Pelo Pardi pamphlet translated/ copies sent to Hudson/ to B. Ab/[1] and Russel[2] suggesting new pamphlet series. Still need brief note saying who was PeloP/ and G/[3] hasn't sent in the introd/ alread on pamph/ re/ date etc.

Mystery re/ Zielinsky job/ STUCK. Have before asked re/ Paolillo. sd/ to be in Milano. Does anyone see (or are they still alive) Arena, yr/? stuffed Copola d'Anna,[4] Bevione (whom I thot better head than Pellegrini). Pellizzi had one or two good sentences tucked into his Tempo art/l.

Can{'}t some serious character blast the historic blackout/ Alzo/ re/ both Del Mar and Benton/ the WHEN/ Benton blasts suppression of circulation of foreign coin in U.S. {"}ON WHICH NO ONE PAID ANY INTEREST.{"} He advocated metal currency WHEN there was abundant supply of metal/ AND menti{o}ned exports as superior even to mining.

B.Ab/ suggest protection of drug racket goes pretty HIGH/ and N.Y. police apparently pick on the weak. Church lax on the part of its own theological tradition that wd/ smash kikietry racket. what else?

Peron has said some true words. as I found from one small leaflet from some crank in England.

I forget if yu said that good doctor who cured Malu,[5] was still in Roma. OR if I have bored yu repeating complaint that whenever there is a SANE movement, eugenics, endocrine study, it gets stopped and some fool craze in medicine supersedes. If the medico is still available ask him WHY there is no effective research for anti-*dopes*. Surely if heroin poisons there is an antidote to unpoison.

OR yu wd/ expect some sort of curiosity among medics to find one.

AND the idea that all these underminings just happen without some driving force running the lot of 'em, seems naive.

Too bad the CLASSICS aren't getting off a bit quicker/ Philostratus on Apollonius of Tyana/[6] Nero just as dirty a swine as Roosevelt/ and Ike not half the man that Domitian was/ in fact nowt new, but a progressive decadence.

Has Rome radio/ mentioned the last bit of kike impertinence/ Moses Ikestein Mendez Rothschild Fwance/[7] premier of the frogs. asking frogliament to give up power of financial legislation and leave it to him. AND I dont suppose the Meyerblatt[8] or semiT (in reverse) will suggest that this contains the germ of dictatorship.

the goy is undoubtedly so godDAMNED stupid that he WANTS chains. You'll like the final books of Phil/ on Ap/ if you get time to read 'em. The classics SHOULD be KEPT in the schools/ lack of 'em leaves people open to surprises/

AND Ike with no combat record/ The IDIOCY of not stating that IF China meddles,[9] the FIRST allied move will be *ALL-out* carpet bombing of Moscow.

elemental, my dear Watkins{son}.

even a mediocre school teacher in 1898, had the sense when confronted with persistent but untraceable disorder to out Sol/ Solomon, with the simple sentence: {"}if there is ANY further disorder in this class, Pound and McClure will leave the room.{"}

And they call these catamites "statesmen" o mundum insipiens et insipiens[10] (guess that grammar is off) latin weakening.

The Pittsburg volcano, now spliced to Luzzato[11] (re/ whom my roman friends do NOT supply me with data) has sent on anodyne Messagero[12] blurb/ evidently the choinulist never heard of the U.S. Constitution, or Dante's views re/ the function of poesy.

[illegible deletion] Stan(islas) YANK(owski) trying to get text of Ric/ St V/ to translate/ so far he wd/ have to do hours tram ride to library in Calif/ as they wont lend him the vol/ of Migne.

Niemojowski,[13] surprised that White Eagle, Polish refugee paper in London, sabotaged when Nij/ tried to print trans/ of E.P. wich I tell him is just plain nacherl/

three divisions of Poland, cause they suffered from O.R.A.-ic blindness[14] re/ causes of national insecurity.

AND yu calling Marx a German[15] (SHAME on you,,, or rather, if il piu non esiste, *la* piu SCALTRAAAAAAA si mostra.[16] It is wot Lenin called "Aesopian" langwidg.

did I say there are cracks (or at least A crack (in enemy front. Lore (16 quarterings, deep-chested child of the Vaterland) said it was IMPossible to conceal her intention so she TOLD the fullBLIGHT what she wanted a fellowship for and GOT it. (To study with Kenner, the works of * * *.[17]

Did yu ever heard of Alfalfa Bill (Murray)[18] possibly in congress when yu were in the U.S. and then governor of Oklahoma. a SOUND man, re/ all except xtianity, having had that old cough losenge pushed into his throat in childhood...BUT..

also Waddell,[19] brit/ archaeolog...any data in the Ros/ti archives??

P.S.// take it from grampaw: ANY touch of the jew book defiles/ note Heydon polluted,[20] Apollonius of TYana UNpolluted. {29 Lug}

1. **Beatrice Abbott.**

2. Probably **Peter Russell.**

3. Possibly **David M. Gordon.**

4. Arena and **Coppola d'Anna** are first mentioned together in letter 33.

5. **Eugenio Morelli.**

6. EP is referring to Philostratus' *Life of Apollonius of Tyana.* He uses the Loeb translation by F. C. Conybeare in *Thrones.* **Apollonius of Tyana** was twice arrested for treason—once by Nero and once by Domitian. He escaped Domitian's court by necromancy. EP obviously identifies with Apollonius; his tormentors are two presidents, Roosevelt and Eisenhower.

7. EP apparently believed Pierre Mendès France was Jewish. See also letter 80.

8. The *Washington Post,* published by **Eugene Meyer.** *Blatt* is German for "newspaper" and commonly appears in titles.

9. Presumably a hawkish reference to the Korean War.

10. Lt.: approximately, "O foolish world."

11. Riccardo Luzzatto, who is also mentioned in letter 70.

12. Lt.: "messenger." Presumably this is a journal or newspaper.

13. **Jerzy Niemojowski.**

14. ORA's failure to participate in EP's belief in a Jewish conspiracy.

15. EP's point is that Marx was ethnically part Jewish. However, he was German speaking, and not a practitioner of the Jewish faith.

16. It.: "a more shrewd pretense is not possible," that is, that Marx was German.

17. Ezra Pound.

18. **William Murray.**

19. **Colonel Lawrence Austine Waddell.**

20. EP refers to this notion in canto 91; he first mentions **John Heydon** in the "Ur-Cantos." What he means here is that Apollonius has no taint of Jewish theology, but Heydon (who does have some part of theosophical wisdom) does.

82. TLU-2   27 July 1954
27 Lug/ 54

O.R.A.

thanks fer them kind words,[1] nacherly UNESCO, dirty organ of usuro-
crats is NOT attempting to promote understanding but to impose the
same swine etc. as have corrupted Europe for 2000 years. Too bad the
interpretress at several dirty convegni[2] has never been able to get a little
love of truth into the buzzards she has had to interpret for. It wd/ have
been useful to TELL snake-face. may be now he is superficially OUT, he
wd/ imbibe a little decency. and/or that halfbaked semiliberal halfwit
"Ciao Luigi." Einaudi, FAKE
~~itl~~ intellectual handing out **** **** to effect yu have to put money
INTO a bank before tha bank can hand it out.
immondicie.[3]

And too bad you still go out of cocciatugine,[4] or however you spell it,
defending that mass of corrupting incoherence forgery, fakery/ the O.T.

You are old enough to have got round to reading a few clean books, such
as poor old Mead (GRS) on Apollonius of Tyana.[5] Plus the Zielinski.

That ALL the clean ideas in Xtianity come via greece (earlier origin may
be india) but at any rate NOTHING of the goddm kikes/ {vid} Tertullian,
Gibbon, the classic authors/ slime always getting xtns/ killed off. FACE
it and dont hide behind Lubin/ of course people shd/ be judged as individuals (as they were NOT at Katyn.)

Just been reading Dazzi's[6] saggi on Mussato/ I spose all them murderers were aryan/ BUT still...

AND as fer the MUTTheadedness of all the pseudointelligentzia IN-
CLUDING Possum Eliot, that none of my correspondents has chucked
Waddell's work in my way/ until the bassi fondi[7] of N.Pork dig up an ex-
governor of Oklahoma, who has read Waddell (and a LOT of other stuff
that the wops OUGHT to read and DIgest.).

Yr. [illegible deletion] artl/ on PeloPs/ most timely/ am forwarding to
F,M,[8] in [illegible deletion] whopes it will purr/suade him to print G.G.'s[9]
trans/ of Pelops/ on Peace. BUTT the damn goy is so stupid.

lack of communication TO ME, of news of Waddell, indicative of the
mush headedness of the fly-brains who write english and woptaliano.

Of course the subversives don{'}t need coherence/ all they need is to
rot, and corrupt, and that spreads, whereas ORDER needs mind.
     * * *

Dont lie down on Richard St Victor/ that verse is the CLEANSING/ it
kiks OUT the god damn freud½rot. System of kiketry, to pick individual bit of filth out of pozzo-nero,[10] thereby concentrating ALL pubk/ attention on pozzo nero.

D.P. thanks me for distinction between posso-n and cloaca.[11] (I was using the term to define a swine, now thank heaven DEAD. but who shd/ have been strangled at birth.)

AND dont lose TIME/ the corruption has rage{d} 50 years/ Thanks for qt/ of definition usura/

THAT shd/ have been made 30 years ago, but one can't ~~thin~~ think of everything.

News that some research is being made into anti-dopes/ sd/ to be complicated/ AND also great variety in individual reactions, following one Paris specialist: "Il n'y a pas de maladies, il n'y a que des malades.".[12]

Epstein,[13] simpatico medico, non-aryan in this bughoUSZ says he is not interest in medics/ who say they had an "interesting t.b. or pneumonia".

Mr Zukofsky[14] brot his ten year old son to play Mozart on the lawn a fortnight ago. ETC. INDIVIDUALS/ BUT......[15]

I shd/ like to arouse ORA'S interest in history/ in biology/ in Luther Burbank,[16] {&} in eugenics/

did yu ever hear of a guy named Murray/[17] aetati/ 81 two years ago/ dunno if still alive/ Congress and then governor of western state/

Nice Marco Polo[18] stamp on yr/ epizl. Tell 'em to do one for the Noh players this august. That is a bit of connection.

1. In a letter of 21 July 1954 ORA had thanked him for his *Classic Anthology* and had added: "You have certainly recreated Chinese poetry for English readers, and it is truly a great achievement; you have done far more for international understanding and friendship than Unesco with all their millions."

2. It.: "meetings."

3. Probably *immondizia*, It.: "rubbish."

4. Probably *cocciutàggine*, It.: "stubbornness."

5. EP is referring to **G. R. S. Mead's** *Apollonius of Tyana.*

6. **Manlio Torquato Dazzi.**

7. It.: "lowest depths"; EP probably means "low life of New York."

8. **Frederick Morgan.**

9. **Giovanni Giovannini.**

10. It.: "cesspool."

11. In Italian *cloaca* and *pozzo-nero* are synonyms but in English or Latin *cloaca* can refer to the common cavity into which the intestinal and urinary canals discharge in birds, fish, and reptiles.

12. Fr.: "there are no illinesses, there are only sick people."

13. A doctor at St. Elizabeths.

14. **Louis Zukofsky.**

15. EP means that Dr. Epstein and **Louis Zukofsky** are two "good" Jews.

16. **Luther Burbank.**

17. **William Henry Murray.**

18. Marco Polo (1254–1324) appears in canto 18.

83. TLU-3   17 August 1954
17 Ag/

ORA

what does La Raiola want with titular glories/ Salazar[1] has no official
job in Portugal/ AND these academic shells think of nothing/ they have
to be told, or as Yeats REmarked "nothing affects these people but our
conversation."/ "Everybody knows it's R8s byby.[2] O.K. Let her set back
and tell 'em. Of course I wd/ hv/ preferred another author as flag/ but that
is a bagatelle/[3] Let her TELL 'em. and if they dont follow CONskruktiv
suggestions, let her raise hell with the other members and "orficers.".

I see NO tendency on Mullins[4] part to ascribe ALL to one infamy/ one
has to treat ONE subject at a time. esp, in view printing costs/ AND for
60 years all of "you" evade le prob/ monnetaire, by that escape mechanism "yes, but it isn't everything."/ man has broken leg and pneumonia/
etc. THE MOST evaded problem has been the MONetary. And as S/[5] remarked: fool to pay psychiatrist when cd/ have free from priest BUT the
church is so corrupt. Boris clear in his mind. they have been to Venezia
for the Noh, con fiocchi.[6] Morgan ~~think~~ thick in head re/ the PeloPar/

Can you tell Eliot WHEN, i.e. at what point a religion is lousy? He
seems a bit bewildered at what point. Boris' Proverbi Egiz, very fine in
parts/ king Kati per es/ At last once again FOUR people in action. First
time since the "twenties." Mr White was in the treasury/ only the american tax payer can produce the credulity necessary to suppose his presence was accidental. Didn't I ~~wh~~ quote my chink/ ~~he~~ re his damblasti-
dor: "Mr Hu Shi did not at that time know Mr Dexter White was a
hrooshun spy." Put Helen onto Apollonius of Tyana/ if yu haven't time
to read either Mead or Philostratus, re that most estimable and unkikified
character. Did I ask re/ Waddell? the god damn brits always manage to
hide their useful citizens.

** coming BACK to it. I have never known, read or heard of a monetary reformer who thought money was ALL, or the whole answer/ five
generations have been CONditioned to AVOID that problem, that disease. At least since 1860/

whole propaganda. including a lot of stincgking xtianity (jewdianity
disguised) included. Ergo the mon/ ref/r{'s} emphasis. And YOU, who
ought not are still conditioned, though yu do recognize money as PART
of the picture. Alzo Lubin has conditioned you to a blindness to the defilement the yidd has brot into EVERY civ/n or religion he has penetrated/
alzo his degradation of ALL thot of sexual relations/ via his stincgking
circumcision, as means to desensitize his shock troops and render them
immune to any finer feeling that wd/ distract 'em from profit motive.

mercantilism/ NOT production/ the exchange based on scarcity, ignoance and monopoly.

To believe god is a yidd requires an insensitivity equal to that of believeing Roosevelt was a gentleman. And to degrade the somma sapienza[7] to level of bad taste implied in picking semites is again an insult both to sd/ Div/ Sap and to any man of average intelligence.

There is probably NO trace in ANY semitic writing of the finer feelings found in Chinese record, OR in egyptian scene of Boris' dust jacket for "Maxims." sentimentality, desensitization for purposes of getting women cheap. EtCetraaaaaa

Yes, heroism, decency/ ALL excited by HIRED press to the wrong ends. Pawn yr/ castles and rescue the HOLY sepulchre from the Moslim. etc. KILL the germans, defend Damnocracy etc. ALL to profit of arms manuf/ and loan kikes. The decent motives which DO function perverted. History falsified.

Anything and every/ to keep public mind OFF the Rothschild and their "fellow Xtn Barings". NO it is NOT the only motivation/ but it is means whereby the decent motivations are made to collaborate with the worst. AND the one the least revealed by rotocalco.

Just heard that a VERY dirty piece of work Peter Viereck has been hired to mis-teach in Firenze. Alert all clean wop critics. This animal really STINCKGS exceptionally ~~EVER~~ EVEN for a third rate american worstifier.

The Meyerblatt radio/ Bill Downs[8] slamming the arabs and yelling WHooray for yr/ ZioKikes. Thank god for the small favour of DeGaspari's demise (tentatively....has not Italy lost an enemy? this not a dogmatic statement/ BUT I shd/ think the peninsula wd/ be more cheerful without that fyce. And Dizzy's canal[9]....getting back to Cleopatra.

Waaal, the arabs are semites/ O.R.A. tends to look on 'em with couleur de rose...A couple back in 1934 were more pessimistic/ news fromDelhi is that the Sears Roebuck catalog is the book most in demand in the Hindoo lie/bury. The arabs haven't got to that point of regress. Pardon me if I lapse from usual high seriousness of this correspondence. I remember Orage[10] once stopped a controversy between me and Pickthall[11] in N.Age when I emitted: {"}My Dear Pickthall, I once SAW a Mohamedan.{"} Of course that was nearer to the Whistlerian era.[12] In fact pre-1914 when persiflage was not so grave an offense vs/ humanity. Radio just now/ Barney Baruch/[13] God curse his religion/ rereading the gk and lat/ classics. Deh vey dem yitts tag along. How the lice expect a European defence army with grampaw in the caleboza[14] is ALZO a question.

P.S. friend IN italy has had small inheritance in U.S. question: How invest? with present exchange wdn't it be ~~best~~ better invest in Italy? at least save bank charges? P.S. continued/ shame to have safe-keeping fee of $650 against probably $200 income. I hv/ no idea what sort of bond dummy-Xtns[15] give their citoyen.[16]

1. Antonio de Oliviera Salazar (1889–1970).
2. Raiola's baby.
3. Fr.: "something of no consequence or importance."
4. ORA had been reading Mullins's *The Secrets of the Federal Reserve* and had remarked: "I think it is always the case with believers and fighters for a cause, there is a tendency to explain all the evils of a period by one cause, whereas the causes are many" (12 Aug. 1954).
5. Most likely **Sheri Martinelli.**
6. Presumably *coi fiocch*, It.: "first rate."
7. It.: "highest wisdom"; equivalent to *divina sapienza* ("Div/ Sap"), "divine wisdom," in other words, God.
8. **William Downs.**
9. "Disraeli's canal," a reference to the Suez Canal.
10. **A. R. Orage.**
11. **Marmaduke Pickthall.**
12. Late Victorian. Whistler was the first American painter to establish a reputation in Europe.
13. **Bernard Mannes Baruch.**
14. It.: "jail."
15. The Christian Democratic party of Italy.
16. Fr.: "citizen."

84. TLU-3   23 August 1954

23 Ag/ 54

O.R.A.

O.Kay Doc Morelli is a gt/ physician/[1] having fought t.b. can you now get him onto dope/ and unblind yourself to the activities of that dastardly RACE which you adore and excuse. AND to a definite method of corruption and destruction of the god damned goy who is too bloody stupid to cooperate with other goys/ while the press is taken over and all sources of information controlled/ AND the definite material poisoning by dope/ accompanies the corruption of MIND, dating ~~from~~ (to) 500 b.C. and in constant augment. While money is issued as interest-bearing debt for the KIKES/while the press sinks more and more into control of the KIKES. heroin is pushed/ and the negro attendant knows that big chews are back of it. AND the son of the rabbi who is not a peddlar finances the "fix"/ i.e. BUYS the stuff for the addict who hasn't the money and is trying to break the habit/ and (i.e. no Jew) has the apparatus, syringe etc/ a typical case. ONLY(,) living in the empyrean(,) the decent member of our generation hasn't heard of the methods and habits of Roosevelt's sequelae.[2] The poor addicts "push" the stuff/ the only way they can get it. That stuffed shirt Gunther[3] "inside" etc. is getting I suppose large sums for exposing the less useful sensational cops/ a year or so AFTER the event/ and Carper, the police chief was copped along with "Cat-Fish" but that was in another year tho in the same city. AND the alleged literati write what will sell NOT what wd/ function for sanitation. AND the kikes go for the WHOLE of the more sensitive section of the younger generation/ "all" jazz musicians" on marijuana/ which "is not habit forming" and leads to heroin/ and "Benzedrine is harmless, they give it to aviators"/ so that after carpet bombing they will go on with some drug habit or other. WHILE one is distracted by trying to lift the historic blackout etc. and allows the eye to rest on the past instead of the present/

Some research is being done for anti-dope/ they claim the personal factor creates difficulty, as it dont take 'em all the same way. HAS Morelli any ideas?

Of course an honest police force wd/ be useful/ AND a greater knowledge of palliatives wd/ be useful.

Arsenic does not destroy, at least it took Sarah Bernhardt[4] into a fair maturity. Vare must have learned SOMETHING.

AND to my certain knowledge dope was being used as a political weapon as far back as 1927. I think I gave you detail on one case. known directly to my informant who considered it funny. (as indeed it{,} as isolated circs{,} was). or as Kung remarked "they do not see implications" which has been smothered by xtn/ translators with the term "omens" to get it off the ground into the fog of the supernacherl.

B/[5] has got some bright detail. back to Etruscans, re falsification of objects/ falsification of mummies for "mummia" mummy powder in mid/age/ falsification of documents/ let us say between a.d. 100 and 300/ the supreme filth that gawd prefers kikes/ after yu swallow that tutto e possibile.[6] BUT yu have mental habits. And the records, as of Antoninus Pius get destroyed.

Can yu put me thru to Morelli/ re/ drugs{?} Judging from local hell the red kikes have given up aphrodisiacs as excitants/ they might lead to affection. If heroin is the main line in opium derivates, it is the one apparently that most kills sex urge/ and THENCE damages ordinary affection/ normal manifestations of friendly affection, as comforting a child/ reverses all the normal magnetisms. and that is something Morelli might think up a cure for.

Pegler/ tonight on Dies/[7] good, also good on Mrs Roosevelt. BUT has got hang over of prejudice re/ Mus/ whom he still calls "the bum of bums" revisionism hasn't got that far/ mebbe Villari cd/ have his book sent to him/ or put Barnes[8] and Devin-Adair[9] onto revising Peg's iggurunce.

ANd yr/ french jew, naturally working fer Moscow/ too bad it wont kill Churchill/

but Napoleon said something about a MAP. In fact he said yu can't conquer a map.

You may have missed Julian Benda[10] some years ago, say 5 or 6 saying "but Europe does not WANT to be united."

AND who sent the gold to Wellington in Spain? HOW did it get there? and so forth.

Take the METHOD of yr/ semitic friends in the dope ring/ French[11] has got his wife out of the country/ having got her loose/ BUT, let us get close up report. Marijuana relatively harmless/ smoked/ then s comes the syringe and heroin/ first shots given free, as dare etc. and when distinguished addict tries to break or goes broke the "fix" is financed to keep 'em on it. Our simple pastoral lives started in another era/ D.G.R.[12] wasn't brain washed into chloral.

1. ORA wrote in response to EP's queries about **Malù**'s impending marriage: "She expects to marry her young Hercules early in October[. . . .] She is now in good health having been dragged from the grave by that great man, Prof. Morelli, turned out of the Senate because he was a Fascist and had started and directed the anti-tuberculosis campaign of the régime" (26 June 1954).

2. Lt.: "aftereffect, secondary result." EP means Roosevelt's followers.

3. Presumably a New York police chief.

4. Sarah Bernhardt (1844–1923), the stage name of Henriette Rosine Bernard, a celebrated French actress. She injured her right knee during a 1905 performance, and by 1915, after gangrene had set in, her leg was amputated. EP seems to believe that she took arsenic as a pain killer. Arsenic was also used as a drug to heighten intellectual powers, which EP may have in mind here.

5. **Boris de Rachewiltz.**

6. It.: "anything is possible."

7. In his radio show Pegler must have focused on the **Martin Dies** committee.

8. **James Thomas Strachey Barnes.**

9. Presumably the New York publishing house.

10. **Julien Benda.** EP is referring to some public statement he made about 1950, which we have not identified.

11. **William French.**

12. **Dante Gabriel Rossetti.**

85. TLU-3   [3 September 1954]

{ORA}
Cara mia SIGnora/

I read the dirty jew book from age of 6 to 17 and have never denied i
that it contains some juicy rather african [illegible deletion] eroticism and
perfervid rhetoric. the chocolate coating over the venom.

Boris I think will track down some of the good stuff the kikes ~~spoi~~
spoiled.

It is NOt the arsenic in the bottle and labled, but the arsenic in the
DEElicious soup than is dangerous.

and the occident mind conditioned/ ~~fgh~~ for 2500 years.

the damn goy/ with his temple initiations, and selecting minds fit to
understand etc/ and his unwritten tradition was poisoned between a.D.
100 and 300/ control of press of the period/ BY the mass edition of the
poisoned text.

No greater blasphemy than to ~~ass~~ accuse the summa sapienza[1] of such
a solecism as preferring kikes to other races/

you wdn't even let the huns consider 'emselves chos{e}n. and [illegible
deletion] SAID they got the nasty idea of superior race from the kikes.

A louse like Waley[2] gets a public by abusing chinese originals and his
coreligionists ~~as they~~ have obliterated other records, we are only getting
some egyptian and sumerian texts to compare with their anthology/

Mrs Stokes (wife of guy who is having a nervous breakdown becau
because he tried to get at some truth in Nurnberg/ and Rhoosians swiped
the documents which are now unfindable even in american files/) told a
good one on "frenchman who said: every f{r}enchman has his GOOD jew.
Fortunately mine's dead.". Hamilton[3] WAS a kike. a red headed scotch
chew. And ~~Llod~~ Lloyd is a welsch name, recently defiled by a David/
~~Thann~~ Thammy may or may not have had a lithp. As a matter of fact I'm
not sure he hadn't reduced it to a single L??[4]

correct me if I err, am not in the least certain.

and a usurer is a spiritual kike whatever his blood count.

as to names, the last bloke who got by {me} in scandanavian fleece
called himself Olson[5] [in margin:] {Kensington}.

Yes, the high point in american dignity was when Hoover voted in W.8
election AND simultaneously the british judge said: Mr Hoover, "I am
sorry that this has been brought as a civil, not as a criminal action.". Old
Tinkham said it wd/ have cost him a million to get the evidence *when
needed,* and at a time when he hadn't the million, but DID get confirmation re/ chinese mines later.[6]

a TACTICAL error on Mullins part to drag in the name unnecessarily,
and prevent a certain amount of circulation for useful volume. AND as

old Ionides said: a greek will do ANYthing till he gets 20 000 stg//[7] after
that it pays him to be honest.

There WAS a tremenjust press build up for Herbie at a time when Bel-
gians were sniping at the bosche[8] and the brit/ press telling about Kadav-
erfabriks.[9]

a{l}zo/ I suppose a crook CAN arrive at point when only legal crimes
appeal to his better nature.

Herbert will certainly NOT mention the infamy of the debt system/
run for the benefit of a gang of individuals who ought to be jailed.

I consider genocide impractical/ and admit in theory each individual
shd/ be judged on his merits.

BUT the cathedrals rose when segregation was in fashion.

and the buzzards have been out of the ghetto only 105 years/ NOT that
I wdn/t wish Metternich and Gentz to go to a lower bolge in hell than
Meyer Amschel[10] IF one ϙ were in that order of idees.

Il nemico è l'ignoranza/[11] and the dam goy is too casual in allowing the
kike to run his press and arrange history to prevent the transmission of
crucial facts.

Benedictions.

deh chreatest gabidol off the woildt mit NO morning baber/ only a [il-
legible deletion] Meyerblatt.[12]

The same congenital idiocy of the goy/ letting the jew book monopolize the occident/ NOW jew banker in Geneva ordering "destroy a farlo
sparire dalla circulazione".[13] Same french authors NOT on sale in shoppe
of that worm Ravenna, Piazza S. Marco Venezia, and NOT printed in
Canada during war. IMbegoddamcility of the goy in allowing jew monopoly of book trade or practically that.

[in right margin:] historic vol/ ett e[14]

1. *Somma sapienza*, It.: "highest wisdom," that is, God.

2. **Arthur Waley.**

3. Because he was born on the West Indian island of Nevis, Alexander Hamilton's (1705–1804) ethnicity was frequently questioned.

4. EP is discussing **David Lloyd George** and **Samuel Jones Loyd.** George affected the spelling of "Lloyd." He was not Jewish.

5. Unidentified, but the marginal remark "Kensington" suggests that he was
an acquaintance of EP's during his London years.

6. EP is referring to two scandals during Herbert Hoover's years in London that
plagued him during the 1928 election: he was unjustly said to have voted twice
in British elections (he was forbidden to vote as a U.S. citizen); and he was involved
in a 1905 trial concerning a land deal in China. "W.8" is a postal district of London, presumably of the constituency in which Hoover voted.

7. 20,000 pounds sterling.

8. *Boche* is the abusive term the French apply to the Germans.

9. Gm.: "corpse factories." It appears from the context that EP is referring to
the period near 1928 before the Nazis were in power and had established govern-

ment-run concentration camps. However, the Nazi Brown Shirts ran their own camps before they came to power.

10. **Meyer Amschel Rothschild.**

11. It.: "the enemy is ignorance."

12. The greatest capital of the world with no morning paper, only a "Meyer-blatt." See letter 81.

13. It.: "to make it disappear from circulation."

14. This marginal note is only partially legible and may be intended to identify the "French books" missing from Signor Ravenna's Venetian book stall and banned in Canada.

86. TLU-1   9 September 1954

9 Sept/

O.R.A.

On the basis of considering the one to 1000 chance that nothing is wholly impossible/ Re. the Raiola and Villa a Napoli/ if a miracle occurred/ what terms wd/ they give/ i.e. FOUR rooms minimum/? free in return for dynamism? An ambiente where D.P. cd/ stay when I visit Brunnenburg? if she cd/ stand south wops after the non-espansivi liguri?[1]

Amaral[2] thinks South America wd/ more appreciate certain talents than the U.S. does? whether any of this wishful thinking wd/ stimulate FURTHER thinking? "Agricultura" possibly premature/ tho good intention/ trouble is they will have the wholeDAMN sugar trust up there cutting down those saplings/ if noticed.

AND the ide{a} of bleeding the trees[3] in 6 years time MAY be sheer iggurunce. They should wait twenty.

eternal vigilance. The California Gesellites[4] whether from design or STEWpidity, yawping for 2 cent stamp WEEKLY/ idiot and outrageous charge for purchasing power/ usury at 104% per annum. That is the kind of muck you get from half baked eer credit cranks.

Douglas{'} A. plus B/ theorem[5] recognized de facto all over the place/ and then perverted/ loaded with bugrocrat red tape/ whereas his per capita distribution did NOT entail paper work or staff/ apart from general survey of production capacity/ as Brookings Inst. in 36 or whenever.

A few gleams in the British press/ whether U.S. will bend without the USUAL 30 year time lag/ OOOOnoZE?

Boris done excellent job on King Kati, 1500 years before Kung/

Will some of yr/ cultured set start on PERVERSION/ 40 years whole occidental attention focused on filth/ and yr/ blinkin church did NOT invoke the clean mediaeval tradition/ contemplatio/ of the divine light. fell for this kikery/ bait yesterday, talmudist trying to get me switched off onto otiose curiosity. Vae qui cogitatis inutile.[6]

awful mind-conditioning as between a.D. 100 and 300. Take an evening off with Philostratus on Ap/ of Ty/[7]

What about Savage, nice cultural suggestion in patronymic, is he human or merely an Harvard man/ does he KNOW the Harvard Univ/ Press is doing the ODES? wd/ he oppose participation in culture by anyone NOT tied up to his beanery?

I had ONE letter from Bowers,[8] then he clammed up/ {years ago} believe he is or has been in South America

Bloomsbury monopoly of brit/ press is weakening/ the buzzards admitting my uplifting in{f}luence on such characters as Yeats and Elephunt/[9] or one even saying they took the wrong turning. merely literary and aesthetic not gittin down to brass tacks

1. It.: "undemonstrative Ligurians."

2. **José Vásquez Amaral.**

3. EP is discussing a project to plant maple trees near Schloss Brunnenburg and tap them for sugar.

4. The individuals are unidentified. The proposal EP criticizes is that holders of currency be required to affix a two-cent stamp to every dollar bill each week. The idea is to increase the "velocity" of the circulation of money, but EP regards this rate as excessive.

5. **Major Clifford Hugh Douglas** argued that goods an economy could not itself consume had to be exported, leading to international conflict and war. The A plus B theorem offends against the principle of equilibrium, which is a foundation of all varieties of mainstream economics.

6. Lt.: "woe to him who thinks vainly."

7. Philostratus' *Apollonius of Tyana.*

8. Probably Claude Gernade Bowers (1878–1958), American journalist and diplomat, author of *Jefferson and Hamilton.*

9. T. S. Eliot.

87. TLU-2 NYPL   4 November 1954

4 Nov.

O.R.A.

worried that chq/[1] or even notice of same sent one day earlier has not reached Brunnenburg/ not sure whether Boris is now there or in Rome.

They seem to be rushing him re/ purchase of land. Cheque to cover new demand HAS been sent. I dont know whether air mail is prompt to Merano.

If Boris is NOT in Rome, I wonder if you know how to phone to the Op/ Combattenti,[2] and tell them that Rachewiltz has the 2½ and will pay, a mere matter of days.

Naturally do NOT tell the Op/ Combat/ where the chq/ is ultimately from/ or rather where it is NOT from as I have no personal giuridica[3] and cdn't sign a cheque for three lire. BUT [illegible deletion] the cheque will not bounce.

I dont know what the designation of the Ente[4] is. Mary quotes the words "Questo Instituto"[5]

I dont know whether some s.o.b. is trying to force Boris to borrow money, and get into debt. at any rate that is not necessary.

also some yarn that some uncle in a bank is arranging loan to wicked contadino/[6] i.e. THAT wd/ be a mortgage and keep on ruining the land. ANYthing to make DEBT, american radio consecrated (black mass) to ever{y} form of loan sharking. publik and privik.

Rumour that Dag Hamerskold[7] quoted Pisans at some Mod/ Museum of Art beano two weeks ago, data not yet to hand.

Has Boris a phone in Roma?

I wrote AT once as soon as I got Mary letter re new terms her letter date{d} 20 Oct/ but dont know date of my reply/ chq/ sent one day later/ should have arrived/ or at least one of the air letters/ that saying it WOULD be sent/ and that saying it HAD been.

benedictions/ and best to Malu and co/

Monotti had good blurb in Il Mare (redivivus)[8] BUT can't seem to get prompt correlation/

shd/ have had six copies by air/ AND of Secolo XIX[9] and of preceding Mare clippings.

Sometime the FOUR steps to the bughousz should be printable/ Slop of Tate's generation/[10] and my own contemporaries in this morass/ NONE of 'em has faced basic issues raised in the Cantos.

1. This letter is apparently about some financial arrangements on behalf of Mary and Boris, about which EP was characteristically nervous.

2. Probably *Opera Combattenti*, It.: "office of veterans' affairs."

3. It.: "legal status." Found mentally incompetent to stand trial for treason in 1945, EP was still legally incompetent in 1954 and thus was unable to have a bank account.

4. It.: "corporation"

5. Mary had apparently not identified "this institution" by name.

6. It.: "peasant."

7. **Dag Hammarskjöld.** A communiqué from **Sheri Martinelli** to ORA includes the following note: "Dag Hammarskjöld, Sec.-gen. of the U.N. in an address at the Museum of Modern Art, Oct. 19th of this year said: 'Modern art teaches us to see by forcing us to use our senses, our intellect and our sensibility to follow it on its road of exploration. It makes us seers—seers like Ezra Pound when, in the first of his Pisan Cantos, he senses "the enormous tragedy of the dream in the peasant's bent shoulders." Seers—and explorers—these we must be if we are to prevail'" (30 Nov. 1954; NYPL).

8. Lt.: "returned to life."

9. EP is referring to excerpts from the first section of "Oro e Lavoro" that were printed in *Il Secolo XIX*.

10. EP presumably means **Allen Tate,** but we do not know to what four steps he is referring.

1955

88. TLU-2   6 January 1955

6 Jan/ 55 annon Dom. AUG.

I dont understand how Helen had the Cantos, they were ordered sent to you. Unless this is some other provenienzaaaa.[1]

I still marvel (changing the subject) at the pussilanimity of some fauna/ the infantilism. etc. You wd/ think that any adult, instead of saying what USE? etc. of something printed in rural paper/ wd/ have sense enough to know that a QUOTATION from same, in far country where NO damn wop paper has ever been heard of (except the vile Corriere)[2] wd/ be as useful as a quote from an official organ in a despised etc[illegible deletion]

And in the same breath bemoaning the lack of spirit in his concitoyens....[3] (YES, I have a case in mind).

My friends are THE most chaRRRRming idiots on earth, among whom about 8 or 10 have traces of intelligence. Among whom, you (I gather, [illegible deletion] Helen) Mary and Boris.

[illegible deletion] New adult arruv/ from Calif/ from la PoLOGne via Australia. Now translating R. de St Victor.[4] I want connections to get him into print as soon as possible/ he can get some of his cash out of Australia AFTER May 1st/ (has to be OUT of there a year before the brit/sods/ will permit transfer.

Baynes and Moss "BYZANTIUM"/[5] Andreades chapter on Byzantine econ/[6] DID anyone in the Ventennio make ANY use of corporatism[7] in Byzantium? LOTS of propaganda value. Prefect's edict re/ trade unions functioned from time of Leo the Wise,[8] right down to Mustapha Kemal/[9] the dirty Manchesterians crabbed ALL Byzantine history, part of black out/ AND Pearson[10] reports that the church of Rome, damned giudianity and perversion, is trying to prevent publication of facts in archives of the greek church. The more one

I seem to remember Villari being damned dull/[11] may be that was some other book of his.

Anyhow, ALL out of date. as atomic energy for industry busts ALL previous calculation/. No use thinking as from the Tin-Lizzy days. Mania of even better radio mutts, for OMITTING Italy in all american yawp re/ Europe/ they have heard of france, the decaying heap/ and EVEN of Spain as a factor. Inferiority complex of all the lousy journalists re/ Mus/ who HAD been a journalist/

Naturally D.G.R. Hand and Soul and Vita Nuova basic in E.P's paideuma/ also that "I have been here before" poem./[12] AND yr/ quote from Dant/[13] the general theme, or Cantos, begining with Pisans/. The first ½ being attempt to set up circle of reference.

Am now trying to learn a little greek/ never had patience to use largest size dic/ before. Whether anyone can read the Odyssey until they have translated the ODES, I don't know. Chang,[14] as per clip that will send to Mary, is tootin fer Kung in 'Frisco.

IF there are any ITALIAN italian{s} left, they ought to make USE of J.Brown's "Panorama de la literature contemporaine aux Etats Unis."[15] to castigate Brown AND illustrate[illegible deletion] the rise of Italy as an intellectual power (however weak and dithering in the 3rd/ decennio AFTER)

TOTAL lack of any controversial writing in the J.S.[16] NO one has noted the improvement by translation in Eva's version:[17]

[illegible deletion] Redefreiheit ohne Radiofreiheit gleich null ist.

OR that knowing what one did, he had a duty, to warn the dupes.

Some {S}panish friend of Jimenez (Juan Ramon)[18] notes the scant solidarity of intellectuales americanos.

NOT noting the contradiction of noun and adjective. Cocteau[19] made a remark when he said: I thought I was among men of letters and was suddenly aware that they a were a group of garage mechanics.

1. *Proveniènza*, It.: "source."

2. *Corriere della Sera*, a Milan-based daily newspaper established in 1876 as an evening paper; except during the years of Fascist rule, it followed an independent-centrist editorial policy until the 1970s.

3. Fr.: "fellow citizens."

4. **Stanislas V. Yankowski**'s translation was published as *Richard of Saint Victor, Benjamin Minor.*

5. Norman H. Baynes and H.St.L.B. Moss's *Byzantium.*

6. There are two chapters by **André M. Andréadès** in *Byzantium:* "The Economic Life of the Byzantine Empire: Population, Agriculture, Industry, Commerce" and "Public Finances: Currency, Public Expenditure, Budget, Public Revenue."

7. See letters 54 and 55.

8. EP is referring to *The Eparch's Book* (see Nicole), which dates from the time of Leo the Wise, Byzantine emperor (866–912). This book of regulations regarding commercial guilds and conditions of sales and purchases in Constantinople is a major source for canto 96. See also letters 95 and 98.

9. Mustapha Kemal or **Kemal Atatürk.**

10. **Drew Pearson.**

11. This is not **Luigi Villari** (as EP may mistakenly think), but Pasquale Villari. EP is responding to the following from ORA: "I have been reading two books, one of which has been on my shelves for 50 years, Pasquale Villari's history of the Barbarian Invasion of Italy" (26 Dec. 1954).

12. "Hand and Soul" is a short story by **Dante Gabriel Rossetti.** *Vita Nuova* is Dante Alighieri's spiritual/erotic autobiography, translated by Rossetti as *The New*

Life. "I have been here before," is the first line of Rossetti's translation of Song IV ("Sudden Light") from Dante Alighieri's *House of Life.*

13. ORA quoted from Dante's *Paradiso* 33.85–87: "Nel suo profondo vidi che s'interna/ Lègato con amore in un volume/ Ciò che per l'universo si squaderna" ("In its [the Eternal Light's] depth I saw that it contained, bound by love in one volume, that which is scattered in leaves through the universe"; trans. John D. Sinclair) (26 Dec. 1954).

14. A visitor to St. Elizabeths, probably Wing-tsit Chan, author of *"The Unwobbling Pivot* and *The Great Digest,"* or perhaps Carson Chang, author of *Third Force in China,* a book EP mentions in a letter to Wyndham Lewis dated 19 November 1954 (see *Pound/Lewis* 281).

15. EP is referring to John Brown's *Panorama de la littérature contemporaine aus États-Unis,* which contains translations of several EP works, including cantos 11 and 45.

16. Unidentified, but also mentioned in letter 90.

17. Eva Hesse's translation of *The Pisan Cantos,* published as *Die Pisaner Gesänge.* EP cites her translation of "that free speech without free radio speech is as zero" (74/426). Presumably the improvement is the superior phonetic balance of "Redefreiheit" and "Radiofreiheit."

18. **Juan Ramón Jiménez.**

19. See canto 77/472. Louis Dudek asked Pound about this passage and reports that Pound "said it was about an incident when Cocteau went to see some fellow surrealist writers. They turned out to be chaps who had never read anything, some of them—'at least nothing before 1870'" (*DK* 29). EP also mentions it in *Guide to Kulchur* and adds, "You can get the meaning of this from Willy's pharmicien" (89). "Willy" is **Henri Gauthier-Villars.**

89. TLU-3 18 February 1955
18 Fb/

ORA.

accuse reception hnbl communication 31st ult.[1] Decline responsibility for neglect of W.M.R.[2] as matter of fact re/ centenary of Leaves of Grass. a few days ago I pointed out to edtr/ that acc/ my belief it was W.M.R. who told the damn brits/ that Whitman had a certain importance, and that AFTER that the damn yanks, a very few, but some, with time-lag, began to glance at the yawper. The radio "Invitation to Learning" on the past sabath was burbling about the hair on W chest being more like the flowing hair of the prophet, than Hemingway kind of hair. YU hv/ to hear the newt{s} to gauge the kulchurl level of Baruchistan in the reign of baby-face No.2. I think alzo that I told yu the ONLY time a pubr/ has ever printed {a} bk/ on my recommendation (if he did actually publish it, and I think he did) was Elkin Mathew's who consulted me in 1909 (or thereabouts) re/ a trans/ of the Convito. by yr/ reverend sire.

Hang onto the spare Cantos until emergency arises/ or give to Helen, that wd/ be most suitable if she has someone to read to her.

Now that there is a decent chink-wop edtn/ of Confucio/ and if Mary hasn't given you a copy YET give her{,} as from me{,} a bat over the head. Beautifully printed with only one idiotic miscorrection/ some imbecile, my own darter not above suspicion, has changed ascia to g asse[3] when W.M.R. would have LOOKED at the ideogram, its shape and refused to think an AX is an axis. p. 39. fer krizache[4] correct it in all copies yu get in reach of. It is CORRECTLY printed in the Rapgllo Ta S'eu, Studio Integrale.

repeating NOW THAT. etc. CouldN8t some qualified person. O.R.A. the only one known to me. EDIT [illegible deletion] my Orientamenti/ at least the saggi on TAXES. Il problema delle tasse/[5]

Now that there are usurers in Geneva howling for the destruction of [illegible deletion] Lavoro ed Usura. etc.

The disease of the occident (all of it) is making LEGAL crimes of simple non-criminal and often useful acts such as sale of beer or transport of diamonds.

This naturally leads to corruption of the ~~poilce~~ police as well as the oedemitous ~~pugg~~ swelling of the bugocracy.

and it is done because idiots like Einaudi do NOT understand monetary issue.

and the lousy gesellites, Aberhart included/ can't distinguish between 104% state usury, and a 12% annual demurrage tax, for elimination of national debt and all other taxes (might make a few exceptions for unusualy reasons, BUT one shd/ understand that such taxes are punitive, or intended as deterrents, or to exclude foreign competition in local labour market, but are NOT necessary to get money for the govt.

this racket was understood at least 300 years before Marco Polo.

Some partial (eng) translations of the Meridiano articles/ ~~hav~~ are in typescript/ but I know of NO eng/ or american public ready for them. IGNORANCE at cabinet level. govt. by illiterate mechanics and traders/

Mary/Boris and Vanni are doing noble BUT they cd/ use some collaboration. Have just been enjoying Varé's Two Imposters. BUT doubt if he is suitable editor for such a selection/ apart from the fact that he wdn't touch it.

IF there ia/ is a spare copy of the selections made in Venice (Villari shd/ know of it), all that is needed is to eliminate ALL matter that wd/ deter reader NOW in 1955. I am in total fog re/ current infamies in Italy.

BUT a b vol/ no larger than Lav/ ed Usura.wd/ be useful/ and after the Confucio they might take E.P. seriously. After all Bevione read the Gesellite articles or at least one and wrote me page and ½ of typescript/ and asked me viv voc to write a book on it which he said he wd/ go thru (when it was too late, of course"} are ~~eri~~ analyze with equal care. Pellizzi goofed/ and printed some twaddle re/ Soddy. by Jim B/.[6] Farinacci printed a gesellite artl/ which is no [illegible deletion] vaseline for the year current. Por also, ~~und~~ in Bot's and Ros's[7] magazines. As Vanni has paid M/ royalties on Kagekiyou,[8] the royalties on such a vol/ ought to pay the editor or editress for his or her time/ no use to me in bughouse so the editor cd/ pay for his or her food during time spent on the operation. You ~~we~~ wd/ bathe satisfactorily in the milk of tolerance [illegible deletion] as you eliminate all reference to the main Xtn myth, namely the crucifiction, or rather the crucifiers. They'll do it{,} or try it{,} every time. joined of course by the dummyXtns[9] and other perverts/ but still you cd/enjoy your "simple fancy" and ELIMINATE such particulars. which it wd/ the worst possible politics to reprint {anyhow}, dicto millesimo.[10] in the year current. WMR/ being aristotelian at that point. at least I think Ari/ says about the same. or else{,} where HAVE I read it during the past 6 months? I NEVER read bks ABOUT art, having started to LOOK at pictures aetat 12. Sheri[11] started at 3, and is therefore getting out of the Picassian muck, and up to pre-Raph contenuto[12] An Isis and Kuanon wont do for Sta Sabina/[13] Yes'm Dante an excellent poet/ probably MORE in Div. Com that was NOT in preceding poetry, than in any other writer. I have just got to saying: Mr Eliot concedes that I hv/ a certain ability as a writer, but never seems to see that ~~is~~ this may be connected with at least something or other IN the MIND, some capacity, let us say, for perception.

I will do something about getting yu the vol/ of translations.

> Benedictions a tutta la Fam/
> Malu Aldo[14] inc/

1. EP is acknowledging receipt (*accusé de réception*) of ORA's letter of 31 January 1955 ("31st ult.").

2. **William Michael Rossetti.**

3. Lt.: "ax" to "axis."

4. For Christ's sake.

5. It.: "the question of taxes."

6. Presumably EP means John Brown; see letter 88.

7. Probably **Edmondo Rossoni.**

8. *Kagekiyo*, a Noh play, was translated into Italian by **Mary de Rachewiltz** and published by Ernest Fenollosa and EP in *Introduzione ai Nô, con un dramma in un atto di Motokiyo: Kagekiyo.* See Gallup, *Ezra Pound* D60.

9. The Christian Democratic party of Italy.

10. Lt.: "I say for the thousandth time."

11. **Sheri Martinelli.**

12. It.: "subject matter."

13. Santa Sabina is an ancient church in Rome mentioned in cantos 93/623 and 109/774 as an example of fine architecture.

14. **Malù's** fiancé, Aldo Mingoli.

90. TLU-3   27 February, 3 March 1955
27 or thaarbouts Fb/

O.R.A.

what yr/ father did say, without any Aristotl, if my memory serves, was that Dant Gabe after translating all them thaar potes Pr/ Sec.[1] remained interested in Dante and Cavalcanti, and not much in the others. Naturally I have no idea WHERE W.M.R. uttered this. Giovannini[2] (Mary will tell yu who is) saying Tuesday, not only re/ Whitman but for Dante studies in general/ so perhaps a tiny minority (and god knows there are NO gt/ masses of fauna who think ANYthing) may not have mislaid yr/ pat/ fam's[3] work as much as you think. Not having access to library cats/ and bks/ of ref/ IF you dont hear from Morgan (who moves slower than hibernating cocodril)[4] have you handy any reference to WHERE yr/ pa boosted Whitman?

Old Montanari[5] has just sent from Ravenna a Asso Bastoni[6] where an unknown to me Lonnigan is waving a bloody but noble shirt. Can't some of yr/ obstreperous students take count of what Italy HAS/ someone to swat the snobism focused on Paris/ (note best material here in U.S. with names like Giovannini and Martinelli)/ When I want a simple reference looked up, I have to write to Venice/ IGGURUNCE. LaDriere[7] brot me some thesis on Fortune (concept) in med/ aev/[8] I may have overlooked it, but as I remember he omitted Inferno vii where the whole thing is set out most lucidly and concisely. Having been concerned with Paradiso, and in less degree with Purgat/ for years, I had completely forgotten that passage, if it ever entered my skull at all/ tho I had the general adumbration. without remembering ubicity of it(s) font.

Naturally the pretini[9] now take NO interest in theology or consequent ethics/ re/ mediaeval Anschauung that passage IMPLIES (bigosh and how).

Boris and Mary working full blast, I cd/ do with a few more serious correspondents, on any one of several useful topics. Intellectual life COULD exist in a geographic area without waiting to re-form a state. four inches of news print, seem to imply that yr/ present govt. has sold you down the river/ bitched the remains of [illegible deletion] autarchia. Whether yr/ local press spreads this news, I dont know. I ought to concern myself with american infamies, and let the dummyXtrs stew in *their* juice. MA!

Can't the pub/cn of Stone Confucio, with woplation be used to start some SERIOUS discussion of basic issues which WOULD have been raised in a civilized country, such as NEED to protest when executive exceeds his legal powers/ Ot Or the proposition that Eva H/ has improved by translating the necessarily more clumsy english into: "Redefreiheit ohne Radiofreiheit gleich null ist."?

The danger of having the world led or hogswoggled by people, not necessarily skunks, but who simply have had NO experience in thinking about government. Take one of the best examples, Charlie Wilson,[10] never had thought about anything but making machines and grabbing the largest possible chunk of the market. WHEN TOLD. he ~~ed~~ chuck{ed} his General Motors stock, not a microcephale. BUT need of contact with people who know a few things he doesn't.

The struggle is to get the discussion ONTO the crucial points. Poland seems to have drifted to hell while governed by the husbands of the Yankowski's, three sisters left there,[11] the Kulchur hub/ jailed for life etc. I hammered before on the IGNORANCE of the governing clawses all over the lot/ Querschnitt/[12] Hull,[13] Stilwell,[14] Leahey,[15] de Chambrun/[16] a fair variety but ALL ham iggurunt of things that had ought to hv/ ben lambasted into 'em in prep/ school. Yu kno anything about the people running french paper "Rivarol"?[17] someone sends it to me free.

Never heard of bloke waving a shirt/ interviewed in 31 Jan. Asso Bastoni.

3 Mz/ hv/ just heard from english (or rader OIrush) friend of Sturzo's?[18] Is the man ANY use? Does ANY damn socialist ever learn? I dont even kno that Stur was a soc/ merely that he disliked something or other.

alZo/ no more news of Virgil/ since B/ mentioned Coselschi?[19] wasn't he at E.I.A.R. (or was that another whpr?)[20] Told tother day that Knights of Pythias[21] are totally separate from murkn masons, and York rite not so corrupted. I dont spose I can get any data re/ that from YU. Another gentle line in conversation is the goofery of the American Acad/ in RomAAAA. A lot of waste space, last 40 years record for mediocrity and augment of misunderstanding between the two countries??? I spose the gentle VanBurens are dead by now??? Did you ever know them? AT any rate when yu think what COULD have been done, if they had had the sense to lodge me in one of the student stewdioz/// or of course still COULD. More central than Cumae. too late for several items. BUTTTT.

another point for gentle parlance/ is the SEDIMENT still in backwaters of the J.S.[22] leavings from the muck of Canby,[23] Hillier,[24] Atlandig Sedgwiks,[25] various degrees of la canaille litteraire/ Afraid Carter[26] is swamped in noble effort to make local centre in Va. AND Ireland reported sunk in black bigotry with all the good authors banned. (no detail...I never cd/ much believe in their kulchurl urge/ OMITTING so much that is needed for mental life. (nasty word mental...wop word: intelligenza. much be'r,. Forgot Inf. VII/ as hv/ for 40 years been objecting to neglect of Purg/ and Parad/

VURRY neat Virgil, there. and so forth. Somebody mentioned knowing Helen but forget who.

1. EP probably means *primo cento*, It.: "1100s."
2. **Giovanni Giovannini.**
3. *Pater familia*'s.
4. *Cocodrillo*, It.: "crocodile."
5. Not **Saturno Montanari**, the poet who died in 1941, but presumably **Philippo Montanari**, who is mentioned in a few other 1954 letters.
6. A Fascist journal.
7. **James Craig La Drière.**
8. Lt.: "Middle Ages."
9. Lt.: "young priests."
10. **Charles Erwin Wilson.** When he assumed office in Dwight D. Eisenhower's cabinet in 1953, he was obliged to dispose of his General Motors stock, valued at about $2.5 million.
11. Sisters of **Stanislas V. Yankowski.**
12. Unidentified but presumably a politician. Also mentioned in letter 120.
13. **Cordell Hull.**
14. **General Joseph Warren Stilwell.**
15. **William D. Leahy.**
16. **Clara de Chambrun.** EP told D. G. Bridson: "While I was in the bughouse, I ploughed through four sets of memoirs—Hull, Leahy, Stilwell and Madame de Chambrun. . . . You get Hull, the plodder, who is well, you must go round him. And then you get Leahy, who is a damn good guy, but who thought Chiang Kai-shek ought to have been an American; and you get Madame Longworth de Chambrun, in the middle of things in Paris . . . and they were all of them ham-ignorant of what ought to have been jammed into them at high school" (176–77). These names also appear together in 1951 and 1956 letters to Wyndham Lewis *(Pound/Lewis* 265, 292). See also letter 98.
17. A Parisian journal.
18. ORA replied: "You ask about Don Sturzo; I read a speech he made in the Senate about a year ago, denouncing rings and monopolies as one of the main causes of the high cost of living [. . .]; the reaction in the Senate was to tell him to appoint a committee and go into the matter and this successfully snuffed him out. He is very old now, but I have always liked his advocacy of decentralisation" (13 Mar. 1955).
19. **Eugenio Coselschi.**
20. Whippersnapper.
21. A men's society modeled after the Freemasons. See Carnahan.
22. Unidentified, but also mentioned in letter 88.
23. **Henry Seidel Canby.**
24. Probably Robert Hillyer, the author of two articles that appeared in the *Saturday Review of Literature* following EP's receipt of the Bollingen Award. A conservative with Harvard connections, Hillyer attacked everyone involved, including the Bollingen Foundation, by claiming that the awarding constituted an insult to the war dead.
25. Probably Henry Dwight Sedgwick (1861–1957), an American lawyer and assistant U.S. attorney for the southern district of New York (1895–98), who in 1890 gave up law practice to devote his time to writing.
26. **Thomas H. Carter.**

91. TLU-3 18 March 1955
18 Mz/

O.R.A.

Please thank Helen for very interesting extract/ Glad to have paid part of debt to R/ family, especially to W.M.R. very neat loop.

Of course D.G.R. was the start {for me}/ never heard of Christina {in the U.S. pre 1907}, it was Fordie who [illegible deletion] used to stomp round insisting, and quoting her in inaudible voice.

And of course thinking the whole pre-Rap gang had ceased in the '80s/ {or along with Sheets + Kelly}[1] it was surprise to young yank[2] to be called in to sponser.

** this in haste (at least started in haste) re/ Orientamenti. A great deal of it out of date or inopportune at this time. I shd/ suggest a half page introduction re the ACCEPTANCE of several of the ideas, mainly Gesellite. Perhaps a mere tabulation.

1. Arbeitswert.[3] Now in common use, in fact the ONLY comprehensible measure when american radio or govt. wants to compare what a russian has to DO to get a suit of clothes, or what part of an american's time he has to use *now* to buy food in proportion to what he had to use 40 years ago.

2. The present production system creates a mass of prices faster than it distributes the power to buy. This is the gist of C.H. Douglas' Social Credit [illegible deletion] perceptions.

The filth of London, the "School of Econ." and Gug Gregory[4] denied it, and tried to conceal it. The infamous F.D.R. based the whole spew deal on it, but used poison.

The answer is not deficit spending UNLESS you use stamp scrip.

The infantilism of Aberheart's[5] measures and Bankhead's proposal[6] offered an intolerable price 104% per year for the use of money. Instead of the {rent} sane 12% per year as used at Worgl.

The Jefferson letter to Crawford[7] is basic. And John Adams had, five years before then, used the term "devaluation for the benefit of the whole people," i.e. not for a small group of swindlers.

Por and I were correlating, Douglas, Gessell, Canonist doctrine of the Just Price (included in Douglas) and fascist practice. The billion $ brain washing is tries to hide about 40 historic facts.

Orage probably the ONLY socialist whose mind ever opened to ANYTHING.

I take it the Yalta publication[8] will make it easier to tell some parts of the truth in ENGLAND.

Dear old Domvile[9] writes on 14th inst,[10] on hearing the U.S. is *about* to publish, opines that W.C. wd/ prefer to blush in secret and that "after perusing them (the papers) Judas Iscariot will be able to pose as a virgo intacta."[11]

Barney Baruch's friend Ike was pushed fairly near to the edge of a thought tother day/ like DelMAr on the monetary UNIT being the total volume of nation's money/ That a new issue cd/ be made ONLY by the govt. and wd diminish the value of each buck already in circulation.

However that don't git round fact that it is NOT necessary to issue all money as INTEREST-BEARING debt. that is another basic line in any summary of E.P. on econ/

I dont think the other material Olga brought to Rome needs to be considered now/ Angold is dead/ the Mencius notes superseded by later work etc. And, as I hv/ sd/ the Orientamenti needs cutting down to what is OPPORTUNE now. with omission of what might give offense without doing any positive good. Mencius main remark being that detailed research is useful because it can conduce, and WHEN it does conduce to brevity and lucidity of statement. clear summary.

With Raiola fading. I dont know how far the utopian vista is open to yr/ correspondent. The PROPER place for E.P. wd/ be the AMERican acad/ in Roma. (NOT in administration but HOUSED.) when yu consider they{ir} poor record for past 40 years/ and what ~~i~~it COULD have been.... THAT is part of the time lag/ AS per Whitman, discovered by W.M.R. in 1854/ still regarded a joke in 1905 by profs/ in Philadelphia

First time I heard him taken seriously ~~b~~ was by a DANE, in 1906 or 7. There is a sediment in minor beaneries hostile to E.P. NOT on econ/ or polit/ grounds even tho the English Institute has gone to exceptional length of using the ~~wole~~ whole of their year book for E.P.'s kudos/ and a bloke named Espey done a whole vol/ on{"} Mauberley{"}[12] (which passed wholly unnoticed when first pub/d.) in 1920. Very interesting book, and some parts HIGH grade writing.

The braghe molle were tactically right 9 years ago to stick to literary (awtistikk) angle, as the american pancreas ({"}brain{"} being a misnomer) has been too completely poisoned to face the 40 historic facts. BUT Whittier,[13] Bryant[14] and co/ were more real than the aesthetes, even if not brilliant pro{sodists}

Wonder if Varé will mention my notes on his Two Imposters to you?

1. Keats and Shelley.
2. EP is alluding to his role in getting **William Michael Rossetti's** *Dante and his Convivio* published by **Elkin Mathews.** See also letters 15 and 89.
3. Gm.: "work-value." A measure of value in hours of work, still commonly used to compare the living standards between countries.

4. Probably Sir Theodore Gregory (b. 1890), Sir E. Cassel Professor of Economics at the University of London (1927–37), economic adviser to various governments, and author of numerous books on banking, the Gold Standard, and the U.S. Federal Reserve System.

5. **William Aberhart.**

6. On Febuary 17, 1933, Senator John H. Bankhead of Alabama introduced a bill into Congress that would authorize the federal government to issue a dated stamp scrip that would operate as legal tender. EP knew of the Bankhead scheme from Irving Fisher's *Stamp Scrip*, which he reviewed in *New English Weekly*.

7. See letter 70.

8. A reference to the release of papers from the 1945 Yalta conference involving Roosevelt, Churchill, and Stalin. These papers were kept secret until the week of 20–26 March 1955. See also letter 92.

9. **Sir Barry Domville.**

10. Of this month.

11. Lt.: "untouched maiden."

12. John Espey wrote *Ezra Pound's Mauberley* (1955).

13. John Greenleaf Whittier (1807–92).

14. William Cullen Bryant (1794–1878).

92. TLU-2   29 March 1955
29 Marzo/

O.R.A.

ThaZZ the stuff for the troops. Yr/ philippik recd/

I don't know about the second quote, in the ~~1st~~ 2nd/ paragraph. I think it wd/ be better to put in a word or two to make it clear that the "tanto benigno"[1] etc/ does NOT refer to yr/ present correspondent. Which wd/ seem to be far from yr/ intention.

I dont know that I can hit the right words at first go/ but something like a ♭ BECAUSE the opposition. etc.

May be a new sentence. AND I don't know that Ooozenstein and W.C. had even a top dressing. Foetus-faced bladder has been used in describing C's moog.

However whether Tempo rises to print, can you send a copy to Denis Goacher,[2] 40 Parkhill Rd. London n.w. 3 s.v.p. He is trying to print TRAX,[3] with some postscripta on life and entanglements etc.

Enc/ the latest from the cultural front/ Classics de-mothball'd. Letter from NHPearson[4] says it went very well.

L'egregia Crosby[5] has dug up some old letters, and proposes publication, all ad maj. [illegible deletion] Ez. glo.[6]

As to Pelop's pamph/ the lunatic who printed it wanted{,} I believe{,} to give me a pleasant surprise. (quite nuts, mixture of american indian, jew and whatnots, been in at least 2 asylums plus dope) printed only 106 copies. Of course it is now there for publication IF the Famille Pelops WANT{S} it diffused, but I have no idea where they can find {\}a publisher.

Newsweek, infuriated by, I suppose, Hudson Rev/ plus Yalta, is printing the old line lie re/ broadcasts for Mus/ etc. and I doubt if they will print a rettifica.[7] tho Dave[8] left here with intention of sending one. A quite decent visitor yester/ still thinking Acheson[9] has a warm heart, and Hiss more sinned Against than sinning.

(trick of getting immature apes into places of responsibility) however E.P.'s incarceration was disapproved/ BUT then this bloke had disapproved of it nine years ago.

Il nemico e l'ignoranza.[10] His wishful thinking prospected Adlai,[11] and he brushed off Mrs Longworth's[12] crack that Adlai was an intellectual in the Dorothy Parker[13] class. He thought the regal Alice wd/ say anything just fer the fun of it.

Mundt on the air, kicked hell out of Sparkman,[14] who was very flustered, shouting out of turn.

Stef/[15] spitting teeth by mail, when I wrut that the Yankowski sisters had busted Poland by neglecting to educate their husbands/ all I had to go on was Stan's revelation that he had MORE sisters, apparently married oo all the Polish govt, except Beck[16] and Pilsuds.,[17] whom one 'em had obviously flustered because he pinned the Holy three headed eagle or Holy Sepulchre or whatever right THRU trappings onto he{r} buZZum thereby causing an "ouch" with attendant excitements. She WON'T write any memoirs, and Stan, to her disgust seems to be making a q.satisfactory trans/ of Ric/ St Victor's De Contemplatio.

As to family vaults. Ingrid's[18] ma-in law{'}s pa was on Q. Vicky's[19] staff, and young Ing/ is struggling vs/ a mind which seems to have jelled at that period.

I have forgotten who Gladwyn Jebb is. And haven't found out which Trevelyans[20] she has been to the boat-race with. the idea of coherence among my well-wishers can not be taken in vain abstraction. I think I told yu I discourage Dave by defining democracy as a place where old VyOler has a vote and even Bock can't get into Congress. Ike has raised the cultural level from Micky Rooney to Irving Berlin. I mean at the Hite Whouse.

Stock has got promise of an hour of Ez on Aurssstraliarn radio. Might be good to send HIM copy of yr/ Quo tandem abutere usque.[21] Noel Stock 20 Mount St. Preston N. 18 Melbourne, Australia.

best to Helen.

1. It.: "so very benevolent." We do not have the document to which EP is referring.

2. **Denis Goacher.**

3. Sophocles' *Women of Trachis*. We do not know if **Denis Goacher** succeeded in printing this play, but EP did publish, as Sofocle-Pound, *Le Trachinie*.

4. **Norman Holmes Pearson.**

5. **Caresse Crosby.**

6. An impish application of the Jesuit motto *Ad majorem Deum gloriam*, "To the greater glory of God."

7. It.: "correction." The 28 March 1955 issue of *Newsweek*'s "Periscoping the Nation," a section containing news bits from across America, contains a brief note on EP's Fascist history and incarceration (16); on pages 25–27 of the same issue is an article entitled "Yalta's Long Shadow." See also letter 91.

8. Probably **David M. Gordon.**

9. **Dean Acheson.**

10. It.: "the enemy is ignorance."

11. **Adlai Stevenson.**

12. **Alice Roosevelt Longworth.**

13. **Dorothy Parker.**

14. **Senator John Sparkman.**

15. Presumably **Lincoln Steffens.**

16. **Jósef Beck.**

17. **Józef Pilsudski.**

18. **Ingrid Davies.**

19. Queen Victoria's.

20. Family of prominent British politicians and scholars. There were three brothers: Charles Phillips (1870–1958), George Macaulay (1876–1972), and Robert Claverley (1872–1951).

21. Lt., roughly: "Which will be useful in the end."

93. TLU-1   [mid-April 1955]

O.R.A.

of course the F. Forum[1] is a hand picked plebiscite/ the crablice do not scribe to FF/

It appears La Luce[2] was very affable at the Scelba reception/[3] yes E.P. wanted in Italy (not by the police), and no need of trial because he WAS crazy when it happened, and cd/ now be released.

One radio yap here or something said La Luce was annoying DullHorse[4] by wanting to bring back Casa Savoia/[5] along I spose with foreign investments at 74% in Po Valley petrol. Problem istituzionale IN Italy none of my business/ transmission of lies FROM Italy as news, always was, and wd/ I think continue to be under any circs whatsodam.

I do not much care about technicalities/ a nolle prosequi[6] need give NO reasons whatever. But shd/ precede shenanigans.

However/...

and Gladys[7] says she heard you were as Fascist, also thought yu had been to Geneva. Well, I never heard that you had a taste for rotten company, and dont know if that misfortune ever befell yu.

When she asked about Sturzo, I said write to YOU as you knew something about what I HAD been doing. She says she thought Sturzo HAD heard of my econ/ ideas. I doubt if he ever heard of anything save Douglas (C,H,) I mean NO precise knowledge of anything I ever actually said.

She didn't know what Sturz' econ/ ideas were cause she allus dropped to sleep when she tried to read 'em. (probably sign of intelligence)/ and that he was not a socialist but a liberal (nota del epistolario)[8] and theref(ore) allergic to usury as an ~~eveil~~ evil, probably a cawflik calvinist/ AND that he had set up some sort of college or school in RoMAAA, to boost the small man and split up the states into bits/

a jew here sends me {a} "catholic anarchist" paper. I spose that hoax mean{s} merely annul all civic govt. and leave the plebs to racketeers in original-sin, ab/ talare.[9]

But nice confusionarioism.

Did I say that mr cummings thinks americans are "so kind" the police here are being SO considerate of Rab{b}i Papier, they don't want to hurt the rab's feelinks by telling him about {his son} Chakey, who says he is koink to gedt a tdental tdgree and tden he vil pe apble to get all the narcotics he wants. (presumably for resale)

it does show tenderness on the part of the minions.

AND dear Pegler with best intentions, has uttered several inexact statements. I never saw that softboil{d} bunch of rural spinace[10] Wallace[11] but once. under VERY funny circs/ indeed.

Much funnier than any hindoo shenanigans/ Tho~~s~~ he did once run to DeKruif[12] for comfort. DeK was writing about the marvels of science, and the HEROIK woik vs/ pelagra/

And I told him he was hunting fer a remedy cheaper than food and that the prob/m appeared to me economik rather than theraputi{c}

You may ~~jw/~~ have {known}, in fact cert did, know more of wop exiles than I did or do/ apart from Sturz who wasn't very bright, weren't they mostly crablice?

That putt him onto econ/ for some months till the Ladies Home Urinal started giving him $3000 an article to change the subject.

The Sat. Eve/ Post has recently raised its culch/ level by the "Loeb Leopold[13] memoirs," I hv/ not seen{/} but the S.E.P.[14] advertises on the radio that the murderer's life story is appearing in there fireside hebdomidaire.[15]

I don't mind being considered eccentric, officially, so long as I am not required to say Roose was other than a dunghill ~~Church~~ ChurSHCILD no better/ Chur- and Rot-; the twins celestial. Peg's[16] column was NOT carried in the Washington tabloid evening leaf, to which Mr Meyer[17] has had him relegated/ but which omits him ~~wher~~ when the temperature

rises. Good on{e} on Tyler Kent yester, no spare copy at hand. with a final
pp/ re E.P. much better artl tha the enc.[18]

best to Helen.

1. EP enclosed a page from a public opinion poll by Facts Forum, whose 11 April
1955 news release, also called *Facts Forum*, EP sent to ORA. The Dallas group is
self-described in its letterhead as a "Non-partisan public affairs organization whose
purpose is to stimulate interest in vital issues of the day, inspiring expression of
informed and enlightened opinion." Among the questions asked in the April poll
are "Should the Birthday of Franklin D. Roosevelt be made a national holiday?"
and "Are Parent-Teachers Associations infiltrated with Reds?" The first achieves
a Yes Rating of 8 percent (a figure circled by EP) and the second 50 percent. Some
of the results are interpreted in the news release, including the following:

> More than interesting is the result of the poll in connection with the ques-
> tion regarding Franklin Roosevelt's birthday. It appears that the late Presi-
> dent's popularity rating has hit an all-time low. One reason for this might be
> the release of the Yalta papers.

> More than half of the American people are aware, according to the April
> Facts Forum Poll, that anyone who attempts to investigate Communism will
> be smeared. The poll indicated that 62% of the people believe that Senator
> McClellan of Arkansas will become a major target of the Communists be-
> cause he is head of the Senate committee presently investigating Red activ-
> ities in the government.

2. **Clare Boothe Luce.**
3. Presumably a reception at the house of **Mario Scelba.**
4. Presumably John Foster Dulles (1888–1959).
5. The House of Savoy, that is, the house of the deposed kings of Italy.
6. Lt: "no wish to pursue," used in legal documents for a stay of proceedings.
7. **Gladys Hynes.** She wrote to ORA (8 May 1955; NYPL) as EP had requested.
8. It.: "note by the letter writer."
9. *Abito talare*, It.: "monk's habit."
10. Perhaps *spinaci*, It.: spinach.
11. **Henry Agard Wallace.**
12. Probably **Paul Henry de Kruif.** EP may be thinking of *Why Keep Them Alive*,
a study of malnutrition and disease in children that included a discussion of pellagra, a common illness in Italy.
13. Nathan Leopold Jr. (1906–71) and Richard Loeb (1906–1936), both of wealthy
families, were convicted of the elaborately planning thrill kidnapping and kill-
ing of fourteen-year-old Robert Franks and sentenced to life in prison, not the death
penalty, due to the pleading of their lawyer, Clarence Darrow. The *Saturday
Evening Post* must have run a story on their lives.
14. *Saturday Evening Post.*
15. *Hebdomadaire*, Fr.: "weekly."
16. **Westbrook Pegler.**
17. **Eugene Meyer.**
18. EP enclosed a review by David R. Slavit of new productions of *Sweeney
Agonistes* and *Women of Trachis.*

94. TLU-3 NYPL   22 May 1955

22 Maggio 55/

O.R.A.

C/ for correlation and Caravella.[1] These 2 boys have given the first careful statement of the facts/ that has got PRINTED. Yr/ noble call to dam the late sowbelly not having got past the copy desk. I am trying to get copies of Potty Dot's column[2] (the widdy of the late clown Sinc. Lewis, who got permanent hold on american choinulism by saying Adolf wd/ never have *a career* in choimunny) at last useful. Her account of Sowbelly joking with Stalin about bumping off only 49,000 instead of 50,000 german officers seemed to shed light even into Mr Eliot's dim mind. He said: {"}He drank the toast?{"}

Of course this may by now have passed OUT of Mr Eliot{'}s motive centre, but at least the idea of FDR being a louse entered it for a moment. I shd say it must have floated around in his consciousness for at least 15 minutes. AND I spose the column was removed from later edtns/ of the Star as McN/[3] didn did not find it. But F/[4] says he will hunt. I recd only one copy without date. The Brazilian note on Pina M/ was also specific if brief. "America" the Catholic weekly here is too pusillanimous to print G.Gs' sober artle re Pina etc/[5]

As Boris has reserves re Caravel/ perhaps you know of some means of communicating with them indirectly. It is good that they concentrated on Lavoro ed Us/ Does Magnino[6] know them. (this letter is for consultation with Boris) Pisani has sent me a copy od Societa Nuova, with a note by Sturzo. I suppose I shd/ try to read some of it. BUT in any case, if Caravella is neo-[7] or suspect of being neo- The Dummy Xristers COULD with advantage reprint Cairoli's "Prezzo Giusto"/[8] and point out the concord with the Secolo artl/ re/ economics rising from justice if it is to be sane.

Also there is, I think, a footnote in the Confucio/ that justice[illegible deletion], the idea of equity rises with agriculture/ the drover getting no further than difference between my sheep and thy sheep. That line wd/ take in the Pelops/ gang. And the slogan: Italianita Mazziniana[9] ought to hold some of the wilder sperrits: the rump end of a fascist party persisting the worst errors of the ventennio cannot be servibile.[10] There can be no leadership unless somebody follows. Let 'em not talk of frontiers. I say {"}TALK{"} of frontiers.. What was sound in fascismo should get neo-names that dont ~~ri~~ raise instant opposition. Even the stuffy fabians with their nurse-pin sta{t}e had sense enough to expect a time lag. Marx and co/ exploited a reality/ i.e. the change in production methods/ ANOTHER change has occurred. It take{s} time to change frontiers. Local control of local purchasing power wd satisfy the Tirol, without dragging in the ghosts of Cecco Beppe and Metternich. Obviously it is a dangerous slogan for yr/ dear goddam'em kikes smell ANY attack on usury 40 years off. Vide the Genevan shyster wanting "[illegible deletion]Lavoro ed Us/" suppressed AT ONCE.

Ergo the neo/s shd AIM at local c/ of local p/p/[11] without too much cackle.

The Secolo art/ls{,} esp that of 4th inst{,} were very good. AND as the brits "don{'}t believe in ideas", Roma has vurry nice chance to rise. Paul the Deacon[12] along 600 and which what a.D. in defining the wop provinces mentions the province of Tuscany "in which is Roma, quae olim"/.[13] Mus/ wiped off the olim. N.Y. crspdt/[14] says the les noirs[15] are now pro hitler but not pro-Mus/ that due to jew poison at time of abyssinia/.[16] Mr Eliump[17] was given a copy of Freedman[18] but mercifully provided with an envelope/ whether he has yet read it I dunno. Do you see Magnino, or is he in another compartment? Is the g.d. church taking any part in the anti-dope racket? Complete cynicism of female medic specialist/ 30 years american filth/ conviction that every man has his price, and that the bureau for narcotic control offers SUCH great chances for lucre. pragmatic Anschauung. with of course feminine destructivity and nacherl negative bent.

the gal seems to me steady as a rock and full of all the best instincts/ BUT the amurkn scene after the great defilement leave THAT. I haven't read much Marxist slosh/ but do the antiMarx make enough use of the ACTUALITY on which he built{?} namely that old agrarian DETAIL had to shift with machinery production. AND with managerial etc/ there is {now a new} reality under politics. BUT the ethos has got to be CANONIST (Confucian), the JUST PRICE. And for 30 years I have been telling the old Whore of Babylon to hang out that sign. It is her sign. The lowest louse in the Fattycan may hoist it without being branded a heretic (however much his cardinals and contractors will try to ditch him if he does it.) Even high prelates have occasionally murmured something about errors due to iggurunce/ at least in prologs aimed at bringing back a bit of the general darkness. A pope who wasn't a s.o.b. and had even a grain of intelligence cd/ immensely strengthen the CHURCH by a little horse sense and honesty. AND the brit/ s.o.b.{s} wd/ at once hire more Keynes to lie in order to block any renewed catholic sanity. Try to let me know who speaks to whom. s.v.p.[19] Note that Eliot had never heard of Waddell, and HE was running the supposedly best quarterly or periodical/ in Britain for 20 years or thaarbouts. It took a Gree{n}wich Village dope to drag in a vol (of rather crude mixture) by Alfalfa Bill[20] of Oklahoma, to restart hunt for Wad/{'s} lost vols/ and the next boy from Ok/ vurry surprised that Alfalfa shd/ have heard of *anything*. The Admiral did a nice pome for the St Geo/ dinner. "Oh to be in Brixton now that April's here.{"} excellent

prosody throughout. But local in reference. I must git a cawpy fer Helen. I wonder if my own satire is always too strong to get across. V.Chan/[21] of new univ of Pakistan" quotin "limbo of chopped ice and sawdust." You may recall Calcutta note: "we have not this Confucius in India."
but these sounds are from quite distant countries.

1. Unidentified, but presumably both Caravellas are members of the **Movimento Sociale Italiano.** They are also mentioned in letters 97, 99, and 104.

2. EP is referring to **Dorothy Thompson's** *I Saw Hitler!*

3. **Robert McNair Wilson.**

4. Probably **William French.**

5. **Giovanni Giovannini's** article on **Jose V. de Piña Martins** had been accepted by *America,* but the editors later decided not to print it; it was eventually published in *New Times* (Melbourne, Australia).

6. Possibly Domenico Magnini, editor and translator of Plutarch's *Vita Ciceronis,* or, more likely, Leo Magnino, the author of *Teatro giapponese.*

7. Neo-Fascist.

8. Cairoli's *Il giusto prezzo mediovale.*

9. It., roughly: "to be Italian is to be pro-Mazzini."

10. It.: "usable."

11. Control of local purchasing power.

12. EP is referring to **Paul the Deacon's** *De Gestis Langobardorum* (collected in *History of the Langobards*), one of two principal sources for canto 96.

13. Lt., roughly: "which is of the past."

14. Correspondent.

15. Fr.: "the blacks."

16. A reference to Mussolini's invasion of Abyssinia in 1935 and the application of economic sanctions by the League of Nations—an action bitterly resented by Italians, who felt it was their turn to acquire colonial dependencies. EP erroneously attributes the hostility of Britain and France to Jewish manipulation.

17. T. S. Eliot.

18. **Benjamin Freedman's** *Facts Are Facts.*

19. *S'il vous plait.*

20. **William Murray.**

21. Unidentified. EP may be quoting criticism of the Indian edition of *Confucius: The Unwobbling Pivot and the Great Digest.*

95. TLU-3   26, 30 May 1955
26 Maggio/

ORA/

Secolo doing nicely/ and without direct direction, which is a comfort.
Whether O.R.A.'s noble thunder will get past any copy desk even translated I dunno. Current Hudson contains some fairly direct statement BUT
absolutely no indication that anyone has seen a copy of it.

I x spose the Secolo marks gain against time lag/ 13 years instead of 30
between book printing and comment. IMpossible to get an{y} communication or indication re/ who speaks to whom. Lack of controversial sense/
can't get ANYone to analyze the diseases. Brown[1] should have been sub-
jected to acid/ as a SPECIMEN, AS a perfect specimen of State Dept. as
of Roose/. And the Slimes of Sodom[2] has hit a new low in review of Kung-
thology. Some one ought to note Kung's OWN summary of the book:
There are 300 Odes (approx) AND they can be summed up in one sentence: Have no twisty thoughts.

That kicks you bigots/ Xtns got so balled up in dogma they have to
wriggle/ Mr Freedman has at last done a nice li'l brochure on the Talmud.
Getting round to Mustapha's remark in 1908.[3]

Varé's optimistic sentence is in a private letter. I wonder if yu hv/ ever
seen the "lost Cantos",[4] i.e. those writ in wop? Whether they were printed
de luxe, as acc/ one report (and nacherly liberated?) Probably wd/have
caused some annoyance at the time. I have, as yu may recall, caused
annoyance. (Always or at least I hope nearly always, to the spawn of hell
and the filth of iniquity, but annoyance.).

I keep hammering/ Gourmont's dissociation d'idées.[5] They confuse the
land and the mortgage, the material means of or fa{c}tor in production,
and the NON*productive claim. The mess "free and equal" from meaning *IN orig/ context:* no special privilege for noble and clergy. Interest and
usury, muddled for 2000 years, or say at least 2500. Can't get any response
on specific points (apparent trifles which are SYMPTOMS.). Mr Bow got
in a good lick, justifying the old brass who were fussing re/ Kief case.
uninteresting in itself.

Funny NObody takes up analogy with Easter Islands/[6] barbarismus. etc.
At last a little sunburn, 2 days, then, FLOP back into winter. If any of yu
feelin' low, let 'em try try Paul the Deacon fer the habits of constantinople and them parts (a.d. 800.)

{30 Mag}

And if that Freedman pamphlet, WITH chap/ and verse gets thru the
murkn and wop mails, I trust ORA will READ it. I dont think she ever
read Rosanov/[7] spose my "Fallen Leaves" is still at Scarfoglios. Not sure.
ANY chan{c}e of publishing the Brooks Adams, which WAS translated

from copies I brot/ to roMA. I dont kno by whom. NOR has ORA said if she meets Magnino.[8] Wd/ Fantappie be interested? There is no need of time-lag on collateral light, even if yu can't spring grampaw, or get the Oozenstinian dirt out of the State department, all at once. One Scotch laird had said (alas privately) that Winston is an absolute bounder and cad, and got where he got by BEING and abs. b & c. And the Admiral's main-law who lives on Gros/ Sq/ says the murkns lose no op/ of spitting on the monument of the great degrader. The Ad/ suggests we send [illegible deletion] 'em one Baruch to go on to the other side of the mantle-piece. A.K.Chesterton[9] optimistic re/ what wd/ happen IF the brits got a honest govt. I think the Egyptians say: WHEN the peach ripens.

Boris sez yu giv a MAGnificent whoop at Cuma/[10] but seems to think you have a blind eye for the bastids that Xified yr Svr.[11] namely the Monds,[12] Morgenthaus, Rothschilds and other filth of the mesopotamian mud flats. If yu are giving war whoops, I think a Confucian tone might take up several slogans. altering them to the just mean.

Le frontiere d si defendono,[13] AND the best defence is honest government, INSIDE the country.

Pity the pore uncawnshus "carrier" whether it be of bubonics, tubercles or the kikerian state of mind, the [illegible deletion] oily and spherical/ the so accurately defined by Wm Shx/etc. Not that the chew shd/ be prejudged/ he shd/ simply be watched for racial symptoms, and not allowed to infect the mind of the non-kike. Genocide? unnecessary. Bar them from three professions/ and when a lump of suet like the late unlamented Gertie offers Malthus as a remedy, namely gen*osuicide* for the goy.[14] Smile. We have heard it before. Do not assist 'em in erecting idola fori[15] to distract the goy from the problem of issue/ or ~~from~~ when they wish to reduce literature to mere ornament, the poor cousin of the art shoppe. And do not think stable prices in unstable money are useful. Whether they act from intent or from nature do not permit the infection of uncontaminated areas. und so VEITER.[16]

I want more copies Secolo for *May 4*/ whether the Lydi from Orstraliar took off my only cawpy by mistake I dunno, Boris might send a couple of clips by air/ Lydi easier to remember as White Lamb than Whitlam/ poetry ought not econ/ Oh Yes, 2nd/ Part of Faust/ WHY yes, a lot about paper money.[17] Gordon[18] hopes bootleg some sense via Literature course as Econ/ dept absolootly blocked. I told the White Lamb better go Italy than Paris/ THAT point shd/ be hammered. frog translations from yank INFERIOR to polish, spanish, german and even wop (admitting I had in that last case to produce the traductrix[19] BUT still... (Admiral Fisher:[20] if we need men...etc.) If I hadn't started this on air letter wd/ enc/ potty Dot on Ooozefeld the joker. Reading "venbl" Beade/[21] apparently the most goldam set of fads and mass hysteria swept over

Europe, some time after fall of Empire or at least after decline of the Exarchate.

best to Helen.

1. Probably Rear Admiral Wilson Brown, a naval aide to Roosevelt, or perhaps Lathrop Brown, a longtime friend of Roosevelt and a Congressman from Long Island (but not connected in an obvious way with the State Department).

2. A reference to the largely negative *Times Literary Supplement* review of EP's *The Classic Anthology Defined by Confucius* (see "Pound and Confucius").

3. Although we do not know which of Mustapha Kemal's, or **Kemal Atatürk's**, remarks EP has in mind, he is no doubt thinking of Kemal's adoption of the corporativist economics of *The Eparch's Book* (see Nicole). See letters 88 and 98 and canto 96/658–69.

4. Cantos 72 and 73, written in Italian and suppressed until 1985.

5. See letter 33.

6. See letter 57.

7. EP's "Rosanov e cruet."

8. See letter 94.

9. **A. K. Chesterton.**

10. A talk ORA gave at Raiola's villa at Cumae.

11. Savior.

12. The family of **Alfred Moritz Mond.**

13. It.: "Borders will look after themselves."

14. EP seems to be saying that Gertrude Stein was a secularized assimilationist, one who assumed that Jews would disappear into the general population through intermarriage. EP and Stein had first met at the latter's Paris home in 1921 but did not get along well. In a 1927 letter to Archibald MacLeish EP wrote: "Gertie Stein is supposed to haff a stdyle pecause she writes yittish wit englisch wordts. That is not the way to did it but it shows how effektif it iss yess" (Carpenter 401). EP also ascribed to her the following statement: "The Jews have produced only three original geniuses: Christ, Spinoza, and myself" (401).

15. It.: "false idols."

16. *Und so weiter*, Gm.: "and so forth."

17. Possibly a reference to act 4, scenes 5–7 of Marlowe's *Dr. Faustus*. Faustus sells a Horse-Courser a horse for "forty dollars" (paper money) but warns him that the horse, though a sturdy, swift beast, must not be ridden into water. The Horse-Courser ignores the warning, rides the horse into the water, and finds it turned into "a bottle of hay."

18. Presumably **David M. Gordon.**

19. *Traduttrice*, It.: "translator." EP is thinking here of the Italian translations of his works by **Mary de Rachewiltz.** By 1955 she had translated several works with EP's collaboration, including cantos 13, 20, and 27 as *Tre Cantos*. See Gallup, *Ezra Pound* D60.

20. Probably Sir John Arbuthnot Fisher (1841–1920), commander of the Mediterranean fleet (1899) and First Sea Lord (1904–10 and 1914–15), whose relations with Churchill broke down over Gallipoli.

21. **Venerable Bede.** EP is presumably reading his *Historia ecclesiastica gentis anglorum.*

96. TLU-1   2 July 1955

2 Lug

che il giudeo fra voi di voi non ride.[1]

and yet again: nuts fer yr/ Lubin.

If there were any doubt about Del Mar's ancestry I think his Hist/ Monetary systems, which I am rereading now that I know more/ wd/ settle it. AND I trust another Sq. $ vol/ will again proclaim him our greatest amurikun historian. AND I have allus sa allus stood up fer Meyer Anselm against such swine as Gentz and Metternich

AND [illegible deletion] SO we come round again to Dante: HE SAID IT.

I think the sonZov destroy all copies of Del Mar and Waddell just like the gent of uncertain origins in Geneva so recently, i.e. ILLustratin their habits: Distruggetelo e far lo sparire dalla circulazione.[2]

A tablet (now doN't jostle Helen too rudely, but a TABlet has been erected or embedded in Fordie's lil house in Winchelsea/ Goach[3] says some 40 in attendance and a darter come from oireland, I spose the lady horse doctor as the cloistered unlikely be let out fer such vanities.

Gordon[4] says they giv him such a dirty look in the Bib/ of Cong/ the Cong Liebury whenever he asks for a copy of Waddell/ it too{k} him a whole day to get a Talmud to verify Freedman, and see that Freed/ has only picked a few of the daisies.

Whether BOTH the kikes and the Fat Can are out against DelMar I dunno/ but he is a vurry in'erestin' author. You did get his "Barbara Villiers" or the Hist. of Monetary Croimes??? I whope.

The stinking Slimes[5] having sunk to a new low of imbecility re/ Confucio {Anthol.}/ am cheered by quote in Listener,[6] allegedly from Hsieh something or other, saying I am the only translator who models his style on the text (i.e. of the original).

Howard Comfort,[7] Prof. at Haverford College, Haverford, Pa think{s} he might start a Catullian Quarterly, hadn't Mrs Raiola better have his address? How long is she to be in New Pork? McN/[8] wd/ be willing, in fact will I think insert a brief ref/ (proportionate to the bulk of his optimistic mensile.[9] Did Coselski[10] have zummat to do with E I A R or something, what ought I to know, or ignore about him?

1. EP is quoting Dante's exhortation to Christians to behave: "*si che 'l Giudeo di voi tra voi non rida!*" (*Paradiso* 81): "so that the Jew among you may not laugh at you" (editors' trans.).

2. It.: "Destroy it and make it disappear from circulation."

3. **Denis Goacher.**

4. Presumably **David M. Gordon.**

5. See letter 95.

6. The reference is to the fairly positive review of *The Classic Anthology Defined by Confucius* in *The Listener* (June 23 1955). On 30 June 1955 *The Lis-*

tener published a letter from David Hawkes of Oxford criticizing the review: "Pound's *Classic Anthology* is a huge and awe-inspiring monument of mistranslation" (1127).

7. Howard Comfort edited the *Corpus Vasorum Arrentinorum: A Catalogue of the Signatures, Shapes and Chronology of Italian Sigillata*, but there is no evidence that the Catullian Quarterly was ever published.

8. **Robert McNair Wilson.**

9. It.: "monthly."

10. **Eugenio Coselschi.**

97. TLU-3   7 July 1955

7 Lug/.

dear O.R.A.

here is a chance to use TACT. My friends are the most chaRRRming people in the world, and of the highest (sometimes) motivations, but they are weak when it comes to collaborating with each other, and sometimes do not wish to admit that irreconcilable views of life ARE incompatible, etc. and when I think of the hell Yeats or old Fordie wd/ have raised during the past decade, etc. At last{,} Caravella has printed serious criticism, precede{d} by that note in ABC signed by the name of a MOST disrespectable Sumerian emperor whom the signator has probably never heard of. Let me turn round three or 4 more times and cut the cackle. Itrat-Husain has been made vice chancellor of Rajshahi University, at the homonymous town of Rajshahi, in E.Pakistan. With what he seems to think is carte blanche to MAKE a university, out of nowt, or from the begining. BUT he may be naive, he may think there are no strings to the job. AT any rate he has asked me to find him a head for his English dept. (Don't USE this a{s} publicity for E.P's glory, at least not YET.) I happened to have the ideal man at hand (fit for just that and NOTHING else, i.e. totally unfitted for any sort job in the U.S.). BUT the bloke may have formulated his application in such vigorous manner as to scare Itrat's back stage direction (IF any). or it may be cosas del palacio.[1] At any rate Stan/[2] proposed to estab/ the dept/ on Ezratic lines. Wich wd/ be O.K. with Itrat. What I want is that you or someone. whats his name at the Minstero Educ/ or some one (yu cd/ consult Boris *if* he gets back to Roma in a few days. Air LETTER{S} to Pakistan on this kind of stamped sheet go for 10c/ yankish. in envelopes 25 c/ and that not necessary Unless some{one} has IMPressive official stationary.

Complimenting Itrat...that delicate matter...probably best say, the Virgilian Soc/ has heard of his active desire to promote knowledge of the BEST work of the occident, ~~in~~ as distinct from the brain-washing prevalent in occidental universities. Mention the aims of the Verg/Soc/NOT

in the rhetorical "Poter della STUMPaaa"[3] vein. And say that you understand that Stanislas Yankowski is only person who has satisfactorily crit-
icised E.P's TRAXINIAI *as a translation,* that is to say showing some
sense of proportion. And that you (or whoever writes the letter to Itrat)
[illegible deletion] commend the idea that the literature of ANY language
shd/ be studied in its relation to the classics of OTHER languages, NOT
in quest of influences and derivations, but as to the proportion between
the final results. The ~~diem~~ the dimensions of intention being considered
as well as mere technical finish. The expansions of the total concept of
literature. for example Dante having ADDED more than perhaps any
other great poet, more actual subject matter.

I have sent Itrat another letter, as Del Mar dug up the one really good
bit of Koran that I have ever seen quoted, namely that the Government
shd/ NOT take in taxes in good money, and pay its expenses in bad or
inferior money.

banzai maHOmet.

Del Mar's Hist Monetary SYSTEMS, really tremendous, I didn8t get
the full power of it when I first read it, done in 1895 when he had been
over a lot of ground, and corrects minor errors in earlier work and ends
with TREMENDOUS summary, which I was either; too tired or distracted
to ~~read~~ (get force of) 7 years ago.

Alzo correlated with Paul the Deacon on Habdimelich, and SATAN-
ICE stimulatus/[4] ie. his lucidity.

Am I clear(?) Stan/ wrote that he wd/ want to organize the Eng/dept
on Ezratic lines...nervous character and may be unduly worried by not
getting appointment by return air mail.

At any rate Itrat is work(th) keeping informed on all plus activities in
Roma/ OMITTING the hoakum that gets printed by parts of the official-
dom. I don(')t know who is Mr Hsieh/ quoted in "Listener"[5] as saying E.P.
only translator who models his style (in translation) ON THE TEXT (of
the Confucian Odes).. Tablet also hit the right note: no twisty thought,
which ~~OUH~~ OUGHT to purge the Slimes and the Gnu Slopsman[6] twist-
ers.

Olga arrived[7] in Wash's worst heat wave, looking very elegant...but the
complications etc/ etc/ etc. question of timing. Hemingway understands
better than she does.

Of course that Univ. at Rajshahi may have (been) started for the express
purpose of MAINTAINING the Historic blackout, and brainwashing the
Pakis/ and Stan may have put his hand into a hornet's nest. Mebbe I shd/
have told him to send a totally passive and innocuous application.

the damn fool is naturally modest and dont see that a man who knows
greek and latin is the ONLY person FIT to teach english in the bloody

orient. His crit/ of TRAX has got past Armstrong/[8] but whether N.Directions will sabotage it I dont know. NOR do I know who will pub/ his trans of Ric. St Victor. not quite in Sq $/ ambit, as the Sq $ is now banking on AMERICAN writers, fit to stand against europeans. Whereas the Ric/ belongs rather of Ezrologie und DanteStudien. Along with Lore's 600 page thesis on the Pisans, ganz Wissenschaftlich-ISSIMO.[9] I sd/ the {Kulch-}walla at Univ. of Mexico (NOT new Mexico) hopes to get their edtn/ spanish Pisans printed BEFORE he gets fired.[10] He is quite solid re the Odes etc. in their bulletin. The palabra[11] is NOT to the sinologs. etc.

> best to Helen, and bless all
> the eugenics in process.[12]

    1. Sp: "palace politics."

    2. **Stanislas V. Yankowski.**

    3. Probably *potére della stampa*, It.: "power of the press."

    4. Lt.: "satanic impulse." EP has reread **Alexander Del Mar**'s *A History of Monetary Systems* and has found that both Del Mar and **Paul the Deacon** (in *De Gestis Langobardorum*) wrote about the Arab caliph Abd-al-Malik (Habdimelek in Paul the Deacon) who coined gold in defiance of the Byzantine imperial monopoly on gold coinage (*History of Monetary Systems* 134). This story is also mentioned in canto 96/657–58. See also letter 110.

    5. See letter 96.

    6. *New Statesman.*

    7. **Olga Rudge** paid her second visit to EP since his confinement. She first visited him in 1952.

    8. Unidentified but presumably an editor, also mentioned in letter 101.

    9. Gm. + It.: "extremely scholarly." EP means that **Lore Marianne Lenbergis**'s dissertation on the *Pisan Cantos* is extremely (*ganz* and "-ISSIMO") scholarly (*wissenschaftlich*).

    10. *Los Cantares de Pisa* was about to be published.

    11. Sp.: "word."

    12. ORA had written that **Malù** was pregnant (2 July 1955). The child died shortly after birth.

98. TLU-2   21 July 1955
Anagrafa/ 21 Lug.

O R A

Stan(islas) Yankowski, was @ Oxford when 1914 bust loose. However, no need to give date as Itrat may have younger (and less suitable) image in mind. His excitable sister is furious with Stan/ because she thinks that a joke of mine was based on Stan's conversation. All HE did was to reveal the existence of MORE sisters than I heard of.

As they were married to everything but Beck and Pilsudski, I maintained that the fall of Poland was due to their inability to educate their husbands. (probably true).

All Stef[1] had mentioned was Pilsud/ pinning a decoration on one of 'em and gittin' so flustered by the promise of pneumatic bliss etc/ that he pinned it right thru the vestures onto the female herself.

Stef/ is undoubtedly full of Fizz/ and may have been responsible for HjamerskJJJld[2] or however he spellzit knowing of my existence/ at least some old lady remembers Dag/ with long golden curls.

Stan is the TOTAL OTHERNESS. How he has been in charge of Polish emigration, before there wasn't any etc. without learning MORE, god knows the whole of that damnd official class/ as I cease not to Yowl/ as Lehay,[3] Hill,[4] Stilwell, Mme de Chambrun[5] etc.

Anyhow Stan's/ english is o.k. and careful. {Jos} Conrad, {Ford's boring pal} was alzo a pollok. It aint THAT kind of english.

Stan/ has done the only critique of my TRAXINIAI which shows any perception of its relation to the greek text. i.e. WHY some expressions ARE correct {as Translation.}

He is finishing a trans/ of Richard s {as translation} of St Victor's "Benjamin Minor"/ a necessary footnote both to Dante and to yr/ present correspondent.

He is asking what greek he ought to translate. And I have [illegible deletion] dug a author out of Del Mar. but fergit its name.

He (Stan) was teaching in Australia/ and mentioned that country in Shenendoah/ BUT after getting to Baruchistan beGAN TO FEEL HE HAD BEEN TOO HARD ON Down Under, and that the Roosevelterian areas were probably WORSE.

D.P.Greene[6] has just sent me Nicole's Trans/ of Livre du Prefet EPARX-IKON BIBLION/[7] wot he has eggstracted from Bastun lieberry. so I better get thru it in time to get it bak to him before he gets muclted.[8]

Dave preparing to reprint another 100 pages of DelMar, and I think Ingrid[9] may get microfilm of all Del M/ and Waddel in Brit/ Mus/ to keep

Lubin's fellow congregationalist{s} from destroying the [illegible deletion] evidence.

The poison of preserved writing of infamous nature, the perversion of mediterranean thought/ Hv/ just got thru DeOfficiis/ look at end of book II,[10] and yu'll see why THAT part of classic studies has been bitched by the kikery.

Do you remember what happened to excitement in France in the 1920 when they were trying to efface history and impose "plans for the future"

Glad you learned from Lubin/

I condemn no man for his parentage/ it is only when he [illegible deletion] begins to act in certain manners.

alas imperfectly defined in widely diffused educational matter, that I start the alarm whistle.

best to Helen, an lemme return to the EPARCH.

Leon the wise, says God did and therefore he; trade union regulations that in 1894 ~~annoy~~ annoyed Prof. Nicole. obviously a Cobdenite[11] pro ~~urusy~~ usury fan.

1. Presumably **Lincoln Steffens.**
2. **Dag Hammarskjöld.**
3. **Admiral William D. Leahy.**
4. EP means **Cordell Hull.**
5. For EP on this collection of people, see letter 90.
6. Probably David Grene, a professor of classics at the University of Chicago and a translator of Greek drama.
7. Nicole's edition of *The Eparch's Book.* See also letters 88 and 95.
8. EP means *mulcted,* "to penalize by fining."
9. **Ingrid Davies.**
10. EP has been reading Cicero's *De Officiis* and probably has the following in mind: "when he [Cato] was asked what was the most profitable feature of an estate, he replied: 'Raising cattle successfully.' What next to that? 'Raising cattle with fair success.' And next? 'Raising cattle with but slight success.' And fourth? 'Raising crops.' And when his questioner said, 'How about money-lending?' Cato replied 'How about murder?'" (2:24).
11. EP writes in canto 96/864 of "professor [Jules] Nicole's annoyance" about Byzantine guild or corporativist organization. Richard Cobden (1804–1865), a British free trader, is invoked here as one who, as a follower of Adam Smith, would be on the side of banks and interest.

99. TLU-3 19 August 1955

19 Ag/

Dear ORA/

[in left margin:] New bit of ingenuity, enemy or fritt frivolity. Send letter to non extant address, but put my name on envelop{e as sender} so it comes here when undeliverable at what ain't.

Lipmann[1] belongs to that numerous band of poisoners who have boxed in the press columns for the past 40 years/ along with Cerf[2] keeping real work out of print. If that bastard suggests the intelligentzia is going to the right/ it wd/ only be to infuriate the extreme left so there wd/ be an assassin ready for ANY member of the intelligentzia who did anything useful. a la Gentile and Henriot/[3] Linc/ Steffens passed for a revealer, one thought him joking, use of paradox, addressing students of Univ of Cal/ tellin 'em to be honest, go on being honest until people trust you and trust yu, and THEN you can betray them. And his perjuring himself in court, and when taxed with it saying: {"}but you put me on oath.{"} He ended up espowsed with another of 'em. Denial from London that Hankey[4] is grandson of the buzzard who DelMar mentions as director of Bunk of Eng/ about 1854. Not sure if this is authenticated. sourse of phrase? Hankey-pankey. Anyhow the son is quoted as sayin Roosevelt was a scwondwel of the blackest water. But whether this is filial rebellion or family opinion I hv/ not yet ascertained. DOES anyone in yr/ esteemed circle see {"}Rivarol{"}/[5] a weekly from same address of Ecrits de Paris and considerably more lively. P.Dominique reviewed G.Ollivier's book on sowbelly in issue for June 30. Shd be translated into wop. Can anyone tell the Cravella boys?

I have been quoting that Bacon[6] for years, think it is in Butchart{'}s vol/[7] which has NOT been reprinted. Mrs B/ physical break down, did want to revise it 9 years ago, got job in ornithological museum etc. BUT dead on her feet.

Condoglienze to Malu.[8] DelMar on Roman and Moslem money supposed to be avviato[9] toward press, gornoze how long/ {it will take to get there} 3 chapters from Hist. Mon/ty SYSTEMS. Let me know if cantos 88/9 don{'}t arrive. CONfound F.M. he omitted the Gaudier cat.[10] NOT India, Pakistan for Stan/ they seem to intend to use him. so no immediate need to bother that somewhat etc/etc/ fluctuant and indeterminate Inst/ Orient/Studs/. Not to shout: vittoria, until the languid pollok actually gets TO the orient. AND if old and trained governing classes rot/ how yu expect a lot of new sprouts to become perfect directors in 20 years{?} There has to be DIRECTION, and yu got to EDucate a few people, {moeurs de Baruchistan},[11] some bright spark/ possibly wanting attention I believe yr/ friends Mazzini had similar idea. 30 vols/ of Del Mar OUT of circulation, {publ} from 1870 onward NO collusion with yr/ anon-Ymouse correspondent, BUT hammering on FACTS re/ money. BUT not touching institutional problem all the time. Hammering on Roman RE-PUBLIC, and objecting to imperatorial usurpations AND yr/ blasted Fattycan. falsifications of history etc/ N.H.P.[12] says same old CAN trying to hold down on a lot of stuff now available in Constantinople. And that louse Gregory[13] (the advertised) burnt the Palatine library, after{,} or simult/ messing up the music so you cant get the sense of the words. Also the damn CAN did NOT oppose Freud's focusing of total attention of occident on bits of filth in the sewer. Dante{'s} a healthier system. Glad yu see Spampanato. Parts of his bk/ esp/ one appendix OUGHT to get printed in english. But it is slow work. Also people get jittery re/ authors' rights etc. Only useful thing I have imbibed re/ Tolstoi was that he did not insist on copyright. My best ~~tp~~ to Spamp/ did I ever meet him? Am no use on names and when there are a dozen strangers in a room they may get the name of one furriner, and he muff all or most of theirs. Might save time to know before hand who holds rights, if any. AND to get ALL the good books sent to Noel Stock for review in Melbourne. Stock is not handicapped by havin the kind of wife who tries to hold down del Valle. at least not so far as I know.

I wont kuss YOU fer not operating @ 100% on jobs I can think up, IF yu wil learn to DEPUTIZE. The few honest men in Melbourne, Parigi[14] etc. OUGHT to exchange what they print. books AND periodicals/ and do it PROMPTLY and not have it have it all routed thru amurk'z leadin bughouse. Have AT LAST got a London correspondent who can putt a postage stamp on a Nvlp inside of 24 hours.

That brute Varé has not answered my extended comment on his exuberant vol/[15] Naturally I don't expect *HIM* to write about difference between 1½% and 16%. Though, as yu insist, he is [illegible deletion] salonfahig.[16]

Yr/ naples story[17] rhymes with another I have been using for 12 years, re why germans will never rule the world. Contrast of severe discipline vs/ looting, AND the cheerful G.I. "we sez to them (another group of G.I.s) there is ANOTHER jewellers down there on the other side of the street. You go LIBERATE that." The bloody huns alienated sympathy by shooting one of their men who had stolen a watch. Inviting the jeweller to witness execution so he wd/ know it, and despite jeweller's plea not to{,} and that he wd/ give him the watch. vs/ Tasca's view that ANY appeal to ethics or honesty was TOTALLY useless ~~on~~ on the air addressed to the U.S.A. [in left margin:] {Thanks for copy giornale d'Ital.}

Del Mar, emphasis on habeus corpus, and lex something or other ONLY one subject in any bill presented to the Senatum. ~~Hab~~

Caecilia Didia, a.u 658./hab/c. Paetalia and a Sempronia 632 of the city.[18]

Can Mrs Vergilian get the De Officiis back into curricula?

as to Whippers/[19] the other {&} antipodal evil is TOTAL lack of any pride in profession/ vide american profs/ NOT annoyed at infamies of their colleagues *as [constituting] a disgrace TO the profession.*

1. EP is responding to ORA's comments about **Walter Lippmann's** *Essays in the Public Philosophy*, sent to her from the United States: "[Lippmann] has come to see that 'democracy' as expressed by majority rule through parliaments elected on the basis of universal suffrage is (a) failure and is leading to the downfall of the West" (14 Aug. 1955).

2. **Bennett Cerf.**

3. Probably **Émile Henriot.**

4. Probably Baron Maurice Pascal Alers Hankey (1877–1963), head of the British Cabinet office from 1916 until his retirement in 1938.

5. A review of Ollivier's *Franklin Roosevelt* by P. Dominique appeared in this Paris journal.

6. In her letter of 14 August 1955 ORA had written: "I came across this the other day: 'Money is like muck; it is no good unless it is spread.' Lord Bacon."

7. Butchart's *Money.*

8. It.: "Condolences." ORA had written EP about the death of **Malù's** baby (14 Aug. 1954).

9. It.: "sent."

10. EP is blaming **Frederic Morgan** for having failed to include a figure of Gaudier Brzeska's sculpture of a cat in printing cantos 88 and 89.

11. Fr. + En.: "morals of Baruchistan."

12. **Norman Holmes Pearson.**

13. Presumably Pope Gregory I (540–604), after whom Gregorian chants are named.

14. It.: "Paris."

15. Varè's *The Two Imposters.* See letter 26.

16. *Salonfähig,* Gm.: "socially acceptable."

17. In her letter of 14 August 1955 ORA had told an anecdote of Neapolitan humanity, and had commented: "This is in keeping with what your friend Spampinato old me. He had been imprisoned in Naples, but said that it was simply impossible to illuse prisoners in those prison(s) as the jailers simply paid no attention to orders, of that kind, brought in anything the prisoners wanted(,) took out letters and messages, etc. Those are civilised people."

18. EP is probably referring to Del Mar's *A History of Monetary Systems* and his discussion of habeas corpus ("/hab/c"). EP seems to be claiming that this piece of British jurisprudence was already part of Roman law and offers citations. Lex Caecilia Didia (perhaps the "lex something or other" of the previous paragraph) was enacted in 98 B.C. "A.u" is *ab urbe,* a Roman system of dating events from the founding of Rome, which is the source of EP's numbers. "Of the city" is a translation of it. Lex Poetelia (not "Paetalia") prohibited imprisonment for debt

and was enacted in 326 B.C. Lex Sempronia de Pecunia Credita (193 B.C.) extended laws governing loans to some categories of plebeians. The laws are presumably mentioned in Del Mar's works, but we have not been successful in tracing
them.

19. EP is responding to the following in ORA's 14 August 1955 letter: "After
much consideration I have found the right translation of the Italizan 'gerarca' of
fascist memory. It is 'Whipper-snapper' defined in the dictionary as a 'noisy, pre-
suming, insignificant person.' But minus the 'whipper-snappers', the corporate
State should work, when completed by a second chamber of persons appointed
for services rendered to the State in all the different fields of activity{,} and who
would therefore represent not unworthily, the nation. The Western world, I believe, will have to come round to this, or die of the creeping paralysis which we
witness today in Italy, France, and to a minor extent, elsewhere."

100. TLU-3 NYPL   4 September 1955
4 Sep/

la lingua s'affatica.[1] O.R.A. still defending the race of the crucifiers and
the rats in Ratican/ anyhow every polish nobleman had one, and ORA
had Lubin, and Kasper[2] has ascertained what I had long deduced, that our
greatest historian, Del Mar was kike/ AND I shall go on reviving his glorious memory. NOT that such impartiality will do me any good. Whenever t some jew DOES something useful, his tribesmen let him drop hotter
than a goy/. Three cases this week/ horrible fat hand from P.veronese/[3]
Mr Laughlin{2}[4] fooled by one I know IN person and HOW/ {3} and a typical case of a Nuevo Christiano/ teaching in cawflik beanery. NOTE the
nature of skunkery. A montana Prof/ named Ferkiss[5] prints a number of
lies/ which are brot me by Mme Stancioff in a Zeitschrift[6] called "Political Journal", 27 pages of it. as it is personal {from her}, I correct 'em.

Is the professorial catholic rat annoyed at the ~~accurae~~ inaccuracy of his
colleague. NOT a dambit. He thinks Mrs S/ shd/ not have SHOWN me
the article.

Hide it. protect his fellow liar. DONT attempt a rettifica.[7] That's where
my friends have done very poorly, NOT taking up *specific* lies, little by little
and nailing the bastards to the barn door. They dont see the infamy of a
cultural attaché continuing to print lies to get pubd/ by Gallimerde.[8]

{no advocy of ethics either just survey} And the SYMPTOMS of Del
Mar/ no guard against centralization and tyranny. against private money. No attention to usury rate, tho he did DEFINE the right nature of
interest. AND this emerges from Byzantine history/ the Ratican now
trying to smother new data unearthed in Constantinople. Antoninus P/
and Leo VI/ legal rate 4%. Trade regulations, guild system/ Naturally from
at least 1694/ {"}Byzantinism{"} has been a word of abuse.

And now in the Sacred Edict of Kang Hi and Yong Ching/[9] legal rate 36/ and those excellent gentlemen struggling against 7 and 8% MONTH-LY, i.e. 84, and 96%. Boxer rebellion in 160 years/

in contrast to Byzantium stability/ 12% maximum for marine "usu-ry" (included the insurance), various limits at 6 and 8% common loans. Naturally Antoninus Pius is OUT, blacked out of the record almost to-tally/ and Byzantium has had a bad press.

the jew is a disease, or like the unconscious "carrier" of turberculosis, He shd/ be treated kindly, cured IF possible, tho it seldom is, even after several generations of conversion (as in Spain). He is sometimes con-scious, often distinctly WORRIED about it.

Having just concluded that catholic toleration of giudaism is due to total loss of any belief in reality either of the mind or the soul/ i.e. that mental and spiritual infection are less a pest than small pox or bubonic plague/ a red headed, simpatico, goth turns up, this time without his fat mesopotamian. AND it turns out his ma has been writing him beautiful letters, re/ NOT marry out of the church. He crosses himself 3 times and then asks if I can use any benzadrine. (Just as kindly as the Honduran ambassador with his sauterne (prohibited by the regulations).

When the church was civilized/ emend that, not civilized BUT a civi-lizing force, it recognized this. forcible conversion to save his alleged {"}soul etc. The vile prot. lost ALL sense (vid. Spirit of Romance) of the stench of dacaying mind. Dante had it.

That is where the cold war has got to/ Alert yr/ little circle/ ANY one coming from N.Y., an american jail or bughouse, FIRST look at 'em to I mean if they show ANY mental activity, ANY curiosity (might almost say: any charm) to see IF they are junkies. The non-dope wooden ma-chines, or blotting paper. Mr Grab[10] just thanked Meyer for his scolarship hand-out. Let us hope to gawd that G/ will dig up something useful that will take the place of a switch blade and be used on "a higher [illegible deletion] plane"/ Wife of highly paid brit/ lecturer ("honour to meet me") {"}Yes of course: BRIBES.{"} i.e. he had stuck to art history. and wd/ NOT notice degree of usury tolerance VISIBLE flagrantly in the reprod of a {fat} she hand by P.Veronese.

Mysticism aimed at getting power/ advertised in the rotocalcos. Now lousily the chuRRRche has defended, pardon irony, betrayed her heritage.

HOWever one serious Englander find{s} Ric. St Vic. better than Kant or Coleridge.

Will any cawflic EVER again have the candour to admit that Xt/ was for some centuries regarded as a symbol and not an individual kike out to monopolize. There ~~bing~~ being INTERNAL evidence that monopoly was NOT part of the message. Yr/ grampaw[11] had some insight. All the good primi sec/[12] poets were Ghibbeline. If I had patience to reread this note I might remember what I started to say yesterday.

mebbe I be'r close with the reminder of that good hindoo on arrival of family of 'em in S.America. the three brothers: one into banking, one into brothels, and the third goes into the Church.

benedictions.

Giovannini's artl/[13] accepted by Cat/Weakly "America" in Dec/ held six months and then returned from vigliaccheria[14] has appeared Down Under.

Is any Roman looking at Geo. Ollivier's vol.[15] on the pestilence/ does ANY one, SPamp/ per es/ see "~~Rivaro~~ Rovarol"/ AT last a breath of frogland.

1. It.: "to tire of the language."
2. **John Kasper.**
3. **Paolo Veronese.**
4. **James Laughlin.**
5. **Victor C. Ferkiss.**
6. Gm.: "journal" or "magazine."
7. It.: "rectification, correction."
8. Gallimard, a Parisian publishing house.
9. Kang Hi, Chinese emperor (1662–1723) of the Manchu dynasty, was succeeded by his fourth son, Yong Tching (1723–35). Both are mentioned in *The Cantos*, especially cantos 59–61.
10. Probably Fred Grab, a professor of English at Yale who is mentioned in a letter of 8 December 1955 that is not included here.
11. **Gabriele Rossetti.**
12. Probably *primo cento*, It.: "1100s."
13. See letter 94.
14. It.: "cowardice."
15. See letter 91.

101. TLU-3   18 September 1955

18 Sep/

dear O.R.A.

sometime or other I suppose yu will start observing the evidence/ Symbol of the apostles etc/ and the source of the gt/ polution/ Cerruti sending panetone[1] and cheese, remarked that "they cannot think anything noble.

Both Spinoza and Montaigne carried poison, takes time to learn to spot WHICH, for as the poster on the french Vespasians[2] used to proclaim, one cannot have all of these but an individual may have several.

Lubin did NOT guard against fixing farm or other prices in anything itself FIXED. It was to be set in something the value of which was unknown. Frank Harris one contribution (or one a very few, as he warn't a snow-white lamb of gawd or of anything else.)

Del Mar, most useful historian, but NO guard against kahal[3] control or central tyranny/ mere(ly} that essence of money is limitation.

The ONE solid myth or symbol in Xtianity is Xrucifixion. As Confucian, one wd/ rather clean the Vatican sewer than destroy it. Truth preserved in the rites/ but the swine put silly interpretation on them. Lucidity left in france and woptaly, cause they haven't the god DAMNED jew book, hotchpotch in every home, sending a cert % of population to bughouse from trying to make sense of it, or get something coherent from the rag bag of venom. Barbarous wangles. NOT ethic.

Fordie complained about its effect on style of eng/ prose. style c'est l'homme.[4] Freedman explains why some jews FEEL, i.e. give the impression of, the immonde.[5] Successive attack on the white population, Marx, Freud, and now Reich[6] for those who have smelt the rat from Vienna. the dirt of caballa, and *any other* swindle which does NOT take words for what they say, but goes in for some monkey shines about interpretation. In Italy yu hv/ escaped I suppose(,} most of the prot/ rot/ And ty the wop has enough clean pagainsm left to take his Xtianity lightly. prot/ rot is hebraic. And Milton a boor. Eliot commits trahison des clercs[7] in telling the young it is once again safe to read him. Zielinski out of print, but I trust Swb/[8] now working on fotostat. 2 copies Waddel Sumer dictionary[9] have been grabbed. Stock says they are available Down Under. but not clear if for sale or in lie/bury.

Manchu emperor exhorting peasants NOT to borrow @ 7 & & 8% MONTHLY. relative duration of that dynasty to Byzantium/ and the bad press given Byzantium becomes clear/ Antoninus Pius 4% annual, naturally he has been wiped out of the record. even business profits held to 16 something % by Leo the Wise, at least in some common trades. Goy, of course from gk/ XOIROS,[10] but one cant learn it all, all at once.

Tease Goacher about parsimony re/ postage stamps. Gordon fotos/ S's start of portrait yester,[11] unfinished but wd/ do for Armstrong frontispiece as is. That Mondo paragraph best yet. Any idea of its source, fons, [illegible deletion] origo,[12] or whatso?

Might correlate with chinks who have sd/ re/ Odes, Only trans/tr who models on style of original, only one who uses rhythms of original. Harvard still SAYS it means to cleanse itself by doing proper edtn.

Can't Villari be started on some of the ISSUES raised on rome radio/ rede freiheit ohne radio freiheit. etc.[13]

when the louse-ecutiv exceeds his powers, what happens if NO one protests? It will have to come from europe you CANNOT expect pragmatic pigs and illiterate business executives to FACE or even know of the existence of principles and ideas (other than mechanical designs. space rockets, get to god by splitting the atom etc. {Tasca} who had been in business here, thought ANY mention of ethic or justice on Rome radio, was mer was mere/ waste of time and breath/ thot my discorsi too like methodist parson. alzo ten minutes maximum of their attention to anything. Villari MAY remember, or he may never have talked with Tasca. bright lad. Ranieri having grown up in woptaly, argued, mostly with his ex-wife, who sad to s{t}ate, Chisholm[14] reports NEVER listened to ANY radio./ as to my audience, One damn fine Maronite,[15] 2 or three blokes in the hell hole. Mr Slavio, and two old ladies in Firenze. AND when I discovered I had talked over the heads of some of the fauna, the jew press quoted it: How could anyone understand me.?

What I said was: COULD anyone understand me. Still very loose sense of polemic/ Pearce furious with the bastard Brown,[16] but may waste his time cursing Brown's lack of taste (incurable) instead of nailing lies.

jew teaching in Catholic univ/ not shocked at Firkess lies, but that Mme Stancioff showed me the article.

"nuevos xtianos"/[17] one shd/ cure 'em but is it POSSIBLE? spics after three centuries crop up with all the racial habits, NO constructivity, no shoulder to any wheel, always riding or abstaining. Basil[18] says: {"}no, the roman were NOT a nice people.{"} Ask Boris about the dates? He has a few useful items re/ fake amulets, and mummy dust. WATCH any from N.Y. art or music world (as Varé knows by now) Shd/ think some NAME like MacLeish[19] or Clarence Manion wd/ be better catch for Raiola than some dead class room grammarian.[20] somebody wanting to GO somewhere, even if not clear WHY we shd/ revive the classics. (Does Raiola herself know what the score is??) Do have all POssible serious stuff, books or periodic/sent to Roger Sharrock,[21] 4 Furzedown Rd. Southampton, England. and if yu see Spampanato before Boris gets to Roma ask about use of his appendices. I shd/ advocate even ~~pig~~ pirating some if too much red tape wd/ delay printing trans/ in N.Pork pay up {royalties} later of course {if any}.

{P.S. Tell Goacher s.v.p. O.K. TRAX @ Brunnenberg; Of course, Helen can have anything she likes for ANY purpose she likes.}

1. Panettone, a spiced brioche with sultanas eaten at Christmas.

2. A French anti-Semite, so named for Vespasius, the Roman emperor (69–79 A.D.) appointed by Nero to suppress Judea in 67 A.D.

3. Local governing body that administered religious, legal, and communal affairs in a former European Jewish community.

4. Fr.: "style is the man."

5. Fr.: "squalid, foul."

6. **Wilhelm Reich.**

7. Fr.: "The treason of the clerics," title of a conservative work by **Julien Benda** (1867–1956) accusing French intellectuals of having betrayed France. EP uses the

phrase to refer to T. S. Eliot's "treason" since in his "Milton II" essay (first published in 1947) Eliot takes back his attack of Milton (on the basis that his "technical influence" has been bad for future poets) in "Milton I" (first published 1936).

8. **Henry S. Swabey.**

9. Copies of Waddell's *Egyptian Civilization.*

10. Gk.: "pig."

11. A portrait by **Sheri Martinelli.**

12. *Fons et origon*, Fr.: "fount and origin."

13. See letter 88.

14. Probably Hugh Joseph Chisholm (1913–72), poet and translator who served as assistant editor at the Bollingen Foundation (1947–52).

15. The Maronites are a Christian community of Arabs in Lebanon in communion with the Pope. We do not know who this individual might have been.

16. Probably Rear Admiral Wilson Brown or Lathrop Brown; see letter 95.

17. EP's Spanish for "new Christian."

18. **Basil Bunting.**

19. Archibald MacLeish (1892–1982).

20. Probably Hugh Kenner. See letter 102.

21. **Roger Sharrock.**

102. TLS-2 30 September 1955

~~29~~30 Sep/

O.R.A.

Kenner the LAST man for THAT job.[1] adapting himself to what he considers the circs/ doing all he dares/ marked as a poundista. but less so than is supposed. Doing his maximum in the Chicago sewing circle.[2]

Incapable of main ideas/ AND a deaf man who lip reads NOT best for public job. As I have just writ Lekakis[3] better a noisy half-wit who wd/ get the Comit/ on the map than some jackass afraid to bray.

I thought there was naiveté somewhere when I saw Coselski's[4] name on the list. The by [illegible deletion] ORA beloved kikery will certain silurate[5] any attempt to debunk their smog.

Whether he is of those, fra voi di voi.[6] or a 4/16th descendent from slave population of different race/ etc.

And Kenner is NOT in classics dept/ ANYhow. and the american prof/ lowest of all forms of animal life when it comes to courage/ is more timorous of MENTIONING affairs in some other *dept* of his instrooshun for suppression of learning than on ANY other line. goodness, merceee emmmee.. w w w w ot can I d d d d d o, about something in a DIFFERENT file-case.(?)

H. Comfort at least likes Catullus/ of course his one idea is to interrupt MY work, and get me to translatin some minor indecency of Cat's...but still he has heard of the latin' language.

Gimme time to look for an arab assassin or something with guts. Gege
says her gk/ prof/ is human. information recd/ yester, no time fer details.
Kasp/[7] shd/ have seen Riola ~~Rolta~~ or whatever her name is, on Wwdns/
Nec bonus christianus ac bonus Tullianus.[8] Freedman at least gives a clue
to why so many of 'em bring that greasy feeling into the air when they
enter a room. Bill Williams{,}[9] protected by havin a rabbi for a gramp/ or
gt/gp/{,} mentions "One of those fresh j...whom one [illegible deletion]
wants to kill on sight." but as he hasn't got to federal reserve nobody
suggests he is anti-filthery.

Gladys[10] says Struzo[11] is a wash-out. And that she is ~~g~~doin a statue of
Angus Og/ the former item no surprise, and the latter an indication of
rising ripple of sincerity..

Wang-iu-p'uh/ comment ~~of~~ on sacred Edict of Kang Hi "The blazing
flame in the mind, is thy heaven."

Remains of lucidity in France and woptal due to *not* having the King
James confusion in every home. american bughouse{s} full of victims who
have tried to make sense out of that dung hill (not ~~s~~ to say there aren{'}t
tulips and crocuses sprouting among the detritus.)

One codetenut/[12] thinks he can write a novel cause he has read it so
much.

You can tease Helen with Fordie's last ditch defence of cafolicism: have
to have that sort of training to get a Voltaire. But Fordie definitely anti-
prot, i.e. anti the augment of kikery. AND did the professional cats/ dislike him. The Chests/[13] and Bel/s[14] who were gettin their rent by flop-
pin' ~~d~~ round in it. No more mental seriousness than re/ rival football
teams. Davies sez he learned more in 3 days at Brun/[15] than in year pre-
vious/ Goach/ full of pre-raph retrospect. xextracted from Helen. Sorry
Ing's Hon/ Prog/ didn't make it, but imagine he is bored stiff by his son-
in-raw, and hoped for more open air. Mary seems to have found 'em all
bearable. Naturally O.R.A. not having licherary bitions hasn't included
vignettes/ mebbe Helen cd/ send on impressions. I have only seen the
male Goacher. One's world {I mean mine now} is populated via epizto-
lary correspondence. Have you any tame art-experts. Walker[16] is out of
town/ I merely KNOW good from bad but haven't collected commissions
on renaissance forgeries.

Probably too late for jury on Monday ANYhow Baruchistan does NOT
want art.

Groucho[17] (loathsome animal) has opined reason so many kids on street
@ night. Afraid to stay home alone. Hem/ on "is it true that wild animals
won't do yu harm if yu carry a torgch?" "Depends on how fast yu carry
it.{"}

Classics Gang ought to try for Manion or MacLeish. not some campus
quietude.

WHAT inducement to anyone to take it?? Free roof in vacation? ANY expense account? Salary, I take, is zero? Chance for someone wanting to make a NAME.

BUT suggest get rid of Coselshki.[18] otherwise what goes on wd/ be instantly reported to kahal. Yu know anything of pollok damblastador who followed Patocki?[19] Ciencianowski[20] or zummat.? Belated eggstraks of Ciano/ two points. Philips[21] annoyed [illegible deletion] when Mus/ told him U.S. was controlled by Kikes (suspect Phillips not 16/ ¼) and Ciano lamenting wops had NO informers inside Britain/ nowt new/ but useful ultimate confirmation on innocence and naiveté of Mus/ Ciano very useful to {To swine who puff the} dictator legend. and NO fascist at any time. M's fault for having him round. vurry non Confucian. Peliz:[22] he sees ALL the wrong people.

Peg/ done some more soda water. one col/ re La Luce. IF ORA hears of ANYone capable to THOUGHT re/ basic principles she let off a siren.

Giovannini suggest Siefert/[23] but Sief has NO guts and no drive. merely a latin or gk/ prof.

{EP}

1. ORA had written: "Boris [de Rachewiltz] thinks that Hugh Kenner of the University of California would be a good choice [to replace the recently deceased Morey as American president of the Committee for the Defence of Classical Culture] as he is in sympathy with your views on 'kulcher' as a vehicle for humanistic thought, an{d} not a mere study of roots and such like Dryasdust conceptions. Before approaching him we should much value your opinion" (14 Sept. 1955). See letter 67.

2. EP is probably thinking of the Modern Language Association, whose conventions used to alternate between New York and Chicago. Kenner would have been a frequent presenter during this time.

3. **Michael Lekakis.**

4. **Eugenio Coselschi.**

5. Anglicized Italian from *silurare*, "to torpedo, dismiss."

6. See letter 96.

7. **John Kasper.**

8. Lt.: "neither Christian virtue nor the virtue of Tullianus." Tullianus is a Roman dungeon built by Servius Tullius.

9. William Carlos Williams.

10. **Gladys Hynes.**

11. Probably **Father Luigi Sturzo.**

12. Co-detainee.

13. G. K. Chesterton (1874–1936) and his cousin **A. K. Chesterton.** EP knew of both of these militant Catholics.

14. **Hilaire Belloc's** family.

15. Brunnenburg.

16. Probably John Brisben Walker (1847–1931), an American journalist and editor who served as director of the National Gallery.

17. Groucho Marx.

18. **Eugenio Coselschi.** ORA wrote on 23 October 1955: "Your aspersions on Colselschi's racial ancestry are I think unfounded, but he is NOT a live wire; too addicted to pacifist unrealities."

19. **Count Jerzy Potocki.**

20. Jan Ciechenowski was Potocki's successor.

21. **William Phillips.**

22. **Camillo Pellizzi.**

23. **George Joseph Siefert Jr.**

103. TLU-3   8 November 1955

8 Nov.

Veritas Praevalebit, ma tres chère Oliviaaaa.[1]

Dante did it "despite the dirty rag tied over his eyes." He did it on Ric. of St Victor who uses ~~the~~ bits of {the} conglomerate with scotch acument MERELY as so many algebraic signs.

AND the curse of the eng/ translation of the whole of the mess, has NEVER deluged woptaly or frogland/ hence some remains of lucidity. even [illegible deletion] under the rump of the Mendez Mendacity ROTschild in Paris.

Already in time of Bede. the intelligent christers deploring concessions to Giudaism. J.C. (or whoever he was) OR the prepauline legend is CLEARLY designed as ANTIdote for the pestilence of the butchers of lesser cattle.

Papini's[2] tears, violet fros deuil,[3] contain ONE good sentence, calzante/[4] whether they will melt what pore Jim B/[5] called "a heaRRt of STone", remains to be seen.

The mind-conditioned Edwards,[6] INCAPABLE of any noble concept has usefully printed yr/ vigorous whoop/.[7] When I told the punk he wd/ be more fittingly employed on a biog/ of Eleanor Horse fyce (that launched a thousand djeeps) his vife saidt: Yew arre mohore himportantd.

I take it parasites have some function in nature. accepting the mechanizms thereof, with more faith that can be got from unhistoric and parasitical confusionism, and a mechanism for imposing fine{s}, having nowt to do with justice or ethics.

The Raiola wrote for permission to visit/ did not arrive/ was not, acc/ Kasp/[8] at her n.y. address, but piles of mail awaiting her. she had been enthusiastic re/Clarence Manion. I have since collected name{s} of 4 or 5 excellent MOMBERS for Clas/ boost, but not suitable for HEAD of am/ section.

The spina dorsale of my rome talks/ Brooks Adams, Law of Civilization and Decay, now in Knop{f}s Vintage series @ 95 cents. The most charrming blue eyed, jewess I have ever met (but whose dirty Talmudic brother is trying to prevent her enlightening the stage) told me sunday it was all over N.York. Kas/ says already 3rd. edtn. AND the first book sold in his new bookeshoppe in Geo/ville (Georgetown, Wash. D.C.)

So that ~~must~~ much is praevalebinG.[9] the Evening Star still repeats LIES, and uses general terminology of abuse.

What some wop COULD do, following Papini, is to start discussing the REAL issue(s), on philosophic basis.

AND what some Roman cd/ do wd/ be to send me interesting articles promptly. As for example the unknown and untraceable whatshis name in Il Nazionale 4 Sept. I though(t) Villari switched my subscription TO Il Nazionale cause he knew 'em and approved of 'em.

Noble author must have misunderstood, or not heard the "NOT"/ if I quoted anything I wd/ have said "this is NOT Milton."

All that is valuable in Dante is from greek or indian or engyptian (probably that from India) sources. AT LAST, a translation of Zielinsky's summary of his life work is being translated. AND some respect for the light and the SYMBOL of Xtianity, in place of the hoax, may be starting. Sunday the first day of WEAK. IF you had had murkn. presbyterian familiarity with the K.Jim's perversion, mebbe yu wd/ have got round to noticing what is in the anterior segment of it. For which the gospels were sposed to be antidote. or not/?

~~And as~~ You will be glad to hear that british benedictines read yr/ present correspondent, at least some of 'em and one of 'em proclaims the Cantos as THE catholic poEM. at least since the catholic era. Hightime to make effective the afro-american phrase: wash up thei' lawd. and clear out the den of thieves and the chair of Judas Iscariot.

The complete pusillanimity of some as claims to be heritors of the martyrs is also comment. People now askin Giovannini if he TRIED to get it printed in the U.S.

Nixon blacking Gene Meyer's[10] boots, etc.

Seriously/ after Papini stickin his nekk out, is there anyone ready to introduce certain basic topics ~~into~~ sulle pagine to qualsiasi rivista or quotidamniano[11] woptalIAN? Of course the question of monetary issue is the most dangerous/ but even quite simple americans are beginning to doubt the omniscience and sapience of Sowbelly's GeopolitiKKKK. such as NOT letting Adolf eggzaust himself AND the muscovites/ AND betraying occidental civilization. Why don(')t Villari review the Geo/ Ollivier/[12] and Use the frog minority when it has more candour than the Corriere della "Serva"[13] (Italia).

(H)ave you had time to pick out the parts of Orientamenti that might now be timely. AFTER Brooks Adams has got into Paper back.

Best to Helen/ magnif/ iconography of Brnbg/[14] recd. I gather yr/ dear sister has a sense of humour. thankGoRRRR.

Glad to see you smack "planned economy"/ that was what Por (socialist marasmus, fell for.) and E.P. NEVER did. Can you rub Odon's NOSE
in it. Socialist muck. NOT Andy Jackson, freeing the U.S, of debt. No
known case of Marxists EVER being more than ¼ cured.

Not even need of govt/ to spread information/ BUT IF it does INFORM
the pore bloody citoyen, the INDIVIDUAL shd/ make his OWN calculation re/ what crops are needed or what goods.

1. Lt. + Fr.: "truth has prevailed, my very beloved Olivia."
2. **Giovanni Papini.**
3. Fr.: "mourning."
4. It.: "fitting.
5. **James Thomas Strachey Barnes.**
6. John Hamilton Edwards visited ORA in July. Together with William W. Vasse
he published *The Annotated Index to the Cantos of Ezra Pound*. EP mocks Mrs.
Edwards's speech.
7. ORA had sent Edwards "2 type-written pages" (23 Oct. 1955). We are not sure
what they were, but probably a plea for EP's release.
8. **John Kasper.**
9. EP has mixed the Latin and English words for "prevailing."
10. **Eugene Meyer.**
11. It. + En.: "on the page to whatever review or daily."
12. Ollivier's *Franklin Roosevelt.*
13. EP turns "Corriere della Sera," *Evening Post,* into "Corriere della Serva,"
Servant Post.
14. Brunnenburg.

104. TLU-3   9 November 1955
9 Nov.

ORA
for Villari or any adult, as well as the more fiery characters/ AS the
London Times 29 Ag/ gave a clean notice of Jim Barnes{'}[1] views/ it might
be useful to contrast them with those of yr/ anonymous correspondent.
Jim wrote universal aspects of fascism. E.P. was opposed to SOCIALISM,
and to the socialist elements IN fascismo.

He believed it the BEST activity possible in Italy in a given time. He
did NOT concede an inch of his Jacksonian principles/ he left the Social
Creditors, or rather as he had never been OF them/ he dropped Social
Credit general plans for Gesell precisely because Gesell fitted in Jeffersonian belief in the MINIMUM government. Douglas{'} system requiring burocracy, even an addition of extran{t} bureaucracy/ Gesell reduc-
ing even waht exists in U.S. practice.

I seem to have started on wrong side but legibility unimpaired.[2] Gesell's theory or rather his MECHANISM, a special case under general formula stated in Jefferson's letter to Crawford 1816. As stated in full front page art/l in Capitol Daily,[3] Washington 1939 one of the clearest essays E.P. ever wrut. AND which Por or O.R.A. ought to have somewhere in their archives for Villari to consult. or even VARE/ Varé might even degin to write comment on the DIFFERENCE between position of Barnes, for whom Mus/ wrote prefance/ and E.P. who never managed to get to talk with Mus/ but ONCE.[4]

Caravella and M.S.I.[5] may not like EP being NON socialist. BUT there it is.

E.P. had views re/ _U.S._ Government. In Italy he was observer. commending expediencies/ politics science of possible/ E.P. protested against falsification of NEWS about Italy printed in foreign papers. and against the historic blackout. He did not participate in struggles of italian factions/ he objected to ignorance.

I think Vil/ is less than just to Jim/[6] {on one point} at least I understood that Jim told Reuter to go to hell, and chucked thousand quid salary, rather than send lies. NOT that they dismissed him for telling the truth, but re/ uncooping yr/ correspdt.

Item/ he {Jim} tackled La Luce/ {secolo 27 Ag} and reported that she had a HEARRRT ov STone. Of course his use of language was always more ezuberant than that of E.P.

Lets see if Papini's gentle tears can melt the outer crusts of it. She was purrlight to La Driere[7] @ the Scelba reception.

Do you know, or does V/ friends of Formichiella/ friend of ½ Soma. His son, nice boy and friend of Igor[8] came in yester, gt/ difficulty to get past door as he apparently started by saying he was an interpreter/ and had not writ for permission. His pa/ consul Gen/ in Boston, but apparently the christers (½) are still on the pester.

What about the Troubetzkoi/[9] Boris dont git round to that item/ I cant complain as he has plenty to do. Alzo I keep enquiring re/ the young Fillipanni.

and wanting means of communication with Caravella/ whose address I can't find. First letter had illegible signatures/ Boris vurry nervous about 'em.

Prezzolini[10] has AT LAST printed something useful/ Bug/easy 14 Oct. narsty squish paper/[11] BUT obviously designed to circulate/

Army paper in Japan, got some nice crit/ of Faulkner and Hem/[12] whom the critic finds unsatisfactory.

AND mentions yr. correspondent with favour.

great joke that the parsimonious Frost[13] has been kicked out the offi-

cial Lie/BRAYs as unamerican/ having all his life exploited the new england background and provincialism. HAW,,, and again HAH!!!

the stinking Star,[14] less putrid than the Meyerblatt says I am an
AVOWED/ etc. might be timely to repeat that I am AVOWED only for J.
Adams, and the U.S.Constitution, plus Jeffersonian MINIMUM of gov-
ernment/ and Jacksonian antidebt line.

and continue to BATTTere/[15] Now that Knopf {has} issued Brooks Adams Law of Civ/ and Dec/ @95 cents, it might be assumed that AT LEAST
THAT part of E.P's discorsi was not anti-semitic must have been about
85% of what I did [illegible deletion] did say.

best to Helen.
Does SHE read wop papers? which?

1. EP's reference is to the 29 August 1956 *London Times* obituary "Major Strachey Barnes, a Paladin of Fascism."
2. EP had started this letter on the wrong side of the air mail paper.
3. EP's "Ezra Pound on Gold, War, and National Money." See Gallup, *Ezra
Pound* C1509.
4. EP is referring to Barnes's *The Universal Aspects of Fascism*, which was reviewed by T. S. Eliot in *The Criterion* in December 1928. The Italian translation
was published as *Gli aspetti universali del fascismo* in 1931 and had a preface by
Mussolini. EP met Mussolini "but ONCE," on 30 January 1933 in the Palazzo
Venezia in Rome.
5. **Movimento Sociale Italiano.**
6. **James Thomas Strachey Barnes.**
7. **James Craig La Drière.**
8. **Siegfredo Walter Igor Raimondo de Rachewiltz.**
9. **Princess Amélie Troubetzkoi.**
10. **Giuseppe Prezzolini.**
11. A "squish paper" is soft or not incisive.
12. Ernest Hemingway.
13. EP is pleased that some of Robert Frost's books have been "kicked out" of
"official" libraries. We do not know to what books EP is referring.
14. Probably the *Washington Evening Star.*
15. It.: "to fight."

105. TLU-3   13 November 1955
13 Nov.

just got W.M.R. "American Poems" Moxon, I suppose about 1872, no
date, but that date on the Cruikshank funny pixchoor.[1] FORTY years
ahead of american taste. Don{'}t recall ANY mention of W.M.R. in university yawp re/ criticism.

Of course Ford didn't try to boost W.M.R. as Ford was 50 years ahead,
re Prose and france, etc. and all the earlier brit/ Kleinstadt[2] trying to head
HIM off.

I dont know whether you possess a copy/ and this probably needed HERE to wash heads of local profs/. WMR thought it the first considerable anthol/ of american poets/ {to appear in England} dedicated to Whitman, whom he calls the greatest of the lot. and I dare say contains all of Walt's best stuff. Not yet time to examine. ANYhow, a WMR revival is due.

Alzo note Hemingway and Papini still going on re/ Ez' erro{r}s, as if Hem's pinkosity in Spain[3] were an answer/ and his sins not being RED. BUT those two at least have nerve to put their names on a ~~ch it~~ chit.

AT risk of losing MSI support, can't someone in woptaly get round to NOTICING that E.P. was virtually excluded from the press during the Ventennio/ apart from special contacts, Saviotti, Indici (local in Genova) Mare, Rapallo, Broletto, Como, due to Linati.[4] Invited but practically NEVER printed in any paper of ANY appreciable circulation/ until di Marzio ~~got~~ started "Meridiano di Roma."

EP, not only NOT avowed fascist, but ANTI-~~socialist~~ socialist/ [illegible deletion] and always for: best government is that which governs LEAST.

Gesell preferred to Douglas (C.H.{'s} Social Credit) because requires LESS burocracy.

Possible for Villari or Varé to RECOGNIZE this. The Dummy Xristers make NO use of INDIVIDUAL leads at least I have seen none/ as in Roma, Crassus[5] (was it) fire department, private racket, before public fire dept. Torlonia BONIFICA???

ORA ought to talk to an ADULT, I mean not merely to Helen. or let Helen talk to an adult. Note Ollivier, talk about the 13% factuality of Rivarol/ about Devin Adair/[6] I can{'}t be total reading committee, but somebody OUGHT to fight the spirit of Kleinstadt INSIDE Italy. Eastman (Max)[7] now admits socialism imperfect.

And several facts get thru Devin/ but they still boycott E.P. lot of yawp about symptoms, and no attention to ROOT. Anyone in woptaly Mention MANION?

The Raiola rose to that idea re/ Classics/ but no news of her for 3 weeks/ Her hotel didn't say she had gone to hospital/ but was out of N.york.

I understand some british benedictines are noticing that the Cantos are a, or THE, catholic poEM.

Shd/ like to keep Sheri out of jail[8] long enough to get some religious art. Ever read H.James "Madonna of the Future"/{?}[9] TREmendous pressure at PIVOT on which the turn AWAY from ignobility and depravity IN PAINTING is made.. Epstein,[10] ground tone, IGnobility/ the later and senile Picasso, TREmenjus technique, but basic depravity. Manus animan pinxit.[11] Sensibility in Marin,[12] marvellous, but only 13% of human heritage. Art in Egypt and Byzantium, right down to 1527 had something _inside_ it.

più a se l'anima tira.[13]

AND from 1927 the bolos thinking of dope as POLITICAL weapon.

The Times{'} obit of Barnes, MIGHT be used to differentiate MY position/ evidently Jim didn't realize the difference as his wife has found draft of an appeal to (yes, yes, guess WHOM…Winston) in Jim's papers, based on error.

Jim for fascism as principle/ E.P. recognizing it as the possible IN ITALY, despite its difference from Jefferson's aim/ AND considering VOCATIONAL representation[14] as constitutional for U.S. lower house.

~~proto~~ Of course I wd/ be DEAD from overwork if I hadn't been jugged, but someone might start serious discussion of what I HAVE thought and written.

Dazzi has ordered some Sq. $ for Querini. o.k. as far as it goes.

ORVAL Watts, attacks U N. but don't give POSITIVE answer/ which IS in note to my Confucian PIVOT/ The principle which HAS functioned.

1. In 1869 **William Michael Rossetti** began editing a series called Moxon's Popular Poets for E. Moxon, Son, and Co. Helen had apparently sent EP a copy of an anthology of american poetry.

2. Gm.: "small city." EP means "provincial Brits."

3. Hemingway fought on the Communist side in the Spanish Civil War (1936–39).

4. Here EP is listing some of the publications that did not exclude him: the Italian literary journal *L'Indice*, edited in Genoa by **Gino Saviotti**, who in 1931 offered EP a special section of the journal to guide "all that concerns foreign contributions"; *Il Mare*, the Rapallo daily newspaper; and *Broletto*, a monthly magazine published in Como, to which EP contributed three articles between April and December 1938 and which had some connection to **Carlo Linati.**

5. See letter 72.

6. American company that published Villari's *Italian Foreign Policy under Mussolini* (1956). Apparently the firm employed Pound as a reader.

7. **Max Eastman.** EP is probably referring to his *Reflections on the Failure of Socialism*.

8. **Sheri Martinelli** had been charged with possession of marijuana after a narcotics raid of a home in Alexandria, Virginia, on 26 July 1955. According to the arrest report, she also took heroin. Evidently all this disturbed EP greatly.

9. James's "Madonna of the Future" (*Complete Tales* 11–52).

10. **Sir Jacob Epstein.**

11. Lt.: "the hand paints the soul."

12. **John Marin.**

13. It.: "the soul draws more to itself."

14. One of the electoral principles of fascism was representation by trade or profession, as opposed to the more usual representation by region or electoral district.

106. TLU-3   11, 15 December 1955

11 Dec/

ORA

am passing on yr/ pa's Anthology of {"}American Poems{"} to the Catholic Univ.[1] as they haven't a copy, and it will be seen ñ by more people. Dedicated to Whitman, preface not as good as the note in memoirs that H. sent on. [illegible deletion] No date, but the Cruikshank drawing in dated 1872 good 30 years before americs took Whitman seriously.

In view of which I wonder whether it was Dante Gabe or Wm.R/ who dug up the Rubaiyat,[2] Said to have lain unnoticed until "Rossetti" picked it off the two penny box in Charing X.Rd.

acc/ my uncertain memory it said merely: "Rossetti" and D.G. having had more publicity, both author and reader may have yumped to conclusion that it was D.G.

You aren't old enough to remember the incident, or did it happen later?

Did a buzzard named Hammond[3] appeal to you? Now letters recd/ by the said Alabama intellectuel are being offered to Jas/[4] for $200 by a jew in Tokyo (whither Mr H/ has repaired.) Apparently Mr Blum and Lupinacci have the same angle of incidence. Montanari[5] don't say just who pays Epoca's printer, but suspects the amerikikes.

The civilized Alvarez[6] says he is english, that his family left spain in 1600 and which what. Pleasant conversation this p.m. I wonder if any of yr/ pious friends is interested in getting printed in Australia where 4 pages of 3 cols each are now open to factual statements.

15th/ I see you have appeared in ABC. You may remember its edtr/ found the foreign items that Boris collected were TOO exotic for the ABC readers. IS there anyone in Rome, now that B/ has left who will exchange information with, let us say, Stock who can apparently print anything he likes in 4 pages (12 columns) of the N. Times, OrrrStraliarrr. six weeks to get it, save by air, which costs 3 shillings/ BUT this not so bad for documents of Polk and Van Buren, which have already been undiffused for 120 years.[7] Varé probably right,[8] but can he APPLY it, let us say to the frottole[9] which a certain Messina, SAYS Cini[10] says la damblastatrice passed to him. Difficult to believe that Cini possesses such an unsuspected fund of naiveté, and I dont know whether Messina is a bloke I once met in Rapallo, where he had been incaricato[11] to supersede a very honest sec/ pol/ who had been denounced by a female connection of a Roma{n} paluka for lack of brio.[12] As the local son of the local baker remarked: Noi altri liguri non siamo espansivi.[13] If that bloke WAS Messina, it wasn't his fault. He was called in from out.

A buzzard name Blum in Tokio offers Laughlin some letters for $200/ which Mr Hammond had received during some alleged efforts to circulate a quite phoney petition, relative to yr/ anon/ crspdt. Mr L/ not knowing that H/ had migrated to the land of the Roising Sun (Sun Root, a better trans/) writes enquiry re. some perfectly unconnected-with-the-event, son of Nippon. Praps Mr Bl/ shd/ have offered 'em to ~~com~~ some cultural foundation, such as is paying Mr T/[14] to collect or at least search for quite immature correspondence of Doc. W.[15] with my olde friend VYoler, who don{'}t see as how the documents shed much light on history of american licherchoor. "The leaves of Aspern P/rs"[16]

The Eng/ Prof/ together with Doc W. et uxor[17] arrive by automobile, I believe a pleasant time was had by all, and that if any erotic{a} are IN the documents, they were in actual fact without result. (or certainly without "issue") carnal or uterine. ALL of which hellups Mr Rockerfeller and Mr Fluublight[18] keep the stew~~?~~dent mind off cardinal facts of american history, and should cause to emerge a satirist in at least SOME language, even if not native born.

Hammer on trivium/ Dante. Guicciardini, Mazzini. E.P. always deplored ventennio's NOT hooking onto Risorgimento. Can Villari report on Stock's reprints? Or etc.etc. Need to form a base for essential historic curriculum.

Research into ends of the eart{h} goes on. Very nice letter from the widow Frobenius. J.F. Rock[19] lively researcher.

Somebody might find out which books of L.A.Waddell are in lib/ of Inst Oriente. A long view MIGHT lead @ least one or two wops to deplore FAILURE of ventennio to send out real news as antidote to smear/ which has been AMAZINGLY effective. by contrast the Meyerblatt is going strong on french inefficiency in Morocco/ 30 years after Albert Londres who was, so far as I know, neither read nor noticed.

Montale has quoted Lav/ ed Usur/ correctly, and NO one will notice the basic nature of his article. I dont suppose ORA saw it, or wd/ admit etc.etc.

In contrast the large display, next to Louis Armstrong, in "ARTS SPECTACLES," does NOT know difference between usury and interest. France going highbrow.

> Best to Helen, Malù e
> compagnia.

---

1. EP had just presented William Michael Rossetti's *American Poems* to the Catholic University of America. See letter 107.

2. EP is remembering the following anecdote from Ionides' "Memories": "It must not be forgotten that we owe to Rossetti . . . the 'Omar Khayyam,' translat-

ed by Edward Fitzgerald, first published in 1859, which Rossetti picked up one day for a penny, outside a bookshop, read and admired it to such a degree that he went to buy some more copies, when he found the price had risen to two-pence, and he was cross with the bookseller. But he talked so much about it that all his friends tried to get copies, and this is how its fame was made" (43–44).

ORA replied: "I believe it was W.M.R. who picked up the Rubaiyat, well before my day. Both he and D.G.R. knew a good thing when they saw it and did not have to wait for the pundits to point it out to them" (24 Dec. 1955).

Dante Gabriel Rossetti discovered the Fitzgerald translation, not ORA's father.

3. **Douglas Hammond.**

4. EP's American publisher, **James Laughlin.**

5. **Philippo Montanari.**

6. Probably Alfred Alvarez, a literary critic who published critical commentary on EP's poetry.

7. Presumably Noel Stock was preparing to publish something on Polk and Van Buren in the Australian journal *New Times*. In a letter to E. E. Cummings dated 8 December 1953 EP had written: "why the HELL don't yu get interested in something interestin/ as fer Zmpl/ all presidents who staved off Civil War from 1830 to 1860 got bum press, and hv. been forgotten. Nont Only V.B/n <but> Tyler, Polk, Buchanan" (*Pound/Cummings* 350).

8. ORA had reported Varé's comment to her on the campaign to get EP released: "It is useless to show the U.S. that they are unjust; they should be made to see that they are absurd; that would make them sit up and take notice" (25 Nov. 1955).

9. It.: "nonsense."

10. **Vittorio Cini.**

11. It.: "in charge."

12. It.: "liveliness."

13. It.: "We Ligurians are not demonstrative."

14. Probably **John Connop Thirwall,** the "Eng/ Prof/" mentioned later in the letter.

15. William Carlos Williams.

16. Henry James's "The Aspern Papers" (*Complete Tales* 6:275–382) features an American literary scholar who causes an old woman's death so that he could have access to a famous poet's papers that she owns. Perhaps Thirwall was trying to discover if there were love letters between Williams and **Viola Baxter.**

17. Lt.: "and wife."

18. J. William Fulbright (1905–95). See letter 70.

19. **Joseph Francis Charles Rock.**

107. TLU-2   [December 1955]

This letter was written on a letter to EP dated 16 December 1955 by Eugene P. Willging, library director of the Catholic University of America, and was received by ORA before her 24 December 1955 letter in which she acknowledged EP's letter. Willging had written to thank EP for his gift of his copy of William Michael Rossetti's American Poems.

Dear O.R.A.

this will show that the Anthol/ has been put where it will be of some use. I shd/n't say that D.G.R. had ever been underestimated here, though that may be merely at level of my own friends. Sparked Swinburne, though that probably not known as the young do not go in for chronology instinctively until they have been processed. Fordie had a positive apostolat[1] re/ Christina[2] whom he thought downtrodden by roaring victorians. Vita Nuova especial{y} made a cult, and only in matter of bulk of product wd. D.G.R. have been held second to Browning. Fitzgerald having left one poem.[3] {vide earlier note re/ fortune ofe that.} Xtna no direct use to me but via Fordie might be said to enter the second boiling of the "advance". Whether she had direct influence on L.Johnson[4] and Alice Meynell[5] who might have learned from her I dont know or whether it wd/ have been conscious or unc-.

{DGR} Perhaps both the painting and the verse influenced by horrible milieu. chronologic and local. DGR not quite getting XII hundred in verse or 1500 in pre-Raph. NOR being exclusively and intensely [illegible deletion] Ottocento[6] with Manet and Degas. But certainly in gt/ wave of fashion before Debussy and Mallarme. Fordie against all the velvet and plush of the period, hence his urge re [illegible deletion] Xtina. AND so forth. DGR making something different. Xtna in some ways closer to primi secoli[7] style in a given area. Wops: heaven and hell as mythology a mythology nearer their temperament, differing from limbo, fog and boiled vegetables.

To understand Fordie/ Helen might consider that he was LOATHED by all the old parochial flubdubs who had never heard of french prose, Flaubert etc. Had no one to play with till my generation arrived, ten years his junior. Was on war path for Xtina and old F.Mad. Brown[8] whom he also thought was underestimated.

so that if he trod on toes he was at least headed for somewhere.

no doubt W,M,R could STAND quite a lot of printed matter that F.M.F saw as rubbish to be cleared away before one cd. get something better.

Then again WMR en famille and in his public functio{ns} may have presented different angle?

He {Fordie} told yr/ gawd's idea, re Gosse[9] and old Ker,[10] AND as usual if his version wasn't millimetricly factual it was what OUGHT bdy/ well to have happened, or perhaps not as usual, in % to past events but certainly decorative sub/ spec/ aet/[11]

After all, german Märchen.[12] What about his ma/ NOT my dish of tay, but Violent[13] used to say (not in denigration) that there was a lot of Ford {"}in that old woman.{"}

Sorry the Parnasso was bicuspid,[14] waste of time not have seen the family vault before its destruction, y compris[15] the inhabitants.

by the way, HAD Dante Gabe ever BEEN to Italy? had he SEEN the preraphs/ i.e. ital/ painting before it started down hill?

Tragedy of Vance's[16] father in Indiana, who finally managed to get his son to Europe to SEE what was painted. Old man WANTED to paint.

The poetry DGR had before him, that can be transported. even in Nat/ Gallery, the light is not ital/

> Capo d'anno[17] to them
> Rossetti girls. and the tribe of
> Malu.

1. *Apostolate*, It.: "the office or position of an apostle." EP means that Ford promoted **Christina Rossetti's** work.

2. **Christina Rossetti.**

3. See letter 106.

4. **Lionel Johnson.**

5. **Alice Meynell.**

6. It.: "1800s."

7. It.: "first centuries."

8. **Ford Madox Brown.**

9. **Sir Edmund Gosse.**

10. **W. P. Ker.**

11. *Sub species aeternitatis*, Lt.: "below eternal beings."

12. Gm.: "fairy tales."

13. **Isabel Violet Hunt.**

14. We do not have a letter from ORA to which EP is responding here. Presumably EP is calling the Rossetti family house ("the family vault") "the Parnasso" in jest. As ORA had reported on 6 August 1950, the house in London "was blown up by a flying bomb" during World War II and thus would have had standing walls but no interior: "bicuspid."

15. Fr.: "and including."

16. **Fred Nelson Vance.**

17. It.: "Happy New Year."

1956

108. TLU-1   31 January 1956
31 Jan/

O.R.A.

Isn't La Pira[1] the man to deal with the matter. I spose Pouj/[2] will see
him?? if not why not? There was a frenchman in here last week/ but
hasn't returned YET. more bloody minded than O.R.A. but in the right
direction. Whether Pouj/ reads any language but his own. I dont see that
I can simplify beyond what I have in Θ Lavoro ed Usura/ extant in wop.
and english

Bugeasy/[3] for 6 Jan/ has a letter of La Pira's slipped in cause some
crablouse was denouncing it. back in 1922 or '3 one of yr/ chosen printed a brief note of mine on Social Credit in Ere Nouvelle, but I doubt if
anyone discovered it and it cert/ had no sequel/ the frogs are the LAST
people to hear of anything that is thought outside their own cloacae.

There was a gesellite called Baral (Jean)[4] died off during the war/
{Marseilles or thar' bouts.}

Yes, it may be time, to reprint the parts of Orientamenti that deal specificly with Il Problema delle tasse.

Corsini[5] might be ready to select 'em/ but copeis are hard to find. I dont
know if even Por has one. Various people do NOT answer letters. Nico-
letti{,} who came I think at least once to yr/ salotto{,} is in Perugia, cd/
be reached via Por. who says N/ is "sempre esaltato".[6] meaning he is
honest.

Whether Riley[7] (the abov. mentioned frog, is descended from Reile/ I
dont know. I shall tell him to translate Lav/ ed Usura IF he ever shows
up again/

M. Slatin[8] has excavated an article by a certain M.B. Cramer[9] in Journal of English Literary History 1941, p. 309/ 10 re/ yr/ pa in the Germ
for 1850/[10] vurry lively.

D.P. has inherited some stray issues of Germ/ don{'}t know if that issue among 'em. Will inspect and pass on to Cat/ Univ/ for adjustment of
credit to WMR fer his acumen.

Cramer's artl/ "What Browning's rep/ owed to Pre-Raphs.

I don't know that Rivarol or Ecrits de Pris wd/ touch problème mon-
netaire/ might just disappear if they did. BUT if ANYbody ever speaks
to ANYone/ dare say they wd only mention yr/ anonymous correspondent re/ geopolitik.

Stock very lively in New Times/ digging up president Johnson afraid
too concentrated to circulate in england, europe or the U.S.

Pavlos[11] at least being useful/ reprinting Portuguese labor ~~low~~ {law} on
his broadside. Current.

1. Probably Giorgio La Pira (1902–77), a politician, a law professor at the University of Florence, a member of the anti-Fascist underground, and one of the signatories of the Italian Constitution in 1947.

2. **Pierre Poujade.** ORA suggested (22 Jan. 1956) that EP get one of his disciples, perhaps Mary or Boris, to send Poujade information on Gesellite schemes.

3. Probably a reference to a recent issue of *Il Borghese.*

4. **Jean Barral.**

5. EP was negotiating with Renato Corsini to reprint parts of his *Orientamenti.* One of Corsini's essays on EP appeared in the Rome daily *Secolo d'Italia* (4 May 1955), was translated (most likely by EP himself), and published anonymously as "Ezra Pound, Economist: Justice the Final Goal," *New Times* 25 (16 Dec. 1955): 7.

6. It.: "always excited."

7. An unidentified Frenchman who visited EP at St. Elizabeths.

8. Myles Slatin, who at this time was writing "'Mesmerism.'"

9. Maurice Browning Cramer, author of "What Browning's Literary Reputation Owed to the Pre-Raphaelites."

10. *The Germ,* a journal (four numbers in 1850) in which the manifesto of the Pre-Raphaelite Brotherhood was printed.

11. A Greek American introduced to EP by **Michael Lekakis.**

109. TLU-3   1–3 February 1956
1 Feb/

Germ/ 1900 reprint. with yr/ pa's preface.[1] {\}ORA
this mostly for Helen/ you not having answered question: DID Dante Gabe ever get to Italy and SEE pre-raph pictures? {"}Hand and Soul{"}/ very applicable to Sheri/[2] that being modus operandi.

Germ inherited mostly uncut/ been lying unread several years cause no immediate incidence/ H & S. is printed separate.

So far I find no ref/ to Landor? Mebbe he didn't get his spikes back into the ultimate Britain till '54

No ref/ bks/ to see if wot HE said re/ Rob. Br[3] preceded crit. in Germ.
NOT WMR crit/ but the "Giants" artl/
If yu and H/ haven't a copy {y}r/ right wd/ precede the Cat/ Univ. idea.
Another point/ the Amor Platonicus/[4] and the monument at Vasto/[5] your grandfather, or great grand?[6]

The father or grandfather of WMR/ D.G/ and which of them the elder? D.G. being 22 in 1850. Christina 19. {?WMR?}
and the ma or grandma, who burnt the remaining copies Am/ Plat.?
2 Feb FOR the record. Dant Gabe @ 22 does {"}H & S.{"}
Mediaeval part horribly writ/ take off for Hewlett's[7] Little Novels of Italy, but D.G. being absolute genius does finale in real prose/ WHEN I read H & S, I was TOTALLY incapable of seeing the differenc{e}, not interested in prose. Must have read it early as i̶s̶ motto is quoted in early poem, alzo the {phrase} "inglesi matti sul misticismo"[8] stayed permanently in

mind, though wholly unconscious of SOURCE. It took Fordie to attack the bad prose, and carry toarch for the real writing.

Landor on Browning already ahead of the bloke who wrote the "Giants in our time", BUT do we spose that P.R.B.[9] didn't or couldn't see Landor precisely ve because he wasn't matto sul misticismo.[10]

For straight phrasing D.G. got to it in "I have been here before" poem/ Will Smith[11] (A Lume Spento" inscribed {To him} in memoriam,) I still remember commenting {his} "He know how", whether he or I had read out the poem I do not remember. He died at 25, painter.

I dont know when I will surrender Germ reprint/ alzo Should {"}Girl among Anarchists" go into Cat/ Univ. with it, to make nucleus fambly mumnument? Or was fambly liburry bombed out of existence, and does H/ want it if you don't? same for Germ?

##have WMR poems ever been collected? if only 10 pages cd/ be included at end of a vol/ by D.G. or Christina. is there an adequate memoir? hanging is a bit non constructive, and obsolete in age of electric chairs and atom bumps.

no partic/ organization devoted to pendulation/ but the English ASS(ociation) gets things printed, as their annual proceedings a year or so ago DEEVoted to yr. crspdt. IF THAT {1900} reprint of Germ is out of print/ a new one could be excogitated/ In fact shall recommend it to Nude Erections.[12] AT which time a new preface along with the BY WMR, cd/ be ON.

Alzo the question of incasso/[13] Giovannini intends to put a student onto subject when he gets a suitable. BUT either H or O[14] wd/ be certainly preferable/ and non exclusive, and/or BOTH plus the stu/Dont (as NHP[15] has now taken to calling 'em).

3 Feb/ am suggesting N.Directions do offset/ fac-sim. Germ 1900 that wd/ give copies for Helen/ Cat/ Univ. and Brun/bg

Mary says can't see how to be clearer re/ econ/ than already in Lav/ ed Usu/ Pouj/ prob. reads only french/ wot about a translator?

re/ revival/ godDAMN fire drill, when one has to waste time in passageway or cellarage, I hv/ pocket edtn/

perché quel popolo è si empio

Incontr'a' mei in ciascuna sua legge?[16]

somebody might get twist out of Arabia colorata in rosso.[17]

etc/ I keep yowling for MORE communication _between_ those who have vestige of horse sense.

1. **William Michael Rossetti** was the editor of _The Germ_ and wrote the manifesto of the Pre-Raphealite movement.

2. **Sheri Martinelli.**

3. Robert Browning.

4. *Il mistero dell' amor platonico del medio aevo* by **Gabriele Rossetti**. Rossetti was persuaded to suppress this work after publication, but some forty copies were preserved. EP is negotiating to sell ORA's copy.

5. The birthplace of **Gabriele Rossetti.**

6. EP is querying information in ORA's memoir, provisionally entitled "Anecdotage of an Interpreter," part of which was eventually published as "Pages of Memoir" in *Edge*. EP comments on other chapters in letters 111, 122, and 123 (and in a letter dated 7 October 1958 but not included here). Although the complete memoir is not extant, the surviving chapters can be found in folder 6241, box 142, series 4, manuscripts, of the Ezra Pound Papers at the Beinecke Library.

7. Maurice Hewlett (1861–1923), who wrote medieval romances in the manner of William Morris.

8. It.: "the English are mad about mysticism."

9. Pre-Raphaelite Brotherhood.

10. It.: "not mad about mysticism."

11. **William Brooke Smith.** EP dedicated *A Lume Spento* to him.

12. EP's pun on *New Directions*.

13. It.: "collection."

14. ORA had suggested that a statement be written on the "money question" and offered to provide **Pierre Poujade** "with ammunition for his fight" (22 Jan. 1956). EP responded by saying that **Giovannini** intended to get a student to make a collection of his statements on the money question, but that "H or O" (probably **Helen Rossetti Angeli** or ORA) would be preferable.

15. **Norman Holmes Pearson.**

16. It.: "why are these people so ungodly / Against me in every one of their laws?"

17. It.: "Araby colored red." The unidentified Italian passage above probably refers to the intrasigence of the Jews, who are identified by EP and many anti-Semites with communism. Hence, "red Arabia" could be the Jewish state of Israel, which, of course, was not communist.

110. TLU-1   3 April [1956]

3 Ap/

Dear O.R.A.

You haven't mentioned Villari for some time, I trust you still see him. If not you might forward this note to him/ or phone him to come read it on the promises and DIScuss it with whatever citoyen compos mentis[1] is available.

I was grateful for his very clear summary of my econ/ only one point needing further elucidation or dissociation.

WORK as the measure of price/ the BASIS of money (and credit) the ABundance of nature and the responsibility of the whole people.

Marx and Mill[2] both flop at this point. godless mutts. Blake wd/ have classified both as atheists, I suppose. I think it wd/ be good strategy to emphasize E.P. as ANTI*MARX and of course VASTLY superior.

Brooks-Adams, useful for contrast between the two temperaments. Idealist and avaricious.

Del Mar gt/ historian, and immensely valuable for pointing out that the fight was NOT between xristers and pagan divinities, but against the worship of Augustus.

Also Donation of Constantine[3] forged from IGnorance, the gold was under the Pontifex Max/

That division of power of issue/ Gold sacred/ silver wangled to senators etc/ bronze to some privileged cities/ local control of local purchasing power.

Abd el Melek's revolt/ vid Canto 96.[4] solidifying tip in Del Mar (Monetary SYSTEMS... V/ has the Netherland pamphlet?[5] have you had it?

Another Sq $/ Del Mar finally on way to press.[6]

St Anselm pivotal for later charters/ evil of central control when it passes urge to justice, especially just price (just rent) tithes vs/ fines.[7]

Anselm didn't want the loot/ but for five centuries the struggle sank into question of WHO GETS IT.

Hen/ VIII finally ending Pete's pence.[8]

All of 'em gettin it in the neck when departing from Confucius.

MENCIUS basic for tithes, i.e. SHARE vs/ fixed rent or tax.

The idea of charter. social contract, finally gets to separation of church and state.

But charter, division of powers starts, or can be studied as emerging from Anselm vs/ Wm.H. Roosevelt Rufus.

Stephen[9] makes a contract but does not keep it.

U.S. Constitution the summit UNTIL revival of or later development from guild basis. Though the guilds in Byzantium had no say in anything outside their own scope.

However, as per Strike X. The indonesian Sookarno[10] has got to idea of representation based on what people DO not merely on where they live.

That, plus the emergence from u,s, colonial system, Guernsey market house,[11] etc. are the ADvances SINCE the U.S.Constitution was set up.

And Social Credit directive very ably summarized (as distinct from Gesell's mercantile Anschauung) by Rev. Lintell in recent issue of Voice.[12] Villari shd/ correspond with [?]uth, Lincs. England. [illegible]/ and thinks [rest of letter missing]

1. Fr. + Lt.: "a citizen of sound mind."
2. John Stuart Mill.
3. See letter 23.
4. Abd-al-Malik (646–705), the fifth Omayyad caliph (685–705), mentioned in canto 96/654. EP learned of him in Del Mar's *A History of Monetary Systems*, in which the name is spelled as EP has it. Del Mar observes that he was the first

Muslim ruler to strike coins not bearing "the stamp of Roman suzerainty," thus declaring his temporal sovereignty.

5. Chapter 12 of Del Mar's *A History of Monetary Systems* published as *A History of Netherlands's Monetary System* in the **Square $ Series**. In the rest of the letter EP is summarizing Del Mar's account of British monetary history.

6. Del Mar, *Roman and Moslem Moneys*. This volume contains the chapter on Abd-al-Malik from *A History of Monetary Systems*.

7. William II, called Rufus, king of England (1087–1100), opposed St. Anselm's insistence on the church's control of the investiture of bishops. Rufus exiled Anselm and raised land rents: "Rufus raised rent 5 to 40/ usu terrae" (canto 105/ 749). EP thought that civil rights derived from Anselm's stand.

8. "Peter's pence," the popular name for papal taxes levied throughout Europe prior to the Reformation.

9. Probably Stephen Spender (b. 1909), British poet.

10. EP apparently read that Sukarno (1901–70) had plans for representation by occupation in Indonesia modeled on Mussolini's Fascist constitution.

11. See letter 32.

12. In the 25 February 1956 issue of *Voice*, A. R. Lintell published a statement. It was reprinted (with the addition of two paragraphs by EP) as "Production and Consumption" in *New Times*.

111. TLU-1   28 April 1956

28 Ap/

O.R.A.

CHEERS!! Now may be if I ask you to find a *THIRD* jew,[1] yu'l do two MORE chapters of autobiog/ VURRY interesting.[2] Too lively for Hudson Rev. I don't know where I can get it PAID for until one knows there will be MORE of it, and *WHEN* it will be available.

I am fairly sure I can get these two bits printed, BUT great waste not to have it PAID for.

Mary sent me "una guida" PND[3] (they have omitted the vowel points()}[4] but appear totally (yes Totally) Jeffersonian, but still bogged in Keynes who is NOT a basis or a guida to anything but wangles. Have you any idea who they are?? All usurers are liberals.

Dick degli UBERTI has done VERY useful art/l in Corriere della Liguria, 14 th April.[5] AT last a few basic facts stated by someone who know(s} them.

Corsini's article[6] was excellent, but based on one booklet. The noble Villari has a couple of errors or at least uses terms a bit loosely. Work the ~~basis NOT~~ measure of prices, not the BASIS for issue.

Nobody cd/ have got more into so short an art/l. And I am grateful to him for clarity on most points.

One shd/ ad mag. glor/[7] go ON keeping words distinct from each other. PURchasing power INCLUDES, money and credit.

You cant monopolize credit, it springs up like grass wherever one man trusts another.

PND seems to be for NO proper control. Villari says I want state MONopoly of issue of money. that is NOT basic in my econ/ CHUNG YUNG.[8]

C.H.D. solid re/ early money: the man who issued the money HAD the goods. {& Del Mar shows social trend in proposito.} it was Lenin and co/ who wanted banking to be monopoly of the state.

woman named Alice Widener seems (on evidence of one ~~issue~~ number, to have best paper (fortnightly) in America, called {"}U.S.A.{"} fine article on UNESCO coupons backed by american $. the usual amurkn suckers.

ON the whole the PND very hopeful sign, if they would only READ a different or ANOTHER set of books. otherwise merely manchester and all the old lack of defences. Given Doug/ {wd. be almost 100% O.K.} and Gesell

AND usual wop care[illegible deletion]lessness. The wobbly Keynes did NOT get to be Governor of the Stank of Eng/ (as far as I recall) He was on the board.[9]

They have the idea that circulation is useful/ so had Gesell before Rossoni's clear remark re/ lo stato.[10] and the second phase of Gesellism. I must examine their GUIDA, BUT waste of time till one knows more of their personal morals. The sceptic Armando[11] remarked that ALL political parties are good (in their programs).

Santayana made similar remark re/ clerical tyranicity. i.e. sim/ to PND. One copy of Feder known to be in this country. fuss about Adolf[12] aimed at concealing Feder. Stok[13] sez Borin had never heard of Ashberg. Pleyber says he knows nowt re/ money and thinks Dominique in same boat. yu go'rr edderkate.[14]

One unintelligible type error in yr/scrip which I will note later as D.P. too{k} chapters home to read. The rest I can correct, alzo praps wrangle re/ thisandthat.

{best to Helen.}

1. EP had challenged ORA to name another honorable Jew besides Henry Lubin in a letter now lost.

2. ORA had sent EP a portion of her memoir for possible publication in the *Hudson Review.* Despite EP's endorsement, the article was not accepted.

3. It.: "a guide to pound." EP means a guide book to money, not himself.

4. The *o* and *u* of *pound.*

5. **Riccardo M. degli Uberti**'s "Why Pound Liked Italy."

6. See letter 108.

7. An irreverent application of *ad majorem gloriam Deum.*

8. One of EP's Confucian touchstones. He translates it as "unwobbling pivot."

9. EP is correct: **John Maynard Keynes** was never governor of the Bank of England.

10. It.: "the state."

11. **Armando Sapori.**

12. Adolf Hitler.

13. **Noel Stock.**

14. "You gotta educate."

112. TLU-3   7 May 1956

7 Maggio/

O.R.A.

Sorry the Raiola keeps smashing her osseus structure/[1] and re/ her status in the Soc/ Verg/ she implied that I wd/ be welcome at Cumae IF I ever get turned loose/ but is this her private bit of wishful thinks? Has she any conception of the purely or impurely NON-political opposition to yr/ anonymous correspondent in academic and plutocratic circles, snobocracy etc. (I hear that Fuller JFC[2] refers to Cadocracy, but that is something else yet again.)

Does she (La Raiola{)} know on what terms I cd/ break into Cumae if ever the occasion of making such a choice, shd/ arise?

I am not a classical philologist. I have small greek and very promiscuous latin, which latter I read to find out what I want to know etc.

Dick Uberti has done a very good article in Corriere della Liguria, 14 th Ap. First one by someone who has known the facts for so long.[3] Translation will appear in Melbourne, Australia. He wrote some years ago that WHEN he cd/ get at his father's papers, there wd/ be data. And evidently a decade has been sufficient to bring that happy result.

Scarfoglio in Nuova Anthologia.[4] An ADULT treatment of the Odes. I think Giovannini{,} and Gordon[5] (now translating Mencius, and correlating that text with a lot of occidental sanity) are going to try to organize a serious means of intercommunication re/ terminology and basic ideas. No idea how long it will take. BUT if they get it going it won{'}t dodge and try to uphold blackout of history and falsification of news. No acquiescence. I don't know how to get the New Times to you. air mail very expensive from down under and surface post takes six weeks to HERE. I wonder how long to Italy.

Do try to keep on with your memoirs, they are of interest ABOVE a certain level. I dont say that that top floor is teeming with inhabitants. BUT the bard of Avon did on @ least one occasion mention quality of the audiences as preferable to mass demonstration. Everyone who has seen these two chapters VERY interested. They are much better than the one

sent two years ago/ let us hope similar interval will not intervene before
the next batch.

I dont know how much you earn per hour on the interruptives, but am
convinced interruption is in long run UNProfitable.[6] Very few people
know ANYthing about real history of past 50 years. No other honest
records of economic thought/ Versailles wangles SEEN from honest
monetary angle are available.

The more Patrologia[7] I read the WORSE the corruption labled Christianity appears/ I dont know that even the kikes can be blamed for all of
it. Atys worship[8] ~~and other~~ etc. Does Villari know anything re/ quantity
of land and slaves owned by pagan temple{s} before the grabby Xters began squabbling over prebende?[9] Del Mar says Half. Julian[10] ameliorated
a bit, and tried to get a little honesty in toaxation. Wm. Rufus a pre-FDR,
a real STINCGker, but Canterbury vs/ York[11] etc. leading to Browning
re/ Spanish Cloister soliloq.

and as for social medicine and hist of opinion. This re/Tommy Ebor.
Superfluit ad Feb. anno 1114, etiam hinc laudandus, quod cum letalem
ejus morbum negarent medici posse sanari absque usu feminae, castus
maluerit mori, quam episcopalem dignitatem tali macula contaminari.[12]

cf/ Mood pills,[13] 1956

The "dark" ages nuts on bones, cf/ Monselice,[14] where they got a chapel
like a pharmacy, largest collection in the world. fads no more intelligent
than atom bombs. {"}Degrading superstition{"} said A.Upward,[15] only it
didn't degrade the savages, and Julian's era, especially when he gets into
the LOUSY near Orient, very bloody. Theology a grammatical exercize,
but theological controversy 98% fight for church income. maybe more.

Best to Helen, an' yu be a good girl and GIT ON with yr. Memoirs.

Two points for L.V.[16] work the MEASURE of just price, but must be
assayed, i.e. picked etc.

and Del Mar, not E.P. interested in state monopoly of issue. so long as
"the man who issues, HAS the goods", money wd/ be valid, state monopoly not necessary, state supervision a protection against excess, but
not fundamental.

Some one in Australia finally got a good sentence out of Tommy
d'Acquin.[17] re/ it being permitted the highbrow to think also about how
a thing wd/ work.

optimum

The BASIS for money, the abundance of nature and the responsibility
of the whole people.

1. ORA had written that Raiola "had a fall in the Villa and broken her wrist and
right arm" (18 Apr. 1956). Four years earlier she had been run over by a car.
2. **John Frederick Charles Fuller.**

3. See letter 111.

4. Scarfoglio's "L'Antologia classica cinese," which appeared in *Nuova Antologia*, is a review of EP's *The Classic Anthology Defined by Confucius* and includes Scarfoglio's literal translations into Italian of a number of EP's English poems.

5. **David M. Gordon.**

6. EP thinks ORA's English tutoring, for which she was paid by the hour, was interrupting her writing.

7. *Patrologia Graeca* and *Patrologia Latina*, edited by J. P. Migne, are collections of the works of the fathers of the church in Greek and Latin, respectively.

8. Atys, or Attis, is the Phyrgian analog of Adonis and a castrated lover of the corn goddess Cybele. Here he appears to be a synecdoche for asceticism rather than for pagan erotomysticism. EP is generally hostile to the former and friendly to the latter.

9. It.: "profits."

10. **Julian the Apostate.** EP approved of his administrative and tax reforms.

11. See letter 110.

12. Lt.: "He passed over in February in the year 1114, deserving of praise also from this [the manner of his death], inasmuch as, even when the doctors said that his fatal disease could not be cured except by the use of a woman, he preferred to die chaste rather than have his episcopal dignity besmirched by such a stain."

13. Presumably tranquilizers, introduced about this time.

14. A town near Padua, apparently containing a chapel with a reliquary of impressive proportions.

15. **Allen Upward.**

16. **Luigi Villari.**

17. Thomas Aquinas.

113. TLU-2   30 June [1956]
30 th GiuGNO/

AU NUTS, fer yr/ Lubin. Here I am boostin Del Mar as america's greatest historian. and It is to be presumed that Del Mar's ancestors had been circumcised for quite as long as Lubin{'}s.

I do not say that Lubin was a sonvabitch because he was a chew? Yu have to watch 'em. I do not say he was a sonvabitch. I say you swallow Lubin cause you liked the bloke. and gawd knows they have got round some keen observers. AND yu swallow him whole and FAIL to see that this sweat for UNIFORM and/or steady prices. stable prices (from the Augean) was in Lub's effort{,} to be stable in one of the most god damned UNSTABLE of measures/ especially in the period of super hoax Lub/ was working in.

And the horrible Xtians/ perverting [illegible deletion] the religion of the universal god of all men, into the tribal punk of a mesopotamian tribe KEPT the occidental mind off honesty for centuries, fooling round with discussions of fads and hair cuts. Particularly fine examples in Bede and in Paul the Deacon.

AND the stench of the church (questionnaire read this week from cat/ stewdent, why dont cat/ univs/ purvide the degraded republic with more and better writers)

Respons[illegible deletion]s, sheer mental cowardice, low character of hierarchy TOTAL indifference to truth.

I trust the degradation as from yr/ pa's ~~thime~~ time is fairly apparent in McN/[1] little (he hopes) monthly. Have any of yr/ friends got ANYthing to say? McN/ tried to get Pine[2] to TELL the young what to do (as of oggi pom/)[3] all he cd/ get was copy of excellent speech by the Judge who stopped the Degraders (at least for a day or so). Mr Molitov[4] lunches with Baruch. and ORA loves the chews and declines to defend the occident against them. all cause she knew a benevolent Lub/

Jerusalem did NOT giv the world religion. it defiled it. The doctrines of the Church (Xtn) are NOT chewisch. vide Zielinski if you can get a copy, or if the eng/ trans/ ever gets printed (or even finished). Why not make another division/ poisoners and those who give food?

best to Helen. Which one is Toto (maschile[5] or fem.) Glad Malu is not accepting Gertie Stein's chewish remedy: genosuicide.[6] recommended by Aragon[7] to the goys.

AND given my admiration for DelM/ AS HISTORIAN, it need 40 years watching to SEE that he is a kike, and that his information cd/ lead to kahal government system/ the STINK model of kremlin tyranny, only nobody KNOWS about it. Even so the kikes prob/y afraid he wd/ bust some of the rackets.

Just what is the naive but candid reader to INFER from the presence of Coselschi in yr/ little band of enthusiasts?

1. **Robert McNair Wilson.**
2. Judge David Andrew Pine; see letter 59.
3. *Oggi pomeriggio*, It.: "this afternoon."
4. **Viacheslav Mikhailovitch Molotov.**
5. It.: "male."
6. See letter 95.
7. **Louis Aragon.**

114. TLU-1   24 November 1956
Thanksgiving day 1956/

in the land defiled by jews and perverted by their most filthy servants.

Am in yr/ debt for ref/ to Augie contra Faustus.[1] Thought with Renan's[2] "n'y rien que la betise qui donne une idee de l'infini"[3] that I was past certain kinds of surprises. BUTT Faustus a very iggurunt man, with gleams of intelligence trying to debunk some of the piffle but Augie the

Hippologian[4] the MOST unmitigated deluge of piffle and hogwash that I have encountered even among Xtn theologians. Found him a damn bore ten years ago/ wondered if I shd/ leave complimentary ref/ in early Canto[5] or erase it.

Then somebody trotted out an intelligent sentence/ BUT the contra Faustum REALLY, ma chere O.R.A. is unmitigated hogwash. Faustus bad enuf/

let us suspend for a moment, as I have only [illegible deletion] got to the start of Chap/ XX.

BUT after a week or so with Plotinus[6]...who has got quality. the descent to reading the idiots leads to this blow-off.

Contrast the delightful afternoon/ miracle of five intelligent ~~people~~ visitors and one highschool article in course of getting educated by Horton/ whether it wd/ be possible to duplicate such a gathering in the Jew-nutted States OUTSIDE a bughouse I don't know.

Found an unexpected Andrewsite this a.m. but when I told him HOW to have a sane tax system, he wondered if [illegible deletion] Andrews[7] knew about it. summary of his earlier reflections. He had stopped doing much outside work/ in 1939 if he bothered to earn ten bucks, he GOT 9.

Now if he earns 10 the tax swine leave him five and the $ is worth only ½ former.

Kasper acquitted of sedition/[8] public cheers/ still got another net spread re/ some technicality, but they cant soak him more than a year for it. His lawyer sd/ he had never heard of anyone accused of doing so many things by remote control. None of the kikecution witnesses stood up under cross Xam. At least got a little publicity for the NAACP being run by kikes not by coons.

Glad to see TelAviv in true colours, and the nature of moscow-Paris-London a bit more in the open.

Have you looked at Mary's translations in Prospetti?[9] shd/ like opinion of someone who know the wop language and is not too much influenced by fond parental etc.

PurrLight bloke in Orissa wants pref/ to their trans/ of Leaves of Grass. My mind works very slowly/ I sent 'em early verses, but forgot to putt in a plug for W.M.R. I think also that the bloke had miscalculated his date line, and the postal service's tempo.

The blithering imbecility of chasing Mus/ out [rest of letter missing].

1. On 8 November 1956 ORA had written: "I do not know that Gabriele Rossetti made any references to Cavalcanti or *I Fedeli d'Amore* reading Greek. I sold my copy of the Amor Platonico and so cannot look it up for you. I feel sure that they were not familiar with Greek but I see in Valli's 'Linguagio Segreto di Dante'

that Dante's knowledge of Plotinus came to him through St. Augustine{,} *Contra Faustum*, in which he developed the whole doctrine of *Rachele Sapienza*. Pascoli saw in *Contra Faustum* one of the chief sources of the Divina Commedia." She was responding to EP's letter of 4 November, which is missing. This remark prompted EP to read Augustine's *Contra Faustum*.

2. **Ernest Renan.**

3. Fr.: "only stupidity gives some idea of the infinite."

4. St. Augustine the Theologian (354–430) was bishop of Hippo.

5. "And Augustine, gazing toward the invisible" (canto 16/68).

6. **Plotinus.**

7. Probably Stanley Andrews (b. 1895), a journalist and editor with a special interest in Agricultural affairs who held several appointments as consultant and director of agriculture government agencies. In the early 1950s he served as the director of Technical Cooperation Administration, a U.S. food agency designed to increase food production in Communist-sensitive areas. The "Andrewsite" discovered by EP is unidentified.

8. Efforts to get EP released from St. Elizabeths were hindered in part by his association with **John Kasper.** EP supported Kasper's activities and regarded him as something of a martyr to his cause. In February 1957 the *New York Herald Tribune* ran a four-part series of articles on Kasper's activities that made several references to EP's friendship with him. See also letter 115, in which EP announces: "Kasper defeated."

9. Translations by **Mary de Rachewiltz** of her father's poems—"De Aegypto," "Ité," "Alba," "Taking Leave of a Friend," section 7 of *Homage to Sextus Propertius*, parts 1 and 3 of *Hugh Selwyn Mauberley*, canto 3, and part of canto 81— appeared as "Poesie" in *Prospetti*, the Italian edition of *Perspectives U.S.A.* The publication also included a translation of canto 45 by Carlo Izzo.

115. TLS-2   6 December 1956
6 Dec 56

Dear O.R.A.

herewith salutation and a christening "moog" or something useful, MORE useful, for Malu's "Olivia".[1]

Helen's letter arruv in singed envelope and french surcharge stating it wuz DAMaged, I spose was on plane that crashed in Babylon or Lutece or somewhere. anyhow the surcharge was in french, so mebbe the wop mail goes that way. {or via Maroc?}

Kasper defeated, same as South was in 1864,[2] cause mind diverted from money and taxes, customs, onto local issue having no broad and defensible theoretical basis save in nature itself.

Villari's mild vol/[3] has some useful points, showing Mus ~~he~~ did not favour mongrelizations.

very hard to stir interest in ~~immediate~~ near past. esp/ with so much needed for the present, in fact 400 times more brains and knowledge than there is lying about on scrap heap.

the WeltWUCHER[4] of Zurich vurry annoyed with Eva's Pisaner Gesange.[5] {Says I over political}

commie printer in Mexico at last dislodged from roadway, and Cantares de Pisa injected into S.AM.[6] blood stream unless the university is keeping all copies in their cellar. marvelous translation full of life, and might guide the wops.

Horrible decay of mental QUALITY can be measured from Plotinus to Augie of Hippo praps worse than the stink introduced between Dante and Milton.

Common source of infection. Arsenic in the soup more dangerous than in the bottle with a plain lable.

Littlefield[7] reports sales of yr/ correspondent in Athens, but his cab driver worried by misplaced greek accents, and wishing he cd TELL the simpatico scrittore[8] and get 'em put right.

naive outlook of modern greek in re/ amurkn and brish printers.

> and so on, banZAI, alala, and
> best to Helen and Malu.
> {E.P.}

I think Fordie must have brought Goldring or some other biondino[9] to the fambly vault. I cert. never met W.M.R. I would have remembered that. But if merely introduced to a Mrs Angeli,[10] would not have known who it was.

the paideutic Fordie cert took me, as far as I cd/ make out, into ever ambience he cd/ get into, DETERmined that I shd/ be made aware of british manners and customs.

{D.H.} Lawrence[11] also has beard, considerably more red, but I think less barbered.

and so on.

> {E.P.}

Later/ having put this in wrong kind of envelope, yr/ Grampaw's Beatrice di Dante, arrives.[12] for which my thanks. I doubt if the Cat/ Un. will get it.

no binderies in this country, una prece,[13] that I will some day be able to get it rebound in woptalia.

still later. yr/ illustrious ancestor speaks of THREE ragionamenti, and ends with "fine del primo". Did he write or print the other 2/ or did yr/ bigoted grandma burn the inedits?? or has everyone forgotten which??[14]

preface {"}non offro tutte e tre in una volta.../ main diversi periodi.{"}[15]

I dont spose yu remember the date the big vol/ was printed.[16] But I can get that from Pearson at Yale. i.e. whether before or after the Beat. di D.

1. **Malù**'s newborn, named after ORA.
2. Actually 1865.

3. Villari's *Italian Foreign Policy under Mussolini*.

4. Gm.: "world profiteering or exploitation."

5. Eva Hesse's translation of *The Pisan Cantos*, published as *Die Pisaner Gesänge*.

6. South America (even though Mexico is in Central America).

7. **Lester Littlefield.**

8. It.: "friendly writer." The writer in question is Zesimos Lorenzatos, who had translated EP's *Cathay* into modern Greek in 1950.

9. It.: "fair-haired boy."

10. Angeli was Helen's married name.

11. EP proposes that Lawrence, not EP, was the young man Helen had been introduced to by Ford.

12. Gabriele Rossetti's *La Beatrice di Dante* was suppressed after its printing in 1842 and was reissued in 1935 with a preface by Balbino Giuliano. ORA had written on 24 September 1956: "Looking over my books I find I have two copies of 'La Beatrice di Dante' privately printed by Gabriele Rossetti in 1842, so I am sending you one; when you no longer wish to have it you might pass it on to the Catholic University, Washington."

13. It.: "a prayer."

14. The 1842 edition of Rossetti's *La Beatrice di Dante* ends with the first argument ("fine del primo") but two more arguments ("ragionamenti") were promised in the preface, as EP quotes in the next paragraph. The other arguments did not remain unpublished (*inèdito*, EP's "inedits"). Rossetti subsequently wrote eight more (for a total of three for each section of the *Commedia*), which were printed for the first time in the 1935 edition.

15. Probably *una volta . . . / mai diversi periodi*, It: "I am not publishing all three [arguments] at one time, but at intervals."

16. Rossetti's *Il mistero dell' amor platonico del medio aevo* was printed in 1840.

116. TLU-3   7 [14] December 1956
7 Dec/

O.R.A.

want to know more of yr/ grand-dad?

Political exile?? escaped from fury and bigotry of vatican? ?? not a mason but student of masonry?

Interested to see he hooks D/ to Swedenborg,[1] as I have done for 50 years, but can't recall having found in the VERY small amount of criticism or Dante-Studien that I have looked at.

Prefer texts to comments. Of course the Dant-Swed hook¾up may have filtered thru footnotes, but I can't recall anything but my own observations of the two writers.

Real masonry, as from China etc. pure down to Mozart.[2] and since flooded with mutts who have NOT the faintest inkling of the mysteries once guarded in an order....

anyhow. IF family tradition..shd/ like it. O.R.A. kill two stones with one bird, as it wd/ make chapter of memoirs, if done in duplicate.

Villari has some gentle words on subject, am doing what I can for his book (Mus/Foreign policy)[3] but dont see that I can much boost the sales. Too much going on. Need for IMMEDIATE ideas, not for retrospect or justice to memories. His qt/ for Weinstein is timely, but cant sell the book on one paragraph, suppressed from the brutish edn. of von Pip.[4]

Did I say Zurich "WeltWUCHER" furious re/ Eva's trans/ of my Pisans.[5] which have also got past the communist watch p̄ bitch in Mexico city, At least 3 copies, the rest may still be in some cellar.

even the retarded H.C.[6] who was with Laughlin in Ford Floundations[7] says he saw there things which "would turn{"} my {"}hair{"}.

WHICH{,} considering that I know a bloke[8] who sat in with Morgenthau and Dex White,[9] seems a eggzaggeration.

That Australia has accepted a huge loan from the Internat/ skunks shows that the life of the mind in that far country has not yet got into the saddle.

Your uncle Dant[10] wrote from direct knowledge. Was yr/ pa a mason? or had he VIEWS? Naturally Caraffa[11] wanted Dante Al/ dug up. quest' e{'}pacifico.[12]

Large gap between Pitagoro[13] and the year 1300. Section d'Or[14] got lost, etc. and renaissance architecture went to...pot an' barocco[15]...latter term derived from what? baro?

14 th/ summary. Augustine, really SCHOCKingly stewpid, poisoned with kike book.[16] Faustus[17] a few Voltarian quips, better than Aug/ but poisoned. Trying to be some sort of Xrsten. Got hold of Swedenborg again/ he at least said jew church bust/ Xtn, no longer moral force, BUT lacking gk/ lat culture and having read jew book... says too much. More intelligent than Plotinus, as more direct experience. Plot. ARGUING about what he dont know. Swed, anthropomorphic from advanced anatomy. In short I see why I stopped reading him. Tho has beautiful passages. Basta.[18]

what I tuk me pen in 'and again for is to say no ref/ library here, and no room in cubicle for one anyhow. CAN some of yr/ INFORmed friends give we list and date{s} of Brutisch damblastadors in Roma. Rennel Rodd?? Ron. Graham[19] whom Villari seems to tolerate... Drummond (a stiff with a wooden head)/ Was Buchanan[20] ever there,, and if so when?? Rodd was sposed to treat Mus/ like a human being..

Bright paper from Detroit with a lot that I have been saying and quoting for 20 and 30 years. labled "Truth and the Constitution". possibly a numero unico for Andrews campaign. ANY bright ideas you and yours may have for interesting ~~interexting~~ people in taxes and money/ the SYSTEM,, wd/ be welcome. Only McNair Wilson's clinical training can have got him thru life of deStael bitch/ whom he perfidiously calls "swiss"/ one jew millionairess largely contributing to mess in la vieille europaaaaa.[21] Ought to be continually emphasised WHAT can be done by ploots/ that even a dirty sow without money cdn't have managed. I spose it{'}s all retrospect. Anyhow he seems to have got to idea of internat finance ALWAYS destructive. [illegible deletion]

Have marked that request for ambassadorial chronology in RED, so you can find it if you fergit it.

What a farce, the Xters give up their main myth/ the god damned jew aims at irresponsible oligarchy, {(}talking demos.{)} that {irresp. olig} is the ONLY social organism, only form of social organization the jew has evolved. NOTHING of Athens, Rome or suffrage. irresponsible hidden control, leaving oprobrium of law enforcement to suckers. Pontius Pilat the original goy out in front. Mob excitement and muddle....

as to the pie in the sky gang....Dant and Swed. {are} both sound in their schema of increasing enlightened consciousness, someone wrote {me} that Thoreau was hep to superiority of greek culture. all the publicity he has had wd/ appear to have picked out civil disobedience as his one bright idea, incongruous in trying to fit in. etc.

basta, buon Natale.. Mary says Freudian filth has taken the devil out of local school {play} celebration, but Tirolean sense still left the kids chasing him out of district.

Freud, Marx, Necker, that sow Mrs de Stael..what a punktheon

1. **Emanuel Swedenborg.**

2. See canto 90/605. EP associated the San Ku of ancient China with Eleusis. It was a sort of Masonic council with an initiation rite called the Widow's Son, "which is also to be found in some of the Romance literature of the Middle Ages and the modern Masonic ritual" (Stock, *Poet in Exile* 23–26). Mozart's *Magic Flute* incorporates Masonic rituals.

3. Villari's *Italian Foreign Policy under Mussolini*.

4. Probably **Franz von Papen's** *Memoirs*.

5. See letter 115.

6. Possibly Huntington Cairns (1904–85), American lawyer, educator, museum administrator, art expert, editor, and author. He became counselor for the U.S. Treasury and later accepted a similar position at the Smithsonian. Following the awarding to EP in 1949 of the Bollingen Prize, which he had helped in setting up, Cairns made regular visits to St. Elizabeths and made notes of EP's conversations.

7. **James Laughlin** worked for the Ford Foundation for five years in the 1950s; he also edited *Perspectives*, the foundation's magazine.

8. Probably **Rex Herbert Lampman.**

9. **Harry Dexter White.** EP had read *Unconditional Hatred*, in which Russell Grenfell argues that World War II was engineered by a Jewish conspiracy in which White participated. In *Italian Foreign Policy under Mussolini* Villari also subscribes to this view.

10. **Dante Gabriel Rossetti.**

11. Probably Gian Pietro Carafa (1476–1559), Pope Paul IV (1555–59).

12. It.: "this thing is peaceful."

13. Pythagoras.

14. Fr.: "golden section." A proportion to demonstrate the mathematical basis of harmony attributed to Vitruvius, an architect and engineer in the first century B.C. In the formula the ratio of the whole to the larger part (such as the area and length of a rectangle) is the same as the ratio of the larger part to the smaller part (such as the length and width of a rectangle). The golden section was revived during the Renaissance.

15. It.: "baroque." *Barocco* is not derived from *baro* ("card shark" or "cheat") but from the Portuguese *barocco* ("rough pearl").

16. The Bible.

17. Augustine's polemical target in *Contra Faustum*, which EP is reading.

18. It.: "Enough."

19. Sir Ronald Graham. See letter 51.

20. Probably Lady Buchanan, one of EP's correspondents during the 1930s.

21. Fr.: "old Europe." **Robert McNair Wilson** had apparently read a biography of Mme. de Staël (1766–1817). Her father, Jacques Necker, was Swiss Protestant, not Jewish.

117. TLS-3   25 December 1956

We include the entire text of ORA's response to EP's letters of 6 and 7 December 1956.

Dear Ezra Pound:

It was a treat to get your interesting letter of 16th December. My grandfather, Gabriele Rossetti, was born at Vasto, {in the Abruzzi,} an old Roman [illegible deletion] Municipium called then Istonia, which remained faithful to Rome during the wars with Hanibal. It is on a cliff overhanging the sea on the coast of the Abruzzi, [illegible deletion] in the midst of very beautiful scenery. I have been there twice{,} first in 1928, and {again} when the little town{,} in August 1954, was commemorating the hundredth anniversary of Gabriele's death. The picturesque old fashioned town is afflicted by landslips and will probably one of these days slide into the sea. The house where G.R. was born came to such an end some years ago; it had been made a national monument, and to celebrate the 100th anniversary that occurred that year, {1954,} the municipality had built a house on the site of the old one and called it La Casa Rossetti, and I gave them a collection of photos of the works of D.G.R. which they hung round the hall. There is a big{,} more than life-size{,} monument to Gabriele in the Piazza with medallions of his 4 children: Maria, D.G.R.; W.M.R. and Christina. EVerything in the town is Rossetti, the piazza, the

Liceo, the Library, the Theatre. The Vastese are a rather strange people; when I was there in 1928, guest of a relative "Gelsomino Zaccagnini by name, a local magnate, he took me to call on the Podestà,[1] and while we were there [illegible deletion] two journalists from North Italy came to complain to the Podestà: they were making a tour for their paper and had made a stop at Vasto, and the inn where they went for a meal refused to serve them because they were *Forestieri!*[2] and another relative of ours, a rather well-to-do man who hoped to develop the very beautiful seashor{e} just below the town{,} forming part of the municipality of Vasto, has built some houses along the shore for summer visitors, but it was not a success as they local fishermen refused to sell them anything for the same reason{:} "Forestieri"! I fancy they have become rather more civilised now, as they were occupied by {the} English during the last war, who looted a lot of shops, ~~and~~ I was told (but I have not ascertained the truth of the statement) that these English went to the Library and Museum and carried off the Rossetti MSS my father had given them, saying, according to what I was told that the Rossettis belonged to England! It sound{s} a rather strange story! In this little town my grandfather was born in 1783, the son of a blacksmith. The Abruzzi were then part of the Kingdom of the Two Sicilies, and Ferdinand IV, {(}afterwards through dynastic changes Ferdinand I), was the ruling monarch. Then came the French Revolution, the Napoleonic wars, Vasto was invaded by the French. The young Gabriele was early distinguished for his poetic gifts and was also gifted to some extent as a ~~draughtsman~~ {artist}. The feudal lord of Vasto whose attention was called to the gifts of his vassal, (he was from the Marchese d'Avalo) of the very ancient Spanish house, transplanted from Spain into Italy, in which Vittoria Colonna, beloved by Michelangelo, married) sent him to complete his studies to Naples. Here he soon became, during the reign of Joseph Bonaparte, and Murat, extremely popular as poet and *improvisatore*.[3] He was made libretto writer to the San Carlo Opera House, and then as the opera stars nearly drove him made with their quarrels and jealousies{,} he had himself transferred ~~to~~ as custodian to the King's Museum, now the Museo Nazionale of Naples{,} in 1816. The Bourbons now had returned, and Rossetti, who had joined the Carbonari, took part in the insurrectionary activities which led King Ferdinand to grant a constitution to his Kingdom. This Rossetti greeted with great enthusiasm in a poem which begins "Sei pur bella con gli astri sul crine" which was immensely popular in its day and sung more or less all over Italy. Then the King, protected by the Austrians, repealed the Constitution, and Rossetti expressed his indignation in other poems in one of which he reminded the King "I [illegible deletion] Sandi ed i Louvelli non sono morti ancor"; the reference to the two ~~French~~ regicides enraged the

King{,} and Gabriele was on the proscription list and lay in [illegible deletion] {hiding} for several weeks ~~or maybe~~ {3} months. Before this event he had become acquainted with the British Admiral, Sir Graham Moore, and his wife Lady Moore who was on the ship with her husband. Lady Moore conceived a great admiration for Rossetti as poet and patriot, and when she heard of his fate and danger she begged her husband to save him{,} and the story goes that the Admiral, who had been informed where Rossetti was hiding, went on shore with a fellow officer and another British naval uniform, which Rossetti donned, and arm in arm with the Admiral went through Naples under the very eyes of the "sbirri"[4] who were hunting for him and was taken on the British war-ship. The King, informed of the event{,} sent to the Admiral to demand his rebellious subject, but receive{d} the answer that he was on British ground and could not be touched. From Naples he was taken by the admiral to Malta where he landed and lived for three years under the protection of the Governor, John Hookham Frere,[5] a learned man, translator of Aristophanes, and it was here that Rossetti began his special studies of the Divine Comedy. He was then a mason, and I expect Frere was also. Rossetti was greeted in Malta by the Italian population as the {"}Tirteo d'Italia{"};[6] his patriotic verse was known to all, but the spies of the Naples Bourbons were always trying to lay traps for him. [illegible deletion] He became famous by improvising in the presence of Sir Hookham Frere and a large audience a long poem on St. Paul in Malta. In 1824, under the protection of Hookham Frere, he went to England and settled in London, earning his living by teaching Italian—then studied by most cultivated people—and devoted himself to his esoteric studies of Dante in which he was financially assisted by Frere and Charles Lyell[7] (father of the famous geologist). They were all masons and my father told me that in his early years Masons were constantly calling at the very modest Rossetti home, coming for financial and other aid.

My father was not a Mason; he was an agnostic (not an Atheist){;} Shelley was his hero both as poet and man.

Shall be seeing Villari in a day or two and shall get you{,} from him{,} a list of Bt. Ambassadors. I do not remember them, beyond Sir Rennel Rod[8] of War I days and Sir Erick Drummond[9] on the eve of World War II.

I am writing to the printer of the Beatrice di Dante by Gabriele Rossetti, who is in Imola. It is a thick book and I feel sure would interest you. Sigra. Giartosio to whom I 'phoned, tells me she thinks the only way of getting a copy is to write to this printer who probably has some copies on hand. As soon as I get it I shall mail it.

I perceive that this is a very badly written letter. I have just come back from Helen's where I had a copious English Christmas dinner which I think has dulled my alread{y} rather senile brains. But you will excuse me.

The little baby, Olivia, is very sweet and is making good progress. On 3rd Jan. she will two months old. I love little babies. Malù is standing the strain of nursing her very well and that is a great comfort.

Am reading a book on [illegible deletion] Churchill by Emrys Hughes, M.P. What a man to have a decisive voice in settling the fate of Nations{!!} He is undoubtedly clever, but an egotistic [illegible deletion] mountebank if ever there was one. What a destiny for the world, at this tremendouns change in everything{,} which will, when completed, make as new a world as that of {which} that arose out of the chaos of the fall of the Roman Empire, to be guided by two such mentors as F.D.R. and W.C. What a figure Eden has made England cut in this Suez fiasco! Enough to make angels weep.

Well, I shall write again soon, as soon as I get the Ambassadorial facts from Villari and the news about the Beatrice di Dante from Imola.

> Meantime, I will bring this creed to an end with all affectionate and admiring good wishes
>
> {Olivia Rossetti Agresti}

Gabriele Rossetti's publications were: 1826–27 Il Comento analitico sulla Divina Comedia (only the Hell published{,} though the others were written); 1832 Lo Spirito Antipapale che prodisse la Riforma; 1840 Il Mistero H dell'Amor Platonico del Medioevo, 5 vol.; 1842 La Beatrice di Dante; and four volumes of poetry published in England Il Tempo, Il Salterio, Il Veggente in Solitudine, and L'Arpa Evangelica. He also wrote in verse "La Vita Mia, il Testamento" printed in Italian for the first time in 1910{,} of which my Father printed an English version in verse with notes in 1901 (London, Sands & Co.)

1. It.: "power," that is, junior judge or magistrate.
2. It.: "foreigners."
3. It.: "one who speaks extemporaneously."
4. It.: "police."
5. **John Hookham Frere.**
6. It.: "the Tirteo of Italy." "Tirteo" is a reference to the Spartan poet Tyrtaeus, so Rossetti had been greeted as a writer of narrative poems celebrating heroic deeds.
7. **Charles Lyell.**
8. **Rennel Rodd.**
9. **Sir Eric Drummond.**

1957

118. TLS-3   20 May 1957
20 Maggio

O.R.A.

Sorry yu'v been under the weather. Name Francis Adams[1] vaguely familiar, ma no l'ho presente,[2] as specific quality in verse. I tho't I HAD thanked yu for Beatrice,[3] which arruv/ long ago/ but may be I had delayed intending to comment.

I don't spose Villari can be got on the LINE for anything specific. I want data re Louis X. of France, who has had bad press/ I want correspondence re Thiers,[4] from any prof, who knows anything.

The ignoramus Sanzo[5] whose artl/ you sent?? know anything of him?? sounds like the enemy pretending amity. At any rate to show that the Ku Klux is not adhering to Confucius or to E.P. Dallam,[6] a much earlier Ezratic than Kasp/[7] has just had a cross burned in front of his church.

The dividing line is not strictly Ez vs. non-Ez. Kasper's REAL ideology is far above ANY [illegible deletion] U.S. audience/ and am not sure it is useful to spread it among those who will NOT understand why Lincoln was shot. (i.e. for understanding what Jeff/ wrote to Crawford in 1816).[8]

Can't Villari FIND me ANYone who will consider ideas/ such as in Academy Bulletin/ another number under weigh. Note bloke named Niebuhr,[9] said to be a kike, at head of Union Theological seminary/?? needs investigation re/ order given 1600 years ago, to get into Xtn organizations and ROT 'em. any side lights? not necessarily a descendent of THE known Nieb/ d. 1831 or thaarbouts/

Note present pseudo msolems, since oil and dead sea minerals.

A line on WHAT decent ideas wops after the betrayal are NOW ready to understand.?? am writing Mary to stir re soja. I think in Meridiano I said: peanuts, sugar maple, soja. R.Duncan then hit kadzu, useful on Ligurian hill tops where soil only an inch deep, if THAT.

Do you know anything ABOUT Sanzo? Bottai's ABC fairly CLOSED to thought. and{,} alas{,} he always had the capacity to make things heavy and dull. Gray[10] just dull without solidity. the neo/s spirited but excitable. There used to be several males present at ORA's sunday p.m. who seemed capable of comprehending something, and wdn't now have much excuse to avoid all vital topics.

The Boston benedictines put out a lively 4 pages/ called {"}The Point,{"} no charge, not on news stands/ and only sent to individuals (supposed catholics). NOT trying to muddle all terminology, or pretend that talmud and St John are identical. It is to be noted that WITH Confucio, China has had 2500 years WITHOUT religious wars/ only the three jew religions (de trebus impositoribus)[11] seem eager to start mass murder for sepulchres and other [illegible deletion] theatrical trappings. The hocking of Normandy by Robt/etc. a LLLovely display of usurer's dexterity.

O.K. I want someone to study Thiers, and Louis X. who lasted 2 years shortly after Templars were busted.

If any one meets Sanzo or any wop-choinulist might say that I have been advising american afros to learn their OWN culture, african genius, as manifest in G.W. Carver, etc.

wrote Langston Hughes[12] re/ Frobenius about 30 years ago/ he replied that the negro-universities {were} not then at that level.

BUT the way out, or a way wd/ be for them to develop their OWN paideuma, and not give 5 an 10 c. imitation of judaized Birmingham.

You can omit ref/ to your chosen in transmitting this.

No study yet made [illegible deletion] of the DIFFERENT african races imported to America.

Booker T.Washington,[13] with sense of humour that his family had saddled him with that celebrated pair of prenoms, conversation at table has degenerated since he got OUT of bughouse, and got drunk and was brot back to a different ward.

at any rate capable of "ah muss get back that school-boy comPLEX-shun"

surprised to learn that the slaves imported had already been slaves in Africa.

in sho{r}t DEFective education all round/ tho Morse[14] has recently compared an alto locato[15] to Dave Beck.[16]

some wop egg-head instead of swallowing Luce[17] and the Meyerblatt might mention that E.P. has been advocating development of their own Afric paideuma/ their own classic,

not Viennese muckracking.

and so on.

> best to Helen, saluti to
> Villari.
> {Benedictions}
> {E.P.}

1. In a letter to **David M. Gordon**, forwarded to EP, ORA had asked: "Did you ever hear of an Australian poet, Francis Adams? In 1857 he sent my Father, William Michael Rossetti, a copy of his first book of poems 'Songs of the Army of the Night'" (1 Apr. 1957).

2. It.: "but I don't have it at the moment."

3. **Gabriele Rossetti's** *Beatrice di Dante*. ORA had sent EP a copy of the Giar-tosio reissue on 17 January 1956.

4. Probably Adolphe Thiers (1719–1877), French journalist, historian, politician, and member of the revolution of 1830 that put Louis Philippe on the French throne. He was arrested and briefly banished during the coup d'état of 1851. EP seems to think that he was punished for opposing banks. See letter 119.

5. Unidentified, but presumably an Italian journalist also mentioned below and in letter 119. ORA complained on 6 June 1957: "I do not know whom you refer to as 'the ignoramus Sanzo whose article you sent.'"

6. **Dallam Simpson.**

7. **John Kasper.**

8. See letter 70.

9. **Reinhold Niebuhr.**

10. EP's epithet for **Luigi Villari.**

11. *De tribus impositoribus*, Lt.: "the cheating tribes." The "three Jew religions" are Judaism, Christianity, and Islam. EP is no doubt thinking of the Crusades and the Israeli-Arab wars.

12. Langston Hughes visited EP at St. Elizabeths and corresponded with him.

13. Booker Taliaferro Washington (1856–1915).

14. Probably Wayne Lyman Morse (b. 1900), U.S. Senator from Oregon, a strong defender of civil liberties during the postwar anticommunist hysteria.

15. Probably *alto locatorio*, It.: "an old or former tenant."

16. **Dave Beck.**

17. The publications of **Henry Robinson Luce.**

119. TLS-3 21 June 1957

{21 Giug 57}

Dear O.R.A.

Yr persistent naiveté in some matters passeth all understanding. If the Encyc. Brit/ slights Louis X[1] it is probably because he freed some serfs/ or committed a non vatican act of some sort/ but to cite a sink of fraud the Enc. Brit/ especially NOW that the chicago kikes[2] have taken it over and blotted out even the modicum of fact it once contained!!

alzo Thiers, who apparently understood the bank filth, and has ~~the~~ therefore been declared null and void even by Andrew White.[3] who is pretty clean on all matters save difference between greenbacks and shin-plasters.

Interest in Louis X/ and Thiers {be}cause {of} suspicion aroused that they have been blacked out of history because they spotted the cloven hoof of bank sodomy.[4] BUT I want specific facts/ The FILTH of the First crusade,[5] also unstressed in the usual hand-out. the amount of BUNK we were fed.. pre-Del Mar..

Has Scaligero[6] noticed the "baros metetz en gatge"[7] or the pawning of

Normandy and consequent rise in taxes in England/ that real Roosevelt
Wm/Rufus. etc.

Mary sends [illegible deletion] confirma, that USIS[8] and similar inste-
rooshuns are run by kikes and when they cant make hand out to chewsz
they gi{v}e it to commies or pinks without guts to be commies.

Note that since Elkin[9] printed the Convito NO estabd/ pubr/ has ever
accepted a book of my recommend, and NONE of these usurocrat foundations given a fellowship to any candidate whom I have recommended.

Sanzo[10] quotes the jew Vivante,[11] if you know whom I mean, shd/ like
to know whethe{r} the Boris bro/in row[12] said it in heat ten years ago or
is continuing his mendacity.

YES precisely/ stato corporativo/ vocational representation[13] the ONE
advance on the U.S.method of representation/ ONE senator sees it/ and
young Chatel[14] has discovered a CONgressman. who knows about money, but thinks NO other me{m}ber of either House or Senate has ANY
perception of same. Unc. G/[15] said "about six".

{anagraphic decline during 19 years}

Did you ever hear of Andrew D.White?[16] probably before you were looking at such matters. Founded Cornell Univ. and his Autobiog shd/ be
required reading for ALL University presidents, in or OUT of the U.S, {vol,
brot me by fellow patient} It is something that the words Stat.corp/ have
been used instead of the usual "fascist" {meaning also communist, and
totalitarian}.

god ROT their infamous bones.

one shd/ also distinguish one kind of mason from another/ they do not
all welcom{e} the B nai Brith control of their order.

Geo. Washington Carver, afrosaxon who started PEANUTS as subject
for intellectual contemplation and fer feedin various people/ source of my
Arachidi articles.[17]

The infant Olivia looks mildly ironical and selective, and the ma evidently several feet larger than as I remember her. Thanks for the foto.

I spose Edge will reach you in time/[18] they have printed the M note{s}
in captivity/[19] anonymous but sufficiently apparent to HORRIFY the
kangaroo soc/ crediters.

a high school paper here has pirated PUNCH admirable skit on Bankers.

Re/ yr/ other letter, opened after the one dated 6. VI. I can't believe
Wordsworth[20] said anything as good. More like Butler,[21] whom I have
never managed to read/ thanks for best quote of Augustine[22] I have ever
read. {g. Cavalcanti} in quella parte dove sta memora[23] other variant, in
quella parte dove sta memora[24]

The manner in which INcommunication is maintained/ like my not know{i}n{g} TSE[25] had known Mrs Jack Gardner/ etc.

and that there are Rossettis and biscuit factories[26] NOT mobilize{d} to/ d run printing presses shocks me and cause my etc. as the fretful porcupine. Sanavio with french wife seems DEtermined to translate Rock Drill/[27] at any rate a pleasanter character than the last wop horror who penetrated this campus, a useful anthropological specimen to SHOW the young yanks then present what Mus had to work against in building a country.

magnif/ portagoose trans/ Canto XX, front page Jornal do Brasil.[28] bilingual jap Mauberley/[29] Whitman in oriya[30] and believe I am to follow in that decorative type face/ on the heels of Mr Eliot O.M.[31] but at any rate in good company.[32]

best to Helen and Malú.

the CONtrasted styles of old Lampman, septuageneraian yank journalist and on a note on stationary of Consiglio Communale[33] of a large wop city/ might aid in orienting the difficulties of intercommunication between men of good will in alien ambience.

{ever dev'/mo}[34]

{EP}

1. ORA had written that she had passed the request for information on Luis X and Thiers—"a rather incongruous couple"—on to Villari, who had then written to EP. She added: "Louis X seems to have been a colourless person, so much so that the Encyclopedia Britannica says very little about him. Should you be interested in that period because of the Templars or the Albigenses I might be able to get some suggestions from Prof. Scaligero who knows a great deal about all the mystic and and heretical movements of the Middle Ages" (6 June 1957).

2. The Encyclopedia Britannica was purchased by Sears Roebuck in 1928 and moved to New York. In 1941 Roebuck offered it to the University of Chicago but was turned down; however, William Benton, the university's vice president, took it over and moved it to Chicago.

3. **Andrew D. White.**

4. See letter 117.

5. Called for by Pope Urban II at Clermont in 1095.

6. Professor Scaligero, mentioned by ORA in her letter of 6 June 1957, to which EP is responding.

7. This phrase occurs in canto 85/548. Terrell identifies it as Provençal and translates it as "barons put up as pawns" (2:472).

8. USI, the Unione Sindacale Italiana, an anarcho-syndicalist labor union that opposed both the pre-Fascist liberal and the Fascist Italian governments.

9. **Elkin Mathews.**

10. See letter 118.

11. Probably Cesare Vivante (1855–1944), an Italian jurist, professor, and foremost authority on commercial law in Italy.

12. Presumably "brother-in-law."

13. The corporate, or Fascist, state. This remark was prompted by ORA's comment on Prime Minister Harold MacMillan's suggestion that British employers form a union to match the Trades Union Congress. She commented: "I have long said that the Corporate State will come back to Italy as an English invention, after the factious Italians have banished the very word from their vocabulary as belonging to the hated régime! The Corporative State to my mind was the one really constructive social-political idea of the century[. . . .] But in his social policies Mussolini was the only constructive and practical statesman of the century." See also letters 54 and 55.

14. **Jean Marie Châtel.**

15. **George Holden Tinkham.**

16. **Andrew Dickson White.** A selection of his two-volume autobiography (1905) was published as *Selected Chapters from the Autobiography of Andrew D. White* in 1939 and reissued in 1956. We presume it was this volume that EP was given. Cornell was controversial for its programs, which were accused of neglecting classical instruction in favor of technical and scientific instruction.

17. EP's "Arachidi."

18. In her 6 June 1957 letter ORA remarked that she "had a nice letter some days ago from a Mr. John Chatel, making some very complimentary remarks about some words of wit and wisdom of mine which he says he read in 'Edge' but which I have not seen and really have no idea what they are." John Chatel and **Jean Marie Châtel** are one and the same. See also letter 109.

19. Mussolini's "In Captivity: Notebook of Thoughts in Ponza and La Maddalena." See letter 42.

20. ORA cited the phrase "all silent and all damned" (11 June 1957) as a characterization of TV viewers and asked if it was Wordsworth's.

21. ORA had asked if EP had read Samuel Butler's *Erewhon.*

22. The best "quote of Augustine" (11 May 1957): "Speaking of his gradual ascent to God he [Augustine] says, 'e giungo ai campi e ai vasti palazzi della memoria dove sono i tesori delle innumerevoli imagini di tutte le cose, portatevi dai sensi..... Grande a questa forza della memoria, straordinariamente grande, O Dio; un ampio, infinito mistero. Chi lo penetrerà fino in fondo? Ed è la forza del mio animo, e appartiene alla mia natura, ed io stesso non comprendo tutto quello che io sono. L'animo dunque è angusto a comprendere se stesso? ...' And he goes on to speak of the memory we have of memory: 'E mi, ricordo di essermi ricordato, come poi sarà per la stessa forza della memoria se mi ricorderò di essermi ricordato adesso.' And then there is the 'memoria dell'oblio:['} {']Se dunque la memoria ritenesse non l'oblio ma la sua immagine, esso dovettes [illegible deletion] esser presente perchè quell'immagine potesse esser colta...' How great are the mysteries within us."

"Having arrived at the fields and vast palaces of the memory where the treasures of an infinite imagination of all things are, the bearer of all the senses. . . . This power of memory is great, exceptionally great, O Lord, a large, infinite mystery. Who could penetrate its depths? It is the energy of my soul; it is natural to me; [but even so] I cannot understand everything that I am. The soul longs to understand itself." "And I, remembering that I remember myself, as then I will remember myself by the same power of memory by which I remember now." "If therefore, the memory does not retain what has been forgotten but its image is present, because that image can be regenerated" (editors' trans.).

23. It.: "in which part the memory dwells." This is line 15 of Cavalcanti's canzone, "Donna mi priegha."

24. A variant of "In memory's locus taketh he [Love or Amor] his state," which is from EP's translation of "Donna mi priegha" (*Translations* 133). EP uses this line as a leitmotif in cantos 36, 54, and 76.

25. T. S. Eliot.

26. ORA had written: "I have my niece Lucy here in Rome, the daughter of my brother Arthur, (who died many years ago). She is married to an Irishman who is the prosperous owner of a well know biscuit factory" (11 May 1957).

27. P. Sanavio and Denise Alexander translated canto 4 as "Canto IV," but we do not have any information about their translation of *Rock Drill* into French.

28. The translation appeared as "Canto XX" in the 28 April 1957 issue of *Jornal do Brasil*.

29. *Hugh Selwyn Mauberley* appeared in English and in Japanese in . . . *Shishu* . . . See Gallup, *Ezra Pound* D169.

30. Whitman's *Leaves of Grass* was translated into Oriya as *Durbadala.* See Gallup, *Ezra Pound* D198.

31. Eliot had received the Order of Merit from the British crown in 1948, the same year he was awarded the Nobel Prize for Literature.

32. Some of EP's poems were translated into Oriya and collected as . . . *Kabita* . . . , which had an introduction by T. S. Eliot. See Gallup, *Ezra Pound* D197.

33. It.: "city council."

34. *Devotissimo*, It.: "very devotedly."

120. TLS-3   23 June 1957
{23 Giug 57}

Dear O.R.A.

Have just sent slow post to L.V.[1] my thanks for yr/ having saved Augustine's respectability/ I had been worried as to need of deleting him from an early Canto,[2] as hadn't found in more recent browse anything up to Ric. St. Vic. or Erigena/ yrs/ a much needed note on the Cavalcanti.

BUT, recent viva voce report on the blithering imbecility of the post-Regime conditions/ the ass in the Fatty can etc. Three gangs of bigots contending re/ which St allowed the banker's nephew (at least I spose it is the Bankhaus Pacelli,[3] who got its homonym into the job) to git his interview with Gawd/ mebbe you can remember whether it was Ignatz,[4] or Dominic,[5] or some minor character persuading Mrs God[6] to wangle it.

what we want/ is some impartial witness to contrast the First decen-

nio/ the conditions in 1940/ with whatever skulduggery now reigns.
Whether the francia o spagna[7]...my visitor sd/ country had been bought
by the U.S. and AT LAST someone resented, tho alas, very mildly, the
quality of the mutts getting the rake off as cultural representatives representatives of american degradation.

I spose Rocke too olde??

I remember the idiocy that cropped up AT ONCE after the betrayal. {3
years ago approx}

There was one article re/ 5 different kinds of Masons. but I didn't make
a record of it. The difference here between York and Scottish not widely
publicised. The prevalence of yr/ beloved kikes has been noticed. ANY
intellectual exercise is a rarity among yanks/ will possibly be confined
to the incarcerated... no I don't think they will ALL be jugged because
the murkn is naturally incommunicative and irrelevant and if does know
or see anything it don't occur to him to mention the fact save in a desul-
tory manner. When I think of those two buzzards on cinema steps, alter-
nating the strophes and antistrophes of Aeschylus in greek, but not taking each others addresses, the possibility of a coherent city..... seem{s} to
need considerable stimulus.

The contrasted styles between a roman editor and ~~an~~ a septuagenari-
an american newspaper man in yester post-bag/ along with yr/ Augustine and a sweedish optimist form a Querschnitt/[8] The first three cert/
aimed for posterity.

Bot/ with talent for putting unreadable heaviness into any paper/
Guareschi only wop readable abroad??

Ian Monro??[9] COULD state the contrast/ 1922/ 32/ 45/ 57/ would he,
and can anyone find him.{?}

ONE U.S.Senator aware that vocational rep/ and sindacalismo[10] (probably never heard the Word) is a development, and the way whereby orderly (constitutional) govt. COULD} ameliorate.

ONE congman/ aware of money. Spampanato and one other Ital/ vol/
forget by whom/ contain some information. I hope you will get Edg/
sometime/ it was yr/ autobiog/ note I think, that Chatel was talking
about. You have probably forgotten it/ but tell Helen to tease a bit more
out of you. Even the young ape who got the Punch satire into his school
pape{r} is quoted as uttering idiocy re/ fascismo. And ABC for once no-
tices the use of words/ and french ignorance on that subject. fascio, fascieux. parroting.[11]

Packhard[12] probably incapable of stating what he knows. Rocke and
Monro only two I can think of who could put down reliable statement
of: then and oggi.

If L.V. still circulates can he find anyone? Varé could have. Do phone

Monotti, he also could and pseudonymously without endangering his income.

During Ventennio I heard NO allusion to guilds in Byzantium. HAD any wop heard of 'em? at least they weren't used paideuticly.

The dummy-xtns/ and theoretic free enterprisers don't so far as I know, trumpet Torlonia's bonifica (if that is the technical term) for his private use.

Like Crassus fire insurance.[13] private enterprise as pilot fish for the state.

My head does NOT retain people's names. There used to be a couple of APPARENTLY intelligent wops at yr/ sunday p.ms. Believe Paolillo is in Turin/ but forget names of the others. Picchio[14] was seen once by Mary and Boris/ no idea how he writes. Andrew D.White mentions Villari's father. Wonder if L.V. remembershim?

Hard to get copies of Edg/ here, but I have some spare copies of translation mimeograph copies of MSs Notes in Captivity[15] if you want copies sent to anyoe one in PARTICULAR

{EP}

1. **Luigi Villari.**
2. See letter 114.
3. See letter 55.
4. **St. Ignatius Loyola.**
5. **St. Dominic.**
6. Presumably the Virgin Mary.
7. It.: "French or Spanish."
8. Gm.: "cross-section." EP is punning on this politician's name. See also letter 90.
9. Probably **Ian Smeaton Munro.**
10. It.: "syndicalism."
11. Here EP is explaining the derivation of the word *fascismo. Fascio* is Italian for "bundle" and *fascieux* is a nonstandard plural of the French *fascine* ("bundle of sticks"). Both derive from the Latin *fascis,* hence EP's comment: "parroting."
12. **Reynolds Packhard.**
13. See letter 72.
14. **Ruggero Pier Piccio.**
15. A reference to "In Captivity: Notebook of Thoughts in Ponza and La Maddalena"; see also letter 42.

1958

121. TLS-1   16 August 1958
BrunnenburgOTirolo[1]
16 Ag

Dear O.R.A.

Villari here {yester} and lively/ only trouble he can't read much. DO you see"Candour"/ or have you anyone who needs to see Stock's art/1 on Del Mar in issue for 13 June?

shall I forward all eng/ and americ/ papers to you for use in Rome/{?} no use their being concealed here. OR only the Stock article??

Helen's bro/ Denis[2] has heard of a little history/ are you keeping him EDucated??

Canto 98/ due in ILLUSTRAZIONE Ital/ for Sept. bilingual.[3] 100[4] may have been putt in printable form this a.m. and more that NEED (hell's bellz) revision.

Re/ printed matter/ if you are too busy, can you phone Monotti or someone else who SHOULD (however unwillingly) be forced to know of the damn little information that gets past the copy or croppy desk?

{99 in Virginia ¼ly}[5]

{EP}

1. EP was released from St. Elizabeths and was living with his daughter at Schloss Brunnenburg in the Tyrol, near Merano.
2. ORA's great-nephew Emmanuel Dennis, brother of Helen Dennis Guglielmini, and son of **Helen Rossetti Angeli.**
3. Canto 98 was published in *L'Illustrazione Italiana*.
4. Canto 100 was published as "Canto C" in *Yale Literary Magazine.*
5. Canto 99 was published in *Virginia Quarterly Review.*

122. TLS-2   1 September 1958
Brunnenburg-Tirolo, Merano
1 Sep.

Dear ORA

In very weak and enfeebled condition. Started on {"}American experience{"} chapter[1] before got to the others.

I think it very important that you shd/ get the stuff down on paper/ i.e. yr/ credentials, and FACT that you did get a hearing.

As you know I think the Lubin story does NOT enter yr/ mind in full. i.e. that the stabilization of food prices, or ANY prices in a god damned ambiguous medium, controlledby by the Rotchschild is a device (con-

scious or unconscious) and not wort{h} a hoot, or at least worth part of a
hoot IF it directs ɡ attention to the [illegible deletion] mechanism of world
domination by manipulators of money.

Not to say Lubin wasn't sincere etc.

Personally object to irresponsible tyranny by any gang.

//As to publication/ I haven't {now} connection with anything but the
deceased or at least suspended Edge. {& the Richmond N. Leader[2] that
wd. want stuff in snappier form.}

FOR publication, it wd/ help find an outlet, if you cd/ group the objective items/ the policeman/ the taxi driver, etc. AND possibly the POINTS
of the lectures.

If you say/ I told these palookas in ChiKago: then putt one idea.

Preferably exposing the worst stink.

Then when you get to the cop in S. [illegible deletion] des Moines/ cop/
vivid item/ then ONE idea from the lecture.

Preferably one that wd. blast the successors of the 1919 hoaxers

something that wd/ show Churchill or FDR as a skunk,

BUT at any rate ONE idea (not more) from each talk (whether it was
actually part of the ~~the~~ talk you then gave.)

{EP}

am getting this off at once before perusal of other chapters.

Essay on the corporate state (da basso)[3] wd/ be useful/ especially as of
'37.

detachable from the rest/ but cd/ be got over somewhere/ launched by
memoir,

1. EP was reading ORA's memoir.
2. *Richmond New Leader.*
3. It.: "from the foundation."

123. TLS-1   23 October 1958

[Brunnenburg]

P. 14 Mussolini chapter/[1] suggest ~~footnote~~ {recast}/ re "trial and shooting members of Gt Fascist Council."

~~I never heard of it~~. and suppose the general brit and yank reader, may
be equally in the dark unless you mean Ciano etc./[2] yes, that is it, but
you cd/ clarify the paragraph.

see NO need in referring to bloody german tyrant.[3]

Am not giving last part of p, 14 Mrs C/[4] to take england/ as they add
nothing in present form to ~~cur~~ allay current phobias. it is not informa-
tive/ or at any rate not opportune

Can you send it recast of page 14. form "O, the pity of it all" to final words: Dongo when.[5]

and I will send after Mrs C/ as as postscript emendation.

{E.P.}

1. EP is continuing his commentary on ORA's memoir.

2. In her revision ORA added "the Fascist Grand Council, a body consisting of the members of the Government, some of the Under-Secretaries, and some appointed members, vested with advisory powers and entitled to be consulted by the Head of the Government." This account is not quite accurate. The Grand Council was a body of the Fascist party and became legally supreme over the government in 1928, as opposed to advisory. In addition to Mussolini, there were four life members: Achille Starace, Roberto Farinacci, Augusto Turati, and Renato Ricci. Another class of members was ex officio—both from the Party and from the government; and a third class was selected at large from the Party.

Dante L. Germino gives the following account of the council's role in the overthrow of Mussollini: "at the instigation of Grandi, Bottai, and Ciano, the Grand Council voted, in that fateful all-night session of July 24–25, by a majority of 19 to 7, in effect to call upon the king to dismiss Mussolini from office and to appoint someone in his place capable of reaching an armistice agreement with the Allies" (116). Twelve hours later the king had Mussolini arrested. German paratroopers rescued Mussolini from his imprisonment at Missolonghi. Members of the Grand Council in the hands of the Salò Republic after the rescue were executed, including Ciano, Mussolini's son-in-law.

3. In her revision ORA retained the references to the "bloody German tyrant."

4. Presumably Rachel Cookson. EP had sent her some chapters of ORA's memoir in the hope that she could find a publisher; Cookson apparently sent them on to **Theodora Bosanquet,** but nothing came of it.

5. The Ezra Pound Papers in the Beinecke Library contain pages 14–15 of her memoir, which appear to be a revision of the page EP is commenting upon since we have the phrase "Oh, the pity of it all!" on page 14 and "Dongo" at the bottom of page 15.

1959

124. TLU-1   [20–31 January 1959]

[Brunnenburg]

Dear O.R.A.

for Villari, but as his eyes are bad, do TALK to him.

Pressa pochismo.[1] Enough to make gods weep. WHY in Vesperi[2] must he make useless and INACCURATE statements, leaving what he KNOWS for airy conjecture.[3]

I didn't even see Pavolini, etc. after etc. Damn it, it is enough, if noticed, to discredit all his careful work re/ the 600 days etc.

the historian who does NOT leave blanks.

Also renders him useless in refuting the perfidy of C. Norman[4] who has just done a magnificent book on cummings, building up my LITERARY position, but using some truth to conceal the ROOT infamies.

so easy to refrain from putting in arabesques.

1. It.: "close enoughness."

2. Why in heaven.

3. ORA did not know what utterance of Villari's EP has in mind, but guessed that it was "the lecture he gave about your work" (31 Jan. 1959).

4. Charles Norman, author of *The Magic Maker: E. E. Cummings* and *Ezra Pound*, the first EP biography. EP's comments are a little difficult to interpret, but we think he is complaining that in his book on Cummings Norman failed to denounce EP's favorite bugaboos and thought EP's positions damaged his literary reputation.

125. TLS-1   20 March 1959

[Rapallo]

20 Marzo

Dear O.R.A.

If I manage to spend a few hours (not days) in Roma during next week or so, may I have use of yr/ salotto.[1]

Also a man I shd/ like you to see, and a number whom I don't want to see just NOW.

Please mention this to NO one, not even to Villari or Boris who may be in Rome when I pass thru.[2]

{EP}

1. It.: "sitting room."

2. ORA's letter in reply (21 March 1959) reveals that they had still not seen one another since his return to Italy on 9 July 1958.

Though we print below a letter from EP to ORA's sister, the following is the last letter of the EP/ORA correspondence and strikes us as a fitting close to the epistolary friendship that was so durable and idiosyncratic.

126. TLS-1   18 December 1959

Dear Ezra Pound:

the years go by and I have become infirm on my legs and dull in my wits. I had news of you a little while ago from Boris and this brings you and Mrs. Pound my best wishes for Christmas and the New Year. I should love to get into a helicopter and be dropped in the grounds of the Castle and sit with you and yours and fold my legs and have a long talk, but most of my conversations now have to be "imaginary Conversations" as I cannot get about, and now that poor old Villari has left this Vale of Tears practically no one comes to see me. By the way, I have been reading a book on "William Wetmore Story and his Friends" put together by Henry James,[1] and find it full of interesting things about worthies of the mid XIXth cent. Among others this dreadful story of poor old Walter Savage Landor: 'One hot summer day towards noon his wife and children turned him out of doors (he was then living at Fiesole) with some 15 pauls in his pocket (about 7/)[2] on the burning highway and told him to be off and never to come back. He was then past 80; and he wandered down to Florence, a broken-down, poor, houseless old man. There, straying aimlessly about the hot streets, exhausted and ill, he had the good fortune to meet Mr. Robert Browning who was to him a good angel and who took him under his protection and did everything he could to make him comfortable and happy.' An extraordinary story is it not? There is a lot about the Brownings in the book, letters, conversations, etc. I remember Browning coming to our old home in Endsleigh Gdns. when I was a little girl.

We have now a delightful baby in this house, Malù's second child, 5 months old; the softest, warmest, dearest little thing you can imagine. 'Cuddle and love me, cuddle and love, crows the mouth of coral pink; oh the bald head, and oh the sweet lips, and oh the sleepy eyes that wink!' (C G. R).[3] Helen has given me Edith Sitwell's Atlantic Anthology;[4] there is a noble tribute to you and the Cantos.

> Goodbye, good old Friend,
> Christmas love and New Year
> wishes.
>
> {Olivia Rossetti Agresti}

1. James's *William Wetmore Story and His Friends.*
2. Seven shillings.

3. This quotation is from **Christina Rossetti's** "I know a baby, such a baby" in *Complete Poems* 2:50.
4. Sitwell's *The Atlantic Book of British and American Poetry.*

ORA lived for another year. She died in Rome on 6 November 1960, not long after her eighty-fifth birthday on 20 September.

1963

127. ALS-2   6 July 1963
Rapallo
6 July 1963

Dear Signora Angeli
   O.R.A.'s varied contacts & the straight sharp action of her mind shd certainly make her reminiscences of value to a publisher.
   Her writing is clear, serene equanimous, dodging nothing, a model that I and others wd have done well to have followed.
   I wish I could help in the matter more than my present condition permits but I am still in hospital recovering from an operation.

> yours with kindest
> remembrances
> EP

Abbott, Beatrice (1898–1991): Bostonian who corresponded with EP during the 1940s and 1950s. She is the source of a conspiracy theory regarding the government's use of chemicals in food and water to control the population.

Aberhart, William (1878–1943): Radio evangelist and politician in Alberta, Canada. He founded the Canadian Social Credit party in 1935 and was premier of Alberta from 1935 to 1943, dying in office.

Acheson, Dean: Secretary of state (1949–53) under Truman. There were allegations that he was soft on communism and that Alger Hiss served as his executive assistant when Acheson was assistant secretary of state.

Adams, Brooks (1848–1927): American historian, younger brother of Henry Adams. His best known work is *The Law of Civilization and Decay* (1895).

Agassiz, Louis (1807–73): Swiss-born and educated, he emigrated to the United States in 1846 as a distinguished naturalist. A pioneer in classification of fossil fish and of glacial deposits and movement, he became professor of natural history at Harvard in 1848. William James and Sir Charles Lyell were among his students. He wrote *Contributions to the Natural History of the United States*. EP tells an anecdote about Agassiz and observation in *ABC of Reading*.

Alden, John (b. 1914): Curator of rare books at the University of Pennsylvania (1946–50) who, at EP's request, arranged for ORA's copy of *Il mistero dell' amor platonico del medio aevo* to be bought by the University of Pennsylvania Library.

Aldington, Richard (1892–1962): English Imagist poet and novelist and H. D.'s husband.

Aldrich, Chester Holmes (1871–1940): American architect who served as director of the American Academy in Rome (1934–40).

Amaral, José Vásquez: A professor of romance languages at Rutgers University who specialized in Latin American literature and translated some of EP's works.

Ambrose, St. (339?–397): Bishop of Milan (374–97) who imposed orthodoxy on the early Christian church. He was learned in both Christian and pagan philosophy. His "Catholic Neoplatonism" led to the conversion of St. Augustine.

Ambrosini, Vittorio Ambrosio (1879–1958): Italian chief of the general staff. Along with Marshal Badoglio he participated in the overthrow of Mussolini and the negotiation of an armistice with the allies in 1943.

Andréadès, André M. (b. 1876): Professor and author of numerous books published in Greek, English, Italian, and German, primarily on economic and political matters. He served as dean of the faculty of law at the University of Athens and president of the Greek League of Nations Union.

Angeli, Helen Maria Madox Rossetti (1879–1969): ORA's sister who married Gastone Angeli in 1903. She and ORA published an Anarchist newpaper, *The Torch*, as adolescents, and they co-authored *A Girl among the Anarchists*. Among her other books are *Dante Gabriel Rossetti: His Friends and Enemies* and *Pre-Raphaelite Twilight: the Story of Charles Augustus Howell*.

Angold, J. P.: English poet, writer on economics, and contributor to A. R. Orage's *New English Weekly*. EP admired his work and translated his unpublished "Work and Privilege" into Italian, but the translation was never published.

Antoninus Pius: Roman emperor A.D. 137–61. He instituted grain laws of which EP approved.

Apollonius of Tyana: A first century A.D. sage and miracle worker. As a Pythagorean and sun worshipper he ate no meat, disapproved of blood sacrifice, and wore clothes of pure linen only, not permitting animal skins or fabrics to touch his own skin. EP celebrates him in cantos 91 and 94.

Aragon, Louis (1897–1982): French poet, novelist, essayist, and one of the founders of the surrealist movement.

Attlee, Clement Richard (1883–1967): Leader of the British Labour party (1935–55) and prime minister (1945–51).

Badoglio, Marshal Pietro (1871–1956): Italian soldier and hero of the Ethiopian invasion. On 25 July 1943, he and Victor Emmanuel forced Mussolini to resign. In August he replaced Mussolini as head of the Italian government and signed the surrender to the Allies on 28 September 1943. His government declared war on Germany on 13 October 1943.

Baratti, Boris: Husband of EP's daughter, Mary. He later took a title and became Boris de Rachewiltz.

Baratti, Mary (b. 1925): EP's daughter by Olga Rudge. She became Mary de Rachewiltz after her husband, Boris Baratti, took a title.

Barnes, James Thomas Strachey (1890–1956): A journalist, born in India, raised in Florence by maternal grandparents, and educated at Eton, Sandhurst, and Cambridge. He was a Reuters agent in India and later secretary general of the International Institute of Fascist Studies, 1927–30. He was a personal friend and supporter of Mussolini as well as a member *honoris causa* of the Italian Fascist party. Barnes is the author of *Fascism* and *The Universal Aspects of Fascism*. As EP's co-broadcaster at Radio Rome and close friend, he once described himself as the "chronicler and prophet of the Fascist Revolution."

Barral, Jean: French author of *La révolution economique,* a book EP reviewed favorably in "Jean Barral with Us."

Baruch, Bernard Mannes (1870–1965): American financier and statesman. An advisor to both Democratic and Republican presidents, beginnning with Wilson, Baruch also advised Roosevelt and Truman. In 1946 he submitted the Baruch Plan for the international control of nuclear energy installations. He is the author of *American Industry in the War.* EP derisively named the United States "Baruchistan" after him.

Baxter, Viola: Referred to as "Vyoler" in the correspondence, she was an early friend of EP who married Virgin D. Jordan (1892–1965).

Beaverbrook, First Baron William Maxwell Aitken (1879–1964): Canadian-born financier, prominent British newspaper publisher, and politician.

Beck, Dave (b. 1894): Labor union official and longtime president of the Western Conference of Teamsters.

Beck, Jósef (1894–1944): Polish army officer and minister of foreign affairs (1932–39) and author of *Dernier Rapport—Politique Polonaise, 1926–1936.*

Bede, Venerable (ca. 672–735): English monk, scholar, historian, and author of *Historia ecclesiastica gentis anglorum* and works of exegesis.

Bedford, Twelfth Duke of, and the **Marquis of Tavistock (William Sackville Russell):** Inherited the title Duke of Bedford in 1940. One of Britain's wealthiest men, and twelfth in line for the English throne, he was well known for his pacifist propaganda during World War II. His controversial actions included a visit to Dublin in 1940 to find out what Germany's peace terms were; upon his return he published "Germany's Peace Terms—Official," which was immediately repudiated by Berlin. In the summer of 1939 he declared himself chairman and founding member of the British People's party, which was pro-German and anti-French. He was killed in a hunting accident on 11 October 1953. He is often referred to by his title. The character Lord Darlington in Kazu Ishiguro's 1989 novel *Remains of the Day* is loosely based on him.

Belgion, Montgomery (1892–1973): Paris-born English journalist, writer, and editor. Author of *The Human Parrot and Other Essays, Reading for Profit, H. G. Wells,* and *David Hume.*

Belloc, Hilaire (1870–1935): A Catholic social critic and friend of G. K. Chesterton.

Benda, Julien (1867–1956): French novelist and philosopher who led the modern neoclassical movement in French criticism, defending reason and intellect against Henri Bergson's philosophical intuitionism. Author of *Le Bergsonisme,* the novel *L'ordination,* and *La trahison des clercs.*

Benét, William Rose: Coediter with Conrad Aiken of the second edition of the *Anthology of Famous English and American Poetry.* In 1946 the publisher first announced that it would not print any of EP's poems (the first edition contained twelve poems by EP) because the poet was a Fascist, but following protestations by Aiken and W. H. Auden, EP's work was included.

Benton, Thomas Hart (1782–1858): Democratic senator from Missouri, 1820–50. As a committed supporter of Andrew Jackson and an opponent of the Bank of the United States he advocated legislation favoring frontier interests and was the leader in the movement for securing federal support for Western exploration. He edited the sixteen-volume *Abridgement of the Debates of Congress from 1789 to 1856*. EP draws heavily on his *Thirty Years' View* for cantos 88 and 89. EP had Benton's *Bank of the United States* published in the Square $ Series.

Berenson, Bernhard (1865–1959): American art critic and collector who lived for a time in Rapallo.

Bevione, Giuseppe (b. 1879): Politician and journalist who wrote for *La Stampa* and *Gazzetta del popolo* and was director of the Milan-based daily *Secolo* (1923–26).

Biddle, Nicholas (1786–1844): American financier and president of the Bank of the United States (1822–39).

Billy, André (b. 1882): French fiction writer and critic who was a regular contributor to *Le Figaro littéraire*.

Blackstone, Sir William (1723–80): English jurist and legal historian best known for his influential *Commentaries on the Laws of England*. EP considered the parts of his work "dealing with history and philosophy of law" essential reading.

Bodrero, Emilio (1874–1949): Italian classical scholar, prominent politician, and member of parliament during the Fascist regime. He is known as a scholar for his Nietzschean interest in the pre-Socratics as the source of Western religious wisdom and as a politician for his assault on Freemasonry. He was a vigorous oponent of the thought of Giovanni Gentile. Among his works are *Inchiesta sulla massoneria, I limiti della storia della filosofia, Italia nuova e antica,* and *La fina di una epoca*.

Born, Bertrand de: Twelfth-century French troubador and soldier.

Bosanquet, Theodora: Henry James's secretary, an editor at *Time and Tide,* and author of *Henry James at Work*.

Bottai, Giuseppe (1895–1959): Fascist journalist and politician, minister of national education (1936–43), and one of the Italian *gerarchi*. In 1943 he was sentenced to death, but escaped. He returned to Italy in 1948 after a general amnesty. He founded the neo-Fascist periodical *ABC* in 1953. Boris de Rachewiltz was for a time on *ABC*'s editorial board, and ORA's articles on David Lubin and EP appeared in the publication.

Bowen, Stella: Australian painter, writer, and common-law wife of Ford Madox Ford. Her *Drawn from Life* contains many portraits of contemporary personalities, including those of EP and Max Beerbohm.

Brannan, Charles (b. 1903): Lawyer who specialized in irrigation and mining law and was appointed secretary of agriculture in May 1948. His 1949 plan, which called for direct government income assistance to farmers and limits on assistance to big farms, was brought to the House floor and incorporated into a high-supports bill sponsored by Representative Stephen Pace, but was defeated in the Senate by a more traditional plan sponsored by Representative Albert Gore.

Bricker, John William (b. 1893): Governor of Ohio (1939–45), Republican candidate for vice president (1944), and member of the U.S. Senate (1945–56).

Bridges, Henry Styles (1898–1961): Republican senator from New Hampshire (1937–61) and unsuccessful candidate for the Republican presidential nomination in 1940. A staunch opponent of Roosevelt's New Deal and later a vocal opponent of Truman's foreign policies, he was fiercely anticommunist and a strong advocate of McCarthyism.

Brown, Ford Madox (1821–93): English painter and ORA's and Ford Madox Ford's grandfather.

Bullitt, William C. (1891–1967): Journalist, ambassador to the Soviet Union (1933–36) and France (1936–40), special advisor on foreign policy and Soviet affairs to Roosevelt (1940–44), and conservative critic of the Roosevelt and Truman administrations' Soviet policies. He is the author of *The Great Globe Itself*, in which he denounces the United States for selling out to the Soviet Union. He also railed against U.S. policy in China, arguing that Marshall left Chiang Kai-shek in the lurch.

Bülow, Prince Bernhard Heinrich von (1849–1929): German politician and diplomat who served as German chancellor, 1900–1909.

Bunting, Basil (1900–1985): British poet and friend of EP.

Burbank, Luther (1895–1974): Botanist and horticulturalist who believed his work to have implications for human genetics. Like Agassiz, he rejected Darwinian natural selection in favor of Lamarckian inheritance of acquired characteristics. He believed in the laying on of hands. Racists such as Alfalfa Bill Murray twisted his work for their own purposes.

Calogero, Guido (b. 1904): Italian philosopher and university professor who was one of the leaders of the Liberal-Socialist movement arrested in 1942 as an anti-Fascist. He held many positions in his career, including those at McGill-Queen's University (1948–49), the Italian Institute in London (1950–55), the University of California at Berkeley (1956–57), Princeton (1962–63), Institut International de Philosophie (1963–66), and Rome University.

Canby, Henry Seidel (1878–1961): Educator, literary critic, and editor. In 1920 he established the *Literary Review*, the literary supplement of the *New York Post*. He and others established, in 1924, the *Saturday Review of Literature*, later the *Saturday Review*, with which he remained associated until 1958. He also served as chairman of the Book-of-the-Month Club (1926–54).

Cantine, Holley: Anarchist who ran the Retort Press in Bearsville, N.Y., with Dachine Rainer.

Capitini, Aldo (1899–1968): Italian author, university teacher, administrator, political organizer, and poet. He became a member of the anti-Fascist underground in the 1930s. He was associated with Guido Calogero, among other dissident intellectuals. His *Elementi di un'esperienza religiosa*, a Gandhi-inspired discussion of nonviolent political action and religion, was admired by Benedetto Croce. He followed no party line, but was dedicated to reform. Imprisoned by Mussolini, he was released in 1943. He was a living link between the antifascism of the thirties and the antiwar movement of the sixties.

Carrel, Alexis (1873–1944): French-born American pioneer surgeon and biologist and winner of the 1912 Nobel Prize for Medicine. He is the author of *Man, the Unknown.*

Carter, Thomas H. (1931–63): An American writer who corresponded with EP in the 1950s. He was a founding editor of *Shenandoah*, a literary journal.

Cavour, Camillo Benso di (1810–61): Conservative statesman who brought about the unification of Italy in 1861.

Cerf, Bennett: President of Random House who decided to expunge twelve of EP's poems from the *Anthology of Famous English and American Poetry*, edited by William Rose Benét and Conrad Aiken. Eventually Cerf changed his mind, EP was paid three hundred dollars, and the poems were readmitted with a note explaining that it would be wrong to allow an opinion of Pound the person to taint an opinion of his work. Cerf, who was Jewish, continued to think that people like EP were despicable.

Chakravarty, Amiya (b. 1901): Literary secretary to Rabindrinath Tagore (1926–33) and professor of English and comparative literature.

Chambrun, Clara de (1873–1945): Sister of Congressman Nicholas Longworth, the husband of Alice Roosevelt Longworth. She became a countess through her marriage to Adelbert de Chambrun, the French ambassador to Rome (1933–36). Her son, Count René de Chambrun, was the husband of Pierre Laval's daughter. Laval collaborated during the Vichy regime. She wrote *The Making of Nicholas Longworth.*

Châtel, Jean Marie: One of EP's retinue at St. Elizabeths. He was a fiction writer and later became a psychiatrist.

Chesterton, A. K.: Cousin of G. K. Chesterton and journalist active in the British Union of Fascists. He was born in South Africa but moved to England in the 1920s. Following World War II he formed the League of Empire Loyalists in opposition to Oswald Mosley's postwar "union movement."

Ciano, Count Galeazzo (1903–44): Mussolini's son-in-law, minister of propaganda (1935), and minister of foreign affairs (1936–43). He voted to depose Mussolini in 1943 and was tried and executed by Mussolini's Salò Republic. Mussolini refused his daughter's plea to commute the sentence.

Cini, Vittorio (b. 1885): Italian industrialist and Fascist follower and key figure in securing support for Mussolini from the landowners and industrialists. In 1943 he served briefly as minister of communications.

Connolly, Cyril (1903–74): Anglo-Irish writer and editor, author of *The Missing Diplomats*, a book on Guy Francis de Moncy Burgess and Donald Duart MacLean, the so-called Foreign Office Spies.

Corti, Count Egon Caesar (1886–1953): Croatian-born author of *The Rise of the House of Rothschild* and *The Reign of the House of Rothschild.*

Coselschi, Eugenio (b. 1889): Poet, Fascist propagandist, and personal friend of Gabriele D'Annunzio. He sat in Parliament (1929–39), was a radio commentator in the 1930s, and headed the Comitato d'Azione per l'Universalità di Roma, a propaganda office formed to spread the myth of Romanità and help create a "universal Fascist movement." He was apparently one of the possible candidates for the presidency of the Classical Committee.

Costa, Giovanni (1826–1903): Italian painter. ORA published a book about him: *Giovanni Costa: His Life, Work, and Times.*

Coughlin, Father Charles Edward (1891–1979): Roman Catholic priest notorious as a Fascist sympathizer in the United States. He had a regular radio program on which he assailed American financiers for causing the Great Depression.

Crassus, Marcus Licinius (115–53 B.C.): Politician who in the last years of the Roman Republic formed the so-called first triumvirate with Julius Caesar and Pompey.

Crosby, Caresse: Founded Black Sun Press with her husband, Harry Crosby (1898–1929), in 1927. In 1930 she published EP's *Imaginary Letters,* which was originally written in 1918 for the *Little Review* and included contributions by Wyndham Lewis. In January 1946 she came to visit EP at the request of the hospital staff, who wanted the impressions of someone who had known EP long ago. She was instrumental in getting EP's translation of Sophocles' *The Women of Trachis* performed on the BBC's Third Programme.

d'Anna, Coppola: Italian economist who published a negative review of an enquiry into unemployment in the south of Italy by a Parliamentary committee.

Davenport, Guy: Literary scholar and poet.

Davies, Ingrid: Young woman introduced to EP by Brigit Patmore with whom he carried on a correspondence mostly from 1954 to 1958.

Davies, W. H.: English poet whom EP knew in London and author of *The Autobiography of a Super-Tramp.* In "William H. Davies, Poet," EP reviewed his *Collected Poems.*

Dazzi, Manlio Torquato: When Dazzi was the director of the Biblioteca Malatestiana at Cesena he showed EP a medal by the pseudo-Pisanello in 1923 and helped EP with his research on Cavalcanti. EP's *Guido Cavalcanti Rime* is dedicated to him. Dazzi later became curator of the Querini Stampalia Collection in Venice and brought to Olga Rudge's attention the collection of Vivaldi manuscript scores in Turin. Dazzi speaks in canto 73 but is also mentioned in canto 72. See also EP's comments on Dazzi in "Possibilities of Civilization." EP's letters to him are included in *Ezra Pound, Lettere 1907–58.*

De Gasperi, Alcide (1881–1968): Italian statesman who played a major role in the formation of the Christian Democratic party and served as premier, 1945–53. He knew ORA and thought her a first-class interpreter. He insisted that ORA accompany him to the peace conference in London in 1945.

de Kruif, Paul Henry (1890–1971): American bacteriologist and writer of popular works on medical science, including *Hunger Fighters,* which EP reviewed in *New English Weekly,* and *Why Keep Them Alive.* EP and de Kruif corresponded and met during EP's 1939 visit to the United States. De Kruif introduced EP to Secretary of Agriculture Henry A. Wallace.

DelCroix, Carlo (b. 1896): One of the best known Fascist propagandists. He lost his sight and both hands in World War I. He became president of the Associazione Nazionale Mutilati e Invalidi di Guerra in 1924 and held the post until 1943. He was elected to Parliament on the Monarchist ticket in 1953. He is mentioned in cantos 88, 92, 95, 98, and 101.

Del Mar, Alexander (1836–1926): American monetary historian much cited by EP in the 1950s. Trained as a mining engineer, he was director of the new Bureau of Statistics in Washington (1866–69). Most of his long series of monographs and pamphlets deal with metallic money, coinage, and mints, including, *The Science of Money, Barbara Villiers,* and *A History of Money in America,* and *A History of Monetary Systems.* His work on coins led him into archeology and the history of religions in such books as *A History of Precious Metals, Roman and Moslem Moneys,* and *A History of Money in Ancient Times.*

Del Pelo Pardi, Giulio (1872–1953): Roman who after completing a classical education applied himself to research in agriculture. He founded the Office of Roman Agricultural Technique in 1899. He was a pioneer in agricultural archeology, especially of Roman agricultural technology and techniques. A collection of his writings were collected by EP's son-in-law, Boris de Rachewiltz, and his own son, Tommaso, in 1971. Mary and Boris de Rachewiltz maintain a small agricultural museum at Schloss Brunnenburg in Del Pelo Pardi's honor.

Demosthenes: Athenian orator and statesman who delivered the Philippic orations (B.C. 348–322).

De Valera, Éamon (1882–1975): American-born Irish revolutionary, politician, and president of Ireland (1959–73).

Dies, Martin (1901–72): Democratic Congressman from Texas who chaired the House Committee on Un-American Activities. Its 1941 report included names of over five thousand government employees suspected of subversive sympathies. Dies disliked the New Deal and the Roosevelt administration.

di Marzio, Cornelio (1896–1945?): Editor of *Meridiano di Roma,* a journal eventually suppressed by Mussolini. He was director of the Fascist Confederation of Artists and Professional Men, which supported avant-garde artists during the Fascist regime. EP was introduced to him by Ubaldo degli Uberti. Di Marzio put EP in touch with the Italian Ministry of Popular Culture. According to Luigi Villari he was apparently shot.

Dominic, St. (ca. 1170–1221): Founder of the Dominican order.

Domville, Sir Barry (1878–1971): Director of Naval Intelligence, 1927–30. In 1937 he founded The Link, an association for promoting good relations between Britain and Germany. He was detained from 1940 to 1943 for conducting acts prejudicial to the defense of the Realm. EP admired his autobiogaphy, *From Admiral to Cabin Boy.*

Donaldson, John (1892–1955): Political economist at George Washington University (1922–47) and cofounder, in 1931, of the Academy of World Economics (later the National Academy of Economics and Political Science).

Douglas, Gavin (1474–1522): Scottish poet and first translator of *The Aeneid* into English, around 1515.

Douglas, Major Clifford Hugh (1879–1952): British originator of the theory of Social Credit. He argued that economic depression was caused by insufficient purchasing power.

Downs, William (1915–78): U.S. newspaper, radio, and television reporter.

Drummond, John (1900–1982?): He and his wife Elsie were British friends of the Pounds in Rapallo and Fascist supporters. Little is known of them. C. David Heyman includes Drummond in a list of "impenitent blackshirts" with Ugo Dadone, Camillo Pellizzi, Odon Por, and ORA. Drummond translated EP's Money Pamphlets into English.

Drummond, Sir Eric (b. 1876): Sixteenth Earl of Perth, Twelfth Viscount of Strathallan, British diplomat, and chief advisor on foreign publicity to the minister of information beginning in 1939.

Duncan, Ronald (Bishop of Marsland, Major-General of Marsland) (1914–82): Rhodesia-born poet, playwright, novelist, author of autobiographies, and editor of *London Magazine* and *The Townsman: A Quarterly Review*. He founded the Devon Festival of the Arts in 1953 and cofounded the English Stage Co. at Royal Court Theatre in 1955. Duncan is the author of *Journal of a Husbandman*, a book admired by ORA.

Dunning, Ralph Cheever (1878–1930): American expatriate poet and EP's neighbor in Paris, 1920–24.

Eastman, Max (1883–1969): Editor with John Reed of the influential Greenwich Village paper *The Masses*. During his visit to New York in 1939 EP met Eastman and had intense arguments with him over Fascist regimentation.

Eden, Anthony (1897–1977): British Conservative party leader and prime minister, 1955–57. He also served as Britain's foreign secretary from 1940 to 1945 and from 1951 to 1955 and had close connections to Winston Churchill.

Edwards, Frank Allyn (b. 1908): Journalist with the Mutual Broadcasting System, 1942–54 and 1959–61. From 1949 to 1954 he served as White House correspondent. He was cited, with Edward R. Murrow and Lowell Thomas, as one of the nation's top three broadcasters in a 1953 *Radio Daily* poll.

Einaudi, Luigi (1874–1961): Economist, politician, and writer. He served as governor of the Bank of Italy and as a minister in the fourth Alcide De Gasperi cabinet and became first president of the Republic of Italy (1948–55).

Epstein, Sir Jacob (1880–1959): American-born British sculptor. EP had seen his *Rock-Drill*, which depicted a human figure astride a mechanical drill hammering into rock, and adopted the title for cantos 85–95.

Erigena, Joannes Scotus (810–ca. 877): Irish Neoplatonic philosopher of light and author of *De Divisione Naturae*. He is frequently invoked by EP in *The Cantos*.

Fack, Dr. Hugo R.: A small-press publisher from Texas who made available an English translation of Gesell's *The Natural Economic Order* and the Neo-Economic Series of Freedom and Plenty, a series of pamphlets. EP calls him "a country physician" (*Guide to Kulchur* 246).

Farinacci, Roberto (1892–1945): Italian journalist, barrister, and member of Parliament. With a powerful voice in the Fascist regime, he had a reputation for being "more fascist than Il Duce." Farinacci served as general secretary of the Fascist movement and represented its anti-Semitic sentiment. He established *La Squilla* and *Il regime fascista*. He was summarily executed by partisans in April 1945.

Feder, Gottfried (1883–1941): Principal economic theoretician of German Nazism. His ideas found expression in Hitler's twenty-five-point program for the National Socialist German Workers' (Nazi) party in March 1920.

Ferkiss, Victor C.: He received his Ph.D. in political science from the University of Chicago. His articles on the populist roots of EP's and American fascism are based on his dissertation.

Fish, Hamilton, Jr.: Politician EP met with to discuss monetary reform during his 1939 trip to the United States.

Fleming, William: Australian poet, translator, and editor associated with Noel Stock's circle.

Ford, Ford Madox (1873–1939): Born Ford Madox Hueffer, Ford changed his name after World War I. He and ORA were first cousins, sharing Ford Madox Brown as a maternal grandfather. Ford lived in Brown's house after his father's death in 1899 and came to know his Rossetti cousins quite well. In 1938 Ford was at Olivet College in Michigan and invited EP to join him there, even offering EP his own position. A lively exchange of letters shows that EP considered the offer seriously but ultimately decided to stay in Italy.

Franz Josef (1830–1916): Emperor of Austria (1848–1916) and king of Hungary (1867–1916). His 1914 ultimatum to Serbia led Austria and Germany into World War I. His wife was assassinated in Geneva on 10 September 1898.

Freedman, Benjamin: Author of *Facts Are Facts*, an anti-Semitic work mentioned numerous times in EP's late 1955 letters to ORA.

French, William: EP acquaintance who, with his wife Gloria, was a frequent visitor at St. Elizabeths. He has published several essays on EP and was also a jazz bassist.

Frere, John Hookham (1769–1846): British diplomat, wit, translator, and author. His nom de plume was John Whislecraft.

Frobenius, Leo (1873–1938): German anthropologist and archeologist, founder of the Institute of Cultural Morphology (1922) in Frankfurt, and author of the seven-volume *Erlebte Erdteile*, which EP considered more important than Frazer's *The Golden Bough*. EP borrowed from him the terms "paideuma" and "sagetrieb." Frobenius has had little influence in postwar anthropology. He has—somewhat unfairly—been identified with the Nazi regime because of his views on the specificity of culture to race.

Fuller, John Frederick Charles (b. 1878): British major general in the army, author of many books on military matters and warfare, and a contributor to military magazines as well as the *Sunday Times* and *Daily Telegraph*.

Galdós, Benito Pérez (1843–1920): Spanish historical and naturalistic novelist.

Garibaldi, Giuseppe (1807–82): Foremost guerilla leader of the Risorgimento, he played a major role in the defense of the Roman Republic and the conflicts that led up to and followed the unification of Italy. His country's favorite nineteenth-century revolutionary hero, Garibaldi recorded his ideals in several popular novels.

Gasset, José Ortega y (1883–1955): Spanish writer and philosopher noted for his humanistic criticism of modern civilization. His publications and lectures contributed to the fall of the Spanish monarchy in 1931. He was a member of the Cortes (the Spanish parliament) that promulgated the republican constitution. He fled on the outbreak of the Spanish Civil War in 1936, but returned to Fascist Spain after the end of World War II. His most renowned work is *The Revolt of the Masses*, in which he argues that the masses must be led by an intellectual elite if totalitarian regimes are to be avoided.

Gauthier-Villars, Henri (1859–1931): French novelist, essayist, and biographer. He is mentioned in canto 80/504.

Genlis, Comtesse de (Felicité du Crest de Saint-Aubin) (1746–1830): Author of novels and books on education. She is mentioned in cantos 103 and 111.

Gentile, Giovanni (1875–1944): Italian idealist philosopher who founded the review *La Critica* in 1903 with Benedetto Croce but broke with Croce in the twenties. His *Theory of Mind as Pure Act* brought him favor with Mussolini, who made him minister of education in 1922. He opposed the Lateran Pacts of 1929, which caused him to lose some favor. But in 1943 he came out in support of the Salò Republic. He was assassinated by Partisans as he drove into his villa in Florence on 15 April 1944.

Gentz, Friedrich von (1764–1832): Influential German political journalist famous for his passionate opposition to the French Revolution and Napoleon and for being a special adviser to Metternich. He moved from the Prussian civil service to the Austrian in 1802. He wrote bitter diatribes against Napoleon.

George, David Lloyd (1863–1945): Leader of the British Liberal party, 1926–31, and an important figure in British politics from 1890 until his death.

George, Henry (1819–78): American economic reformer. He advocated a single tax on land to replace all other taxes in *Our Land and Land Policy* and *Progress and Poverty*.

Gesell, Silvio (1862–1930): Minister of finance of the second Munich Republic (1919), monetary reformer, and advocate of stamp script, a scheme in which a stamp representing a percentage of the face value of the paper bill must be attached each month. The scheme could be thought of as reverse interest or institutionalized inflation on currency. Gesell's principal publication was *The Natural Economic Order*, which EP reviewed in the *New English Weekly*.

Giartosio de Courten, Maria Luisa: Author of *Percy Bysshe Shelley e l'Italia* and *I Rossetti: Storia di una famiglia*. She was responsible for the reprinting of Gabriele Rossetti's *La Beatrice di Dante*, which contains her essay "Storia del manuscrito."

Giovannini, Giovanni (1906–1985): Professor of English at the Catholic University in Washington, D.C., he was a regular visitor during EP's stay at St. Elizabeths and is the one who arranged for the EP/ORA correspondence to be sold to the Beinecke Rare Book and Manuscript Library at Yale University.

Girl among the Anarchists, A: Fictionalized memoir written by ORA and her sister Helen and published under the pseudonym Isabel Meredith. ORA gave an account of the work in a letter of 27 October 1950: "I wrote it jointly with my sister Helen: we had lived the experience together. Our Anarchist days began when I was 14 and she was 10 and ended as far as active participation went, when I was 20 and she was 16. Of the 12 chapters of the book Helen wrote 5 and I 7; we were not together at the time; she was in London, and I was married (to an anarchist) in Rome, but though they were written quite separately and neither revised the work of the other, it seems to me quite homogeneous. I remember I wrote the 1st and the last chapters, but have not a very distinct recollection of the authorship of the others. As you see, we both entered political life when other girls are in high school."

Goacher, Denis (b. 1925): Poet, BBC actor, and broadcaster who recorded EP at St. Elizabeths. He wrote the foreword to EP's translation of Sophocles' *Women of Trachis*.

Goldring, Douglas (1887–1960): Author of *South Lodge: Reminiscences of Violet Hunt, Ford Madox Ford, and the "English Review" Circle.* He was Ford Madox Ford's editorial assistant on the *English Review* (1908–9), an intimate of the South Lodge Circle, and an acquaintance of EP's during his London years.

Gollancz, Victor (1893–1967): British publisher and founder in 1936 of the Left Book Club. He published the English translations of Egon Caesar Corti's books.

Gordon, David M. (b. 1929): One of the young men who supported EP during his St. Elizabeths years. He published the *Academia Bulletin*. He is the editor of *Ezra Pound and James Laughlin: Selected Letters.*

Gosse, Sir Edmund (1845–1928): English poet and critic.

Gourmont, Rémy de (1858–1915): French poet and literary journalist and sensualist who stands between the Symbolists and the Modernists. He was one of the founders of *Mercure de France.* EP translated the postscript to his pseudo-scientific *The Natural Philosophy of Love,* a tendentious eroticization of J. H. Fabre's *Souvenirs entomologique.*

Graziani, Rodolfo (1882–1955): Italian chief of staff and combat general during World War II. He also fought in World War I, was viceroy of Ethiopia in 1936, commanded Italian forces in east Africa in 1941, and served in Mussolini's Salò Republic as a military commander. After surrendering to the Allies on 1 May 1945, he was tried and found guilty of collaboration by the supreme Italian military tribunal and was condemned to nineteen years of solitary confinement. After being granted amnesty in 1950, he wrote his apologia, *Ho difeso la patria.*

Green, John Richard (1837–83): Historian and author of the four-volume *A History of the English People.*

Guareschi, Giovanni (1908–68): Italian novelist and editor of the magazines *Bertoldo* and *Candida.* He was imprisoned by the Salò Republic (1943–45). Among his other works are *La scoperta di Milano, Il destino si chiama Clotilde, Mondo piccolo,* and *Il dilemma di Don Camillo.*

Gucciardini, Francesco (1483–1540): Florentine statesman, diplomat, historian, and author of the most important contemporaneous account of sixteenth-century Italian history, *Storia d'Italia.*

Guenther, Charles: EP acolyte whose reviews and articles appeared in the *St. Louis Post-Dispatch.*

Guerriero, Augusto: Journalist for *Epoca* and *Corriere della sera,* known as Ricciardetto. Among his book publications are *Guerra e dopoguerra: Saggi politici.*

Hammarskjöld, Dag (1905–61): Swedish economist and statesman and second secretary of the United Nations (1953–61) who was posthumously awarded the Nobel Prize for Peace (1961) after his death in a plane crash. He was the son of Hjalmar Hammarskjöld, prime minister of Sweden (1914–17) and chairman of the Nobel Prize Foundation (1929–47).

Hammond, Douglas: EP admirer from the University of Alabama who wanted to lead a campaign for EP's release.

Hankey, Baron Maurice Pascal Alers (1877–1963): Secretary of the British Cabinet from 1916 until his retirement in 1938.

Harris, Frank (1855–1931): Literary critic and editor of the *Forthnightly Review, Saturday Review,* and *Vanity Fair* and founder and editor of *Candid Friend.* His books include *The Man Shakespeare, The Women of Shakespeare, Oscar Wilde,* and his autobiography, *My Life and Loves,* which was banned for a time in England and the United States.

Helen: See Angeli, Helen Maria Madox Rossetti.

Henriot, Émile (1889–1961): Novelist, poet, critic, scholar, and member of the Académie Français.

Herbert, Edward, Baron of Cherbury (1583–1648): English philosopher known as the father of English Deism and brother of George Herbert, the metaphysical poet. His principal works are *De Veritate,* which presents an anti-empirical (anti-Lockean) theory of knowledge, and *De Religione Gentilium,* a comparative study of pagan religions. He is mentioned in cantos 100 and 109.

Hesse, Fritz (b. 1897): Representative of the German News Agency (DNB) as well as press attaché at the German embassy in London from 1935 to 1939. From 1939 to 1945 he was *rapporteur* and adviser on British affairs at Hitler's headquarters. His *Das Spiel um Deutschland* was published in English as *Hitler and the English.*

Heydon, John (1629–?): English astrologer and occult writer, author of *The Holy Guide* and other occult books.

Hiss, Alger: Nicholas Murray Butler's successor as head of the Carnegie Endowment for Peace. In 1948 he was tried for perjury after he denied Communist affiliation before the McCarthy commission. He was unsuccessfully defended by Lloyd Stryker, EP's Hamilton classmate. Whittaker Chambers, a former member of the Objectivist circle of poets and the editor of *Time Magazine,* testified against him. Hiss was prosecuted by Richard Nixon, convicted of perjury after denying his Communist affiliation, and spent forty-four months in jail.

Holley, Horace (b. 1887): Writer associated with *Others: A Magazine of the New Verse* (1915–19), a New York poetry magazine. Alfred Kreymborg

(1883–1966) was its principal editor; William Carlos Williams was an associate editor.

Horton, Thomas David: Poet, journalist, EP acolyte, frequent visitor at St. Elizabeths, and founder (with John Kasper) of the Square $ Series.

House, Colonel Edward Mandell (1858–1938): Advisor to President Woodrow Wilson and author of *The Intimate Papers of Colonel House.*

Hull, Cordell (1871–1955): U.S. secretary of state, 1933–44.

Humboldt, Alexander von (1769–1859): German naturalist, explorer, and major force in the classical period of earth sciences and ecology.

Humboldt, Karl Wilhelm von (1767–1835): German statesman and philologist. Best known for his work in comparative linguistics and his theory that languages determine the worldviews of speakers.

Hunt, Isabel Violet (1860–1942): English novelist and biographer. She lived at South Lodge from her girlhood until her death. She and Ford Madox Ford lived at South Lodge together from 1910 to 1915, despite the refusal of his wife, Elsie Martindale, to divorce him.

Hynes, Gladys: Acquaintance of Father Luigi Sturzo during his exile in England. She wrote to Sturzo on EP's behalf. She also wrote to ORA as EP had requested.

Ionides, Luke (1837–1924): A Greek-British painter and man-about-town in London. All we know of him is from the "Memories" Ford Madox Ford published in *The Transatlantic Review* (1924) in eight installments. EP's mother-in-law, Olivia Shakespear, apparently acted as his amanuensis. He was in his eighty-seventh year and died while the series was in progress. In *Guide to Kulchur*, EP describes him as one of the "men who were old *enough* [to be] all right" (227). He is also mentioned in *The Cantos.*

Jenkins, Ray H.: Tennessee lawyer who appeared before the House Committee on Un-American Activities.

Jenner, William E.: Republican senator from Indiana and chairman of the Internal Security Subcommittee of the Senate on the Judiciary. He shared McCarthy's rabid anticommunism.

Jiménez, Juan Ramón (1881–1958): Spanish poet of the influential modernist movement "generation of 98" who began as an impressionist painter but quickly shifted to writing poetry. In the wake of the Spanish Civil War he moved first to the United States and then to Puerto Rico, where he resided until his death in 1958.

Johnson, Lionel (1867–1902): English poet and member of the Rhymers' Club, founded by William Butler Yeats and others in 1890–91. EP mentions Johnson in *Hugh Selwyn Mauberley.*

Juin, Alphonse (1888–1967): French field marshall and war hero who served first in the Vichy government and then in the Free French Forces.

Julian the Apostate (331–63): Nephew of Constantine the Great who became emperor in 363. An avowed paganist, he regarded Christianity as a persecuting force and championed a curious, eclectic amalgam of active polytheism, the mysteries, and Neoplatonism. He undertook various administrative and tax reforms of which EP approved.

Kasper, John Frederick: American right-wing activist, EP acolyte, regular visitor at St. Elizabeths, and founder (with David Horton) of the Square $ Press. Kasper organized the Seaboard White Citizens's Council, billed himself as "Segregational Chief," and addressed racist gatherings in the South following the 1954 U.S. Supreme Court decision on the desegregation of schools. Kasper believed that Jews were behind integration. Arrested on numerous occasions during the late 1950s, he was sentenced to several jail terms.

Katue, Kitasono (1902–78): Japanese avant-garde poet and founder of *VOU*. EP and Katue began corresponding in 1936. He provided EP with an audience and much needed income from the *Japan Times* during the late 1930s and early 1940s.

Kemal Atatürk (1881–1938): Statesman and reformer, founder and first president (1923–38) of the Republic of Turkey. He appears in cantos 22 and 96.

Kenner, Hugh (b. 1923): Canadian-born American literary critic. The doyen of EP scholars.

Ker, W. P. (1855–1923): Scottish specialist in medieval studies.

Keynes, John Maynard (1883–1946): English economist best known as the author of *General Theory of Employment, Interest, and Money*, which brought about a revolution in economic thinking that dominated policymaking in the Western democracies from 1945 to the 1970s, when it was displaced by "monetarism."

Kitson, Arthur (1860–1937): Monetary reformer and author of *The Bankers' Conspiracy*.

Kravchinski, Sergei Michailovich (1852–95): Exiled Russian Anarchist and nihilist who used Stepnyak as his pseudonym.

Kropotkin, Prince Peter (1842–1921): Prominent Anarchist ORA knew in London. He wrote variously on anarchism, revolution, Russian literature, and geography.

La Drière, James Craig: Professor at the Catholic University of America in Washington, D.C., and a regular visitor to St. Elizabeths. He defended EP's actions in a letter published in the *Washington Star*. After his release, EP spent several days at his house.

Lampman, Rex Herbert: Washington reporter who had worked in the U.S. Treasury Department during the 1930s.

Landor, Walter Savage (1775–1864): English writer known for *Imaginary Conversations of Literary Men and Statesmen* (1824–29). EP's *Imaginary Letters* is an effort in this genre.

La Pira, Giorgio (1902–77): Politician, law professor at the University of Florence, member of the anti-Fascist underground, and one of the signatories of the Italian Constitution in 1947.

Laski, Harold Joseph (1893–1950): English political scientist at the London School of Economics, 1920–50. Laski adopted Marxism in 1931 and became chairman of the Labour party in 1945. He wrote numerous books, first expounding a pluralist doctrine of the state and later accepting the Marxist interpretation of history and arguing that social revolution of some form was inevitable. Among his friends were Oliver Wendell Holmes and Roosevelt.

Laughlin, James (1914–97): Founder and president of New Directions Publishing Corporation and friend of EP since 1934 when he arrived in Rapallo to enroll in the "Ezuveristy." An important poet in his own right, he is the author of several articles on EP and of *Pound as Wuz*.

Leahy, William D. (1875–1959): Fleet admiral and chief of staff to Roosevelt and Truman. His memoir, *I Was There*, contains many references to Pétain and one to EP (464).

Lekakis, Michael (1907–87): Greek-American sculptor whose work is in many American museums, including the Museum of Modern Art. He was a friend of EP and visited him at St. Elizabeths.

Lenbergis, Lore Marianne: Young German graduate student who had received a Fulbright scholarship to study EP's work under Hugh Kenner and eventually produced a Ph.D. dissertation.

Leone, Enrico: Neapolitan and major spokesman for syndicalism who edited the first conspicuously revolutionary syndicalist paper in Italy in the early 1900s.

Leopoldine Reforms: EP celebrates the Sienese reforms of Pietro Leopoldo I, Grand Duke of Tuscany (1765–90) in cantos 42–44. These reforms were continued by Leopold II, Holy Roman Emperor (1790–92), and were designed to alleviate the economic problems of Tuscany.

Lewis, Fulton (1903–66): National affairs radio commentator for the Mutual Broadcasting Company. Known for his right-wing attacks on Roosevelt's New Deal policies and for his support of McCarthyism, he broadcasted "The Top of the News from Washington."

Lewis, Wyndham (1884–1957): British novelist, painter, and essayist. He and EP launched Vorticism in the short-lived periodical *Blast* in 1914. Lewis published *Hitler*, a very sympathetic view of the rising Nazi party, in 1931, and a sort of retraction, *The Hitler Cult*, in 1939. EP read the latter work and wrote to Lewis defending Hitler.

Linati, Carlo (1878–1949): Italian lawyer and literary critic who corresponded briefly with EP.

Linder, Tom: Georgia agriculture commissioner accused in 1951 of lobbying in Congress for higher farm prices without having registered as a lobbyist.

Lippmann, Walter (1889–1974): Well-known American columnist from World War II until the sixties. He is the author of *Essays in the Public Philosophy*.

Littlefield, Lester: Friend of Marianne Moore and New York bibliophile who sent EP books he could not get from Washington libraries.

Lloyd, Ernest Sampson (d. 1945): Chair of the U.S. War Agricultural Committee, president of Madras Corporation (1906–10), revenue secretary, financial secretary, and acting chief secretary (1923).

Londres, Albert (d. 1932): Author of sociological studies, among them *A Very Naked People, Terror in the Balkans*, and *The Road to Buenos Aires*, a book on white slavery.

Longanesi, Leo: Editor, writer, and painter. He was an admirer of Mussolini and coined the phrase "Mussolini is always right." Following World War

II he founded the Longanesi publishing house and in 1950, along with In-
dro Montanelli, founded the right-wing journal *Il Borghese.*

Longworth, Alice Roosevelt (1884–1980): Daughter of Theodore Roosevelt
and wife of Congressman Nicholas Longworth. A famous Washington political hostess, she was a regular visitor at St. Elizabeths.

Loyd, Samuel Jones (1796–1883): English banker and economist of Welsh
extraction. He succeeded his father, Lewis Loyd, as partner in the London
and Westminster Bank. From 1833 he was a strong advocate of the gold
standard, that is, a fixed ratio between the government's gold reserves and
the issuing of paper money. The Bank Act of 1844 was largely based upon
his principles.

Loyola, St. Ignatius (1491–1556): Founder of the Jesuit order.

Lubac, Henri de (b. 1896): French author on religious subjects.

Lubin, David (1849–1918): Polish-born U.S. agricultural reformer and founder
of the International Institute of Agriculture (IIA) in Rome in 1906. ORA
was his translator from 1904 until his death on 31 December 1918 and
wrote his biography. He was praised by H. G. Wells and corresponded with
Wells and Max Nordau. That he was Jewish colored EP's attitude toward
him.

Luce, Clare Boothe (1903–87): American writer, congresswoman, and wife of
Henry Robinson Luce, the editor-publisher of *Time, Life,* and *Fortune*
magazines. She served as U.S. ambassador to Italy, 1953–56.

Luce, Henry Robinson (1898–1967): Publisher of *Time, Life,* and *Fortune*
magazines.

Luchini, Alberto: Helped EP with translating *The Great Digest* of Confucius
into Italian.

Luzzatti, Luigi (1841–1927): During his fifty years of parliamentary life he
served as prime minister (1910–11) and five times as minister of the treasury.

Lyell, Charles (1767–1869): British botanist, Dante scholar, and father of the
geologist Sir Charles Lyell, who opposed the catastrophic theory of geologic
change.

Malatesta, Errico (1853–1932): Influential Anarchist, journalist, and revolutionary who proposed "propaganda by the deed," or insurrection, as the
most efficacious political action. Exiled from Italy after the insurrection
at Benevento in 1877, he lived in London until 1919.

Malù: ORA's adopted granddaughter who had been diagnosed with tuberculosis and treated by Eugenio Morelli. EP sent money and medical advice
as well as a wedding gift when Malù married Aldo Mingoli in 1954.

Manin, Daniele (1804–57): Leader of the Venetian Revolution of 1848. The
Austrian-backed Venetian provisional government was ousted and the
Republic of St. Mark was proclaimed with Manin as president. He was also
a prominent supporter of Cavour's diplomacy during the 1850s.

Manion, Clarence (b. 1896): Professor of constitutional law, dean of the College of Law at Notre Dame, and founder and builder of the Natural Law
Institute. He received the Freedom Award in 1950. In *The Key to Peace* he

argues that ownership of property is a duty and an obligation rather than a right and that there should be no limit to property accumulation.

Manning, Ernest Charles (b. 1908): Social Credit premier of Alberta (1943–68).

Maranini, Giuseppe: Social science and political science professor and author of *Istoria del potere in Italia, 1848–1967.*

Marin, John (1870–1953): American artist who worked mostly in watercolors.

Marinetti, Emilio Filippo Tommaso (1876–1944): Founder of Futurism. An early Fascist, he joined the party in 1919 and was elected on the Fascist ticket in that year. Mussolini never liked Futurist aesthetics, nor Marinetti's defense of Jewish painters. Nonetheless, Marinetti stuck with Mussolini and the Salò Republic. He was given a state funeral on his death in 1944. EP eulogizes him in canto 73.

Martinelli, Sheri (d. 1997): Painter and intimate of EP's at St. Elizabeths beginning in 1951. EP tried to get some notice for her work and wrote a preface for her *La Martinell.* Like other EP protégés, she spent quite of bit of time in the old house of Ivan Stancioff and his wife in Urbana, near Washington. ORA saw some of her paintings at Brunnenburg and was "much struck by their mystic intensity," which reminded her "of the spirit that inspires many of D.G.R.'s heads" (25 Sept. 1955).

Martins, Jose V. de Piña: Professor of Portuguese at Rome University whose pen name was Duarte de Montalegne. On 30 March 1954 the Vatican Radio aired his appeal for the release of EP. The appeal was later broadcasted by Italian radio and published under the title *Prometheus Bound.*

Mathews, Elkin (1851–1921): London publisher of EP's *A Quinzaine for This Yule, Personae, Exultations, Canzoni,* and *Lustra.* Shortly after EP arrived in London he persuaded Mathews to publish William Michael Rossetti's *Dante and His Convito.*

Mazzini, Giuseppe (1805–72): Leader of the Italian national struggle for the unification of Italy under a republican form of government.

McCormick, Robert Rutherford (1880–1955): Editor and publisher of the *Chicago Tribune.* He was a critic of Roosevelt's New Deal and Fair Deal economic policies.

Mead, G. R. S. (1863–1933): Secretary to Madame Blavatsky, president of the Theosophical Society from 1881 until her death in 1891. Mead broke with Theosophy over a homosexual scandal involving Charles Leadbeater in 1908. He founded in that year the Quest Society with those Theosophists who had followed him. This society organized lectures at the Kensington Town Hall. EP, Wyndham Lewis, and T. E. Hulme participated in these lectures in 1912. Olivia Shakespear and her daughter, Dorothy (the future Dorothy Pound), were regular attenders. EP met Mead in 1911 and published "Psychology and Troubadours" in Mead's journal, *The Quest,* the following year.

Mencius or **Meng-tzu** (372–289 B.C.): Chinese philosopher and follower of Confucius and author of the second of the Confucian classics, the *Book of Mencius.*

Meridiano di Roma: Fascist weekly founded in 1936 that ceased publication following Mussolini's downfall in 1943. Among its regular contributors were EP, Giovanni Papini, Emilio Marinetti, G. Ansaldo, C. Pavolini, and Giovanni Gentile. It was edited by Cornelio di Marzio. Many of EP's articles in *Meridiano* were collected in *Orientamenti*, which was subsequently suppressed. One of the few surviving copies was seized, in May of 1945, by agents of the Federal Bureau of Investigation and translated.

Merlino, Francesco Salverio (1856–1930): He began as an Anarchist but later moved toward more Socialist ideals.

Metternich, Klemens Wenzel Nepomuk Lothar von (1773–1859): Austrian statesman and minister of foreign affairs (1809–48). He was instrumental in forming an alliance against Napoleon I and was a leading figure in European politics, hosting the Congress of Vienna (1814–15).

Meyer, Eugene (1875–1959): He held several government posts, was editor and publisher of the *Washington Post*, and was one-time governor of the Federal Reserve Board. EP quotes from Senator Smith Brookhart's speech against the nomination of Meyer to the Federal Reserve Board in canto 30.

Meynell, Alice (1847–1922): English essayist and poet.

Michel, Louise (1830–1905): French political agitator. Her Anarchist activities led to her deportment (1871) and, after an amnesty (1880), to repeated imprisonment. She lived in London between 1886 and 1895.

Mihailovitch, General Draza (1863–1946): Leader of the non-Communist resistance in Yugoslavia. He was executed by Tito in 1946.

Mille, Pierre (1865–1941): French civil servant and author of many novels and historical works on the colonial empire.

Mistral, Gabriela (1889–1957): South American poet and critic who organized a petition for EP's release.

Molotov, Viacheslav Mikhailovitch (1890–1986): Soviet premier and foreign commissar.

Mommsen, Theodor (1817–1903): German archaeologist, historian, and professor of ancient history at the University of Berlin from 1858. He published *The History of Rome* and other works related to Roman chronology, coins, and law. He was politically active and a member of Prussian House of Delegates.

Mond, Alfred Moritz (1868–1930): Chemical manufacturer and politician who fired editor Ford Madox Ford upon buying the *English Review* in 1910. EP mentions him in canto 104.

Monotti, Francesco: Italian journalist and regular contributor to *L'Indice*, a Genoese bimonthly literary journal edited by Gino Saviotti to which EP also contributed in 1930 and 1931.

Montale, Eugenio (1896–1981): Poet, editor, translator, critic, and journalist associated with the *ermetismo* movement. He won the Nobel Prize for Literature in 1975. He had been forced to resign as director of the Gabinetto Vieusseux Library in Florence in the late 1930s because he refused to join the Fascist party.

Montanari, Philippo: Father of Saturno Montanari. EP corresponded with him from 1941 to 1961.

Montanari, Saturno (1918–41): Italian poet. EP translated a few of his poems.

Moreau, Gustave (1826–98): French symbolist painter whose erotic renderings of mythological and religious subjects have often been viewed as decadent.

Morelli, Eugenio (1881–1960): Professor of medicine, from 1928 director of the Forlanini Institute, and from 1938 head of the Medical Association. An expert in pneumotherapy and author of numerous books on the subject. He treated Malù, ORA's adopted granddaughter, for tuberculosis.

Morgan, Frederick: One of the editors of the *Hudson Review*.

Morgenthau, Henry, Jr. (1891–1967): U.S. Secretary of the Treasury, 1934–45, under Roosevelt.

Moulton, Harold G. (1883–1965): American economist, member of the Brookings Institution, and author of, among many other works, *The Dynamic Economy: A Dialogue in Play Form*.

Movimento Sociale Italiano: Neo-Fascist political party of Italy founded 26 December 1946 by former Fascists who participated in the Salò Republic. It was first led by Giorgio Almirante and later by Augusto De Marsanich.

Mullins, Eustace (b. 1923): A member of EP's St. Elizabeths circle. He published the journal *Three Hands* for a while. He called himself director of the Aryan League of American. Mullins wrote *The Secrets of the Federal Reserve* and *This Difficult Individual Ezra Pound*.

Mundt, Karl E. (1900–1974): Republican representative from South Dakota and member of the House Un-American Activities Committee. As acting head of the committee, he interrogated Alger Hiss.

Munro, Ian Smeaton: Foreign correspondent for the *Evening Post* who was stationed in Rome during the 1930s and may also have worked for the *Manchester Post*. He is the author of *Beyond the Alps, Through Fascism to World Power: A History of the Revolution in Italy*, and *Youth of Yesteryear*. He is the "Monro" mentioned in canto 109.

Murray, William (Alfalfa Bill) (1860–1956): Agrarian who, like "Pitchfork Ben" Tillman, Tom Watson, and Ignatius Donnelly, advocated a more equitable distribution of cultivated land. He served as a Congressman and governor of Oklahoma. He ran unsuccessfully for president in 1936. In his sixties he wrote a number of strongly racist books, claiming among other things that Roosevelt was a Jew, that the New Deal was a program actually written by "Israel Mose Sieff," and that the United Nations was a Communist plot. He found "scientific" support for his racist ideas in the work of Luther Burbank and introduced EP to the works of the eccentric scholar Lawrence Austine Waddell.

Murray, William Henry (1869–1956): Democratic Representative from Oklahoma (1913–17), governor of Oklahoma (1931–35).

Mussato, Albertino (1261–1329): Author of *L'ecerenide*, a Latin tragedy based on the life of the tyrant Ezzelino translated into Italian by Manlio Torquato Dazzi. EP recurrently links him to Dante.

Neame, Alan (b. 1924): British writer and translator whose *The Adventures of Maud Noakes* was published by New Directions.

Nicoletti, Giaccino: Fascist intellectual attached to the Ministry of Popular Culture in the Salò Republic who avoided persecution following the war.

Niebuhr, Reinhold: American Protestant theologian and member of the American Committee for Cultural Freedom, which included such men of letters as Bertrand Russell and Stephen Spender. In 1955 the committee considered applying for EP's release but the attempt was blocked by Dr. Winfred Overholser, the superintendent of St. Elizabeths during EP's stay.

Niemojowski, Jerzy: Translator of EP's work into Polish.

Notari, Umberto (1878–1950): Italian journalist and author whose *I tre ladri* was published in English as *The Three Thieves*.

Orage, A. R. (1873–1934): Publisher of the *New Age* and founder of the *New English Weekly*. EP published at least one hundred articles in the *New Age*. It was in the *New Age's* office that EP met Major Clifford Hugh Douglas in 1917 and was converted to Social Credit economic theories. Orage quit the *New Age* in 1922 to join Gurdjieff at *Le Prieuré* in Fontainebleau and then served as his emissary in New York from 1923 until he returned to London and founded the *New English Weekly* in 1932. He immediately welcomed EP back into his pages.

Overholser, Willis A.: Author of *A Short Review and Analysis of the History of Money in the United States*, a book EP valued highly in the late 1930s.

Pacelli, Eugenio (1876–1958): Pope Pius XII, 1939–58.

Packard, Reynolds (1904?–1976): Director of the United Press bureau in Rome. EP knew Packard from his Paris years.

Pantaleoni, Maffeo (1857–1924): Economist, journalist, and political figure. He supported Mussolini's Fascist regime and in 1923 served in the Italian Senate.

Panter-Downes, Mollie (b. 1906): English author and journalist who contributed to the *New Yorker* from 1939.

Papen, Franz von (1879–1969): German politician and diplomat; he served as vice chancellor (1933–34).

Papini, Giovanni (1881–1956): EP's old acquaintance who was a regular contributor to *Meridiano di Roma* prior to 1943, a writer, and a Dante critic.

Paribeni, Roberto (1876–1956): Italian scholar of ancient Greece, Tuscany, and the Leopoldine Reforms with close connections to the Fascist movement.

Parker, Dorothy: Great wit in the 1920s whose stories appeared in the *New Yorker* and *Vanity Fair*. In the 1930s she went to Spain and wrote for the Communist weekly *New Masses* and was chair of the Joint Anti-Fascist Refugee Committee.

Paul the Deacon or **Paulus Diaconus** (ca. 725–800): Historian and author of *Historia Miscella* and *De Gestis Langobardorum*, collected in *History of the Langobards*, both sources for the opening of canto 96.

Pavolini, Paolo (1903–45): Regular contributor to *Meridiano di Roma*. He was minister of popular culture (1939–43) and Fascist party secretary in the Salò

Republic. He insisted on the execution of Count Galeazzo Ciano. He was subsequently captured and executed by partisans at Dongo.

Pearson, Drew (1897–1969): American radio personality and co-author (with Robert Allen) of "The Washington Merry Go-Round," a newspaper column that was read on NBC radio.

Pearson, Norman Holmes (1909–75): Literary scholar who taught at Yale during EP's St. Elizabeths years. He was on the editorial board of the Square $ Series.

Pegler, Westbrook (1894–1969): American conservative columnist whose syndicated column "As Pegler Sees It" appeared from 1944 to 1962. Beginning in 1933, he also wrote a syndicated column, "Fair Enough," for the *New York World-Telegram*. He received the 1941 Pulitzer Prize for exposing labor racketeering.

Pella, Giuseppe (1902–81): Prime minister of Italy in 1953 who was the chief architect of Italy's economic miracle through his participation in Alcide De Gasperi's governments.

Pellegrini-Giampetro, Domenico (b. 1899): Minister of Finance in Musssolini's Salò Republic.

Pellizzi, Camillo (b. 1896): Journalist, university professor, and literary critic. He worked in England for long periods of time between 1920 and 1939 and was professor of Italian literature and language at the University of London. He was a Fascist "new technocrat" and advocate of a moderate wing of fascism headed by Giuseppe Bottai. He was once the director of the Fascist Institute of Culture. Among his works are *Una rivoluzione mancata*. A friend of EP, he made it possible for EP to collaborate with the *British-Italian Bulletin* and supported his candidacy as a political commentator for Rome Radio.

Perkins, Frances (1882–1965): U.S. secretary of labor (1933–45) during Roosevelt's presidency and the first woman to be appointed to a Cabinet post.

Pétain, General Philippe (1856–1951): World War I hero and president of Vichy France. After the war, he was put on trial for treason and convicted. His death sentence was commuted to life imprisonment on the island of Yeu.

Phillips, William (1878–1968): Undersecretary of state, U.S. ambassador to Italy, Roosevelt's personal representative to India, and political advisor to Eisenhower.

Piccio, Ruggero Pier (1880–1965): World War I ace and air force general. A Fascist sympathizer, he served as chief of staff (1925–27) and as Italy's air attaché in Paris (1927–39), but broke with fascism in 1943.

Pickthall, Marmaduke (1875–1936): English Orientalist and novelist. He supported Turkey against the independence movements in Armenia and the Balkans in a series of articles in *New Age*, collected in *With the Turk in War-Time*. His first novel, *Saïd the Fisherman*, remains his best-known work.

Pigou, Arthur Cecil (1877–1959): Chair of political economy at Cambridge University (1908–44) best known for his contribution to welfare economics. John Maynard Keynes singled him out as the leading advocate of classical economics.

Pilsudski, Józef (1867–1935): President of the first Polish Republic established in 1918. Retiring in 1921, he engineered a coup in 1926 and became dictator for life.

Pini, Georgio (b. 1899): Mussolini's official biographer. A Fascist journalist who directed several papers and in 1936 became editor in chief of *Il Popolo d'Italia*, he was almost in daily contact with Mussolini. Following the July 1943 coup, Pini adhered to the Salò Republic and in October 1944 was made undersecretary of interior.

Pisani, Monsignor Piero: Archbishop of Constanza who was in fact living in Rome, where EP and Mary met him in the mid-1930s. He is mentioned in cantos 93 and 97.

Plethon, Gemisthus (1355–1450): Late Byzantine Neoplatonic philosopher. He attended the Council of Ferrara and Florence (1438) convened to heal the schism between Rome and Constantinople. EP thought Plethon responsible for transmitting the pagan wisdom of Greece to the West. He is mentioned in cantos 8, 23, 26, 83, and 98 and in *Guide to Kulchur*.

Plotinus (?203–62): Alexandrian philosopher. EP was familiar with his spiritual idealism as expressed in the *Enneads*, Plotinus' lectures as collected and published by his student Porphyry. Plotinus is mentioned several times in *The Cantos*, including canto 15/64, where he acts as EP's guide and leads him out of contemporary hell.

Pomeroy, Eugene C.: Vice president of the Defenders of the American Constitution.

Por, Odon (b. 1883): Hungarian-born Italian economist whose *Politica economico-sociale in Italia anno XVII–XVIII* EP translated as *Italy's Policy of Social Economics 1939–1940*. Por had been part of the *New Age* circle in London during World War I. His own *Guilds and Co-operatives in Italy* and *Fascism* were translated by E. Townshend and published in England in 1923. He held a minor position in the Fascist government.

Potocki, Count Jerzy (1889–1940): Poland's ambassador to the United States (1936–40). EP had lunch with him during his 1939 visit to the United States and told him not to trust Churchill.

Poujade, Pierre (b. 1920): Organized the stationers of the small town of Saint-Céré, France, in resistance to the tax inspectors on 22 July 1953. Poujade went on to become a significant force in French politics of the 1950s.

Pound, Dorothy (1886–1973): EP's wife, née Shakespear.

Pound, Omar (b. 1926): EP's son by Dorothy Shakespear-Pound, born in France.

Prezzolini, Giuseppe (1882–1982): Writer, organizer, and disseminator of Italian culture. He directed *La Voce* (1908–14); co-founded and directed, with Giovanni Papini, the cultural review *Leonardo* (1903); wrote for *Il Borghese*, *Il Tempo*, and *La Nazione*; and published some fifty-seven books and seventy anthologies. An early admirer of Mussolini, to whom he gave a national forum in *La Voce* in the pre-1914 years, he chose to spend the years between 1930 and 1950 in the United States as a professor of Italian literature at Columbia University and as director of its Casa Italiana.

Quisling, Vidkun (1887–1945): Founder of the Norwegian Nazi party in 1933 and prime minister of occupied Norway. His name has become synonymous with "traitor." Like Pétain, he was tried for treason, but unlike him, was executed.

Rachewiltz, Boris de (d. 1997): The husband of EP's daughter, Mary. He was Boris Baratti before he took a title.

Rachewiltz, Mary de (b. 1925): EP's daughter by Olga Rudge. She became Mary de Rachewiltz after her husband, Boris Baratti, took a title.

Rachewiltz, Siegfredo Walter Igor Raimondo de (b. 1947): EP's grandson and son of Mary de Rachewiltz and Boris de Rachewiltz.

Radek, Karl (1885–1939): Author of *The Development of Socialism from Science to Action.*

Rainer, Dachine: Anarchist who ran the Retort Press in Bearsville, N.Y., with Holley Cantine. Rainer corresponded with EP during the late 1940s and 1950s and circulated a petition for his release.

Raiola, Mary: Founder of the Vergilian Society in the United States, who offered her villa at Cumae for the society's activities. EP frequently refers to the possibility that he might be able to establish himself there as a resident guru. ORA spent Easter of 1954 at her villa.

Ramperti, Mario (1887–1964): Journalist, fiction writer, and essayist active in the Futurist movement. He was a Fascist and an ardent supporter of the Salò Republic. He was tried after World War II but was not sentenced.

Rampolla, Mariano, Marchese del Tindaro (1843–1913): Cardinal and secretary of the Vatican state under Pope Leo XIII (1887–1903). During the conclave of 1903 it appeared that Rampolla might be elected Pope, but Cardinal Puscyna of Austria-Hungary blocked his election.

Randolph, John (1773–1833): American statesman whom EP admired. He is mentioned in several cantos, especially 87–89.

Reich, Wilhelm (1897–1957): Austrian psychiatrist and biophysicist and Freud's associate at the Psychoanalytic Polyclinic in Vienna. He broke with Freud and later was forced to leave Nazi Germany. He resettled in New York in 1939 and in 1942 founded the Orgone Institute. His research into "orgone energy" was declared fraudulent by the Food and Drug Administration. In 1956 he was convicted of contempt of court and died in a federal penitentiary.

Renan, Ernest (1823–92): French religious historian. EP read his *Averroès et l'averroisme* very carefully during his work on *Guido Cavalcanti Rime* in the late 1920s.

Reuther, Walter (1907–70): American labor leader, president of the Congress of Industrial Organizations (1952–55), and president of the United Auto Workers (1946–70).

Rhodes, Cecil (1853–1902): Financier, politician, and empire builder of British South Africa. He is principally known for having bequeathed approximately three million pounds for the Rhodes scholarships at Oxford.

Ribbentrop, Joachim von (1893–1946): German politician who served as Hitler's foreign policy advisor, masterminded the German-British Naval Agreement of 18 June 1935, was the German ambassador to England (1936–38), and served as the German foreign minister (1938–45). He was sentenced to death at the Nuremberg Trials and executed on 16 October 1946.

Rock, Joseph Francis Charles (1884–1962): Botanist, explorer of China, and research fellow at the Harvard-Yenching Institute of Cambridge, Massachusetts. He was the author of many works on Na-khi culture from which EP borrowed for the later cantos.

Rocke, Cyril Edmund Alan Spencer (1876–1968): English colonel and author of *The Truth about Abyssinia* (1935), a pro-Fascist account of Italy's involvement in the Abyssinian war.

Rodd, Rennel (1858–1941): British author.

Rolland, Romain (1866–1944): French historian, critic of music, and novelist who exiled himself to Switzerland during World War I.

Rosamaria: ORA's adopted granddaughter.

Rossetti, Christina (1830–94): English poet and sister of William Michael Rossetti, ORA's father.

Rossetti, Dante Gabriel (1828–82): Pre-Raphaelite poet and painter, brother of William Michael Rossetti, ORA's father.

Rossetti, Gabriele (1783–1854): Father of Dante Gabriel Rossetti and William Michael Rossetti, ORA's father. He was a prominent Jacobin in Naples and was forced to flee in 1821. He received the protection of John Hookham Frere, English viceroy in Malta, and eventually secured a position teaching Italian at King's College in London. He married the daughter of Byron's Dr. Polidori and had four children, Maria, Dante Gabriel, William Michael, and Christina. In 1825 he published *La Divina Commedia di Dante con commento analitico,* in which he allegorized Dante's poem as an antipapal, or Ghibelline, allegory. Although his thesis was ill-received he devoted two subsequent works—*Il mistero dell' amor platonico del medio aevo* and *La Beatrice di Dante,* both suppressed—to defending and radicalizing it.

Rossetti, William Michael (1829–1919): ORA's father.

Rossoni, Edmondo (1884–1965): Leading exponent of Fascist syndicalism and head of the Fascist unions. He was also an author and editor of journals, including the influential *La Stripe.* He fought, unsuccessfully, to make his own theories of corporativism the basis of the Mussolini administration. Rossoni served as minister of agriculture (1935–39) and was a member of the Fascist Grand Council. In 1943 he voted for the Dino Grandi motion that unseated Mussolini. First sentenced to death in absentia, he was later sentenced to life imprisonment. He fled to Canada, where he remained until his sentence was revoked in 1947, when he returned to Italy.

Rothschild, Meyer Amschel (1743–1812): Founder of the Frankfurt-based financial house of Rothschild. He lent money to the British, Prussian, and Austrian allies opposed to Napoleon. His eldest son, Anselm Meyer (1773–1855) succeeded him at Frankfurt; Solomon (1774–1855) established a branch at Vienna; Nathan Meyer (1777–1836) one in London; Charles (1788–1855) one in Naples; and James (1792–1868) one in Paris.

Rudge, Olga (1895–1997): American violinist whom EP met in Paris in 1923. She became his mistress and bore him a daughter, Mary de Rachewiltz, in 1925. She was involved, with EP, in preserving Antonio Vivaldi's manuscripts.

Rush, Benjamin (1746–1813): Medical doctor and one of the signers of the Declaration of Independence.

Ruspoli, Father Francesco: EP acquaintance mentioned in several of his 1952 letters but otherwise unidentified.

Russell, Peter (b. 1921): Poet, translator, editor, and EP disciple. As owner of Pound Press in England, 1951–56, he published *Nine,* a little Poundian magazine, as well as EP's Money Pamphlets.

Santayana, George (1863–1952): Spanish-born American philosopher and writer who studied philosophy at Harvard with William James and Josiah Royce and taught there as well. One of his most celebrated students was T. S. Eliot. He resigned his Harvard post and moved to England in 1912. After World War I he settled in Italy, eventually residing in a Roman Catholic nursing home run by the Blue Sisters.

Sapori, Armando (b. 1891): Italian economics professor and senator (1948–53). He is the author of *Studi di storia economica.*

Saumaise, Claude de (1588–1653): French classical scholar. EP mentions him in canto 87.

Saviotti, Gino: Editor of the Italian journal *L'Indice* for which EP wrote in 1930–31.

Scarfoglio, Carlo (1887–1969): Anti-Fascist journalist, translator, and author of *Il mezzogiorono e l'unita d'Italia* and *"L'Antologia classica cinese."* He defended EP's Radio Rome activities.

Scelba, Mario: Interior minister in the Christian Democratic government of Alcide De Gasperi.

Schacht, Hjalmar Horace Greeley (1877–1970): President of the Reichsbank (1929–39) and minister of economics in Hitler's government (1934–37). He was imprisoned in 1944 after he was implicated in the July bomb plot. Acquitted of war crimes at Nuremberg, he resumed his career as an international banker.

Scheiwiller, Vanni (b. 1934): Italian publisher of books by and about EP. He is the son of Giovanni Scheiwiller, the publisher of EP's *Profile.*

Serao, Matilde (1857–1927): Italian author of *Fantasia, Il ventre di Napoli,* and other books. She was an anti-Fascist.

Sharrock, Roger: British literary scholar who started corresponding with EP in 1955.

Siefert, George Joseph, Jr.: Professor at the Catholic University of America in Washington. His University of Pennsylvania dissertation appeared as "Meter and Case in the Latin Elegiac Pentameter."

Sieff, Baron Israel Moses (1889–1972): Businessman and secretary to Chaim Weizmann of the Zionist Commission. Sieff joined his brother-in-law, Simon Marks, as vice chairman and joint managing director of Marks and Spencer in 1926. He was active in the Political and Economic Planning discussion group founded to collate current knowledge in economic, industrial, and social fields for the benefit of the government and the business world. His wife, Rebecca Dodo Marks (1891–1966), was a co-founder of the Women's International Zionist Organization (president until 1963), a founder of the World Jewish Congress, and instrumental in the establishment of the Daniel Sieff Institute at Rehovoth, which became the nucleus of the Weizmann Institute of Science.

Silone, Ignazio (1900–1978): Italian journalist, political activist, and one of the major novelists of his time. Though initially a Communist, he turned against communism after converting to socialism in 1930. In 1949 he helped found the Socialist Unified party.

Simpson, Dallam (b. 1926): Founder and first editor of *Four Pages,* a little magazine published in Galveston, Texas, that ran for fifteen issues from 1948 to 1951. EP contributed frequently, but usually anonymously, to the magazine. In the 1950s Simpson lived in Washington, D.C., and was a regular visitor of EP at St. Elizabeths.

Smith, William Brooke (d. 1908): EP knew him when both were undergraduates at the University of Pennsylvania. Smith introduced EP to the London aestheticism of the 1890s. EP dedicated *A Lume Spento* to him.

Soddy, Frederick (1877–1956): English chemist who graduated from Oxford and became lecturer in radioactivity at Glasgow University in 1904. In 1914 he became professor of chemistry at Aberdeen University and in 1919 professor of inorganic and physical chemistry at Oxford. He won the Nobel Prize for Chemistry in 1921 for his experiments in radioactivity. This work led to his formulation of the theory of isotopes. In addition to scientific publications, he also wrote works advocating economic change, such as *Wealth, Virtual Wealth, and Debt.*

Soldato, Giuseppe: One of the four Italian writers who, along with EP, was signatory to two "Scrittori del Tigullio" manifestos that appeared in *Il popolo di Alessandria,* 27 Feb. 1944, and 23 March 1945.

Spampanato, Bruno: Italian journalist, politician, and author of *L'ultimo Mussolini (Contromemoriale).*

Sparkman, Senator John: Member of a group formed at Dean Acheson's instigation whose purpose was to limit the damage McCarthy was doing by investigating and refuting allegations of Communist affiliations.

Spivak, Lawrence Edmund (b. 1900): Editor and publisher of the *American Mercury* (1939–50) and radio and television producer and panalist. He was cofounder, permanent member of the panel, and producer of *Meet the Press* (founded in 1945), a Sunday evening news program of the National Broadcasting Company with an estimated audience of 10 million in the mid-1950s.

Square $ Series: Publication venture run by Thomas David Horton and John Kasper (until the latter's arrest for inflammatory attacks on African Americans and Jews in 1956 and 1957). The series included some of EP's works and translations and works by many of his favorite authors, such as Alexander Del Mar and Thomas Hart Benton.

Stancioff, Anna (1861–1955): American-born wife of Dr. Dimitri Stancioff, a Bulgarian politician and diplomat who served as minister in London (1920–25). She escaped from Bulgaria in 1945 on the day the Russian invasion began. The Stancioffs, who were among EP's prewar friends, settled in Urbana, near Washington. EP occasionally sent his acolytes to their home.

Starace, Achille (1889–1945): Fascist leader and longtime secretary of the Partito Nazionale Fascista. A Mussolini loyalist, he was responsible for incorporating regimentation and military symbolism, such as the Fascist salute and the goose step for party marches, into daily life. He was captured by partisans in 1945 and executed.

Steed, Henry Wickham (1871–1956): British historian, journalist, and head of the foreign department (1914–19) and editor of the *London Times* (1919–22). He was in charge of Allied propaganda during World War I and throughout World War II advised British statesmen on problems of Austrian diplomacy. After leaving the *London Times* in 1922 he lectured widely abroad, attended regularly the Assemblies of the League of Nations, and was lecturer at King's College in London on central European history (1925–38). From 1937 to 1947 he was one of the chief broadcasters on world affairs for the BBC overseas service.

Steffens, Lincoln (1886–1939): Influential journalist best known for his eyewitness reports on the Russian Revolution. A Christian Anarchist and "intellectual Communist," he was a hero of the popular front against fascism. Among his protégés were Walter Lippmann and John Reed. EP and Steffens met in London, and EP introduced him to writers and artists. EP found his grass-roots radicalism attractive. He appears in *The Pisan Cantos*.

Stevenson, Adlai Ewing (1900–1965): Democratic nominee for president of the United States in 1952 and 1956. Eisenhower defeated him both times.

Stilwell, General Joseph Warren (1883–1946): Commander of U.S. forces in the China-India-Burma Theater of Operations for more than two years during World War II and an important figure in Sino-American relations at the time.

Stock, Noel: Australian admirer and EP scholar. In 1946 he founded and edited the Poundian little magazine *Edge* (1956–57), which had a run of eight issues. The magazine included many of EP's pieces (some anonymously) as well as works he recommended, including ORA's "Pages of Memoir" and "The Most Unforgettable Chracter I've Known."

Sturzo, Father Luigi (1871–1959): Sicilian Catholic priest and founder of the Partito Popolare Italiano in 1920. His party was a rival of Mussolini's Fascist party, and Sturzo refused to ally with the Fascists when they achieved power. He opposed the Concordat, which granted the Vatican political independence, thus earning for himself the Vatican's enmity. He was forced into exile in 1924. He spent the next nine years in London, then moved to the United States. He returned to Italy in 1946 to found the Democrazio Cristiana Partito and in 1952 he became a senator. He is the author of several books, including *Church and State* and *Italy and the Coming World*.

Sulzberger, Cyrus Leo, II (b. 1912): Chief foreign correspondent, beginning in 1944, of the *New York Times*. In 1940 and afterwards, he angered Italian leaders with his reports of Italian troop movements in Albania. He also wrote a number of books on international affairs.

Suvich, Fulvio (b. 1887): Italian statesman who participated in the negotiations that led to the Franco-Italian Rome Agreements (1935) which helped Mussolini in Ethiopia. He also served as ambassador to Washington. He is mentioned in canto 94.

Swabey, Henry S. (d. 1996): British Anglican clergyman, Social Crediter, friend and EP acolyte, founder of *Voice*. Swabey also translated Tadeusz Zielinsky's *La Sibylle* for Noel Stock's *Edge*.

Swedenborg, Emanuel (1688–1772): Swedish scientist and mystic often described as the "scientist who became visionary." After completing academic studies at the University of Uppsala, Swedenborg traveled abroad to study science and its technical applications. He returned to Sweden in 1715 and became assessor in the Royal College of Mines (1715–47). He showed a flair for scientific invention. After a profound religious crisis in 1743–44, he abandoned his scientific work and commenced to teach the true meaning of the scriptures. His most influential idea was the doctrine of correspondences, adopted by Baudelaire and the Symbolist movement. EP was introduced to Swedenborg in the United States in 1905 or 1906, studied Swedenborg's writings during his stay with Yeats at Stone Cottage in 1913–14, and again returned to him in the 1950s.

Tagore, Rabindrinath (1861–1941): Bengali poet, dramatist, and mystic who won the Nobel Prize for Literature in 1913. His work was championed in the early 1910s by Yeats and EP.

Tansill, Charles Callan (1890–1964): Professor of American history at the Catholic University of America (1918–39) and later at Georgetown University. He is the author of several books on history and diplomatic relations, including *Back Door to War*, in which he argues that Roosevelt conspired to bring the United States into the war on the British side.

Tasca, Angelo (1892–1960): Italian Socialist leader, historian, and founder and leader of the Italian Communist party, 1921–29. He was expelled from the party by Stalin for rightist deviations. He became a French citizen in 1936 and in 1940 collaborated with Vichy while simultaneously working for the Belgian and British Resistance. His best-known work is *The Rise of Italian Fascism*.

Tate, Allen (1899–1979): American essayist, teacher, and poet.

Taylor, Henry C.: American friend of ORA's from her days with David Lubin.

Taylor, Henry Junior (b. 1902): Industrialist, journalist, U.S. ambassador to Switzerland (1957–61), delegate to various international conferences, economist, and writer.

Thirwell, John Connop (1904–71): English professor at the City College of New York who published many articles on William Carlos Williams and edited *The Selected Letters of William Carlos Williams*. He visited EP at St. Elizabeths in 1956.

Thompson, Dorothy (1893–1961): American journalist and political commentator. She was married to Sinclair Lewis from 1928 to 1942.

Tinkham, George Holden (1870–1956): Republican isolationist Congressman from Massachusetts (1915–43). EP met him in Italy and visited him during his 1939 visit to the United States.

Troubetzkoi, Princess Amélie (1864–1945): American writer, born Amelie Rives in Richmond, Virginia. EP knew her in London. EP heard her speak on the American Hour on Rome Radio. Troubetzkoi introduced EP's daughter, Mary, to her husband, Boris de Rachewiltz. She appears in canto 74.

Tweddell, Francis I. (1863–1939): Indian-born British doctor who lived in the United States (1905–39). His cure for tuberculosis included breathing powdered gypsum. EP corresponded with him in 1937 and 1938.

Uberti, Riccardo M. degli: Son of Ubaldo degli Uberti and author of works about Pound.

Uberti, Ubaldo degli (1881–1945): Chief naval press officer in Rome who met and befriended EP in 1934. He translated some EP pieces and wrote letters in support of EP's work. He succeeded Andea Pais as editor of *La marina republicana* (in which EP's canto 72 first appeared) in 1945.

Ungaro, Andriano: Minculpop official described by EP as "an Italian liberal who had the guts to initial my broadcasts" (Carpenter 583).

Ungaro, Filippo: Journalist who wrote for *Il Secolo* and a member of parliament during the Fascist era. He is mentioned in canto 97.

Upward, Allen (1863–1926): English barrister, amateur sinologist and religious historian, novelist, playwright, poet (one of his poems was included by EP in *Des Imagistes*), and world traveler. EP read, reviewed, and was influenced by Upward's *The New Word* and *The Divine Mystery*. Upward moved in the same London Theosophical circles as G. R. S. Mead, A. R. Orage, and EP.

Valli, Luigi (1878–1931): Author of *Il linguaggio segreto di Dante e dei "fedeli d'amore."* EP responded to the first volume of this work in an addendum in "Cavalcanti" (*Literary Essays* 149–200) and in *Guide to Kulchur* (221, 294–95). EP was distressed that Valli argued that the "secret" of Dante's poetry was that he was an ultra-orthodox Catholic.

Vance, Fred Nelson (b. 1880): Indiana artist EP met in Crawfordsville in 1907. Vance had studied painting in Chicago, Paris, and Rome and lived, painted, and worked in his hometown during EP's stint at Wabash College.

Vanderpyl, Fritz-René (b. 1876?): Dutch avant-garde writer and art critic who lived in Paris and knew both EP and James Joyce.

Varè, Daniele (1880–1956): Italian author, diplomat, and traveler. Author of *The Two Imposters*. Varè died while *Ghosts of the Rialto* was in press. He complains in that work of EP's absence from a 1954 Venice poetry conference because "the American government . . . kept their most famous contemporary poet shut up in a lunatic asylum" (143). Varè was broadcasting over Rome Radio along with EP during the war as is clear from ORA's letter of 26 August 1943: "Varè, with whom I had a long talk yesterday, tells me he is now speaking constantly on the radio and doing his best to show up to the anglo-american public the monstrosities they are guilty of here."

Veronese, Paolo (1528–88): Italian painter of the Venetian school whose real name was Paolo Caliari.

Vicari, Giambattista: Italian journalist and literary critic, associated with *La gazzetta del popolo* and *Il Cortile.*

Viereck, Peter Robert Edwin (b. 1916): American poet and political writer. His father, Sylvester Viereck, attracted notoriety during both world wars for his pro-German views. A leading spokesman for the "New Conservatism," Peter did not share his father's views. His first book, *Metapolitics,* is an uncompromising indictment of Nazism. He was awarded the Pulitzer Prize for his 1948 collection of poetry, *Terror and Decorum.* In 1945 he became instructor in the U.S. Army University at Florence, and in 1955 he was apppointed to the chair in American poetry and civilization at Florence.

Villari, Luigi (1876–1959): Italian author, diplomat, and member of the Fascist bureaucracy. He served as a cavalry officer in World War I and then joined the staff of the League of Nations at Geneva. Among his books is *Italian Foreign Policy under Mussolini,* in which he defended Mussolini. EP and Villari met in Italy in the 1930s and they remained friends until Villari's death. Villari was the official who rejected the plan EP proposed in 1939 for a propaganda series aimed at American readers.

Voorhis, H. J.: Politician EP met with to discuss monetary reform during his 1939 trip to the United States.

Waddell, Colonel Lawrence Austine (1854–1938): Scottish linguist, archeologist, and professor of Tibetan at University College in London. EP admired his *Egyptian Civilization: Its Sumerian Origin* and *Real Chronology and Sumerian Origin of Egyptian Hieroglyphs* despite their questionable scholarship.

Waley, Arthur (1889–1966): British orientalist and translator of Chinese poetry and Japanese Noh plays.

Wallace, Henry Agard (1888–1965): Agriculturalist who served as Roosevelt's vice president (1941–44) and secretary of commerce (1945–46). Roosevelt was too busy to see EP during his 1939 trip to Washington, D.C., and thus EP ended up seeing Wallace, at that time secretary of agriculture (1933–40). EP was given an introduction to Wallace by Paul de Kruif.

Warren, George F. (1874–1938): Professor of agricultural economics and farm management at Cornell University. A member of Roosevelt's "Brain Trust," he proposed a "commodity," or "rubber dollar," whose value would fluctuate with the level of economic activity instead of being fixed to a gold standard.

Watson, Tom (1856–1922): Populist leader and journalist from Georgia and "agrarian avenger" who ran *Watson's Jeffersonian Magazine.* He served as a Democrat in the House of Representatives, was a Populist candidate for vice president (1896) and president (1904), and a Senator. In 1899 he retired from politics and wrote *The Story of France*. He opposed American intervention in World War I. He admired Alfafa Bill Murray and shared his admiration for Napoleon.

Watts-Dunton, Walter Theodore (1832–1914): English poet who nursed Algernon Charles Swinburne and encouraged him to continue writing.

White, Andrew Dickson (1832–1918): American professor, New York senator, and first president of Cornell University (1868–85). He and the millionaire philanthropist Ezra Cornell, also a state senator, saw a bill founding Cornell University through the state legislature. Cornell was controversial for its programs, which were accused of neglecting classical instruction in favor of technical and scientific instruction. A selection of his two-volume autobiography was published as *Selected Chapters from the Autobiography of Andrew D. White*.

White, Harry Dexter (1892–1948): Unofficial assistant secretary of Henry Morgenthau, U.S. treasurer, and executive director of the International Monetary Fund (1946). He was accused in 1948 of spying for the Soviet Union. One of EP's more obscure villains, he is mentioned in canto 85. For EP he symbolized Jewish infiltration of the U.S. government.

Wilkie, Wendell Lewis (1892–1944): Republican nominee for president in 1940.

Wilson, Charles Erwin (1890–1961): Industrialist, president of General Motors (1941–53), and U.S. secretary of defense (1953–57).

Wilson, Robert McNair (1882–1963): British writer and correspondent for the *London Times* and one of EP's favorite authors on money and banking. Among his books are *Monarchy or Money Power* and *Promise to Pay*, which EP reviewed for the Paris edition of the *Chicago Tribune*. Wilson is mentioned in cantos 101 and 104.

Woodward, William E. (1874–1950): American journalist and historian who was on several advisory boards during Roosevelt's presidency. EP read his *A New American History* and found much in it to admire. They exchanged several letters between January 1933 and May 1936.

Yankowski, Stanislas V.: Oxford-educated Polish academic who met EP after going to the United States from Australia. EP convinced him to translate Richard of St. Victor.

Zielinski, Tadeusz (1859–1944): Polish professor of Greek at the University of Warsaw and prolific writer of almost eight hundred scholarly works. EP read and particularly admired his *La Sibylle: Trois essais sur la religion antique et le christianisme*, a book in comparative mythology whose major thesis, dear to EP, is that pure Christianity has its roots in the pagan rather than bibilical tradition.

Zukofsky, Louis (1904–78): American poet and frequent visitor at St. Elizabeths. He is the founder of Objectivist poetry, exemplified by *A*, his long autobiographical poem that he began in 1928.

Bibliography

Works by Ezra Pound

Fenollosa, Ernest, and Ezra Pound. *Introduzione ai Nô, con un dramma in un atto di Motokiyo: Kagekiyo.* Trans. Mary de Rachewiltz. Milan: All'insegna del pesce d'oro, 1954.

Pound, Ezra. *ABC of Reading.* New Haven, Conn.: Yale University Press, 1934. New York: New Directions, 1960.

———. "A che serve il danaro?" Trans. Olivia Rossetti Agresti. *Meridiano di Roma* 6.30 (27 July 1941): 1, 6–7.

———. *A Lume Spento.* Venice: A. Antonioni, 1908.

———. "Anonymous Contributions to *Strike.*" Ed. David Gordon. *Paideuma* 3.3 (1974): 389–400.

———. "Arachidi." *Meridiano di Roma* 6.40 (5 Oct. 1941): 1.

———. ... *Los Cantares de Pisa* ... Trans. José Vásquez Amaral. Mexico: Imprenta Universitaria, 1956.

———. "Canto C." *Yale Literary Magazine* 126.5 (Dec. 1958): 45–50.

———. "Canto IV." Trans. P. Savanio and Denise Alexander. *Tel Quel* 11 (Autumn 1926): 21–24.

———. "Canto 98." *L'illustrazione Italiana* (Milan) 85.9 (Sept. 1958): 34–39.

———. "Canto 99." *Virginia Quarterly Review* 34.3 (Summer 1958): 339–54.

———. *The Cantos of Ezra Pound.* New York: New Directions, 1972.

———. "Canto XX." Trans. Augusto de Campos, Haroldo de Campos, and Décio Pignatari. *Jornal do Brasil* Suplemento Dominical (28 Apr. 1957): 1.

———. *Canzoni.* London: Elkin Mathews, 1911.

———. *Carta da visita.* Rome: Edizioni di Lettere D'Oggi (Giambattista Vicari), 1942. Published in English as *A Visiting Card.* Money Pamphlets by £, No. 4. Trans. John Drummond. London: Peter Russell, 1952.

———. *The Classic Anthology Defined by Confucius.* Cambridge, Mass.: Harvard University Press, 1954.

———. *Collected Early Poems of Ezra Pound.* Ed. Michael John King. New York: New Directions, 1976.

———. *Confucian Analects*. New York: Square $ Series, 1951.

———. *Confucio Ta S'eu Dai Gaku Studio Integrale*. Rapallo: Scuola Tipografica Orfanotrofio Emiliani, 1942.

———. *Confucius: The Unwobbling Pivot and the Great Digest*. Norfolk, Conn: New Directions, 1947. London: Peter Owen, 1968.

———. *Confucius: The Unwobbling Pivot and the Great Digest*. Bombay, Calcutta, Madras: Orient Longmans, 1949.

———. *"Dear Uncle George": The Correspondence between Ezra Pound and Congressman Tinkham of Massachusetts*. Ed. Philip J. Burns. Orono, Maine: National Poetry Foundation, 1996.

———. *DK: Some Letters of Ezra Pound*. Ed. Louis Dudek. Montreal: DC Books, 1974.

———. *Eleven New Cantos: XXXI–XLI*. New York: Farrar and Rinehart, 1934.

———. *EP to Lu: Nine Letters Written to Louis Untermeyer by Ezra Pound*. Ed. J. A. Robbins. Bloomington: Indiana University Press, 1963.

———. *Exultations*. London: Elkin Mathews, 1909.

———. *Ezra Pound: Lettere 1907–58*. Milan: Feltrinell Editore Milano, 1980.

———. *Ezra Pound: Letters to Ibbotson, 1935–1952*. Ed. Vittoria I. Mondolfo and Margaret Hurley. Orono, Maine: National Poetry Foundation, 1979.

———. *Ezra Pound: Selected Poems*. London: Faber and Gwyer, 1928. London: Faber and Faber, 1968.

———. *Ezra Pound and James Laughlin: Selected Letters*. Ed. David M. Gordon. New York: Norton, 1994.

———. *Ezra Pound and Margaret Cravens: A Tragic Friendship, 1910–1912*. Ed. Omar Pound and Robert Spoo. Durham: Duke University Press, 1988.

———. *Ezra Pound and Senator Bronson Cutting*. Ed. E. P. Walkiewicz and Hugh Witemeyer. Albuquerque: University of New Mexico Press, 1995.

———. *Ezra Pound/Dorothy Shakespear, Their Letters: 1909–1914*. Ed. Omar Pound and A. Walton Litz. New York: New Directions, 1986.

———. *Ezra Pound/Japan: Letters and Essays*. Ed. Sanehide Kodama. Redding Ridge, Conn.: Black Swan Books, 1987.

———. *Ezra Pound/John Theobald Letters*. Ed. Donald Pearce and Herbert Schneidau. Redding Ridge, Conn.: Black Swan Books, 1984.

———. "Ezra Pound on Gold, War, and National Money." *Capitol Daily* 89 (9 May 1939): 1, 4–5.

———. *"Ezra Pound Speaking": Radio Speeches of World War II*. Ed. Leonard W. Doob. Westport, Conn.: Greenwood, 1978.

———. *Ezra Pound's Poetry and Prose: Contributions to Periodicals*. Ed. Lea Baechler, A. Walton Litz, and James Longenbach. 11 vols. New York: Garland, 1991.

———. "Ezra's Easy Economics." *Chicago Tribune*. Paris edition. 2 Apr. 1934. 2.

———. *The Fifth Decad of Cantos*. London: Faber and Faber, 1937.

———. *Gaudier-Brzeska: A Memoir*. London: John Lane, 1916. New York: New Directions, 1970.

———. *Gold and Labour*. Trans. John Drummond. London: Peter Russell, 1952.

——. *Guide to Kulchur*. London: Faber and Faber, 1938. New York: New Directions, 1970.

——. *Guido Cavalcanti Rime*. Genoa: Edizione Rappezzata, 1932.

——. "Hunger Fighters." Review of Paul de Kruif's *Hunger Fighters*. *New English Weekly* 4.19 (22 Feb. 1934): 451–52.

——. *Imaginary Letters*. Paris: Black Sun Press, 1930.

——. *Des Imagistes: Anthology*. New York: Albert and Charles Boni, 1914.

——. *Impact: Essays on Ignorance and the Decline of American Civilization*. Ed. Noel Stock. Chicago: Henry Regnery, 1960.

——. *Instigations of Ezra Pound: Together with an Essay on the Chinese Written Character by Ernest Fenollosa*. New York: Boni and Liveright, 1920.

——. "Jean Barral with Us." *New English Weekly* 8.8 (5 Dec. 1935): 146–47.

——. *Jefferson and/or Mussolini*. London: Nott, 1935. New York: Liveright, 1970.

——. . . . *Kabita (. . . "Selected Poems")*. Trans. Gyanindra Verma. Cuttack, Orissa, India: Prafulla Chandra Das, 1958.

——. *Katai, Metaphrase apo to Aggliko*. Trans. Zesimos Lorenzatos. Athens: Typographia S. M. Tarousopoulou, 1950.

——. *The Letters of Ezra Pound to Alice Corbin Henderson*. Ed. Ira B. Nadel. Austin: University of Texas Press, 1993.

——. "Letters to Woodward." *Paideuma* 15.1 (1986): 105–20.

——. *Literary Essays of Ezra Pound*. London: Faber and Faber, 1954. Ed. T. S. Eliot. New York: New Directions, 1972.

——. *The Little Review: The Letters of Ezra Pound to Margaret Anderson*. Ed. Thomas L. Scott and Melvin J. Friedman. New York: New Directions, 1988.

——. *Lustra*. London: Elkin Mathews, 1916.

——. *Make It New*. London: Faber and Faber, 1934.

——. *"Noh" or Accomplishment*. London: Macmillan, 1916.

——. *Orientamenti*. Venice: Casa Editrice Delle Edizion Popolari, 1944.

——. "Oro e lavoro." *Il Secolo XIX* (Genoa) (6 Apr. 1944): 1.

——. *Oro e lavoro*. Rapallo: Tip. Moderna (Canessa), 1944. Published in English as *Gold and Labour*. Money Pamphlets by £, No. 2. Trans. John Drummond. London: Peter Russell, 1952.

——. *Patria Mia*. Chicago: Ralph Fletcher Seymour, 1950.

——. *Pavannes and Divisions*. New York: Alfred A. Knopf, 1918. New York: New Directions, 1958.

——. *Personae*. London: Elkin Mathews, 1909.

——. *Die Pisaner Gesänge*. Trans. Eva Hesse. Zurich: Verlag der Arche, 1956.

——. "The Poems of Cavalcanti." *Times Literary Supplement* (5 Dec. 1912): 562.

——. *Polite Essays*. London: Faber and Faber, 1937. Norfolk, Conn.: New Directions, 1940.

——. "Possibilities of Civilization: What the Small Town Can Do." *Delphian Quarterly* 19.3 (July 1936): 105.

———. *Pound/Cummings: The Correspondence of Ezra Pound and E. E. Cummings.* Ed. Barry Ahearn. Ann Arbor: University of Michigan Press, 1996.

———. *Pound/Ford: The Story of a Literary Friendship.* Ed. Brita Lindberg-Seyersted. New York: New Directions, 1982.

———. *Pound/Joyce: The Letters of Ezra Pound to James Joyce, with Pound's Critical Essays and Articles about Joyce.* Ed. Forrest Read. New York: New Directions, 1967.

———. *Pound/Lewis: The Letters of Ezra Pound and Wyndham Lewis.* Ed. Timothy Materer. New York: New Directions, 1985.

———. *Pound, Thayer, Watson, and The Dial: A Story in Letters.* Ed. Walter Sutton. Gainesville: University Press of Florida, 1994.

———. *Pound/Williams: Selected Letters of Ezra Pound and William Carlos Williams.* Ed. Hugh Witemeyer. New York: New Directions, 1996.

———. *Pound/Zukofsky: Selected Letters.* Ed. Barry Ahearn. New York: New Directions, 1987.

———. *Profile.* Milan: Giovanni Scheiwiller, 1932.

———. "Psychology and Troubadours." *Quest* 4.1 (Oct. 1912): 37–53.

———. *A Quinzaine for This Yule.* London: Elkin Mathews, 1908.

———. "Rosanov e Cruet." *Meridiano di Roma* 7.50 (13 Dec. 1942): 1–2. Reprinted in *Ezra Pound's Poetry and Prose: Contributions to Periodicals.* Ed. Lea Baechler, A. Walton Litz, and James Longenbach. New York: Garland, 1991. 8:190–91.

———. *Selected Letters of Ezra Pound, 1907–1941.* New York: Harcourt, Brace, 1950. Ed. D. D. Paige. New York: New Directions, 1971.

———. *The Selected Letters of Ezra Pound to John Quinn.* Ed. Timothy Materer. Durham: Duke University Press, 1991.

———. *Selected Prose, 1909–1965.* Ed. William Cookson. New York: New Directions, 1973.

———. . . . *Shishu* . . . Trans. Ryozo Iwasaki. Tokyo: Arechi Shuppansha, 1956.

———. "Sovereignty." *European* 1 (Mar. 1953): 51. Reprinted in *Ezra Pound's Poetry and Prose: Contributions to Periodicals.* Ed. Lea Baechler, A. Walton Litz, and James Longenbach. New York: Garland, 1991. 8:550.

———. *The Spirit of Romance.* London: J. M. Dent and Sons, 1910. New York: New Directions, 1968.

———. "Stamp Scrip." *New English Weekly* 7 (31 May 1934): 167.

———. *Thrones.* Milan: All'insegna del pesce d'oro, 1959. New York: New Directions, 1959.

———. "Tinkham Suggested for President." *Boston Herald* 7 Feb. 1939: 10.

———. *The Translations of Ezra Pound.* London: Faber and Faber, 1934. New York: New Directions, 1963.

———. . . . *Tre Cantos* . . . Trans. Mary de Rachewiltz. Milan: All'insegna del pesce d'oro, 1954.

———. *A Visiting Card.* Trans. John Drummond. London: Peter Russell, 1952.

———. "William H. Davies, Poet." Review of William H. Davies's *Collected Poems. Poetry* 11.2 (Nov. 1917): 99–102.

————, and Alberto Luchini. *Testamento di Confucio.* Venice: Casa Editrice, Delle Edizioni Popolari, 1944.

————, and Gino Saviotti. "Appunti. XV. Nunc dimittis." *L'Indice* 2.9 (10 May 1931): 1.

Other Works

Accame, Giano. *Ezra Pound economista: Contro l'usua.* Rome: Edizione Settimo Sigillo, 1995.

Ackroyd, Peter. *Ezra Pound and His World.* New York: Thames and Hudson, 1980.

————. *T. S. Eliot: A Life.* New York: Simon and Schuster, 1984.

Adams, Brooks. *The Law of Civilization and Decay: An Essay on History.* New York: Macmillan, 1895. New York: Knopf, 1943.

————. *The Theory of Social Revolutions.* New York: Macmillan, 1913.

Adams, John. *Statesman and Friend — Correspondence of John Adams with Benjamin Waterhouse, 1784–1822.* Ed. Worthington Chauncy Ford. Boston: Little, Brown, 1927.

Agassiz, Louis. *Contributions to the Natural History of the United States.* 4 vols. Boston: Little, Brown; London: Trubner and Co., 1857–62.

Agassiz, Louis, and Elizabeth Cabot Cary Agassiz. *A Journey to Brazil.* Boston: Ticknor and Fields, 1868.

Agresti, Olivia Rossetti. "The Red Romantics." Folder 6241, Box 142. Series 4, Manuscripts. Ezra Pound Papers. Yale Collection of American Literature. Beinecke Rare Book and Manuscript Library, Yale University. New Haven, Conn.

————. *David Lubin: A Study in Practical Idealism.* Boston: Little, Brown, 1922.

————. *Giovanni Costa: His Life, Work, and Times.* London: Grant Richards, 1904.

————. "The Most Unforgettable Character I've Known: David Lubin of California." *Edge* 8 (Oct. 1957): 2–20.

————. "Pages of Memoir." *Edge* 4 (Mar. 1957): 1–3.

Aldington, Richard. *Life for Life's Sake.* New York: Viking, 1941.

Alighieri, Dante. *De vulgari eloquentia.* Ed. and Trans. Steven Botterill. Cambridge: Cambridge University Press, 1996.

Amery, Leopold. *My Political Life.* London: Hutchinson, 1953.

————. *Thoughts on the British Constitution.* London: Oxford University Press, 1947.

Anceschi, Luciano. "Palinsesti del protoumanesimo poetico americano." *Poetica americana e altri studi comtemporanei de poetica.* Pisa: Nistri-Lischi, 1953. 13–50, 131–33.

Anderson, David. "Breaking the Silence: The Interview of Vanni Ronsisvalle and Pier Paolo Pasolini with Ezra Pound in 1968." *Paideuma* 10.2 (1981): 331–45.

Andréadès, André M. "The Economic Life of the Byzantine Empire: Population, Agriculture, Industry, Commerce." *Byzantium: An Introduction to*

East Roman Civilization. Ed. Norman H. Baynes and H.St.L.B. Moss. Oxford: Clarendon, 1948. 51–70.

———. "Public Finances: Currency, Public Expenditure, Budget, Public Revenue." *Byzantium: An Introduction to East Roman Civilization*. Ed. Norman H. Baynes and H.St.L.B. Moss. Oxford: Clarendon, 1948. 71–85.

Angeli, Helen Rossetti. *Dante Gabriel Rossetti: His Friends and Enemies*. London: H. Hamilton, 1949. New York: B. Blom, 1972.

———. *Pre-Raphaelite Twilight: The Story of Charles Augustus Howell*. London: Richards Press, 1954.

———. *Shelley and His Friends in Italy*. London: Methuen, 1911. New York: Haskell House, 1973.

Aristotle. *Nicomachean Ethics*. Trans. H. Rackham. Loeb Classical Library 73. 1926. Cambridge, Mass.: Harvard University Press, 1947.

Arrian. *Anabasis Alexandri (Anabasis of Alexander)*. Trans. E. Iliff Robson. 2 vols. Loeb Classical Library 236, 269. Cambridge, Mass.: Harvard University Press, 1929–33.

Augustine. *Contra Faustum*. Venice: F. Temsky, 1891. New York: Johnson Reprint, 1972.

Bacigalupo, Massimo. *The Forméd Trace: The Later Poetry of Ezra Pound*. New York: Columbia University Press, 1980.

Barnes, James Strachey. *Fascism*. London: Butterworth, 1931.

———. *Gli aspetti universali del fascismo*. Rome: Liberia del Littorio, 1931.

———. *The Universal Aspects of Fascism*. London: Williams and Northgate, 1928.

Barral, Jean. *La révolution economique*. Paris: Nouvelles Editions Latines, 1935.

Baruch, Bernard. *American Industry in the War*. New York: Prentice Hall, 1941.

Baynes, Norman H., and H.St.L.B. Moss, eds. *Byzantium: An Introduction to East Roman Civilization*. Oxford: Clarendon, 1948.

Beck, Jósef. *Dernier Rapport—Politique Polonaise, 1926–1936*. Neuchâtel: Editions de la Baconniere, 1951.

Bede, Venerable. *Historia ecclesiastica gentis anglorum*. Oxford, Clarendon, 1891.

Begnac, Yvon de. *Palazzo Venezia: Storia di un regime*. Rome: La Rocca, 1950.

Belgion, Montgomery. *David Hume*. London: Longmans, Green, 1965.

———. *H. G. Wells*. London: Longmans, Green, 1953.

———. *The Human Parrot and Other Essays*. London: Milford, 1931.

———. *Reading for Profit*. Chicago: Regnery, 1950.

Belloc, Hilaire. *The Servile State*. London: T. N. Foulis, 1912.

Benda, Julien. *Le Bergsonisme, ou, Un philosophie de la mobilité*. Paris: Mercure de France, 1912.

———. *L'ordination*. Paris: Emil-Paul, 1913.

———. *La trahison des clercs*. Paris: B. Grasset, 1927.

Benedetta. *Viaggio di Gararà: Romanzo cosmico per teatro*. Milan: Morreale, 1931.

Benét, William Rose, and Conrad Aiken. *Anthology of Famous English and American Poetry*. 2d ed. New York: Modern Library, 1945.

Benton, Thomas H. *Abridgement of the Debates of Congress from 1789 to 1856.* 16 vols. New York: D. Appleton, 1857–61.
———. *Bank of the United States.* New York: Kasper and Horton, 1954.
———. *Thirty Years' View; or, A History of the Working of the American Government for Thirty Years, from 1820–1850.* New York: D. Appleton and Co., 1854.
Bernstein, Michael. *The Tale of the Tribe: Ezra Pound and the Modern Verse Epic.* Princeton: Princeton University Press, 1980.
Blackmur, R. P. "An Adjunct to the Muses Diadem." *Poetry* 68.4 (Sept. 1946): 338–47.
Blackstone, Sir William. *Commentaries on the Laws of England.* 4 vols. Philadelphia: Lippincott, 1898.
Blaug, Mark, ed. *Economists after Keynes.* Brighton: Wheatsheaf Books, 1986.
———, ed. *Economists since Keynes.* Brighton: Wheatsheaf Books, 1985.
Böckh, August. *Public Economy of Athens, to which Is Added a Dissertation on the Silver Mines of Laurion.* Trans. George Cornwall Lewis. London: J. W. Parker, 1842. London: J. W. Parker, 1942.
Bodrero, Emilio. *La fina di una epoca.* Bologna: L. Cappelli, 1933.
———. *Inchiesta sulla massoneria.* Sala Bolognese: A. Fori, 1919. Milan: Mondadori, 1925.
———. *Italia nuova e antica.* Bologna: N. Zanichelli, 1919.
———. *I limiti della storia della filosofia.* Rome: A. F. Formiggini, 1919.
Bondanella, Peter, and Julia Conway Bondanella, eds. *Dictionary of Italian Literature.* Westport: Greenwood, 1979.
Booth, Marcella Spann. "Ezrology: The Class of '57." *Paideuma* 13.3 (1984): 375–88.
Bosanquet, Theodora. *Henry James at Work.* London: Hogarth Press, 1924.
Bosco, Umberto, ed. *Dizionario enciclopedico italiano.* 12 vols. Rome: Istituto della Enciclopedia Italiana, 1935–61.
Boswell, James. *The Journal of a Tour to the Hebrides with Samuel Johnson.* Ed. L. F. Powell. London: Dent, 1909. New York: E. P. Dutton, 1958.
Bowen, Stella. *Drawn from Life.* London: Collins, 1941.
Bowers, Claude Gernade. *Jefferson and Hamilton: The Struggle for Democracy in America.* London: Constable, 1925.
Bridson, D. G. "An Interview with Ezra Pound." *New Directions in Prose and Poetry* 17 (1961): 159–84.
Brown, John. *Panorama de la littérature contemporaine aux États-Unis: Introduction, illustrations, documents.* Paris: Gallimard, 1954.
Bryant, Keith L., Jr. *Alfalfa Bill Murray.* Norman: University of Oklahoma Press, 1968.
Bullitt, William C. *The Great Globe Itself: A Preface to World Affairs.* New York: Scribner's, 1946.
Bülow, Prince Bernhard Heinrich von. *Memoirs, 1897–1903.* Trans. F. A. Voigt. New York: Putnam, 1931.
Burns, James MacGregor. *Roosevelt: The Lion and the Fox.* New York: Harcourt, 1956.

Bush, Ronald. *The Genesis of Ezra Pound's Cantos.* Princeton: Princeton University Press, 1977.

Butchart, Montgomery, ed. *Money: Selected Passages Presenting the Concepts of Money in the English Tradition, 1640–1935.* London: Stanley Nott, 1935.

Butler, Samuel. *Erewhon.* London: Trubner, 1872.

Cairoli, Luigi Pasquale. *Il giusto prezzo medievale.* Brianza: Merate, 1913.

Cannistraro, Philip V., ed. *Historical Dictionary of Fascist Italy.* Westport: Greenwood Press, 1982.

Capitini, Aldo. *Elementi di un'esperienza religiosa.* Bari: Laterza, 1947.

Carnahan, James R. *Pythian Knighthood: Its History and Literature.* Cincinnati: Pettibone Bros. Manufacturing, 1909.

Carpenter, Humphrey. *A Serious Character: The Life of Ezra Pound.* Boston: Houghton, 1988.

Carrel, Alexis. *Man, the Unknown.* New York: Halcyon, 1938.

Casillo, Robert. *The Genealogy of Demon: Anti-Semitism, Fascism, and the Myths of Ezra Pound.* Evanston: Northwestern University Press, 1988.

Cerf, Bennett. "The Case of Ezra Pound." *Saturday Review of Literature* 29.6 (9 Feb. 1946): 26–27.

———. "The Case of Ezra Pound." *Saturday Review of Literature* 29.11 (16 Mar. 1946): 32–36, 49–53.

Chace, William M. *The Political Identities of Ezra Pound and T. S. Eliot.* Stanford: Stanford University Press, 1973.

Chambrun, Clara de. *The Making of Nicholas Longworth: Annals of an American Family.* New York: R. Long and R. D. Smith, 1933.

Chan, Wing-tsit. "*The Unwobbling Pivot* and *The Great Digest.*" *Philosophy East and West* 3 (Jan. 1954): 371–73.

Chang, Carson. *Third Force in China.* New York: New York Bookman Associates, 1952.

Churchill, Winston. *The Second World War.* 6 vols. Boston: Houghton Mifflin, 1948–53.

Cicero, Marcus Tullius. *De Officiis.* Trans. Walter Miller. Loeb Classical Library. 1913. London: Heinemann, 1928.

Cione, Edmondo. *Storia della republica sociale italiana.* Caserta: Il Cenacolo, 1948.

———. *Tra croce e Mussolini.* Naples: SEPA, 1946.

Clark, Martin. *Modern Italy: 1871–1982.* London: Longman, 1984.

Cole, G. D. H. *The World of Labour.* London: Bell, 1913.

Comay, Joan. *Who's Who in Jewish History after the Period of the Old Testament.* London: Weidenfeld, 1974.

Comfort, Howard, ed. *Corpus Vasorum Arretinorum: A Catalogue of the Signatures, Shapes and Chronology of Italian Sigillata.* Comp. August Oxé. Bonn: Habelt, 1968.

Connolly, Cyril. *The Missing Diplomats.* London: Queen Anne Press, 1952.

Conrad, Joseph. *The Secret Agent.* Ed. Martin Seymour-Smith. London: Methuen, 1907. London: Penguin, 1984.

Contini, Ennio. *L'alleluja: Poesie di Ennio Contini e la prima decade dei cantos di Ezra Pound.* Mazara, Sicily: Societa editrice Siciliana, 1952.

Coppa, Frank J., ed. *Dictionary of Modern Italian History.* Westport: Greenwood Press, 1985.

Corsini, Renato. "Ezra Pound, Economist: Justice the Final Goal." Trans. Ezra Pound. *New Times* 21.25 (16 Dec. 1955): 7.

Corti, Egon Caesar. *The Reign of the House of Rothschild.* Trans. Brian Lunn and Beatrix Lunn. London: Victor Gollancz, 1928.

———. *The Rise of the House of Rothschild.* Trans. Brian Lunn and Beatrix Lunn. London: Victor Gollancz, 1928.

Coston, Henry. *Dictionnaire de la politique française.* Paris: Publications H. Coston, 1967.

Cramer, Maurice Browning. "What Browning's Literary Reputation Owed to the Pre-Raphaelites 1847–1856." *A Journal of English Literary History* 8.4 (1941): 305–21.

Dante Alighieri. *The Divine Comedy.* Trans. John D. Sinclair. 3 vols. New York: Oxford University Press, 1961.

Davies, William Henry. *The Autobiography of a Super-Tramp.* London: A. C. Fifield, 1908.

de Angelo, Jaime. "Indians in Overalls." *Hudson Review* 3.3 (1950): 327–79.

De Felice, Renzo, ed. *La Carta del Carnaro: Nei testi Alceste de Ambris e di Gabriele D'Annunzio.* Bologna: Il mulino, 1974.

de Kruif, Paul. *Hunger Fighters.* New York: Harcourt, Brace, 1928.

———. *Why Keep Them Alive.* New York: Harcourt Brace Jovanovich, 1936.

Del Mar, Alexander. *Barbara Villiers; or, A History of Monetary Crimes.* New York: Cambridge Encyclopedia, 1899. Hawthorne, Calif.: Omni Publications, 1967.

———. *A History of Monetary Systems.* Chicago: Clark Kerr, 1895. Reprinted as *A History of Netherlands's Monetary System.* Washington, D.C.: Square $ Series, 1956.

———. *A History of Money in Ancient Times.* London: G. Bell, 1885. New York: B. Franklin, 1968.

———. *A History of Money in America.* New York: Cambridge Encyclopedia, 1899. New York: B. Franklin, 1969.

———. *A History of Precious Metals.* London: G. Bell, 1880. New York: B. Franklin, 1968.

———. *Roman and Moslem Moneys.* Washington, D.C.: Square $ Series, 1956.

———. *The Science of Money.* London: G. Bell, 1885. Hawthorne, Calif.: Omni Publications, 1967.

Del Pelo Pardi, Giulio. *Agricoltura e civiltà.* Ed. Tomasso del Pelo Pardi and Boris de Rachewiltz. Turin: Boringhieri, 1971.

———. *Per la pace del mondo.* Rome: Maglione and Strini, 1924.

Dickason, David Howard. *The Daring Young Men: The Story of the American Pre-Raphaelites.* Bloomington: Indiana University Press, 1953.

Dickinson, G. Lowes. *The Autobiography of G. Lowes Dickinson and Other Unpublished Writings.* Ed. Dennis Proctor. London: Duckworth, 1973.

————. *Causes of International War.* Ed. Catherine Ann Cline. New York: Garland, 1972.

————. *Letters from a Chinese Official: Being an Eastern View of Western Civilization.* New York: McLure, Phillips, and Co., 1907.

Diggins, John P. *Mussolini and Fascism: The View from America.* Princeton: Princeton University Press, 1972.

Dilligan, Robert J., James W. Parins, and Todd K. Bender. *A Concordance to Ezra Pound's "Cantos."* New York: Garland, 1981.

Dobbs, Geoffrey. *On Planning the Earth.* Liverpool: K. R. P. Productions, 1951.

Domville, Barry. *From Admiral to Cabin Boy.* London: Boswell, 1947.

Douglas, C. H. *Credit Power and Democracy.* London: C. Palmer, 1921. Rev. ed. London: Nott, 1934.

————. *Social Credit.* London: C. Palmer, 1924. Rev. 3d ed. London: Eyre and Spottiswoode, 1934.

Drabble, Margaret, ed. *The Oxford Companion to English Literature.* New York: Oxford University Press, 1995.

Dreyer, Peter. *A Gardener Touched with Genius: The Life of Luther Burbank.* New York: Coward, McCann, and Geoghan, 1975.

Drummond, John. "La verita sul caso Pound." *Fiera Letteraria* 1 (Jan. 7, 1951): 1.

Duncan, Ronald. *Journal of a Husbandman.* London: Faber and Faber, 1944.

Eastman, Max. *Reflections on the Failure of Socialism.* New York: Gosset and Dunlap, 1955.

Edwards, John Hamilton, and William V. Vasse. *Annotated Index to the Cantos of Ezra Pound: Cantos I–LXXXIV.* Berkeley: University of California Press, 1957.

Eisenhower, Dwight D. *Crusade in Europe.* Garden City, N.Y.: Doubleday, 1948.

Eliot, T. S. *The Letters of T. S. Eliot.* Ed. Valerie Eliot. Vol. 1. New York: Barnes, 1970.

————. "Milton I." *Poetry and Poets.* London: Faber and Faber, 1957. 138–45.

————. "Milton II." *Poetry and Poets.* London: Faber and Faber, 1957. 146–61.

————. *Selected Essays.* London: Faber and Faber, 1951.

————. *Sweeney Agonistes.* London: Faber and Faber, 1932.

Erigena, Joannes Scotus. *De Divisione Naturae.* Oxford: E. Theatro Sheldoniano, 1681.

Espey, John. *Ezra Pound's Mauberley.* London: Faber and Faber, 1955.

Fabre, J. H. *Souvenirs entomologique.* Paris: C. Delagrave, 1874–1907.

Feder, Gottfried. *Das Programm der N.S.D.A.P. und seine weltanschaulichen Grundgedanken.* Munich: F. Eher, 1931.

Ferkiss, Victor C. "Ezra Pound and American Fascism." *Journal of Politics* 17 (May 1955): 173–79.

"Financial Notes." *The Economist* (5 June 1937): 572.

Finlay, John L. *Social Credit: The English Origins.* Montreal: McGill-Queen's University Press, 1972.

Fisher, Irving, asssisted by Hans R. L. Cohrssen and Herbert W. Fisher. *Stamp Scrip*. New York: Adelphi, 1933.

Fisher, John. *Burgess and MacLean: A New Look at the Foreign Office Spies*. London: Robert Hale, 1977.

Fleming, William. "The Melbourne Vortex." *Paideuma* 3.3 (1974): 325–28.

Flory, Wendy S. *The American Ezra Pound*. New Haven: Yale University Press, 1989.

Flynn, John Thomas. *The Roosevelt Myth*. New York: Devin-Adair, 1948.

Ford, Ford Madox. *Parade's End*. New York: Knopf, 1950.

———. *Return to Yesterday*. New York: Liveright, 1932.

———. *Rossetti*. London: Duckworth, 1902.

———. *Simple Life Limited*. London: John Lane, 1911.

France, Anatole. *L'Île des pingouins*. Paris: Calmann Levy, 1908.

Fraser, Hugh Russell. *Democracy in the Making: The Jackson-Tyler Era*. Indianapolis: Bobbs-Merrill, 1938.

Frazer, Sir James George. *The New Golden Bough: A New Abridgment of the Classic Work*. Ed. Theodor H. Gaster. New York: Criterion, 1959.

Freedman, Benjamin. *Facts Are Facts*. Pamphlet.

French, William, and Timothy Materer. "Far Flung Vortices and Ezra's 'Hindoo' Yogi." *Paideuma* 11.1 (1982): 39–53.

Frobenius, Leo. *Erlebte Erdteile*. 7 vols. Frankfurt: Frankfurter Societats druckerei, Abt. Buchverlag, 1925–29.

Gallup, Donald. *Ezra Pound: A Bibliography*. London: Rupert Hart-Davis, 1963. Charlottesville: University Press of Virginia for the Bibliographical Society of the University of Virginia and St. Paul's Bibliographers, 1983.

———. "The Ezra Pound Archive at Yale." *Yale University Library Gazette* 60.3–4 (1986): 161–77.

———. *Pigeons on the Granite: Memories of a Yale Librarian*. New Haven: Yale University Press, 1988.

Garçon, Maurice. "Voyage d'une Hollandaise en France." *Mercure de France* 1033 (1949): 37–54.

Gasset, José Ortega y. *The Revolt of the Masses*. London: G. Allen and Unwin, 1932.

Gentile, Giovanni. *Theory of Mind as Pure Act*. Trans. H. Wildon Carr. London: Macmillan, 1922.

George, Henry. *Our Land and Land Policy*. San Francisco: White and Bauer, 1871.

———. *Progress and Poverty*. Middleton: John Bagot, 1879.

"German Onlooker." Review of Fritz Hesse's *Das Spiel um Deutschland*. *Times Literary Supplement* (Feb. 5 1954): 84.

Germino, Dante L. *The Italian Fascist Party in Power: A Study in Totalitarian Rule*. Minneapolis: University of Minnesota Press, 1959.

Gesell, Silvio. *The Natural Economic Order*. Trans. Philip Pye. Berlin: Neo-Verlag, 1929. Reprinted in 2 vols. San Antonio, Tex.: Free Economic Publishing, 1934–36.

Giartosio de Courten, Maria Luisa. *Percy Bysshe Shelley e l'Italia*. Milan: Fratelli Treves, 1923.

———. *I Rossetti: Storia di una famiglia*. Milan: Alpes, 1928.

Gibbon, Edward. *History of the Decline and Fall of the Roman Empire*. 6 vols. New York: Collier, 1899–1901.

Giovannini, Giovanni. *Ezra Pound and Dante*. Utrecht: Dekker and Van De Vegt, 1961.

Goldring, Douglas. *The Last Pre-Raphaelite: A Record of the Life and Writings of Ford Madox Ford*. London: MacDonald, 1948. Published in the United States as *Trained for Genius*. New York: Dutton, 1949.

———. *South Lodge: Reminiscences of Violet Hunt, Ford Madox Ford, and the "English Review" Circle*. London: Constable, 1943.

Gontard, Friedrich. *The Chair of Peter: A History of the Papacy*. Trans. A. J. Peeler and E. F. Peeler. New York: Holt, Rinehart, and Winston, 1964.

Gordon, David, ed. "*Academia Bulletin* 1 and 2." *Paideuma* 3.3 (1974): 381–88.

Gourmont, Rémy de. *The Natural Philosophy of Love*. Trans. and with a postscript by Ezra Pound. London: Cassanova Society, 1926.

Graziani, Rodolfo. *Ho difeso la patria*. Milan: Garzanti, 1948.

Green, John Richard. *A History of the English People*. 4 vols. New York: Harper, 1879–80.

Grenfell, Russell. *Unconditional Hatred*. New York: Devin-Adair, 1953.

Guareschi, Giovanni. *Il destino si chiama Clotilde*. Milan-Rome: Rizzoli, 1941.

———. *Il dilemma di Don Camillo*. Milan: Rizzoli, 1953.

———. *The Little World of Don Camillo*. Trans. Una Vincenzo Troubridge. London: Victor Gallancz, 1951.

———. *Mondo piccolo: "Don Camillo e il suo gregge."* Milan: Rizzoli, 1951.

———. *La scoperta di Milano*. Milan: Rizzoli, 1941.

Gucciardini, Francesco. *Storia d'Italia*. Bari: G. Laterza, 1967.

Guerriero, Augusto. *Guerra e dopoguerra: Saggi politici*. Milan: Bompiani, 1943.

———. *La teoria della sovranita: Contributo alla dommatica del diritto pubblico*. 1919.

Haines, C. Crove, and Ross J. S. Hoffman. *The Origins and Background of the Second World War*. New York: Oxford University Press, 1947.

Hall, Donald. *Writers at Work: The Paris Review Interviews*. 2d Series. New York: Viking, 1963.

Handlin, Oscar, ed. *Harvard Guide to American History*. 2 vols. Cambridge, Mass.: Belknap Press of Harvard University Press, 1954.

Han Shu. *Food and Money in Ancient China: The Earliest Economic History of China to a.d. 25, Han Shu 24 with Related Texts, Han Shu 91, and Shih-Chi 129*. Trans. and ann. Nancy Lee Swann. Princeton: Princeton University Press, 1951.

Harris, Frank. *The Man Shakespeare*. New York: Kennerley, 1909.

———. *My Life*. New York: Frank Harris Publishing, 1925.

———. *My Life and Loves*. Ed. John F. Gallaher. London: W. H. Allen, 1964.

———. *Oscar Wilde*. New York: Brentanos, 1916.

———. *The Women of Shakespeare*. London: Methuen, 1911.

Harris, William H., and Judith S. Levoy, eds. *The New Columbia Encyclopedia*. New York: Columbia University Press, 1975.

Hayes, Paul M. *Quisling: The Career and Political Ideas of Vidkun Quisling, 1887–1945*. Bloomington: Indiana University Press, 1972.

H. D. *End to Torment: A Memoir of Ezra Pound by H.D.* Ed. Norman Holmes Pearson and Michael King. New York: New Directions, 1979.

Herbert, Edward. *De Religione Gentilium*. Stuttgart-Bad Connstatt: F. Frommann, 1967.

———. *De Veritate*. Stuttgart-Bad Connstatt: F. Frommann, 1966.

Hesse, Fritz. *Hitler and the English*. Trans. F. A Voigt. London: Allan Wingate, 1954.

———. *Das Spiel um Deutschland*. Munich: Paul List Verlag, 1953.

Heydon, John. *The Holy Guide*. London: Thomas Whittlesey, 1662.

Heymann, C. David. *Ezra Pound: The Last Rower*. New York: Viking, 1976.

Hillyer, Robert. "Poetry's New Priesthood." *Saturday Review of Literature* 32 (18 June 1949): 7–9, 38.

———. "Treason's Strange Fruit." *Saturday Review of Literature* 32 (11 June 1949): 9–11.

Hitler, Adolph. *Hitler's Table Talk, 1941–1944*. Trans. Norman Cameron and R. H. Stevens. London: Weidenfeld and Nicholson, 1953. Oxford: Oxford University Press, 1958. Published in the United States as *Hitler's Secret Conversations, 1941–1944*. New York: Farrar, Straus, 1953.

Homberger, Eric, ed. *Ezra Pound: The Critical Heritage*. London: Routledge, 1972.

Homer. *Homer: The Odyssey*. Trans. A. T. Murray. Loeb Classical Library 104 and 105. 1919. Cambridge, Mass.: Harvard University Press, 1966.

———. *The Odyssey of Homer*. Trans. Richmond Lattimore. New York: Harper, 1965.

House, Colonel Edward Mandell. *The Intimate Papers of Colonel House*. Ed. Charles Seymour. Boston: Houghton Mifflin, 1926–28.

Hughes, Emrys. *Winston Churchill: British Bulldog, His Career in War and Peace*. New York: Exposition Press, 1955.

Index to Literary Biography. Ed. Patricia Pate Harlice. London: Scarecrow Press, 1975.

International Who's Who. London: Europa Publications, 1935–.

Intorcetta, Prospero. *Sinarum Scientia Politico-Moralis, a P. Prospero Intorcetta, siculo, S.J. . . . in lucem edita*. Paris, 1672.

Ionides, Luke. *Memories*. As recorded by Olivia Shakespear. *Transatlantic Review* 1–2 (Jan.–Sept. 1924). New York: Kraus Reprint Corporation, 1967.

Ishiguro, Kazu. *Remains of the Day*. Toronto: Lester and Orpen Dennys, 1989.

James, Henry. *The Complete Tales of Henry James*. Ed. Leon Edel. 12 vols. New York: Lippincott, 1962–64.

———. *William Wetmore Story and his Friends: From Letters, Diaries, and Recollections*. London: Thames and Hudson, 1903.

Jenks, Jorian Edward Forwood. *From the Ground Up: An Outline of Real Economy.* London: Hollis and Carter, 1950.

Johnson, Thomas H. *Oxford Companion of American History.* New York: Oxford University Press, 1966.

Jones, Jesse Holman. *Fifty Billion Dollars: My Thirteen Years with the RFC, 1932–1945.* New York: Macmillan, 1951.

Katz, Irving. *August Belmont: A Political Biography.* New York: Columbia University Press, 1968.

Kenner, Hugh. *The Poetry of Ezra Pound.* New York: New Directions, 1951.

———. *The Pound Era.* Berkeley: University of California Press, 1971.

———. "Remember That I Have Remembered." *Hudson Review* 3.4 (1951): 602–11.

Keynes, John Maynard. *The General Theory of Employment, Interest, and Money.* London: Macmillan, 1936.

Kitson, Arthur. *The Bankers' Conspiracy.* London: Stock, 1993.

Knudsen, Harald Franklin. *Jeg var Quislings sekretær.* Copenhagen, 1951.

Koestler, Arthur. *Darkness at Noon.* Trans. Daphne Hardy. New York: Macmillan, 1941.

Kraus, Rene. *The Young Lady Randolph: The Life and Times of Jennie Jerome, American Mother of Winston Churchill.* New York: Putnam, 1943.

Lamb, Charles. *Specimens of Early Dramatic Poets Who Lived about the Time of Shakespeare.* London: H. G. Bohn, 1854.

Landor, Walter Savage. *Imaginary Conversations of Literary Men and Statesmen.* London: Taylor and Hessey, 1824–29.

Laughlin, James. *Pound as Wuz: Essays and Lectures on Ezra Pound.* St. Paul, Minn.: Graywolf, 1987.

Leahy, William D. *I Was There.* New York: Whittlesey, 1950.

Legge, James, ed. and trans. *The Chinese Classics.* 5 vols. Hong Kong: Legge; London: Trubner, 1861–72.

———, trans. *The Four Books: Confucian Analects, The Great Learning, the Doctrine of the Mean, and the Works of Mencius.* Shanghai: Chinese Book Co., 1933.

Lenbergis, Lore Marianne. "The Coherence of the *Pisan Cantos* and Their Significance in the Context of Ezra Pound's 'Poem of Some Length.'" Ph.D. diss., University of Freiburg, 1958.

Leto, Guido. *Ovra: Fascismo, antifascismo.* Bologna: Cappelli, 1951.

"Letters from Dorothy Pound and Shakespear and Parkyn." *Mercure de France* (1 Apr. 1949): 764–65.

Leverdays, Emile. *Les assemblées parlantes: Critique du gouvernement représentatif.* Paris: C. Marpon and E. Flammarion, 1883.

Levy, William Turner, and Victor Scherle. *Affectionately T. S. Eliot: The Story of a Friendship, 1945–1965.* Philadelphia: Lippincott, 1968.

Lewis, Wyndham. *Hitler.* London: Chatto and Windus, 1931.

———. *The Hitler Cult.* London: Dent, 1939.

Liddel, Henry George, and Robert Scott, eds. *A Greek-English Lexicon.* 8th ed. New York: American Books, 1897.

Lindberg-Seyersted, Brita. "Letters from Ezra Pound to Joseph Brewer." *Paideuma* 10.2 (Fall 1981): 269–82.

Lintell, A. R. "Production and Consumption." *New Times* 22.10 (18 May 1956): 7.

Lippmann, Walter. *Essays in the Public Philosophy.* Boston: Little, Brown, 1955.

Londres, Albert. *The Road to Buenos Aires.* Trans. Eric Sutton. London: Constable and Co., 1928.

———. *Terror in the Balkans.* New York: Horace Liveright, 1935.

———. *A Very Naked People.* New York: Horace Liveright, 1929.

Longobardi, Cesare. *Land-Reclamation in Italy: Rural Revival in the Building of a Nation.* Trans. Olivia Rossetti Agresti. London: P.S. King and Son, 1936.

Louis, François. *Recollections of a Parisian (Docteur Poumies de La Siboutie) under Six Sovereigns, Two Revolutions, and a Republic (1789–1863).* Ed. A. Branche and L. Dagoury. Trans. Theodora Davidson. New York: Putnam, 1911.

Lubac, Henri de. *Le drame de l'humanisme athée.* Paris: Editions Spes, 1944.

Lubin, David. *Let There Be Light.* New York: G. P. Putnam's Sons, 1900.

Mackenzie, Norman, and Jeanne Mackenzie. *The Time Traveller: The Life of H. G. Wells.* London: Weidenfeld and Nicolson, 1973.

Magnino, Leo. *Teatro giapponese.* Milan: Nuova Accademia Editrice, 1956.

Magnini, Domenico, ed. and trans. *Vita Ciceronis* by Plutarch. Florence: Nuova Italia, 1963.

Malone, Dumas, ed. *Dictionary of American Biography.* New York: Scribner's, 1933.

Manion, Clarence. *The Key to Peace: A Formula for the Perpetuation of Real Americanism.* Chicago: Heritage Foundation, 1950.

Maranini, Giuseppe. *Istoria del potere in Italia, 1848–1967.* Florence: Vallecchi, 1967.

Marcus Porcius Cato on Agriculture and Marcus Terentius Varro on Agriculture. Trans. William Davis Hooper. Loeb Classical Library 283. Cambridge, Mass.: Harvard University Press, 1934.

Marlowe, Christopher. *Dr. Faustus. The Complete Works of Christopher Marlowe.* Ed. Fredson Bowers. 2 vols. Cambridge: Cambridge University Press, 1973. 2:121–271.

Martinelli, Sheri. *La Martinell.* Preface by Ezra Pound. Milan: Vanni Scheiwiller, 1956.

———. "A Memoir." *Paideuma* 15.2–3 (1986): 151–62.

Martins, Jose V. de Piña. *Prometheus Bound: Vatican Radio Broadcast on the Case of Ezra Pound.* Trans. Olivia Rossetti Agresti. N.p.: 1954.

Matthews, T. S. *Great Tom: Notes towards the Definition of T. S. Eliot.* New York: Harper, 1974.

Mazgaj, Paul. *The Action Française and Revolutionary Syndicalism.* Chapel Hill: University of North Carolina Press, 1979.

Meacham, Harry M. *The Caged Panther: Ezra Pound at Saint Elizabeths.* New York: Twayne, 1967.

Mead, G. R. S. *Apollonius of Tyana*. London: Watkins, 1901.

Milton, John. *Paradise Lost*. Ed. Scott Elledge. New York: Norton, 1993.

Missiroli, Mario, and Olivia Rossetti Agresti. *The Organization of the Arts and Professions in the Fascist Guild State*. Rome: Laboremus, 1938.

Miyake, Akiko. *Ezra Pound and the Mysteries of Love*. Durham: Duke University Press, 1991.

Mizener, Arthur. *The Saddest Story: A Biography of Ford Madox Ford*. New York: World Publishing, 1971.

Mommsen, Theodor. *The History of Rome*. Trans. W. W. Dickson. London: Dent, 1911.

Moore, Virginia. *The Unicorn: William Butler Yeats' Search for Reality*. New York: Macmillan, 1954.

Morford, Mark P. O., and Robert J. Lenardon. *Classical Mythology*. New York: David McKay, 1971. New York: Longman, 1977.

Moulton, Harold G. *The Dynamic Economy: A Dialogue in Play Form*. Washington: Brookings Institute, 1950.

Mullins, Eustace. *The Federal Reserve Conspiracy*. 2d ed. Union, N.J.: Common Sense, 1954.

———. *The Secrets of the Federal Reserve*. New York: Kasper and Horton, 1952. Staunton, Va.: Bankers Research Institute, 1993.

———. *This Difficult Individual, Ezra Pound*. New York: Fleet, 1961.

Munro, Ion Smeaton. *Beyond the Alps*. London: A. Maclehose, 1934.

———. *Through Fascism to World Power: A History of the Revolution in Italy*. London: A. Maclehose, 1933.

———. *Youth of Yesteryear*. London: W. Hodge, 1939.

Mussato, Albertino. *L'ecerenide*. Trans. Manlio Torquato Dazzi. Città di Castello: S. Lapi, 1914.

Mussolini, Benito. "In Captivity: Notebook of Thoughts in Ponza and La Maddalena." *Edge* 4 (Mar. 1957): 10–26.

Neame, Alan. *The Adventures of Maud Noakes*. New York: New Directions, 1961.

———. "Ezra Pound Reconsidered." *Blackfriars* 32 (May 1951): 222–27.

Nelson, Benjamin N. *The Idea of Usury: From Tribal Brotherhood to Universal Otherhood*. Princeton: Princeton University Press, 1949.

The New York Times Obituaries Index. 2 vols. New York: New York Times, 1970–80.

Nicole, Jules, ed. *Eparchikon biblion: Le livre du préfet*. Geneva: H. George, 1893.

Norman, Charles. *Ezra Pound: A Biography*. New York: Macmillan, 1960. London: Macdonald, 1969.

———. *The Magic Maker: E. E. Cummings*. New York: Macmillan, 1958.

Notari, Umberto. *I tre ladri*. Published in English as *The Three Thieves*. London: Gerald Howe, 1930.

Obituaries from the Times, 1951–1960. Comp. Frank C. Roberts. Reading, England: Newspaper Archive Developments, 1979.

Obituaries from the Times, 1971–1975. Comp. Frank C. Roberts. Reading, England: Newspaper Archive Developments, 1978.

Ogden, August Raymond. *The Dies Committee: A Study of the Special House Committee for the Investigation of Un-American Activities, 1938– 1944.* 2d rev. ed. Washington, D.C.: Catholic University of America Press, 1945.

Ollivier, Georges. *Franklin Roosevelt: L'homme de Yalta.* Paris: Librairie Française, 1955.

Olson, Charles. *Charles Olson and Ezra Pound: An Encounter at St. Elizabeths.* Ed. Catherine Seelye. New York: Grossman, 1975.

Overholser, Willis A. *A Short Review and Analysis of the History of Money in the United States.* Libertyville, Ill.: Progress Publishing, 1936.

Oxford English Dictionary. 2d ed. Oxford: Clarendon, 1989.

Packard, Reynolds. *Rome Was My Beat.* Secaucus, N.J.: L. Stuart, 1975.

Packard, Reynolds, and Eleanor Packard. *Balcony Empire: Fascist Italy at War.* Oxford: Oxford University Press, 1942.

Palmer, Alan. *Who's Who in Modern History, 1860–1980.* London: Weidenfeld and Nicolson, 1980.

Panter-Downes, Mollie. *At the Pines: Swinburne and Watts-Dunton in Putney.* London: Hamilton, 1971.

Papen, Franz von. *Memoirs.* Trans. Brian Connell. New York: Dutton, 1953.

Papini, Giovanni. *Lettere agli uomini di Papa Celestino VI.* Florence: Vallechi, 1946.

Paul the Deacon. *History of the Langobards.* Trans. William Dudley Foulke. New York: Longmans, Green, 1906.

Pausanias. *Pausanias's Description of Greece.* Trans. with commentary by J. G. Frazier. 6 vols. London: Macmillan, 1898.

Pauthier, M. G., trans. *Confucius et Mencius: Les quatre livres de philosophie morale et politique de la Chine.* Paris: Charpentier, 1886.

Pellizzi, Camillo. *Una rivoluzione mancata.* Milan: Longanesi, 1949.

Philostratus. *The Life of Apollonius of Tyana.* Trans. F. C. Conybeare. 2 vols. Loeb Classical Library 16, 17. 1912. Cambridge, Mass.: Harvard University Press, 1960.

Pickthall, Marmaduke. *Saïd the Fisherman.* London: Methuen, 1903.

———. *With the Turk in War-Time.* London: J. Dent, 1914.

Pierce, Franklin. *Federal Usurpation.* New York: D. Appleton and Co., 1908.

———. *The Tariff and the Trusts.* New York: Macmillan, 1913.

Plutarch. *Plutarch's Lives: Pericles and Nicias and Crassus.* Ed. Bernadotte Perrin. Loeb Classical Library 65. New York: Putnam's, 1916.

———. *Plutarch's Moralia.* Trans. Frank Cole Babbitt. Loeb Classical Library 197. New York: Putnam's, 1927.

Por, Odon. *Fascism.* Trans. E. Townshend. London: Labour Publishing, 1923.

———. *Guilds and Co-operatives in Italy.* Trans. E. Townshend. London: Labour Publishing, 1923.

———. *Italy's Policy of Social Economics, 1930–1940.* Trans. Ezra Pound. Bergamo: Instituto Italiano d'arti grafiche, 1941.

Pound, Omar. "Cantos 113: Tweddell, Men against Death, and Paul de Kruif." *Paideuma* 22.1–2 (1973): 173–79.

"Pound and Confucius." *Times Literary Supplement* (29 Apr. 1955): 191.

Rachewiltz, Boris de. *Scarabei dell'antico Egitto*. Milan: Scheiwiller, 1957.
Rachewiltz, Mary de. *Discretions*. Boston: Little, Brown, 1971.
———. "Poesie." *Prospetti* (Florence) 16 (1956): 110–27.
Radek, Karl. *The Development of Socialism from Science to Action*. Chicago: Communist Party of America, 1920.
Raleigh, Sir Walter. *The Works of Sir Walter Raleigh*. Ed. William Oldys and Thomas Birch. Oxford: Oxford University Press, 1829.
Rebora, Piero. "Ezra Pound: *Canto Pisani*." *Italia che scrive* (Rome) (Jan. 1954).
Reck, Michael. *Ezra Pound: A Close-Up*. New York: McGraw-Hill, 1967.
Redman, Tim. *Ezra Pound and Italian Fascism*. Cambridge: Cambridge University Press, 1991.
Rees, Philip. *Biographical Dictionary of the Extreme Right since 1890*. New York: Harverster Wheatsheaf, 1990.
Renan, Ernest. *Averrroès et l'averroisme*. Paris: A. Durand, 1852.
Ricks, Beatrice. *Ezra Pound: A Bibliography of Secondary Works*. Metuchen, N.J.: Scarecrow Press, 1986.
Rioux, Jean-Pierre. *The Fourth Republic: 1944–1958*. Cambridge: Cambridge University Press, 1987.
Robbins, John E., ed. *Encyclopedia Canadiana*. 12 vols. Toronto: Grolier of Canada, 1972.
Roosevelt, Franklin D. *Looking Forward*. New York: John Day, 1933.
Rossetti, Christina. *The Complete Poems of Christina Rossetti: A Variorum Edition*. Ed. R. W. Crump. 5 vols. Baton Rouge: Louisiana State University Press, 1979–86.
Rossetti, Dante Gabriel. *The Early Italian Poets*. London: Anvil Press, 1981.
———. "Hand and Soul." *The Germ: Thoughts towards Nature in Poetry, Literature, and Art* 1 (Jan. 1850): 23–33. Reprinted in *The Germ: A Pre-Raphaelite Little Magazine*. Ed. Robert Stahr Hosmon. Coral Gables, Fla.: University of Miami Press, 1970.
———, trans. *House of Life*. Boston: Copeland and Day, 1894.
———, trans. *The New Life (La Vita Nuova) of Dante Alighieri*. London: Ellis and Elvey, 1899.
Rossetti, Gabriele. *La Beatrice di Dante: Ragionamenti critici*. London: Stampats a spese dell'autore, si vende da P. Rolandi, 1842. Ed. Maria Louisa Giartoso de Courten. Imola: Paolo Galeati, 1935.
———. *La Divina Commedia di Dante con commento analitico di Gabriele Rossetti*. London: John Murray, 1825.
———. *Il mistero dell' amor platonico del medio aevo*. London: R. e G. E. Taylor, 1840.
Rossetti, Olivia, and Helen Rossetti. [Isabel Meredith.] *A Girl among the Anarchists*. London: Duckworth, 1903.
Rossetti, William Michael, ed. *American Poems*. London: E. Moxon, 1872.
———. *Dante and His Convito*. London: Elkin Mathews, 1910.
Rostovzeff, Michael Ivanovitch. *The Social and Economic History of the Roman Empire*. 2d ed., rev. Oxford: Clarendon, 1957.

Ruggeri, Cosimo. "Invece del capestro il premio 'Bollingen.'" *Momenta-Sera* (2 Feb. 1949).

Runciman, Stephen. *A History of the Crusades.* 3 vols. Cambridge: Cambridge University Press, 1951–54.

Santayana, George. *George Santayana: Letters.* Ed. Daniel Cory. New York: Scribner's, 1955.

Sapori, Armando. *Le marchand italian au moyen age.* Paris: Colin, 1952.

———. *Studi di storia economica.* Florence: Sansoni, 1955.

Scarfoglio, Carlo. "L'Antologia classica cinese." *Nuova Antologia* 466.1863 (Mar. 1956): 409–20.

———. . . . *Confucio. Antologia classica cinese.* Milan: All'insegna del pesce d'oro, 1964.

———. *Il mezzogiorono e l'unita d'Italia.* Florence: Parenti, 1953.

Schafer, R. Murray, ed. *Ezra Pound and Music.* London: Faber and Faber, 1978.

Schultz, John A., and Douglas Adair, eds. *The Spur of Fame.* San Marino, Calif.: Huntington Library, 1966.

Scott, Pamela, and Antoinette J. Lee. *Buildings of the District of Columbia.* New York: Oxford University Press, 1993.

Serao, Matilde. *Fantasia.* Turin: F. Casanova, 1892.

———. *Il ventre di Napoli.* Naples: F. Perrella, 1906.

Shaw, Edward Stone. *Money, Income, and Monetary Policy.* Chicago: Richard D. Irwin, 1950.

Siefert, George Joseph, Jr. "Meter and Case in the Latin Elegiac Pentameter." *Language: Journal of the Linguistic Society of America* 28.4 suppl. (Oct.–Dec. 1952): 1–126.

Sinclair, Upton. *My Lifetime in Letters.* Columbia: University of Missouri Press, 1960.

Sitwell, Edith. *The Atlantic Book of British and American Poetry.* Boston: Little Brown, 1958.

Skildesky, Robert. *Oswald Mosley.* London: Macmillan, 1975.

Slatin, Myles. "'Mesmerism': A Study of Ezra Pound's Use of the Poetry of Robert Browning." Ph.D. diss., Yale University, 1957.

Slavit, David R. "Eliot, Pound Played in Three Quarter Round." *Dallas Daily News* 24 Mar. 1955.

Soddy, Frederick. *Wealth, Virtual Wealth, and Debt.* London: Allen and Unwin, 1926.

Sofocle-Pound. *Le Trachinie.* Trans. Margherita Guidacci. Florence: Centro Internazionale del Libro, 1958.

Sophocles. *Electra.* Trans. F. Storr. Loeb Classical Library 21. New York: G. P. Putnam's Sons. 2:121–251.

———. *Women of Trachis.* Trans. Ezra Pound. 1956. New York: New Directions, 1957.

Spampanato, Bruno. *L'ultimo Mussolini (Contromemoriale).* 3 vols. Rome: Revista romana, 1964.

Stock, Noel. *The Life of Ezra Pound.* New York: Random, 1970.

———. *Poet in Exile.* Manchester: Manchester University Press, 1964.

Stokes, Adrian. *Stones of Rimini.* New York: G. Putnam's Sons, 1934. New York: Schocken Books, 1969.

Sturzo, Father Luigi. *Church and State.* Trans. Barbara Barclay Carter. New York: Longmans, Green, 1939.

———. *Italy and the Coming World.* New York: Roy Publishers, 1945.

Surette, Leon. *The Birth of Modernism: Ezra Pound, T. S. Eliot, W. B. Yeats, and the Occult.* Montreal: McGill-Queen's University Press, 1993.

———. *A Light from Eleusis: A Study of Ezra Pound's Cantos.* Oxford: Clarendon, 1979.

Swabey, Henry. "The Church and Usury." *Edge* 4 (Mar. 1957): 4–7.

Tansill, Charles Callan. *Back Door to War: The Roosevelt Foreign Policy, 1933–1941.* Chicago: Regnery, 1952.

Tasca, Angelo. *The Rise of Italian Fascism.* London: Methuen, 1938.

Taylor, A. J. P. *English History: 1914–1945.* New York: Oxford University Press, 1965.

Terrell, Carroll F. *A Companion to the Cantos of Ezra Pound.* 2 vols. Berkeley: University of California Press, 1980–84.

Thayer, William Roscoe. *The Life and Times of Cavour.* 2 vols. Boston: Houghton, 1911.

Thompson, Dorothy. *I Saw Hitler.* 1932.

Tocqueville, Alexis de. *De la démocratie en Amérique.* Paris: Librarie de C. Gosselin, 1835–40.

Torrey, E. Fuller. *Roots of Treason: Ezra Pound and the Secret of St. Elizabeths.* New York: McGraw-Hill, 1984.

Turati, Augusto. *A Revolution and Its Leader (Benito Mussolini).* Trans. Benedict Williamson. London: Alexander-Ouseley, 1930.

Tytell, John. *Ezra Pound: The Solitary Volcano.* New York: Doubleday, 1987.

Uberti, Riccardo M. degli. "Ezra Pound and Ubaldo degli Uberti: History of a Friendship." *Italian Quarterly* 64 (1973): 95–107.

———. "Why Pound Liked Italy." *Academia Bulletin* (1956): 63–66.

Upward, Allen. *The Divine Mystery.* Letchworth: Garden City Press, 1913. Santa Barbara, Calif.: Ross-Erikson, 1976.

———. *The New Word.* London: A. C. Fifield, 1910.

Vallette, Jacques. "Quelques poètes américains récents." *Mercure de Francè* 302 (1 Jan. 1948): 147–49.

Valli, Luigi. *Il linguaggio segreto di Dante e dei "fedeli d'amore."* 2 vols. Biblioteca di Filosofia e Scienza, no. 10. Rome, 1928–30.

Varè, Daniele. *Ghosts of the Rialto.* London: John Murray, 1956.

———. *The Two Imposters.* London: John Murray, 1949.

Viereck, Peter. *Metapolitics: The Roots of the Nazi Mind.* New York: Capricorn Books, 1961.

———. *Terror and Decorum.* New York: C. Scribner's Sons, 1948.

Villari, Luigi. *The Fascist Experiment.* New York: AMS Press, 1972.

———. *Italian Foreign Policy under Mussolini.* New York: Devin-Adair, 1956.

Visconti-Venosta, Giovanni. *Ricordi di gioventa.* Milan: Cogliati, 1904.

Vlaminck, Maurice. *Paysages et personnages.* Paris: Flammarion, 1953.

Volpe, Gioacchimo. *L'Italia moderna.* 3 vols. Florence: G. C. Sansoni, 1946–52.
————. *Storia del movimento fascista.* Milan: Instituto perglishedi di politica internazionale, 1939.
Waddell, Lawrence Austine. *Egyptian Civilization: Its Sumerian Origin.* London: Luzac, 1930.
————. *Real Chronology and Sumerian Origin of Egyptian Hieroglyphs.* London: Luzac, 1930.
Watson, Tom. *The Story of France.* New York: Macmillan, 1899.
Webster, John. *The Duchess of Malfi.* Ed. F. L. Lucas. London: Chatto and Windus, 1958.
Webster's American Biographies. Ed. Charles Lincoln Van Doren. 12 vols. Springfield, Mass.: G. and C. Merriam, 1974.
Webster's New Biographical Dictionary. Springfield, Mass.: G. and C. Merriam, 1983.
Weintraub, Stanley. *Four Rossettis: A Victorian Biography.* New York: Weybright and Talley, 1977.
White, Andrew Dickson. *Selected Chapters from the Autobiography of Andrew D. White.* Ithaca: Cornell University Press, 1939. Ithaca: Cornell University Press, 1956.
Whitman, Walt. *Durbadala (. . . Walt Whitman's Leaves of Grass).* Cuttack, Orissa, India: Prafulla Chandra Das, 1957.
Who Was Who, 1929–1940. Vol. 3. London: A. and C. Black, 1952.
Who Was Who, 1941–1950. Vol. 4. London: A. and C. Black: 1961.
Who Was Who, 1951–1960. Vol. 5. London: A. and C. Black: 1961.
Who Was Who, 1961–1970. Vol. 6. London: A. and C. Black, 1972.
Who Was Who, 1971–1981. Vol. 7. London: A. and C. Black, 1981.
Wilhelm, J. J. *Dante and Pound: The Epic of Judgement.* Orono: University of Maine Press, 1974.
————. *Ezra Pound: The Tragic Years, 1925–1972.* University Park: Pennsylvania State University Press, 1994.
————. *Ezra Pound in London and Paris, 1908–1925.* University Park: Pennsylvania State University Press, 1990.
————. *The Later Cantos of Ezra Pound.* New York: Walker, 1977.
Williams, William Carlos. *The Selected Letters of William Carlos Williams.* Ed. John Connop Thirwall. New York: McDowell, Obolesnky, 1957. Reprint. New York: New Directions, 1984.
Wilson, Robert McNair. *Monarchy or Money Power.* London: Eyre and Spottiswoode, 1933.
————. *Napoleonic Wars.* London: Routledge, 1934.
————. *Promise to Pay: An Inquiry into the Principles and Practice of the Latter-Day Magic Called Sometimes High Finance.* London: Britons, 1934.
————. "When Credit Wears the Crown." *Edge* 3 (Feb. 1957): 13–26.
Wistrich, Robert S. *Who's Who in Nazi Germany.* New York: Macmillan, 1982.
Woodcock, George. *Anarchism: A History of Libertarian Ideas and Movements.* New York: Meridian Books, 1962.

Woodward, William E. *A New American History.* New York: Farrar and Rinehart, 1936.

Wykes-Joyce, Max. *Triad of Genius.* London: Peter Owen, 1953.

Yankowski, S. V., trans. *Richard of Saint Victor, Benjamin Minor.* Ansbach: Elisabeth Kottmeir and E. G. Kostetzky, 1960.

Zeldin, Theodore. *France: 1848–1945.* Oxford: Oxford University Press, 1973.

Zielinski, Tadeusz. *The Sibyl.* Trans. Henry S. Swabey. *Edge* 2 (Nov. 1956): 1–47.

———. *La Sibylle: Trois essais sur la religion antique et le christianisme.* Paris: Redier, 1924.

Zukofsky, Louis. *A.* Berkeley: University of California Press, 1978.

Index

The numbers refer to letter numbers, not page numbers. Only the information in the letters has been indexed, but if a name or subject is not clearly identified in the letter, the index entry refers the reader to the notes to the appropriate letter.

Leon Surette has published *A Light from Eleusis: A Study of Ezra Pound's Cantos, The Birth of Modernism: Ezra Pound, T. S. Eliot, and the Occult,* and many articles on Pound and fascism. He is a professor of English at the University of Western Ontario.

Demetres P. Tryphonopoulos has published *The Celestial Tradition: A Study of Ezra Pound's "The Cantos"* and is a professor of English at the University of New Brunswick.